Restorative justice and criminal justice

RESTORATIVE JUSTICE AND CRIMINAL JUSTICE

THE CASE FOR PARALLELISM

DEREK R. BROOKES

eleven

Published, sold and distributed by Eleven International Publishing
P.O. Box 85576
2508 CG The Hague
The Netherlands
Tel.: +31 70 33 070 33
Fax: +31 70 33 070 30
e-mail: sales@elevenpub.nl
www.elevenpub.com

Sold and distributed in USA and Canada
Independent Publishers Group
814 N. Franklin Street
Chicago, IL 60610
USA
Order Placement: (800) 888-4741
Fax: (312) 337-5985
orders@ipgbook.com
www.ipgbook.com

Eleven International Publishing is an imprint of Boom uitgevers Den Haag.

ISBN 978-94-6236-418-9
ISBN 978-94-0011-236-0 (e-book)

© 2023 Derek R. Brookes | Eleven International Publishing

TABLE OF CONTENTS

About the series

Restorative justice offers a unique approach to crime and victimisation and a change of course from the traditional preoccupation with retribution and transgression of rules in the criminal justice system. It focuses on acknowledging and amending the hurt and injustice experienced by victims, support for offenders to promote desistance from wrongdoing, and the concerns of the society for safety and efficient conflict resolution. Essentially, restorative practices involve a facilitated, voluntary and respectful dialogue between the parties affected by crime. Many different practices have been developed that meet restorative justice requirements, including, but not limited to, victim-offender mediation, restorative conferencing, peace-making circles, and peer mediation. These practices are being utilised in response to property and violent crime, adult and youth offending, school bullying and workplace conflicts, cultural conflicts and mass victimisation. This book series aspires to highlight the many accomplishments achieved through the use of restorative justice practices in response to crime and social conflict. It is a collection of ground-breaking theoretical essays on the principles, uses and versatility of restorative justice as well as state-of-the-art empirical research into the implementation of restorative justice practices, experiences in these programmes and evaluation of their impact on victim recovery, reoffending and community capacity building. Contributors include established scholars and promising new scholars.

Co-editors-in-chief: Estelle Zinsstag (Edinburgh Napier University, UK and KU Leuven, Belgium) and Tinneke Van Camp (California State University, Fresno, USA)

The chief-editors are supported by an international advisory board composed of: Ivo Aertsen (KU Leuven, Belgium), Daniel Achutti (University of La Salle, Brazil), Daniela Bolivar (Pontifical Catholic University of Chile, Chile), John Braithwaite (Australian National University, Australia), Albert Dzur (Bowling Green State University, USA), Jennifer Llewellyn (Dalhousie University, Canada), Shadd Maruna (Queen's University Belfast, UK), Joanna Shapland (University of Sheffield, UK), Ann Skelton (University of Pretoria, South Africa), Heather Strang (University of Cambridge, UK), Lode Walgrave (KU Leuven, Belgium), Dennis Wong (City University of Hong Kong, Hong Kong).

The series in practice: While the primary aim of the series is to publish different types of academic books, thereby giving the floor to researchers, both emerging and well-established ones, we also wish to use it to support and give a platform to painters we admire and who have accepted that we use their unique work for our covers. Each is mentioned within the four different branches our books fit under as described below:

Branch 1: MONOGRAPHS and EDITED COLLECTIONS
These are original academic works based on particular empirical or theoretical research into restorative practices, and edited collections around a specific topic in the field of restorative justice.

The covers for this branch are paintings by Sasa Saastamoinen. Further work by this painter can be found at https://www.sasasaastamoinen.com.

Branch 2: ANTHOLOGY
This branch aims to publish 'anthologies' of work by invited authors, who choose a number of their own publications that have shaped the discourse and debates on restorative justice. They will, within the anthology, be able to reflect on their impact on the field, on the controversies and debates that they have contributed to and how they have responded and evolved. They will also reflect on the future of restorative justice.

The covers for this branch are original portraits by Abigail McGourlay. Further work by this painter can be found at https://www.instagram.com/mcgourlayart/.

Branch 3: TRANSLATIONS
This branch will publish translations of seminal books in the field of restorative justice having originally been published in other languages than English.

The covers for this branch are paintings by Kittie Jones. Further work by this painter can be found at http://www.kittiejones.com/.

Branch 4: THE INTERNATIONAL ENCYCLOPAEDIA OF RESTORATIVE JUSTICE by general editors Ivo Aertsen and Jennifer Llewellyn and a large group of regional editors

The International Encyclopaedia of Restorative Justice will present, for the first time, an encompassing picture of restorative justice worldwide. The origins, development, legislation and practical implementation of restorative justice will be described and critically analysed for a broad range of countries in Africa, Asia, Europe, Latin America, Anglo-America and Oceania, while a variety of challenges and issues related to the developments in the respective regions will be discussed comparatively. The *International Encyclopaedia* explores the complexity of information and analysis into six volumes that will both broaden and deepen our understanding of this innovative field of justice practices.

The covers for this branch are original paintings by Michelle Campbell. Further work by this painter can be found at https://www.chellecampbell.co.uk.

Please see the last page of this book for a list of published volumes in this series.

ACKNOWLEDGEMENTS

There are many people who have, over the past twenty years, inspired and supported my work and enhanced my understanding of restorative justice. They include colleagues in NGOs and justice departments, restorative justice participants, practitioners, criminal justice professionals, trainees and restorative justice scholars. I owe a special debt of gratitude to Keith Simpson for his vision and trust. I have benefited immeasurably from the insight, wisdom and friendship of John Bottomley, David Doerfler, John Kleinig, Alyson Halcrow, Marg Neith, Rhonda McRorie and Bette Phillips-Campbell. Many thanks to Steve Kirkwood for reading and commenting on an early draft of this work and for suggesting that I submit it to the Studies in Restorative Justice series. I would like to express my appreciation for the three anonymous reviewers and especially the Series Editors Tinneke Van Camp and Estelle Zinsstag for their very helpful and perceptive suggestions. My thanks also to Selma Hoedt, Audrey McMahon, Ingrid Knotters at Eleven for their professionalism and care in overseeing the publication, the meticulous copy editors, and Sasa Saastamoinen for her beautiful cover painting. Above all, I will be forever grateful to Lynelle for her unfailing love and support.

Preface

Over the past few decades, many jurisdictions have shown a growing interest in using restorative justice as a means of responding to criminal behaviour.[1] In taking such an approach, they have invariably needed to find a workable solution to the question of how restorative justice processes should be situated in relation to the existing criminal justice system. The most common approach has been to incorporate restorative justice into the justice system as a conditional diversionary mechanism.[2] The offender is given an opportunity to take part in restorative justice instead of being subject to the usual legal consequences, such as prosecution or a traditional sentence. If they agree to take part and do so successfully, then the legal consequences they would otherwise have faced are usually waived, amended or substantially reduced.

There are other possible approaches that could be used, but restorative justice advocates have tended to focus their energy on this diversionary model. And they have had considerable success. As William Wood and Masahiro Suzuki report, 'most RJ programs have been institutionalized within conventional criminal justice systems, often coupled with diversionary practices or as an alternative sanction within them' (2016: 154). However, is the diversionary model the best solution? It does seem to be generating largely positive results. But what if there was an alternative and this option was not only workable but also grounded in a more secure theoretical basis? What if this alternative could result in a higher level of quality and effectiveness for both restorative justice and the criminal justice system? Granted, it would require a considerable effort to transition away from the existing diversionary paradigm. Nevertheless, given the potential benefits, would not such an alternative be worth taking seriously?

It was precisely this set of questions that motivated the journey of research and reflection presented in this book. I have worked for over twenty years as a restorative justice practitioner, policy maker, trainer, researcher and advocate. But over a decade ago,

---

1   There are many definitions and theories of restorative justice, not all of which are entirely compatible (for a useful catalogue, *see* Olson and Sarver, 2022: 947). I take it that the primary aim of restorative justice is to provide an opportunity for those responsible for wrongdoing and those who have been harmed by their actions to enter into a safe and voluntary dialogue for the purpose of working towards moral repair. *See* §1.2.2 for more details, and Brookes (2019a) for a theoretical explanation of this account.

2   My use of the blanket term 'diversionary' in this book is not restricted to pre-charge or pre-trial diversion programmes (e.g. Black, 2009: 546). Rather, it includes *any* judicially authorised mechanism or approach that diverges from or is an alternative to the usual criminal justice outcome. I will also assume, unless otherwise specified, that a diversionary approach is conditional. Thus, an approach is diversionary if it occurs prior to a legal decision – for example, charge, prosecution, sentence or parole – with the intention that, should the offender meet certain specified conditions, the relevant authority may (and usually will) waive or alter the legal consequences to which the offender would otherwise have been subject.

I began to realise that the difficulties and compromises that plagued the diversionary model were far more challenging than I had wanted to believe. So I decided to investigate the possibility of a different approach, one that has received surprisingly little attention.[3] The more I considered this option – sifting through the theoretical frameworks, the ethical issues, the empirical evidence and the practical concerns – the more it became apparent to me that this was indeed a viable alternative. On this model, restorative justice would operate as a legally independent process. There would be no legal consequences, whether or not the offender participated. Neither the process itself nor any outcome agreement would be reviewed, authorised, imposed or enforced by the judicial system. Given this kind of dual track separation between restorative justice and criminal justice, it seemed appropriate to call the alternative model 'Parallelism'.

At first, I assumed that putting in place various safeguards would ensure that restorative justice could operate independently regardless of when it occurred within the criminal justice process, including prior to the judicial decision to prosecute or sentence the offender. But over time, it became clear that, given the number of obstacles to such an approach, the optimal solution for a Parallelist model would be to make restorative justice available in only two circumstances: (1) after the case had exited the justice system entirely or (2) when it had, in legal terms, effectively done so, as in a post-sentence setting. This restriction would guarantee independence given that the legal consequences of the crime will have already been fixed. A decision about whether to make an arrest, file charges, prosecute or amend a sentence could not be influenced by the outcome of a restorative justice process.

To be clear, the use of restorative justice in such a way is not a new phenomenon: there are many jurisdictions that offer restorative justice in a prison setting, for instance. But using an exclusively Parallelist approach across the board has, to my knowledge, never been offered, let alone conceived of as a way of mainstreaming restorative justice. My own introduction to the possibility came by way of working within a system that was already effectively independent of the criminal justice system. I had the good fortune of spending seven years (2001-2008) in Scotland – working with a community justice organisation called *Sacro* – to develop and implement restorative justice largely within the context of the Children's Hearing System.[4] This is an institution for which the legally independent

---

3   Jennifer Brown's 1994 article 'The Use of Mediation to Resolve Criminal Cases: A Procedural Critique' is, to my knowledge, the only other extended defence of a parallelist approach – one that I discovered only after completing much of this book. Her case is encouragingly similar, in many respects, to my own. She writes: 'This Article seeks to shift [Victim-Offender Mediation] firmly into the private sphere, and calls for a decoupling of mediation from the criminal justice system. The mediation should not affect public proceedings against the offender. A Chinese wall is necessary to protect the integrity of the criminal justice system and the integrity of mediation as a fundamentally voluntary process. [P]ublic power should be used only to vindicate public interests' (Brown, 1994: 1308-1309).

4   'Sacro' is an acronym for 'Safeguarding Communities, Reducing Offending'. *See* www.sacro.org.uk.

use of restorative justice could not have been a more natural fit. The Hearing System has a welfare-based framework, and so the young people who participated in restorative justice were able to do so without any legal carrots or sticks to motivate them.[5] Experiencing first-hand the many advantages of offering restorative justice in such a context has had a significant impact on my openness to Parallelism. But it was only in the last few months of my time in Scotland that I began to think about whether this level of independence could be viable in the very different context of the criminal justice system.

Since then, it has been a long journey. I was side-tracked for a number of years when I was given the opportunity to design a restorative justice policy framework for a government body in Australia. I spent countless hours consulting with local stakeholders on how best to minimise the problems that infected the diversionary model. This involved speaking with criminal justice professionals, legal scholars, victim groups, restorative justice advocates, First Nations peoples, community leaders and so on. Every group I encountered shared a significant receptiveness to the idea of restorative justice. However, the same objections kept reoccurring, and the vast majority, from every sector, were directed against the diversionary approach, rather than restorative justice itself. I eventually realised that, if restorative justice was ever to stand a chance of fulfilling its potential as a mainstream option, there would need to be an alternative. And so, I returned to thinking about Parallelism.

Articulating and defending the Parallelist model turned out to be far more complicated than I expected, with innumerable questions and concerns that called for a substantive response. Three of these issues – which I discuss in more detail throughout the book – may be worth briefly mentioning at the outset. They were perhaps the most significant obstacles to my own acceptance of Parallelism, so there may be others who have the same preliminary concerns.

1. I initially embraced the use of restorative justice as a diversionary mechanism largely because I saw it as a way of avoiding or at least curtailing the most damaging aspects of the criminal justice system.[6] Yet Parallelism seemed to leave the status quo in place. However, I came to see that this concern was misplaced. Parallelism is only viable as a normative framework on the assumption that criminal justice has an essential and legitimate role in society. Its foundational remit is to serve the public interest by upholding the rule of law, thereby protecting the freedom and equality of all citizens without fear or favour.[7] But it

---

5   For details, *see* Restorative Justice Services in the Children's Hearings System (2005).

6   This seems to be a common motivation. As Howard Zehr notes: 'The Western idea and implementation of restorative justice developed initially as a response to problems within the Western legal system' (Zehr, 2019: xxvii).

7   The rule of law, like much else, is a contested idea. However, Richard A. Epstein, a professor of law, has argued that, for most purposes, the following can be taken to include its most essential elements: (i) individual cases are decided by reference to general rules; (ii) the general rules apply equally to all, including to the state; (iii) the general rules are sufficiently certain so that, at the least, they apply in such a way that

follows that Parallelism cannot be fully implemented unless the criminal justice system is fulfilling this role. Thus, far from being a negligent bystander, Parallelism has a built-in incentive to reform (or even transform) the system, as well as being part of the solution itself.

2. It once seemed to me that the case for Parallelism would depend on showing that the diversionary model was incapable of delivering positive outcomes. Yet such a claim would contradict the large number of empirical studies that show otherwise. I eventually realised this was not a zero-sum calculation, but rather a matter of weighing up the comparative advantages of each model. It is possible to make a case for Parallelism as the *optimal* model, without thereby making the highly dubious claim that the alternatives are wholly ineffective.

3. One pragmatic concern I had with Parallelism was that I could not envisage any well-established diversionary restorative justice scheme being dismantled, at least not overnight and not without more empirical research. But then it occurred to me that a gradual evidence-based transition was available. Any jurisdiction wishing to test the Parallelist approach could simply add one or more extralegal referral routes to its existing diversionary scheme. Once the case numbers were sufficiently large, the quality and effectiveness of the two approaches could then be compared in a statistically meaningful way. If the evidence indicated that Parallelism was the optimal model, then the diversionary protocols could be phased out over time.

I subsequently discovered many more issues that a Parallelist model would need to address – hence this book.[8] But with these three initial concerns out of the way, I was able to move forward. In the end, the case for Parallelism, as I came to see it, boils down to this: Restorative justice and criminal justice involve fundamentally incompatible processes and priorities. Yet the diversionary approach requires that the two are merged together into a single justice mechanism. This confused hybrid cannot help but make it considerably more difficult for both restorative justice and criminal justice to realise their full potential in terms of quality and effectiveness. Since Parallelism would remove this impediment, it is likely to be the optimal model.

To be clear, this book is offered as a preliminary theoretical exercise. While my arguments are informed by existing empirical studies, there is, as yet, no empirical evaluation of Parallelism in comparison to alternative models. Hence, my intention here is only to show that the case for Parallelism is, in theory, sufficiently plausible to warrant further empirical investigation.

---

like cases are treated alike; (iv) the general rules are prospective and not retrospective; and (v) the decision-making procedures used are fair (Epstein, 2005: 1-15).

8   For a quick overview, *see* 'Parallelism, concerns addressed' in the Index.

1 INTRODUCTION

This chapter presents an overview of the variety of differing approaches to situating restorative justice in relation to the criminal justice system. It introduces Parallelism and proposes that this model could resolve the debates between the other contenders. It then presents the nature of the case that will be made for Parallelism by specifying its limitations, defining key terms, explaining its methodology and how its main components are reflected in the structure of the book.

1.1 THE DEBATE

1.1.1   Integrationism

In most jurisdictions that employ restorative justice to address criminal behaviour, cases are referred as a diversionary option. A judicial authority – police officer, prosecutor, judge or magistrate – offers the offender the opportunity to take part in restorative justice instead of being subject to the usual legal consequences, such as an arrest, prosecution, a traditional sentence, supervision conditions, parole release conditions and so on.

   This offer is always provisional. If the offender agrees to take part in a restorative justice process and does so in a way that the authority regards as successful, then the legal consequences they would otherwise have faced are normally waived, amended or significantly reduced. The offender is not arrested or charged, they avoid prosecution, their prison sentence is reduced, the usual sanction is replaced or modified so as to incorporate the restorative justice outcome agreement and so on. The offender may choose not to accept this offer, or they may not cooperate with the restorative justice process. For instance, they may not show up for meetings, or they could fail to complete the outcome agreement as required. In such cases, the diversionary approach will normally be deemed unsuccessful by the judicial authority, and they are then very likely to impose the legal consequences that the offender would ordinarily have received.

   I will call this kind of relationship between restorative justice and criminal justice the 'Integrationist' model. It is sometimes called a 'Diversionist' model, but the term 'integration' seems to be a more accurate representation. The term 'diversion' means a 'deviation or alteration from the natural course of things' (Black, 2009: 546). Hence, labelling this kind of relationship as a 'diversion' could suggest that, once a referral has been made, the restorative justice process will then travel down its own path, entirely independent of the criminal justice system. But legally speaking, this is not how most diversionary mechanisms work.[1] Judicial authorities do not generally refer a case to restorative justice and then wash their hands of the matter, since they will not yet have made a final ruling with respect to the case: it is classed as 'pending' or unresolved. And so they will oversee the process and review the outcome. If the offender fails to comply with the terms of the diversion, they cannot simply walk away. They will then be subject to the legal consequences they would ordinarily have received. So, in this model, restorative justice remains inextricably tied to the criminal justice decisions, procedures and objectives (Figure 1.1).

Figure 1.1 The Integrationist Model

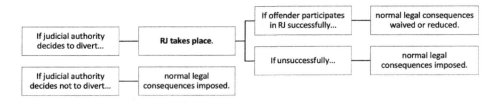

1.1.2   *Maximalism*

There is a far more ambitious view about how restorative justice should be situated vis-à-vis the criminal justice system. This position has been called 'Maximalism'.[2] But to understand what it is that differentiates this model, we first need to explain another central tenet of Integrationism.

For the Integrationist, a process will only count as 'restorative justice' if those who participate in it do so voluntarily. The participation of the victim and any support persons must also be voluntary. But the focus of this requirement is normally directed towards the offender since their legal situation makes them more vulnerable to coercion. The voluntarist requirement, according to Integrationists, entails the following: the offender must be given the opportunity (1) to speak honestly and openly about what they did and how they now feel about it, and (2) to collaborate with the other participants in devising an agreement about how they can make amends for the harm they have caused.

---

1   Diversion to restorative justice can be 'unconditional' in the sense that, once the referral has been made, the case is effectively closed. But aside from this approach being very rare, the decision to divert rather than prosecute is still conditional upon the offender admitting responsibility for the crime, and so this would be an Integrationist, rather than a Parallelist approach (*see* §3.1 for more detail).

2   'Maximalism' is typically contrasted with a model that has been called 'Minimalism', but since Minimalism is identical to Integrationism as I have defined it, I shall continue to use 'Integrationism' instead.

Integrationists also take the view that these core voluntarist parameters are not sacrificed when restorative justice is used as a diversionary option. This means that, from an Integrationist perspective, a restorative justice process will still count as 'voluntary' even when the state threatens to impose the legal consequences that the offender would otherwise have received should they fail to complete the restorative justice agreement as required.

Some Integrationists have even argued that the voluntarist line has not been crossed when the judicial authorities *mandate* that an offender take part in restorative justice and then incorporate the agreement into the offender's sentence. This is because, in such a context, the state has not thereby ordered the offender to admit responsibility, offer an apology or say anything they do not want to say within the meeting itself. This *would* violate the voluntarist requirement, and so the process could no longer be legitimately classified as 'restorative justice'. Likewise, if the judicial authority alone determines what the sentence will be, thus refusing to take into account the participants' agreement, then this too would, in their view, not count as 'restorative justice'. For example, New Zealand's use of conferencing as a diversionary mechanism allows the state to compel an offender to take part in restorative justice. However, since the outcome agreements are not determined by the court, Paul McCold – who calls Integrationism 'the Purist model' – argues that conferences held under these conditions would nevertheless satisfy the voluntarist requirement for restorative justice:

> Conferences are held prior to court appearance where the offender fails to deny charges and the cases are disposed (diverted) at that time. Those who deny responsibility are adjudicated in court, and if found responsible are mandated to participate in a conference to determine sentence conditions. While offenders may be directed to participate by the court and the terms of the conference are sanctioned by the court, outcomes are not determined by the court.... New Zealand has [thereby] created [a] restorative juvenile justice system without abandoning the informal collaborative approach suggested as a hallmark of the Purist model. (2000: 385-386)

Advocates of the Maximalist model argue that the Integrationist's voluntarist requirement effectively prevents restorative justice from having any place in the way that the criminal justice system deals with the majority of cases. Many crimes will be deemed too serious or unsafe for diversion, and many offenders will either be unwilling or unsuitable for a voluntary approach. As Lode Walgrave puts it:

> [R]estricting restorative justice to voluntary deliberations would limit its scope drastically.... The criminal justice system would probably refer only a selection

of the less serious cases to deliberative restorative processes, thus excluding the victims of serious crimes who need restoration the most. (2007: 565)

Thus, in their quest for the most comprehensive application of restorative values possible, Maximalists are willing to jettison the voluntarist requirement. This allows them to expand what counts as 'restorative justice' to include sanctions that have been entirely determined by the court, so long as they have a reparative orientation. This type of sanction might require the offender to pay restitution or compensation either to the victim directly or a victim's fund. Again, the offender might be ordered to engage in reparative work that would benefit the victim or, where there is no identifiable victim, the community (Duff, 2003: 57, Walgrave, 2003: 62). As Jim Dignan suggests:

> [I]n cases for which informal restorative justice processes may be inappropriate, inapplicable or inadequate by themselves, it is possible to envisage a range of non-custodial court-imposed punishments that could be adapted to promote restorative outcomes. (2003: 151)

Most Maximalists even allow for the possibility of compulsory detention being classified as 'restorative', but they argue that the justification would, again, need to be oriented around reparative objectives. For instance, Walgrave argues that incarceration might be used to 'enforce compliance with the restorative sanctions' (2003: 62). Dignan writes that offenders could 'undertake adequately paid work in prison in order to provide financial compensation for or on behalf of victims' (2003: 151). David Boonin suggests that the state could imprison an offender with the intent of restoring the victim (and/or the affected community) to the level of security they enjoyed prior to the offence, rather than in order to make the offender suffer or undergo hard treatment. This rationale, according to Boonin, would radically alter the conditions of incarceration:

> [W]hen offenders are incarcerated on punitive grounds, they are routinely deprived of goods such as cigarettes, television, exercise equipment, and a long list of other things that might make life in prison less unpleasant. If the goal of incarcerating an offender is to make him suffer, these deprivations will often be justified. But if the goal is simply to ensure that his community is restored to the level of security it enjoyed prior to his offense, then there will be no justification for making his life any less pleasant than is required by his incarceration. (2008: 234)

Reparative sanctions already play a role in most criminal justice systems. But the problem, according to Maximalists, is that they are relatively insignificant compared to retributive sanctions, such as financial penalties and imprisonment. Reparative sanctions should, in their view, replace the current retributive philosophy that dominates sentencing. As Dignan argues, 'restorative justice could form the basis of a replacement discourse in which the emphasis would be on more constructive and less repressive forms of intervention' (2003: 151).

It is important to note that Maximalists do not reject voluntary forms of restorative justice. Indeed, they usually concede that voluntary participation produces a higher quality of restoration and that there should therefore be a presumption in favour of diversion wherever possible. But voluntariness, in this view, is not a defining attribute of restorative justice. As Walgrave puts it, for Maximalists, 'cooperation is not a value on its own, but rather a means of enhancing the quality of possible restoration' (2003: 62). Even when the judicial authority has alone determined the nature of a reparative sanction, this can nevertheless achieve a measure of restoration. The Maximalist holds that what is essential to restorative justice is that, in the aftermath of a crime, the harms that were caused are repaired. And this objective, in their view, should become the primary focus of the criminal justice system, using whatever forms of restorative justice are most suitable. If a voluntary approach is viable, then the diversionary option should be used. If not, then a coercive (court-imposed) reparative sanction could be employed so as to achieve the same restorative end (Figure 1.2).

Figure 1.2 Distinguishing Features

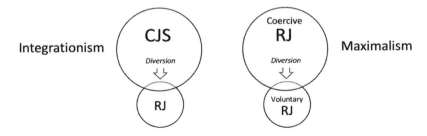

1.1.3   Substitutionism

The most radical position on how restorative justice should be situated in relation to criminal justice might be called 'Substitutionism'.[3] According to this view, the criminal

---

3   It might also be called 'Penal Abolition', but this term only refers to what should happen to the criminal justice system. Whereas 'Substitutionism', as I am using the term, identifies restorative justice as its replacement, and so is better able to capture how this model, like all the others, is concerned with the *relationship* between restorative justice and criminal justice.

justice system is seen in an entirely negative light, and so it aims to replace the system with restorative justice over time. To be clear, this is not the same kind of 'replacement' advocated by Maximalists. For Substitutionists, restorative justice must be entirely voluntary, and so they would not accept that the term 'restorative justice' can be extended to include reparative sanctions. Indeed, Substitutionists go a step further than Integrationists insofar as they hold that the coercive elements of a diversionary mechanism will effectively undermine the voluntariness of a restorative justice process.

Substitutionism is unlikely ever to eventuate. It is difficult to imagine any modern state electing to rid itself of the rule of law, together with the institutional apparatus by which that rule is upheld – police, courts, lawyers, compulsory detention and so on. Substitutionism is nevertheless held as a matter of principle by many restorative justice advocates, if not explicitly then by implication. For example, many would argue that restorative justice is morally superior to the typical deliverances of criminal justice. It is hard to interpret this as anything other than a call for the justice system to be wholly replaced by or transformed into restorative justice. As Robinson puts it, most of the leading advocates of restorative justice 'conceive of restorative processes not simply as a potentially useful piece of, or complement to, the criminal justice system, but as a *substitute* for it' (2003: 377).

Having said this, many advocates are Substitutionists in principle but Integrationists in practice. Zehr, for instance, writes:

> Restorative justice advocates dream of a day when justice is fully restorative, but whether this is realistic is debatable, at least in the immediate future. More attainable, perhaps, is a time when restorative justice is the norm, while some form of the legal or criminal justice system provides the backup or alternative. Possible, perhaps, is a time when all our approaches to justice will be restoratively oriented. (2002: 59)

This incongruity could be justified as a long-term strategy of infiltration and eventual conversion. Carolyn Boyes-Watson, for instance, argues that 'the incompatibility between institutions of the justice system and restorative justice may generate a kind of creative tension that opens space for the transformation of those institutions' (2004: 216). But Integrationism is also a pragmatic necessity. It is the only model that most governments have, so far, been prepared to fund, or that criminal justice agencies and other stakeholders have been willing to endorse. Hence, Substitutionists have had little choice but to toe the line in the hope that the diversionist strategy will eventually 'starve the beast'. As Jorge Perán argues:

A clear RJ strategy aimed at implementing restorative diversion programmes would lead to more social benefits than a strategy of prison reform. While it is true that any honest attempt to improve prisons is positive, I believe that the best and most feasible way of improving prisons is to empty them. (2017: 194)

1.1.4   Resistance to integrationism

There is one position that might be thought of as the flip side of Substitutionism. This is the view that restorative justice should be excised from the criminal justice system, or at least severely restricted. Low referral rates and a political reticence to expand the use of restorative justice as a diversionary mechanism suggest that this position is widely shared, particularly among criminal justice professionals, legal scholars, public servants and politicians. Advocates of the Integrationist model typically explain this resistance in pejorative terms. They refer to territorialism, fear of change, unrealistic demands for evidence, political risk-aversion or a deep-seated belief that the only kind of justice worth the name is retributive. Walgrave, for instance, writes:

All institutions display some form of institutional inertia, a kind of resistance against change, based on fear of the unfamiliarity of the proposed innovation and on the perceived risk of loss of power and influence. (2007: 575)

Some of this may well be true. But it is not clear that the integration of restorative justice is being held back for these reasons alone. In light of the evidence of low recidivism rates and the positive experience of most victims, one would expect these forms of resistance to give way. As researchers Lawrence Sherman and Heather Strang reported over a decade ago:

The evidence on RJ is far more extensive, and positive, than it has been for many other policies that have been rolled out nationally. RJ is ready to be put to far broader use. (2007: 4)

More recently, in 2017, following a review of 84 evaluations of restorative justice services for young offenders, David Wilson, Ajima Olaghere and Catherine Kimbrell concluded:

The bottom line for restorative justice programs and practices is that the evidence is promising, suggesting possible but still uncertain benefits for the youth participants in terms of reduced future delinquent behavior and other non-delinquent outcomes. Victim participants in these programs, however, do appear to experience a number of benefits and are more satisfied with these programs than traditional approaches to juvenile justice. (2017: 3)[4]

Perhaps, then, we need to look for another explanation for the political and institutional hesitancy. It could be that decision-makers can see that the way in which restorative justice has, thus far, been incorporated into the criminal justice system cannot avoid compromising due process protections, such as the right to legal representation, proportionality constraints, the presumption of innocence and equality before the law. As Ann Skelton argues:

> [T]he need to protect the puny individual against the might of the state was certainly the main reason why fair trial rights and due process rights developed in the criminal justice system and became part of our human rights protections, and why lawyers, in particular, are nervous about letting go of them. (2019: 32-33)

Integrationists routinely argue that these concerns can be adequately met by a combination of training and legislation.[5] But this remedy has not been universally accepted as sufficient. Concerns about due process safeguards continue to be raised by legal professionals, victim groups and criminologists. As Braithwaite notes, 'the strongest opposition [to restorative justice] has come from lawyers, including some judges, under the influence of well-known critiques of the justice of informal crime processing' (1997: 3).[6]

Another explanation might be that decision-makers have been listening to the research that shows how, when the Integrationist approach is used, restorative justice processes are routinely co-opted, undermined, delayed and diluted by criminal justice priorities. For instance, Stefanie Tränkle writes that Victim-Offender Mediation (VOM) in Germany and France 'is not able to put into practice its specific modus operandi'. And this, she argues, is due 'mainly to its structural link to the penal law':

> The informal and pedagogical logic of mediation is constrained by the penal framework, namely its power to impose its formal and bureaucratic logic on

---

4   It should be noted that the authors of this report were also critical of the general quality of recidivism research in the restorative justice field, as were Nadine Smith and Don Weatherburn, who, a few years earlier, stated that the studies they reviewed 'provide little basis for confidence that conferencing reduces re-offending at all' (Smith & Weatherburn, 2012: 6).

5   For example, '[The solution to concerns about Integrationism is to require] highly trained personnel ... underpinned by a legislative framework to ensure accountability and transparency' (ACT Restorative Justice Sub-Committee, 2003: 11).

6   Quoted in Clairmont (2005: 249).

the mediation process. The penal law dominates the procedure and impedes the interaction process. (2007: 395-396)[7]

How should the advocates of Integrationism deal with these concerns? Could it be argued that they are nothing more than teething issues? Are they merely crinkles that will get ironed out over time as restorative justice and criminal justice learn how to accommodate each other? Or is there a need to acknowledge that the resistance of decision-makers is not unfounded? Could it be that any attempt to integrate restorative justice into the criminal justice system will invariably generate these kinds of tensions?

My proposal here is that these problems are indeed unavoidable. Restorative justice and criminal justice are inherently designed to achieve different ends. Thus, any attempt to integrate the two by using a diversionary approach cannot help but produce a 'tug of war' situation. When restorative justice is made the priority, the normal demands of due process will tend to be relaxed. But then it is soon recognised that compromising the rights of the participants is unacceptable. So, new guidelines or legislation is introduced to preserve the relevant safeguards. Yet this can only be done if some essential element of restorative justice gives way. The battle rages, back and forth, each side legitimately anxious to retain as much of its terrain as possible. If we were to portray this situation pictorially, it might look like the following (Figure 1.3):

Figure 1.3 Competing Priorities

The resulting amalgamation can, and often does, achieve positive outcomes on both sides. I have no intention of contradicting the empirical evidence. Nor do I wish to impugn the

---

7   As the name implies, VOM employs a rationale, a set of techniques and a structure that is specific to mediation. As argued in Brookes and McDonough (2006), there are a number of problems with using mediation in the context of crime or wrongdoing. Tränkle also identifies these concerns but unfortunately argues that they are endemic to restorative justice, rather than simply the misapplication of mediation. Her point about the detrimental impact of a penal framework nevertheless remains intact.

expertise and dedication of restorative justice practitioners who are currently operating within an Integrationist framework. Again, by highlighting flaws in the Integrationist model, I am not denying or minimising the positive experiences that participants in restorative justice have gained in the context of this approach. The Integrationist model is capable of producing exceptional results. My contention is only that, when restorative justice and criminal justice are intermingled in this way, each is more likely to fall short of its own distinctive benchmarks and priorities. Integrationism is inherently restrictive. It has multiple built-in obstacles to the goal of reaching the highest standards possible for both restorative justice and criminal justice. Such a limitation cannot help but encourage the resistance of decision-makers, and rightly so. It is for this reason that we need to search for a different way of situating restorative justice in relation to criminal justice.

1.1.5   Parallelism

There is one alternative that would seem to offer a promising solution to many of the problems that inflict Integrationism. I will call this approach the 'Parallelist' model. The foundational principle upon which Parallelism is based is this:

> Restorative justice should be legally independent: the criminal justice system must not determine, impose or enforce the decision to participate in restorative justice, what happens in the process itself or the outcome.

The advantage of this model is that it avoids almost all of the compromises that are intrinsic to Integrationism. In other words, it is a win-win solution for both restorative justice and criminal justice. If these two processes were to operate independently, it is more likely that their respective principles and values would not clash with or undermine each other. Instead, they would be free to operate at the highest levels of quality and effectiveness.

Parallelism might also provide a win-win solution to the debates that have raged between restorative justice advocates. For example, Parallelism is consistent with Substitutionism insofar as both propose that, in order to preserve what is essential to restorative justice, it should operate in complete independence of the criminal justice system. Substitutionists will, of course, continue to reject the legitimacy of criminal justice. But they could see Parallelism as an interim position that is less likely to realise their fears of restorative justice becoming co-opted or compromised by criminal justice.[8]

---

8   Václav Havel offers a similarly parallelist suggestion on how best to replace totalitarian systems. 'One of the most important tasks the "dissident movements" have set themselves is to support and develop [parallel social structures].... What else are those initial attempts at social self organization than the efforts of a certain part of society to ... rid itself of the self-sustaining aspects of totalitarianism and, thus, to extricate

Parallelism is also able to incorporate some of the key principles that motivate both Integrationism and Maximalism, and, hence, offers a resolution to the disagreement between the two. With respect to Integrationism, Parallelism not only preserves the voluntarist requirement but does so in a more credible manner. Unlike the Integrationist approach, it allows the offender to make decisions about whether and how they participate in restorative justice without needing to weigh up the potential legal costs and benefits. The absence of this kind of Sword of Damocles, as I argue later, is likely to increase the quality of restorative justice substantially.

With respect to Maximalism, the Parallelist model does not entail a hands-off approach to criminal justice. Far from it, Parallelism includes principled reasons for wanting to ensure that the criminal justice system carries out its primary function of serving the public interest to the best of its ability. Since there is good reason to think that replacing the current retributive philosophy with a reparative orientation is most likely to achieve this end, as the Maximalist suggests, it follows that any transition to the use of reparative sanctions will be strongly supported by the Parallelist. The key difference is that Parallelism does not thereby erode the important distinction between restorative justice and criminal justice. On the Parallelist view, it is unnecessary and unhelpful to classify reparative sanctions as 'restorative justice'. State-imposed sanctions, as we shall see, serve a very different purpose, and so, even if they have a reparative orientation, they should still be categorised as 'criminal justice' disposals, with all that this entails in terms of applying the rule of law, due process, proportionality constraints and so on.

Parallelists will also be strongly motivated to make sure that what might have been gained by a restorative justice process is not 'destroyed by the alienating and negative effects of adversarial justice', as Tony Marshall puts it (2003: 31). Hence, Parallelism will be supportive of criminal justice reform or even radical transformation where necessary. It will not be my purpose to suggest detailed proposals here, but there are well-known changes that would no doubt increase the overall compatibility between restorative justice and criminal justice. For example, victimless acts, such as traffic violations and other minor regulatory offences, could be decriminalised and transferred to a 'system of administrative sanctions' (Blad, 2003: 203). The application of therapeutic jurisprudence would render the system less confrontational and relationally destructive. Offenders could be offered the opportunity to take part in a victim awareness programme as a voluntary adjunct to every criminal justice disposal. Victims of crime could, as Susan Herman proposes, be assigned a case manager 'who would have the authority to ensure that

itself radically from its involvement in the [totalitarian] system? ... The ultimate phase of this process is the situation in which the official structures ... simply begin withering away and dying off, to be replaced by new structures that have evolved from "below" and are put together in a fundamentally different way' (Havel, 1978: 102, 108).

wherever possible, victims seeking resources and services have priority access to them' (2004: 81). Governments could deploy far more resources into addressing the underlying discriminatory and socioeconomic causes of crime, as in justice reinvestment schemes.[9] Prisons could be eliminated entirely or transformed into something more like the Norwegian model.[10]

Having said this, it is important to be clear about the extent to which Parallelism would endorse or require changes to the criminal justice system. First, Parallelism is predicated upon the assumption that criminal justice plays a legitimate role in bringing about core aspects of justice in the aftermath of a crime, but only if it does so by upholding the rule of law. Parallelism would not, therefore, support any reform which sought to remove or devalue this essential ingredient. Second, a full-blown Parallelist model is likely to require significant reforms to any existing criminal justice system. However, the restorative justice arm of this model is entirely independent, and so it can be implemented without needing to wait for such fundamental changes.[11]

This is not to say that setting up a Parallelist approach to restorative justice will have no impact. There is, for instance, evidence that it could help to repair some of the damage experienced in the preceding judicial process. Susan Miller, for instance, found that victims who met with the offender in a post-sentence (pre-release) setting saw the restorative justice process as 'essential' in 'providing a mechanism to combat feelings of being trivialized, condescended to, and disempowered by the criminal justice process' (2011: 187). Similarly, in their interviews with victims who had also participated in a post-sentence context, Tinneke Van Camp and Jo-Anne Wemmers found that, for some, the process, served to 'overcome the frustrations' that they suffered in the court:[12]

> For example, the court record or the criminal trial did not allow them to have all the answers they were looking for in relation to the facts and the motives of the offender. The criminal trial did not bring the same understanding of the facts and motives as the direct dialogue with him. The only way to know the truth was to speak with him in an informal setting independent of the judicial system, so that he could tell the real things without legal repercussions. (2011: 189, my translation)

---

9 This approach is explored in, for example, Bonig (2013), Schwartz (2010), Wood (2014).

10 As suggested in Andvig, Koffeld-Hamidane, Ausland and Karlsson (2020). For a critique of this model, *see* Smith and Ugelvik (2017).

11 Similarly, if a criminal justice system was reformed (or transformed) along the lines suggested earlier, then this arm of Parallelism could likewise be regarded as fully operational even if extralegal restorative justice services had yet to be set up or rolled out across the relevant jurisdiction. But this sequence of implementing Parallelism would, I take it, be considerably less likely than the reverse.

12 Both of these sources also found that victims expressed the desire that the judicial process should therefore be reformed so as to avoid these kinds of frustrations occurring in the first place. *See* §2.1.2 for details.

Even so, it is important to be clear about the primary role of restorative justice in a Parallelist model. While it may help to 'clean up the mess' left by a criminal trial, restorative justice per se is not designed to rescue a dysfunctional criminal justice system. Indeed, as we shall see, when restorative justice is co-opted for this purpose, it is far more likely to be damaged itself as a result. What is needed to ensure that victims do not feel 'trivialized, condescended to, and disempowered' in a court process is not a workaround or a band-aid solution but major systemic reform.

1.1.6   *Logistical questions*

Any implementation of Parallelism will require answers to important pragmatic questions. How and when would referrals be made? Who would deliver restorative justice services? On what basis would restorative justice services be funded, and by whom? How would key administrative difficulties be resolved, such as making contact with victims, informing participants of the availability of restorative justice, finding suitable venues, carrying out the process within a reasonable time frame, monitoring outcome plans and so on? The answers to these questions will, for the most part, depend on specific political contexts, local partnerships and negotiated agreements. Nevertheless, I will suggest some general answers to such questions by drawing upon Parallelist principles and the empirical evidence to date (see §3.2).

The most important logistical question, of course, is how to ensure that restorative justice can in fact operate as a legally independent service. The answer to that question, in my view, is unlikely to be solved by the kind of legislative protections that have thus far been used in diversionary contexts. My proposal here will be that, in the absence of significant legal innovation, the goal of legal independence will require that restorative justice is only offered after the case has actually or effectively exited the justice system. In practice, this will mean that it must take place (1) after the case has been formally closed or unconditionally dismissed or (2) as a voluntary adjunct to either a sentence or a lengthy non-restorative justice (henceforth 'non-RJ') unconditional diversionary programme (see §3.1 for details).

It might be questioned whether the term 'Parallelism' is appropriate for such a model, given that restorative justice would not always be operating at the same time as the criminal justice process. However, two lines can be parallel without being situated side-by-side at every point. One parallel line can, for instance, be located before and continue after the other line ends. Moreover, what is essential to the concept, as I am using it, is the kind of relationship that holds between the two approaches. Restorative justice will operate in parallel to the criminal justice system when they operate independently, but without any implication that one is superior to or takes priority over the other. This is why a term like 'Supplementalism' is less accurate, since it suggests that restorative justice is an add-on or extension of criminal justice, and, as such, carries less importance or value with respect to what is required for justice to be done in the aftermath of a crime.

1.2   THE CASE

1.2.1   Scope

The case for Parallelism presented here involves a claim about how restorative justice should be situated vis-à-vis the criminal justice system. But there are several definitions of 'restorative justice' available, each of which is grounded in a distinct theoretical perspective. Likewise, most countries or regions will have a 'criminal justice system' of some kind, but these are based upon quite different legal systems – Civil Law, Common Law, Religious Law or combinations thereof – as well as having distinct legal cultural values and structures. These differences are very likely to affect how restorative justice is integrated into any particular criminal justice system. Given this variety, it would be unrealistic to claim that this case for Parallelism will be universally applicable as it stands. Nevertheless, I would hope that, with appropriate adjustments and occasional exceptions, it could potentially apply to most jurisdictions and on most accounts of restorative justice.

Take the issue of jurisdictional differences: when I provide examples of issues that arise for Integrationism, these are typically drawn from a particular legal system and culture, namely, Common Law as practiced in liberal democracies. I do not specify the adaptations that would need to be made for the issue in question to apply, if it does, within any alternative legal system or culture. Thus, if, for instance, it turns out that I have identified a problem with Integrationism that would not apply in the same way, or not at all, in some other jurisdiction, then I would concede the exception. But I would maintain that there will nevertheless be a suite of problems – mostly similar to those I have identified – that plague any attempt to integrate restorative justice into a criminal justice system regardless of its legal and cultural particularities, and that these problems are most likely to be solved by ensuring that restorative justice can operate as a legally independent (or 'extralegal') service.

1.2.2   Terminology

As mentioned earlier, there are many definitions of 'restorative justice'. I have nevertheless tried to use this term in a way that will be relatively uncontroversial to most restorative justice advocates and practitioners, at least as it is used within an Integrationist context.

Thus, I take it that restorative justice is fundamentally about *enabling those responsible for wrongdoing and those who have been harmed by their actions to enter into a safe and voluntary dialogue for the purpose of working towards moral repair.*[13] This kind of dialogue will usually cover three basic topics, roughly in the following order: the *facts* (what happened), the *consequences* (how people have been harmed) and the *future* (what needs to happen to repair or make amends for the harm). Towards the end of the exchange, an outcome agreement will be negotiated. This will typically include details such as how the person responsible will provide material or symbolic reparation to the person harmed, a commitment not to reoffend, resources that might support their desistance and so on.

There are several ways in which this kind of facilitated dialogue can take place. The person harmed and person responsible can meet on their own, assisted by a facilitator, in a *face-to-face meeting*. If support persons are also invited – such as friends, partners, parents, social workers and so on – then a *conference* or *circle* can be arranged. If such a meeting is not considered safe or appropriate by the facilitator, or if those involved decide against it, then a *shuttle dialogue* process can be used. This is where the facilitator acts as a go-between, conveying information, letters or audio/video recordings from one participant to the other.

There are also cases in which either the person harmed or the person responsible is unable or unwilling to participate in a dialogue of any kind, or they cannot be identified. It nevertheless remains possible for the remaining participant(s) to engage in a process that embodies restorative values and objectives. This might involve enabling a person who has committed an offence to take responsibility by carrying out a reparative task in the community or meeting with victims who have suffered from the same type of crime. However, this should not be regarded as the norm. Processes that do not involve any dialogue between the person responsible and the person harmed are used only when at least one participant has already committed to taking part in a restorative justice process and a dialogue turns out to be unfeasible. Rather than end a process that could still enable them to engage in whatever measure of moral repair is possible for them as an individual, the participant may choose to hold the same kind of dialogue – covering the facts, consequences and future – with only the facilitator and relevant others attending. But if no such commitment has been made, it is best to refer the case to other services and programmes that are not specifically designed to facilitate this kind of dialogue, such as specialised victim support, reparative schemes or programmes that focus on behavioural change.

Either way, these alternatives should not, in my view, be labelled as 'restorative justice' processes, since they do not involve any dialogue between the person responsible and a person who was (directly or indirectly) harmed. When either one or the other has made a

---

13   For more detail on restorative justice theory and practice as I understand it, *see* Brookes (2019a).

commitment to participate but a dialogue proves unfeasible, then a restorative justice service may be best placed to work with them as an individual. But the service should carefully distinguish such activities from its core business of facilitating restorative justice processes, especially when communicating with funders, evaluators, participants and other stakeholders.

This account of restorative justice does not, therefore, include processes such as conflict resolution, mediation, problem-solving, stand-alone victim awareness programmes, family group decision-making (where no offence has been committed), trauma counselling, cognitive behavioural therapy, rehabilitation schemes, mentoring, coaching, participatory democracy, active listening and so on. Any restorative justice process may, where relevant, draw upon the techniques and methods of these other processes. And most of these processes will share values and principles in common with restorative justice. But each of them also has its own distinctive focus and set of primary objectives. So it is unhelpfully confusing and unnecessary to rebrand them as 'restorative justice'. As Wood and Suzuki put it:

> [T]he future of RJ as we see it depends significantly on whether a focus on *interactions* between parties who have caused harm and those who have been harmed remain central to such a definition, or whether RJ continues to expand into piecemeal programs and outcomes where the difference between 'restorative' and other types of programs becomes increasingly blurred. (2016: 154)

The same is true of programmes or movements that are focused primarily on political or social-structural changes. As I will argue later (§4.8), restorative justice participants can, as they are addressing the personal harm that was caused, also confront wider social issues that were relevant to the behaviour in question. They might, for instance, want to discuss and challenge the discriminatory attitudes, cultural prejudices or historical injustices that help to explain or contextualise the wrongdoing, without thereby excusing or rationalising it.[14] They could also choose to supplement the restorative justice dialogue with extended conversations and activities that involve collaborating with other grassroots social justice organisations or movements. But it does not follow that *these* organisations and movements should be reclassified as 'restorative justice'. It is possible to collaborate, form alliances and

---

14 Restorative justice differs from purely welfarist responses to crime insofar as it can acknowledge and address the often profound impact of an offender's disadvantaged circumstances without thereby denying them any moral agency. As Hans Boutellier puts it, 'Offenders themselves also often disapprove of their own conduct ... [and so] they are surprised when their evil acts are simply explained away ... [as if] they [had] no say in what they did' (Boutellier, 2006: 40).

identify overlapping values, methods and objectives without muddying important distinctions.

In sum, restorative justice is not the solution to every conceivable social, relational or psychological problem. As Margarita Zernova writes:

> No doubt the application of restorative values may lead to positive results in some – perhaps even many – situations. Yet, endorsing restorative justice as a universal response to all conflicts, problematic situations and injustices will not help identify, let alone prevent, undesirable consequences. In dealing with some problems and situations restorative values and methods may not be the best ones or may even be inappropriate. (2016: 142)

To suggest otherwise by liberally spraying the term 'restorative justice' over anything to which it bears the slightest resemblance will soon render the term meaningless. To give an example, Shannon Sliva and Carolyn Lambert discovered a Missouri statute which stated that 'community-based restorative justice projects' include the following:

> [P]reventive or diversionary programs, community-based intensive probation and parole services, community-based treatment centers, day reporting centers, and the operation of facilities for the detention, confinement, care and treatment of adults. (2015: 90)

As the researchers then noted, it is unclear whether the state intended to offer restorative justice within each of these settings or whether it regarded them as restorative justice processes in their own right.

The problem here is not merely the lack of taxonomic restraint. As the term 'restorative' is increasingly prefixed to instruments of state power – prisons, police, parole and so on – there is the danger, as John Platt argues,

> that RJ might simply become one element of a much stronger, coercive body designed to more efficiently control deviant youth. The very imprecise nature of what RJ actually is lends itself to such possibilities. (2006: 63)

Yet much of this imprecision could be easily avoided by observing that, while certain features – for instance, an informal dialogue or the opportunity to process emotions – might be *necessary* for restorative justice, they are not, on their own, *sufficient*. The benefits of clarity and consensus for all concerned – researchers, advocates, practitioners, policy-makers, legislators and participants – would far outweigh the analytical effort.[15]

It might be argued that setting clear boundaries around the concept of restorative justice will lead to a stultifying conformity, inflexibility and standardisation. Granted, this could easily occur. But there is no reason why this should be the only possible outcome or even the most prevalent one. We can all agree on a basic definition of what will count as an 'automobile' – for instance, 'a wheeled motor vehicle used for transportation'[16] – without thereby blocking human ingenuity or limiting our creative freedom. On the contrary, setting clear boundaries can be a powerful stimulus for the imagination. Think of the bewildering variety of objects that now fall under the conceptual rubric of 'automobile'.

Likewise, the account of restorative justice suggested above is sufficiently general to allow for a myriad of diverse and innovative forms that such a process could take. For instance, many First Nations communities use processes that are consonant with this characterisation of restorative justice, but they employ a range of distinctive procedures, conceptual categories and terminologies, as well as a wider set of goals (see §4.9). And there is a constant stream of new potential applications of restorative justice that advocates are exploring, such as addressing the harms caused by the climate crisis or reparations for African American descendants.[17] Even so, we cannot even begin to assess the comparative quality and effectiveness of any such application unless we can agree on the essential features of restorative justice.

1.2.3   Methodology

Suppose we intend to evaluate whether one form of implementing restorative justice (call it 'A') might be more optimal than another ('B'). Then suppose that we could, for instance, show that A will, by design, ensure that the decision to participate in a restorative justice process will be voluntary for the participants, whereas this guarantee is not possible under B. Suppose we also agree that the voluntariness of such a decision is an essential feature of restorative justice, and so it is one of the factors that determines whether or not a restorative justice process can reach its full potential. In that case, we can infer that A is more likely to result in a higher quality of restorative justice than B. Hence, A is *in this respect* the optimal

---

15   Alessandra Cuppini provides a useful case study of this kind of analysis. She demonstrates how, contrary to the claim of many scholars, the International Criminal Court does not exemplify the core elements of restorative justice practice and, thus, argues 'for a much greater degree of caution to be used when employing the restorative label in relation to the justice approach of the ICC' (Cuppini, 2021: 341).

16   Source: https://wiki2.org/en/Car.

17   For examples of these two initiatives, *see* Robinson and Carlson (2021) and Jones and McElderry (2021), respectively.

approach to implementing restorative justice.[18] And this inference will be legitimate even if a range of other non-restorative benefits might result from *B* that are absent from *A*.

Throughout this book, I will be presenting a series of comparative arguments of precisely this kind. The intention is thus to build a cumulative case, showing that there are good ethical, institutional, psychological, legal and political reasons for thinking that, when compared to the alternatives, Parallelism is, on balance, likely to be the optimal model. This view has not yet been confirmed by an empirical study comparing the quality and effectiveness of each model. Nor have I been able to draw upon any statistically meaningful studies of this kind, since, to my knowledge, they do not yet exist. My aim, instead, has been to produce a testable theory which has sufficient plausibility to warrant further empirical investigation. As I later suggest (§3.2.4), such a study might, in the first instance, involve an existing Integrationist scheme continuing as usual, but with one or more Parallelist options being made available as an *additional* approach, and then comparing the outcomes.

This is not to say that there is no empirical support for the comparative advantages of Parallelism. Indeed, I frequently draw on qualitative research and case studies where relevant. But in doing so, my focus is limited to the question at hand. It might, for instance, be thought that I would want to draw extensively on the evidence that is now available for the benefits of post-sentence restorative justice. However, such evidence, on its own, would not serve to establish the advantages of Parallelism *as compared* to Integrationism. This would require a side-by-side trial involving the two models in operation. In the meantime, however, I can draw upon existing evaluations in order to show that Integrationism is beset with a number of problems. If, as I argue, Parallelism is very likely to solve such problems, then it will follow that there is indirect empirical support for its optimality.

1.2.4   Structure

To make this work as user-friendly as possible, I have tried to create chapters and sections that can be read more or less independently, depending on the starting point or interests of the reader. In Chapter 2, I present key theoretical reasons for preferring Parallelism, namely, its capacity to address, in equal measure, both the public and private dimensions of crime, the acquittal of both active and passive responsibility, and the public and private denunciation of wrongdoing. In Chapter 3, I present a set of Guiding Principles that are

---

18   Such an argument will not, of course, persuade those who think that the voluntariness of this decision is not essential to restorative justice. Thus, as with all arguments, the persuasiveness of this case for Parallelism will depend on the extent to which its basic premises are shared, and this includes its views on the essential features of restorative justice.

designed to show what would be required to implement a Parallelist model. I then address logistical questions, such as how a Parallelist approach would organise referrals, source funding and plan for its implementation and evaluation. I conclude by suggesting that Parallelism offers a more viable vision for how restorative justice could become a mainstream response to crime.

In Chapter 4, I present the key advantages of Parallelism as compared to Integrationism, which is currently the majority position. This chapter is thus mostly devoted to showing how Parallelism avoids the detrimental impact that Integrationism is having on both criminal justice and restorative justice – although I do, on occasion, address the various ways in which Maximalism might be thought to offer a solution to the problems created by Integrationism. In the first four sections of Chapter 4, I argue that, since Parallelism is detached from the legal system, it is immune from the way that Integrationism invariably undermines the core principles of equality before the law, proportionality, consistency and due process, as well as Integrationism's tendency to expand the state's coercive powers in ways that are unjustifiable. In the next four sections, I argue that Parallelism is more likely to optimise the quality and effectiveness of restorative justice, since, unlike Integrationism, it avoids the unethical and potentially revictimising impact of enforcing the offender's participation; it does not subject the process to criminal justice priorities (such as timescales and caseloads); and it is less likely to be contaminated by the discriminatory practices that currently infect many criminal justice institutions.[19] In the final section, I argue that, since Parallelism entails that restorative justice services would not be governed or regulated by the state's legal system, it offers a framework whereby, in settler-colonialist countries, First Nations peoples could operate their own independent 'restorative justice' services. This alone would achieve a significant measure of self-determination and sovereignty in relation to criminal justice matters. But such an outcome would be even more likely, I suggest, if, at some point, First Nations peoples were to operate these services in parallel with their own separate legal system.

In Chapter 5, I present a series of key challenges to the Parallelist model that were not addressed in previous chapters. I focus on a range of concerns that could be raised in relation to the needs and interests of victims, offenders and the criminal justice system. I suggest that these challenges, while not insignificant, are, on balance, not as severe or intractable as the problems faced by Integrationism.

The overall structure of the book, then, is designed to set out the case for Parallelism in a way that makes it more amenable to assessment. In presenting the underlying theory of Parallelism and how it might be implemented in Chapters 2 and 3, my aim is to ensure

---

19   Whilst sections 4.1 to 4.4 are *focused* on criminal justice priorities and 4.5 to 4.9 on restorative justice priorities, the 'tug of war' between the two means that there will inevitably be a number of overlaps in the discussion.

that the reader is in a better position to evaluate whether this model does indeed have the advantage of solving the problems faced by Integrationism, which I identify in Chapter 4; and whether it can respond adequately to the challenges that are presented in Chapter 5.

2   FOUNDATIONS

This chapter articulates and defends the theoretical basis upon which a Parallelist model rests. It argues that Parallelism is preferable to alternative models insofar as it takes the view that a just response to crime should address, in equal measure, both the public and private dimensions of crime, the acquittal of both active and passive responsibility, and the public and private denunciation of wrongdoing.

2.1   PUBLIC VS. PRIVATE INTEREST

Restorative justice has often been depicted by its advocates as superior, in key respects, to criminal justice. Howard Zehr, for example, originally presented the two as opposing paradigms in his book *Changing Lenses* (1990: 184-185). To illustrate this, he created parallel lists exhibiting the key distinguishing features of each approach, which he has summarised in the following way (2002: 21) (Figure 2.1):

Figure 2.1 'Two different views'

Criminal Justice	*Restorative Justice*
• Crime is a violation of the law and the state.	• Crime is a violation of people and relationships.
• Violations create guilt.	• Violations create obligations.
• Justice requires the state to determine blame (guilt) and impose pain (punishment).	• Justice involves victims, offenders and community members in an effort to put things right.
• *Central Focus: offenders getting what they deserve.*	• *Central Focus: victim needs and offender responsibility for repairing harm.*

Zehr does recognise that the criminal justice system has an important, if 'circumscribed' role to play, such as 'investigating facts, facilitating processes, and ensuring safety' (2002: 65). And he accepts that, while the contrasting lists, like the one above, 'illuminate important elements differentiating the two approaches, they also mislead and hide important similarities and areas of collaboration' (2002: 58). However, his strategy, like that of many Integrationists, is still to argue that restorative justice is fundamentally more important than or should take priority over criminal justice. He writes, for instance, that '[o]bligations to victims, such as restitution, take priority over other sanctions and obligations to the state, such as fines' (2002: 66). This kind of evaluative positioning has had a powerful and lasting effect on restorative justice theory. As Kathleen Daly observes, it is also routinely used by advocates 'to sell the superiority of restorative justice and its set of justice products' (2002: 59).

2.1.1   Complementary roles

There is an alternative way of understanding Zehr's parallel lists. One of the reasons why they are useful is that they illustrate the ways in which restorative justice and criminal justice focus on different aspects of crime. On the face of it, these two approaches might seem ideologically opposed to each other, leaving us with an either/or decision as to which paradigm we must align ourselves with or prioritise. However, it seems clear that these perspectives are not logically incompatible: both could be true. Criminal violations, for example, might create both legal guilt *and* moral obligations towards the victim. They would only be incompatible in the pragmatic sense that it is extraordinarily difficult for both aspects of crime to be addressed in the same place, at the same time, using the same processes. But if they are done at different places and times, using the distinctive approaches of criminal justice and restorative justice, respectively, then the either/or scenario dissolves.

Moreover, why should one paradigm be regarded as superior to the other? Why should they even be thought of as competitors? It may be true that the criminal justice system is, at present, the dominant player, while restorative justice operates on the side lines. But why should the solution be to create a win-lose scenario? Why expand restorative justice at the expense of a (properly reformed) criminal justice system? Why can they not work as equal partners, each carrying out its own unique role? To be sure, the balance between the two is, at present, skewed in favour of criminal justice. But then why not instead work to restore the balance?

This is precisely the approach embodied in the Parallelist model: the criminal justice system is designed to attend to the public or societal dimensions of crime, while the main focus of restorative justice is to address the private or personal dimensions. On the Parallelist view, both roles are equally essential to a just outcome in the aftermath of a crime.[1] As Zehr himself puts it:

---

[1]   Other voluntary approaches that attend to the private needs of citizens in the aftermath of crime might include community-based rehabilitation schemes for offenders and counselling services for victims. Susan Herman, for example, advocates for a 'set of victim-oriented responses' offered in 'parallel' to the criminal justice system, and that provide 'a focused effort to help ensure the victim's safety, to help the victim recover

[C]rime has a societal dimension, as well as a more local and personal dimension. The legal system focuses on the public dimensions; that is, on society's interest and obligations as represented by the state. However, this emphasis downplays or ignores the personal and interpersonal aspects of crime. By putting a spotlight on and elevating the private dimensions of crime, restorative justice seeks to provide a better balance in how we experience justice. (2002: 12)

And yet, many restorative justice advocates continue to embrace the oppositional framework presented in Zehr's lists. One explanation, I believe, is that the primary function of the criminal justice system is routinely misunderstood – a phenomenon which is perhaps due, in large part, to the multiple ways in which this institution frequently fails to live up to its own raison d'être. The criminal justice system has, in principle, an essential and legitimate role to play and so should not be undermined. It should instead be reformed (or transformed) and regulated so that it can fulfil its core purposes consistently and effectively. But to make a case for this view, it will be necessary to clarify the nature of this role.

2.1.2   Legitimacy of criminal justice

One of the most important developments in political thought has been the principle that the state must assume responsibility for dealing with those who break the laws of society. The rationale behind this principle is not difficult to appreciate. If the process by which guilt is determined and the sentencing that follows are to be fair and just, then they should not be undertaken or controlled by private individuals. If that were the case, then some victims could demand a harsh and disproportionate punishment, motivated primarily by a desire for retaliation.[2] Alternatively, those with powerful connections could punish their enemies for crimes they did not commit. They might also use their influence to avoid a guilty verdict or a sentence for themselves or their family and friends.

The historical development of this principle bears out this underlying rationale. For example, in Scotland, prior to the 15th century, victims and their relatives were responsible

---

from the trauma of crime, and to provide resources to help the victim rebuild his or her life' (Herman, 2004: 79).

2   To be clear, not every victim of crime is seeking a punitive outcome, nor are they always motivated by revenge in wanting a criminal justice response. Judith Herman, for instance, found that the survivors of sexual and domestic violence she surveyed were 'virtually unanimous' in wanting 'to see the offenders exposed and disgraced'. But their motive, she discovered, 'was not to get even by inflicting pain. Rather, they sought vindication from the community as a rebuke to the offenders' display of contempt for their rights and dignity' (Herman, 2005: 597).

for instituting criminal proceedings. The main purpose of the criminal courts was thus to provide a remedy to private individuals who were looking for compensation or vengeance:

> Powerful criminals escaped justice as weak victims were afraid to institute proceedings, while the wealthy purchased immunity from sentence; certain crimes had no specific victim and hence no one had a title to prosecute. ... As a consequence of these failings the concept of a public prosecutor began to emerge in the fifteenth century. (Sheehan & Dickson, 2003: 14)

It is worth noting, at this point, a key argument that is often used to advance the cause of restorative justice: the problem with the criminal justice paradigm, it is argued, is that the state employs 'disinterested' public prosecutors and defence lawyers to speak on behalf of victims and offenders. Why are they not allowed to speak for themselves? Should not the voices of those who were directly involved be heard, rather than those of 'proxy professionals'?[3] However, this objection misses the rationale that gave rise to this practice. Legal professionals were employed to oversee and safeguard the proceedings and, thereby, defend the rights of private individuals who lacked the power, education or resources to do so themselves. Their role was to ensure that, despite the vast number of variables, all citizens could nonetheless be rendered equal before the law. This remains one of the foundational principles of the criminal justice system.

There is another reason for the state's assumption of responsibility for addressing crimes. Many victims do not want the burden or the risks associated with greater participation in justice processes. As Gerry Johnstone puts it:

> Restorative justice advocates often take it for granted that, in the aftermath of a crime, the victim will want to be part of the decision-making process concerning what happens next. However, it is just as likely that many victims would prefer to delegate this decision-making process wholly to officials and professionals. ... [M]any victims would experience this as the state fulfilling its proper function. (2017: 390-391)

Indeed, according to Sheehan and Dickson, the official prosecuting system, not to mention a state-funded police force, was developed, in part, to alleviate these very burdens. In

---

3   It should be acknowledged here that victims often feel side-lined and frustrated by the way that their voice is effectively dismissed or silenced by current forms of legal representation. They also frequently feel revictimised by cross-examinations that deploy 'aggressive argument, selective presentation of the facts, and psychological attack' (Herman, 2005: 572). However, as I will later argue, there are reforms that could address these problems without thereby dismantling or undermining the principle of legal representation itself.

Scotland, towards the end of the 15th century, the Lord Advocate took over, almost entirely, the duty of prosecuting all serious crimes by way of indictment. One might argue that this change was a disastrous shift towards the disempowerment of victims. But such a criticism ignores the historical fact that this approach was taken in the interests of private victims. For instance, the court could not compel the Lord Advocate to provide the name of their informant, which allowed the victim or other witnesses to testify without fear of revenge. In addition, the availability of a public prosecutor who could act on behalf of the victim allowed private individuals to bring a case to court even where they might otherwise have been pressured or coerced by the offender to drop the case. Moreover, if the accused was acquitted, then because the state was responsible for the prosecution, the victim would not be subject to a claim for expenses. The effect of these innovations over time was not surprising:

> [P]ublic confidence in the ability and impartiality of the public prosecutor grew and, moreover, as the investigation of crime became more sophisticated, it became difficult for a private individual to match the resources made available by the state for this purpose. (Sheehan & Dickson, 2003: 16)

In short, the criminal justice system as we know it today was designed to ensure that proper procedures for establishing guilt are followed and that any sentencing of a proven offender is proportionate to their culpability and the seriousness of their crime. And it does so in a way that would be virtually impossible for private citizens to achieve.[4] As Adam Crawford argues:

> The 'rule of law' emerged out of centuries of struggle – with its emphasis upon due process and individual rights – by imposing effective inhibitions upon power and the defence of the citizen from powerful claims. (2002: 107)

It might be argued that, ironically enough, the wealthy and the powerful have, to a significant extent, gerrymandered the criminal justice system to work in their favour. And this is unlikely to be a recent phenomenon. It is a near certainty that, from the outset, members of the ruling class would have found some way of manipulating the legal process to their advantage. But this would still have been a corruption of the system. Its inherent

---

4   Cf. 'While it is true that prior to the establishment of state prosecutors victims played a much more significant role in the criminal justice system, such accounts often gloss over the intolerable burden this system imposed on many victims. They were not just responsible for prosecuting, they had to gather witnesses, attend preliminary examinations in front of magistrates and pay the expenses of the constables and the various officers of the courts' (Roche, 2003: 13-14).

purpose – even if more honoured in the breach than in the observance – is to remove the distorting effects of power and privilege. As Mona Rishmawi writes:

> [T]he rule of law is not the same as rule by law. The use of laws and regulations to oppress people, abuse power and violate human rights is against the rule of law. (2018: 366)

Likewise, it might be argued that the criminal justice system was, and continues to be, used as a tool of colonisation, serving to 'justify' the brutal subjugation and genocide of First Nations peoples in Australia, New Zealand, Canada and the USA. As Juan Tauri argues:

> The implementation of a Western European legal jurisdiction and criminal justice system were fundamental platforms of the colonial enterprise … in two specific ways: (1) it ensured that the definitions of what constitutes crime, social harm and victims were based on Eurocentric interpretations of those terms; and (2) it provided a ready platform for the deployment of structural violence by the state against Indigenous peoples who could not, or chose not, to adhere to Western standards of behaviour – most especially those who dared challenge the hegemony of the colonial state, or who were simply residing on good pastoral and/or mineral-rich land. (2019: 349)

Yet this use of criminal justice was, and still is, contrary to the rule of law, which is designed to recognise, honour and protect the sovereignty of independent nations and the right of their people to self-determination. When a state colonises another territory and its people and then uses the powers of its criminal justice system to crush their resistance and suppress their right to self-determination, it cannot, by definition, be operating under the rule of law. These acts are in violation of the very principles that give any criminal justice system its foundational purpose and moral legitimacy. Even colonial states will hypocritically insist on the universality of the rule of law when another state dares to threaten their right to self-determination. As Martin Krygier and Adam Winchester illustrate:

> The American colonists … felt betrayed by their British rulers for very British reasons; the Americans insisted that no government was above the law, but the English had moved beyond them to regard the lawmaker as legally sovereign, outstripping though (and perhaps thus) losing its about-to-be-former colony. The Americans still defended, and in their written constitution made an

institutional innovation to resurrect and strengthen, an older understanding of law and the rule of law. (2018: 80-81)

In short, if history can teach us anything, it is that relying entirely upon informal mechanisms of social control will not automatically make the world a better place. As Declan Roche argues:

[R]eparative, negotiated traditions of informal justice are only one edge of a double-edged sword, the other of which is one where the poor who cannot access the formal justice of the wealthy are forced to face swift, oppressive, humiliating, brutal, and often barbarous justice. (2003: 13)

Eradicating or circumventing the criminal justice system is not the answer. We need to put our energy into reforming (or transforming) the system so that it can better serve its core values and principles.

For instance, we could, as I suggested earlier, work towards a court system that employed the principles of therapeutic jurisprudence. We could seek to eliminate politically motivated legislation and sentencing policies that do not permit disadvantage to be a mitigating factor, thus going some way to eradicating the effect that poverty, mental health, disability and race routinely have on judicial outcomes. As Michael Tonry, for instance, argues:

[J]uries and judges should have greater leeway to acquit defendants on the basis of deep disadvantage, and ... judges should be encouraged to mitigate sentences for that reason when they believe it appropriate to do so. (2014: 142)

Criminal justice agencies and institutions – police, probation, prisons, the judiciary, and so on – could be regularly reviewed by independent, impartial and transparent bodies with the power to impose and enforce their recommendations. There may be also ways in which the volume of the victim's voice might be increased without undermining due process. For example, David McKenna, as the chief executive of Victim Support Scotland, suggested:

The victim could be legally represented in court, so that they could cross-examine or examine witnesses. The victim could be a party to the case, so that they sit with the prosecutor and give information to the prosecutor – for example, 'That is not right. It was X, Y and Z'. (Scottish Parliamentary Corporate Body, 2002: 1478)

Again, we can agree with Dennis Sullivan and Larry Tifft who argue that the law, as it stands, cannot or refuses to hold accountable 'the perpetrators and benefactors' of the harms that are caused by 'structural violence, hierarchical relations, and an economy that is geared toward deficit creation for some in the interest or surplus enhancement for others' and that it instead focuses on 'the acts of those who are marginalized or disenfranchised by power' (2001: 157). But it does not follow that we should give up on the criminal law. It is utterly fanciful to suppose that an informal restorative justice process could have either the power or the investigative and adjudicatory capacities required to untangle the complexities of structural violence, identify who was culpable and then administer a proportionate outcome in accordance with due process. Unless we want to risk a return to 'might makes right', we need to have some kind of legal system in place. This constitutes one of the strongest objections to a class-based critique of the rule of law. As Bryan Magee puts it:

> Marxists' attacks on legality for allegedly representing only the interests of the ruling class ... have the effect of removing from everybody, not least the poor and powerless, their chief defence. Without law, everything becomes a matter of arbitrary power. (1998: 38)

But in that case, the way forward is not to abandon or circumvent the criminal justice system but rather to reform (or transform) it so that the wrongs of structural violence are indeed criminalised and sufficient resources are devoted to ensuring that the perpetrators are held accountable. We need to engage in the political struggle required to ensure that the criminal justice system operates in accordance with its foundational purpose: to uphold the rule of law. Only then will we be able to stand up to and protect ourselves from the abuses of power and privilege. We cannot effectively confront structural violence – or any other kind of serious wrongdoing – unless we have a system in place that is capable of finding evidence-based answers, without fear or favour, to questions like: Who did it? What laws have they broken? What is the fair and proportionate response to this behaviour? Does this response adequately reflect the culpability of the offender and the seriousness of their crime? And we need a system that can then take these answers and use them to deliver a response that the polity would recognise as 'justice'. As Zehr acknowledges:

> Society must have a system to sort out the 'truth' as best it can when people deny responsibility. Some cases are simply too difficult or horrendous to be worked out by those with a direct stake in the offence. We must have a process that gives attention to those societal needs and obligations that go beyond the one held by the immediate stakeholders. We also must not lose those qualities

> which the legal system at its best represents: the rule of law, due process, a deep
> regard for human rights, the orderly development of law. (2002: 60)

If this is right, then there are profound implications for how restorative justice should be situated in relation to criminal justice. The Integrationist model, as we have seen, entails that restorative justice should function as a diversion from the usual legal consequences to crime. But this positioning cannot help but imply that there is something fundamentally flawed with criminal justice. It suggests that the core principles upon which it rests – the rule of law, proportionality, consistency, legal representation, state-controlled sanctions and so on – are not essential to justice after all. On this view, little of any value would be lost if the judicial system, or at least certain aspects of it, were bypassed entirely.

Parallelism, by contrast, situates restorative justice alongside criminal justice as a complementary process, rather than as a competitor. And it does so for principled reasons: Parallelism is the view that enacting the foundational purposes of the criminal justice system is a necessary part of what it means to 'do justice' in the aftermath of a crime. The system needs to be retained and reformed (or transformed), not eliminated, bypassed or degraded. And yet, Parallelism also holds that criminal justice is not sufficient for 'justice' in the fullest sense. It does not adequately address the personal and relational harm caused by crime. That is the role of restorative justice.

It is worth noting that there is evidence that this perspective is consonant with the views of those who have experienced restorative justice.[5] For example, Van Camp and Wemmers interviewed victims of violence from Canada and Belgium who had taken part in a restorative justice process in both pre- and post-sentence settings. Most of these victims thought that restorative justice should not 'replace' the criminal justice system. Instead, they should be seen as 'complementary' since they each 'served different purposes'.

> Rather than wanting to fully or partly replace the criminal justice system with
> restorative practices, or have the criminal justice system operate as a safety net
> for unsuccessful default restorative processes, the victims of violence that were
> interviewed for this study describe restorative justice as an important
> complement that functions independently of the criminal justice system. (Van
> Camp, 2014: 164)

But the interviewees also expressed two caveats: the criminal justice system, they suggested, needs to be 'reoriented' so that it can 'better meet the needs of victims' (2011: 193, my

---

5   The number of interviewees in the two research studies mentioned here (i.e. Van Camp & Wemmers and Miller) was relatively small, and limited to victims of interpersonal violence, and so the evidence presented here is only suggestive, not conclusive.

translation). And they did not 'agree with the punitive focus of the conventional criminal proceedings.' The 'judicial authorities and system', they felt, should be 'less punitive' and incorporate more 'restorative values' (2013: 137).

To give another example, Miller studied a post-sentence restorative justice programme in Delaware that was designed to address crimes of severe violence. She found that all of the participating victims expressed 'unqualified support' for the state's 'initial punitive response'. It gave them 'a sense of vindication for the wrong done to them' and the reassurance that they had 'public recognition and support'. The offender's imprisonment 'conveyed that the individual committed a terrible wrong', it 'restored the balance disrupted by their cruelty', it held the offender 'accountable', it protected 'other potential victims', and it gave offenders 'the time to contemplate and develop empathy for the victims' (2011: 160, 161, 237, n. 13).

And yet, ultimately, these victims felt that the state's response was not sufficient to help them recover from the crime. Healing remained 'elusive'. For instance, they still needed to 'get answers' to questions about what happened and why. They needed to know that the offender fully understood the devastating impact of what they had done. The victims needed to hear the offender take responsibility and express genuine remorse. And so they chose to take part in a pre-release restorative justice process (pp. 165-167). Yet, even after the process, the victims 'still would *not* have favoured a diversionary RJ program'. As Miller puts it, 'despite how meaningful the exchanges with the offenders were, remorse did not substitute for punishment – they wanted both' (p. 161).

However, this did not mean they had no concerns about the criminal justice system. For instance, the victims were 'frustrated' by 'their relative lack of input' during the court proceeding, the way they were forced to sit nearby or even next to the offender in court, the scarcity of information about the offender and their motives, the 'no contact' policies and so on (p. 164). They also came to hold critical views about the effectiveness of imprisonment, such as the 'ways it infantilizes and marginalizes offenders' (p. 161).

2.1.3   Who owns crime?

In 1977, Nils Christie published an article, 'Conflicts as Property', that has had a profound effect on restorative justice theory. He argued, essentially, that criminal justice professionals and experts were 'stealing' crime from its rightful owners, namely, those individuals and communities who were directly involved (1977: 4). It is not difficult to see why many restorative justice advocates might have adopted this perspective. However, in doing so, they have thereby positioned criminal justice in a particularly negative, even ignominious light.[6]

But is this view warranted? Would it not be more accurate to describe crime as 'subdivided property'? The criminal justice system rightly owns the *public* dimension of crime, while those who were directly involved are the rightful owners of the *private* dimension.[7] Under this description, the problem with the way in which the state currently deals with crime is not one of 'theft', but rather neglect. What is missing is the recognition that attending to the private dimension is essential to 'justice', in its fullest sense. But the criminal justice system is hardly to blame for this lacuna. Even if it were to acknowledge the private dimension, there would be little that it could do, on its own, to remedy the situation. Criminal justice is not designed to take account of the personal and interpersonal aspects of crime.[8] Indeed, as many studies have found, such as the two mentioned earlier, it is so ill-equipped in this regard that it tends to exacerbate and intensify the personal harm that is experienced, particularly by victims. As Zehr puts it:

> Many [victims] speak of a 'secondary victimization' by criminal justice personnel and processes. The question of personal power is central here. Part of the dehumanizing nature of victimization by crime is the way it robs victims of power. Instead of returning power to them by allowing them to participate in the justice process, the legal system compounds the injury by again denying power. Instead of helping, the process hurts. (1990: 30-31)

But it does not follow that criminal justice should be required to overstep its boundaries and absorb the private dimension, thereby creating a kind of hybrid species. That *would* constitute a theft, insofar as this dimension is not legitimately owned by the criminal justice system. Rather, we need to acknowledge the inherent limitations of criminal justice and set up legally independent services, such as restorative justice, that are designed to attend to the private dimensions of crime. Yet at the same time, offences against individuals

---

6   To be fair, Christie does briefly mention the 'honourable' reasons for the development of the criminal justice system, such as 'the state's need for conflict reduction and certainly also its wishes for the protection of the victim' (pp. 3-4). And in his introduction, he seems to suggest that the problem is one of an imbalance between public and private needs insofar as the state's focus on the former has been at the expense of the latter: 'Without [officials], private vengeance and vendettas will blossom. We have learned this so solidly that we have lost track of the other side of the coin' (Christie, 1977: 1).

7   Sherman and Strang suggest an alternative metaphor of joint problem-solving, but this is more reflective of their Integrationist orientation than it is Parallelism: 'A 21st-century view of this question need not view crimes as "property" owned by victims or states, but rather as problems to be addressed jointly by nation-states and their citizens most directly affected by specific crimes' (Sherman & Strang, 2007: 45).

8   Therapeutic jurisprudence would, if widely adopted, serve to ameliorate the de-personalising effects of the legal system. But even here, there will be inherent limitations, given that this is an essentially coercive institution whose primary remit is to serve the public interest.

need to be understood and dealt with as not only a private wrong but also as a wrong that concerns the whole of society. The offender's crime creates one kind of debt that is owed to the individual victim, and another debt that is owed to society. As Antony Duff writes:

> [C]rimes are 'public' wrongs ... in the sense that, while they are often wrongs against an individual, they properly concern 'the public' – the whole political community – as wrongs in which other members of the community share as fellow citizens of both victim and offender. They infringe the values by which the political community defines itself as a law-governed polity: they are therefore wrongs for which the polity and its members are part-responsible in the sense that it is up to them, and not just up to the victim and offender as private individuals, to make provision for an appropriate response. ... Where there is an identifiable victim, she is the obviously appropriate recipient of reparation, since it is she who was harmfully wronged: but the political community as a whole is also owed something, since it shares in the victim's wrong as a violation of its public values. (2003: 47, 48)[9]

Hence, the solution is for both criminal justice and restorative justice to work in partnership, but in a way that will optimise the quality of their respective roles. The Parallelist claim is that this is best achieved by ensuring the legal independence of restorative justice. In this way, we are more likely to meet the full range of personal and societal needs that can arise in the aftermath of crime.

2.1.4   The social contract

Some might object to the foregoing arguments on the grounds that granting top-down regulatory power to the state is an unnecessary and oppressive curtailment of human liberty. They would argue that restorative justice processes, if sufficiently widespread, offer a bottom-up way by which communities can self-regulate the behaviour of their members. This would be more consistent with our evolutionary history and, thus, with human nature. Intelligent hominids living in small groups regulated each other's behaviour by ensuring that cooperation, kindness and generosity within the group was rewarded, while those who committed selfish or cruel acts, such as murder and theft, would be shamed,

---

9   Cf. 'Just because a person commits an offence against me, however, that does not privilege my voice above that of the court (acting "in the general public interest") in the matter of the offender's punishment. A justification for this lies in social contract reasoning, along the lines that the state may be said to undertake the duty of administering justice and protecting citizens in return for citizens giving up their right to self-help (except in cases of urgency) in the cause of better social order' (Ashworth, 2002: 585).

punished and even cast out of the group unless they performed acts of repentance and redemption.[10]

These social emotions and rituals are still very much with us. They are indeed what makes restorative justice processes so effective and powerful. As Michael McCullough argues:

> Humans were able to appease and forgive long before the contemporary restorative justice movement, but restorative justice works because it enables people to use their evolved moral intuitions to address the pain of crime in the mega-societies in which most of us live. (2008: 179-180)

So why bother with state mechanisms of social control, when informal processes like restorative justice are more consistent with our nature, and are thus more effective?

The problem is that the conditions in which these social rituals and emotions evolved are no longer with us – at least not to the extent that would be required for the abolition of the criminal justice system. If we belong to any community, it is one that consists entirely of our social network: family, friends, work colleagues and neighbours. But it is also increasingly easy to switch communities at will, just by moving to another state or country. Many of us live in one community and work in another. Strangers with whom we have no strong emotional attachment or bonds of loyalty surround us. In such conditions, it is considerably easier to prioritise one's own self-interest to the detriment of others. The social shame that deterred our ancestors from harming another member of their clan has been significantly weakened in our large-scale, dislocated, pluralist and individualistic societies.

But if the regulatory mechanisms of the clan are virtually absent, what is the substitute? The best answer to date, imperfect as it is, is the social contract.[11] Citizens can democratically elect – and, to some extent, hold accountable – a government that will perform this regulatory role on their behalf. The role of the state is, then, to simulate, as best it can, the

---

10   *See*, for example, Joyce (2006) and de Waal (2006).

11   This view does not entail, let alone endorse, John Locke's mistaken view that pre-colonial lands lacked the sovereignty necessary for ceding power to another sovereign through a social contract – a view that was used to rationalise the European colonisation of North America, Australia, New Zealand, Canada and so on. As Mattias Ahren puts it, 'Locke held that the Native Americans were living in a state of nature lacking political society, legislation, and law enforcement ... [and so] were incapable of transferring the power to a sovereign through a social contract' (Ahren, 2004: 83). But in fact, as Val Napoleon and Hadley Friedland write, 'for a very long time, all Indigenous groups had self-complete, non-state systems of social ordering that were successful enough for them to continue as societies for tens of thousands of years' (Napoleon & Friedland, 2014: 227). Even though settler-colonialist states have 'officially' come to regard the Lockean view as false, they have, as we shall see (§4.9), generally maintained the policies and legislative frameworks to which it gave rise.

social scrutiny, rituals and emotions that once regulated the hominoid clans of our evolutionary past.[12]

2.1.5   Simulating informal regulation

Few would claim that the criminal justice system is a perfect instrument. But many of its imperfections arise due to the fact that it cannot fully simulate the regulatory processes of small hominid clans. For example, it cannot assume that citizens will have a close emotional attachment or bond of loyalty to the state and its impersonal institutions. So if the state condemns and ritually outcasts a citizen on account of their criminal behaviour, this citizen is unlikely to feel shame, at least not on account of how the state views them. The criminal justice system may intend to represent or communicate the law-abiding public's denunciation and moral disapproval of criminal acts. But this is unlikely to have much impact on the attitudes and emotions of those who commit the crimes. Assuming they have not already done so, offenders can simply shift their loyalties to another 'clan' within which they *can* find ready acceptance and self-esteem, namely, a criminal subculture. Even prison is not necessarily a source of social shame. One's social networks might be such that incarceration is a sign of achievement and pride. As Braithwaite has argued, 'stigmatization … can be counterproductive by breaking attachments to those who might shame future criminality and by increasing the attractiveness of groups that provide social support for crime' (1989: 81).

Since strong emotional ties and loyalties cannot be assumed, the best that the state can do is to operate at the more abstract level of human freedom and equal rights. Even if it cannot fully satisfy our emotional or personal needs, it can at least try to ensure that a range of other important needs are met, including the need for fairness, equality before the law, proportionality, due process and so on. The result may be emotionally unsatisfying for creatures with our evolutionary history. But it makes no sense to demand that the criminal justice system produce outcomes for which it was not designed. We need to find additional complementary processes that can meet our more personal and emotional needs. This is precisely the arena in which restorative justice finds its distinctive rationale and purpose.

Finally, it is not a deficit of criminal justice that it cannot fully simulate the regulatory processes of small hominid clans. That is one of its primary benefits. As already mentioned,

---

12   George Monbiot makes a similar case: 'The democratic challenge, which becomes ever more complex as the scale of human interactions increases, is to mimic the governance system of the small hominid troop. We need a state that rewards us for cooperating and punishes us for cheating and stealing. At the same time we must ensure that the state is also treated like a member of the hominid clan and punished when it acts against the common good' (2007).

there is a darker side to the self-regulation of small communities. The regulatory techniques that operated within small clans may have been largely oriented towards repairing relationships and peace-making. But when hostilities arose between rival clans, the methods used were likely to be violent. Anthropologists Marc Kissel and Nam Kim, for instance, have found that 'altruistic cooperation within a group can sometimes lead to aggression and violence directed against another group' (2018: 143a). Similarly, Roche notes:

> [I]n many forms of indigenous law, reconciliation was sought primarily where parties shared continuing, valuable relationships (e.g. through marriage, kinship, or economic exchange), but where no such relationship existed, parties were much more likely to have recourse to violent self-help. (2003: 14)

Even in cases where the offence occurred within a community, attempts to implement justice outside a formal legal system do not inspire confidence. For instance, Douglas Fry and Patrik Soderberg examined ethnographic data from a sample of 21 mobile forager band societies. They found that 'of the lethal aggression events … almost two-thirds resulted from accidents, interfamilial disputes, within-group executions, or interpersonal motives such as competition over a particular woman' (2013: 270). The horrific practice of lynching in the American South is a more recent example of 'informal justice':

> Lynching is a form of mob-inspired murder when a group acts in the name of perceived justice without conforming to any standard legal procedures. As was often the case, the law, the Constitution, and civil rights were disregarded in favour of emotions, immediate action, and violence. (Covey & Eisnach, 2021: 218)[13]

Thus, the purpose of criminal justice is *to moderate the excesses of informal justice*. Its underlying rationale is to mimic the governance system of the small hominid clan insofar as it holds to account those who violate community norms, but without thereby simulating the vengeful extremes of those regulatory processes. The results of this approach have been impressive. When criminal justice systems were emerging across Europe between the 16th and 17th centuries, there was a significant reduction in the rates of homicides. As Braithwaite explains, 'The capability of the courts in the eyes of citizens to deter violence was one reason they abandoned the private deterrence of blood feuds' (2018: 72).[14]

---

13   On the history of lynching, *see* Berg (2011) and the Equal Justice Initiative (2017).

14   Cf. 'Remove people's legitimate ability to take revenge, and assure them that you'll look out for their rights through less vengeful means, and life consequently becomes much safer for everybody' (McCullough,

It goes without saying that this foundational objective seems to have escaped the notice of most jurisdictions. The methods by which criminal justice systems hold offenders to account are frequently inhumane, stigmatising, racist, malicious, humiliating and cruel. Examples abound: the death penalty, 'life means life' sentences, supermax prisons, solitary confinement, shaming penalties and so on. It might be argued that the jurisdictions which implement such penalties probably see them as restrained or even humane, in comparison to the kind of extreme vengeance that might have otherwise been inflicted by victims or the wider community. While there are victim groups that oppose harsh sentencing practices, such as the death penalty and mass incarceration, there are also plenty of victims who feel that current sentences are too lenient.[15] And the ramping up of punitiveness is, in part, due to political lobbying from pressure groups, even if much of this can be accounted for in terms other than a desire for vengeance.[16] David Reutter, for instance, argues that some judges who impose shaming penalties are no doubt motivated by the desire to 'become little Caesars that make citizens perform demeaning acts and shaming acts'. But such penalties also appear to have been motivated by the desire to win elections. For instance:

> Harris County, Texas state judge Ted Poe ... would order [defendants] to do such things as shovel manure. While those punishments had little to do with justice, they did help Poe secure a Congressional seat in 2004, and he remains in Congress today. (2015: 38)

But this level of public endorsement is no excuse. The extent to which the criminal justice system does not uphold the dignity and human rights of offenders is precisely the extent to which it has neglected its moderating rationale. There is no logical or moral connection between holding an offender accountable and violating or degrading their humanity, even if the latter might be more emotionally satisfying for some portion of the population.[17]

2008: 183-184).

15 For example, a 2007 English pilot study on restorative justice in the criminal justice system found that around half of the victims surveyed felt the sentence given was too lenient (Shapland et al., 2007: 41).

16 As Erin Kelly notes, 'To understand [why the American criminal justice system is so brutal or why it so disproportionately affects certain social groups], we must look to a multitude of factors ... specifically, racial injustice and the demonization of Black men, excessive fear of crime, income and wealth inequality, retrenchment of the welfare state, and other political and social problems' (Kelly, 2021: 246). *See also* Elias (1993) on the political manipulation of victims.

17 Gresham Sykes articulated the 'pain' of imprisonment in a similar normative way: '[T]he confinement of the criminal represents a deliberate, moral rejection of the criminal by the free community' (Sykes, 1958: 65). John Braithwaite likewise argues that 'formal criminal punishment' functions as 'a degradation ceremony with maximum prospects for stigmatization' (Braithwaite, 1989: 14).

2.1.6   *Balance between victim and offender*

Removing restorative justice from the domain of public interest has another key advantage: it is far more likely to restore the balance between how the victim and the offender ought to be treated. It is well documented how criminal justice focuses primarily upon the offender, with the consequence that the needs and interests of victims are routinely neglected or side-lined. While various reforms could address this imbalance to some extent, it is clear that criminal justice will remain fundamentally and intrinsically offender-oriented. Its rules, procedures and underlying rationale are driven by the objectives of crime prevention and detection, due process, delivering sanctions, rehabilitation and so on – all of which are about what is done to or for the offender by the state in the public interest. The victim may participate as a witness to the crime, but thereafter they are little more than an observer to the proceedings.

It is true that in some jurisdictions, victims are given the opportunity to deliver a victim-impact statement. This practice might be justified in terms of its therapeutic benefits, insofar as it gives victims a sense of validation and the opportunity to communicate to the court the harms they have suffered. But as Julian Roberts and Edna Erez argue, this should be its only rationale, given that these statements are, for principled reasons, largely ineffectual in terms of sentencing decisions (Roberts & Erez, 2004).[18] Indeed, this ineffectiveness is often made explicit. For instance, one Australian 'Sentencing Information Package' states that 'all crimes are regarded as crimes against the Crown, or the state', not the victim. This is why 'victims of crime are not a legal party in criminal proceedings and therefore have no right to appeal a conviction or sentence of an offender' (Victims Services and Criminal Law Review, 2014: 12). To give another example, Sergey Vasiliev observes that, within the International Criminal Court, 'Trial Chambers have held repeatedly' that 'the role of victims at trial is to contribute to the truth-finding objective of the trial', and so, their 'participation is not to be pursued for the sake of its "restorative" effects the promise of which is elusive' (2015: 1196-1197).[19]

One of the most frequently employed arguments for the Integrationist model is that incorporating restorative justice processes into the criminal justice system will help to shift its focus from offenders to victims. For instance, when the UK's Home Office funded its restorative justice schemes, one of its key aims was to retain 'a significant focus on the

---

18   Nor are they likely to bring about attitudinal change in offenders, especially if the statement is read out or summarised by the prosecution. As Roberts and Erez explain, 'the offender may … regard the victim impact information simply as a continuation of evidence adduced at trial, or additional information used by the prosecutor while attempting to secure a harsher disposition. The prosecutor is a legal professional discharging his or her professional duty to represent the state. For defendants, this role may dilute the unique character of the [Victim Impact Statement] and strip the statement of its human qualities, and hence its impact' (Roberts & Erez, 2004: 232).

19   *See also* Brookes and Kirkwood (2007).

needs and rights of victims' (2001: 43). Again, in the Australian Capital Territory, one incentive for setting up a restorative justice scheme was that it would: 'Enhance the rights and place of victims in the criminal justice process' (ACT Restorative Justice Sub-Committee, 2003: 13).

However, there is another side to this coin. Integration into an offender-oriented system is just as likely to shift the focus of restorative justice towards the needs, rights and interests of offenders. Given the comparative power, authority and status of criminal justice, integration is far more likely to divert the attention of a relatively new approach, such as restorative justice, away from the needs of victims and towards criminal justice priorities. As we shall see, there are already signs that Integrationism is creating restorative justice programmes that are essentially offender-oriented, despite the best intentions of advocates and practitioners. As Simon Green observes:

> [T]he advancement of restorative justice is predominantly focused around attempts to improve the way in which we treat offenders rather than victims and as a result has been treated with a good degree of wariness by those pursuing victim entitlements. (2007: 179)

Why else would victim advocacy groups feel the need to stipulate that restorative justice should put the needs of the victim first? For instance, the Council of the European Union *Victims' Directive* stipulates that 'Restorative justice services … [should] have as a primary consideration the interests and needs of the victim, repairing the harm done to the victim and avoiding further harm' (2012: §46).[20]

By contrast, Parallelism is more likely to ensure that restorative justice processes are equally focused upon the needs and interests of victims. First, it is not situated within or formally linked to the judicial process. So criminal justice priorities would have virtually no impact on how a restorative justice process operates. Second, the Parallelist model entails that the justification for funding restorative justice services would need to change. Service providers would not be able to focus almost entirely upon the offender-oriented benefits that typically appeal to criminal justice funding sources, such as reducing caseloads, court costs, noncompliance with orders, recidivism rates and so on. Likewise, restorative justice services are unlikely to be largely situated, as they currently are, within offender-oriented agencies or NGOs, such as the police, youth justice services, rehabilitation agencies and so on. As Johnstone notes:

---

20   Cf. Victim Support UK states: 'We believe that the needs of the victim should be put first, ensuring that victims know how restorative justice can benefit them and that they can get involved when it is right for them' (www.victimsupport.org.uk/more-us/why-choose-us/specialist-services/rj/).

[A]lthough in theory restorative justice seeks to restore both offenders and victims, and does not regard one of these aims as having priority over the other, in practice restorative justice schemes tend to be based in services whose traditional and still primary mission involves working with offenders. (2017: 389)

On a Parallelist framework, restorative justice services would need to pay equal attention to the benefits for victims and local communities. They would therefore need to include or partner with victim-focused government bodies, victim support agencies and community groups. This kind of reorientation would, in itself, provide the impetus for a more balanced approach to the delivery of restorative justice.[21]

It might be argued, in response, that this kind of issue could be resolved by training restorative justice practitioners not to prioritise the needs of offenders. For instance, Jung Choi, Gordon Bazemore and Michael Gilbert identified a number of research studies which suggest that 'RJ programs, whether intended or not, have become more or less offender-centered' (2012: 39). One key explanation for this, they found, is the emphasis on reducing recidivism. However, they then argue that this issue can be adequately addressed by ensuring that 'practitioners do not place primary emphasis on this outcome' (p. 37).

This approach would undoubtedly have an ameliorating effect. But it seems unfair to attribute this kind of problem to 'inadequacies in practice' (p. 41), given that the context makes it virtually unavoidable. Any practitioner working within an Integrationist model will be fully aware of how the program's survival ultimately depends on whether referrers and funders are assured that it is meeting key criminal justice priorities, the most important of which is reducing recidivism. Hence, it seems unrealistic to expect, let alone require, that practitioners in this context refrain from focusing on such an outcome. As one facilitator is reported to have said, 'Let's face it, the money is there because of crime agendas rather than victim agendas' (Zernova, 2016: 110).

2.1.7   *Public interest and state coercion*

There is one important objection to restricting restorative justice to a matter of private interest: First, it is clearly in the public interest to reduce the reoffending rate. And there is good evidence that restorative justice reduces recidivism, at least when the referral crimes have had a serious impact on the victim. Second, it is also in the public interest if victims are able to recover from the harms they have experienced. Again, the evidence suggests

---

21   Simon Green makes a similarly victim-oriented case for Parallelism: 'Perhaps one direction to take restorative justice that would … make the process more accessible to more victims, would be to divorce it from formal sentencing processes' (2007: 186).

that restorative justice can be an effective means of achieving this goal. But if this is the case, and if the role of criminal justice is to meet the public interest in matters relating to crime, then this would justify using an Integrationist model. The justice system, on this account, would only be fulfilling its mandate were it to impose or enforce the offender's participation in restorative justice.

But there are two related problems with this objection:

1. It fails to recognise a crucial distinction between a restorative justice process and its outcomes. What happens within the *process* is a private matter. It is a conversation that occurs between individuals for the purposes of working towards repairing the moral harm they have caused or experienced. This is why the state should not be mandating their participation, let alone monitoring their conversation and enforcing any agreements they make. But there are potential *outcomes* of this kind of process that are a matter of public interest, especially when taken as an aggregate, such as a reduction in the recidivism rate and the recovery of victims.

2. Even if the outcomes of restorative justice are a matter of public interest, it does not follow that the coercive powers of the state should be involved. To assume otherwise fails to recognise a crucial limitation on the power of the state. In this chapter, I have effectively been arguing that 'public coercion should only be used to vindicate public interests', as Jennifer Brown puts it (1994: 1309). However, being in the public interest is not sufficient to justify the use of public coercion. The fact that certain social goods are in the public interest does not, by itself, justify the use of the state's coercive powers to achieve those goods. For example, given the financial and social costs of poor health, it is clearly in the public interest for people to eat a healthy diet. But no liberal government would take this to justify using its coercive powers to compel its citizens to eat the recommended daily portions of fruit and vegetables. The backlash would be overwhelming.

There are any number of similar social goods that are in the public interest, and yet the use of state coercion to achieve them would be largely counterproductive. These goods are far more likely to be realised if the target population is given a choice. In such cases, the only tools that a state can employ will be rational persuasion, education, removing logistical obstacles to the desired behaviour and so on. This is precisely the situation with respect to the kinds of social goods that can arise from restorative justice. As I will argue, these goods are far less likely to be achieved – or at least not as effectively – if the coercive power of the criminal law is involved. The offender's motivation will be compromised, the victim will have good reason to be sceptical about their sincerity and so their level of trust will diminish, and so on. These are not the optimal conditions for moral repair. It follows, then, that, even if some outcomes of restorative justice are in the public interest, this would not in itself vindicate the Integrationist approach.

2.2   PASSIVE VS. ACTIVE RESPONSIBILITY

There is an important distinction between active responsibility (taking responsibility) and passive responsibility (being held responsible).[22] In relation to criminal behaviour, passive responsibility is determined by the state. Active responsibility is determined by the offender's voluntary acknowledgment of their wrongdoing. Passive responsibility is acquitted by the state imposing and/or enforcing a response that is proportionate to the culpability of the offender and the seriousness of their crime. Active responsibility is acquitted by the offender apologising to the victim, making amends or repairing the harm they have caused and taking steps not to repeat their offending behaviour.

This distinction highlights the different approaches to responsibility taken by restorative justice and criminal justice. But it also enables us to gain further clarity on Parallelism and how it compares to the two main alternatives – Integrationism and Maximalism. To this end, I distinguish six ways in which the relationship between passive responsibility and active responsibility is characterised or implied by Integrationism or Maximalism and, in each case, offer reasons for preferring a Parallelist view. I conclude by noting that Parallelism does not entail that offenders will always acquit their passive responsibility unwillingly. Indeed, this model, if fully implemented, would do much to encourage the opposite.

2.2.1   *Active superior to passive*

The Integrationist model privileges active responsibility over passive responsibility. It takes the view that passive responsibility only serves as a backup when active responsibility fails. As Braithwaite puts it:

> [W]e need the jurisprudence of passive responsibility to guide what is the maximum punishment we should be able to impose when active responsibility is spurned. But restorative justice is about a major shift in the balance of criminal jurisprudence from passive to active responsibility. (2006: 43)

Parallelism, by contrast, is the view that a just response to crime requires both passive responsibility and active responsibility. It is not an either/or situation. One is not superior to the other. A just response should include attempts to enable the individuals involved, if they so choose, to find ways of healing their private hurt and engaging in the work of moral repair. But it is also in the public interest that the rule of law be upheld. This is done,

---

22   This terminological distinction appears to have originated in Bovens (1998).

in part, by holding the offender to account in a proportionate and consistent manner in all cases, not only when offenders refuse to take (active) responsibility. Put another way, the Parallelist view is that passive responsibility belongs to the *public* dimension of crime, and active responsibility, to the *private* dimension. Since a just response to crime should address both dimensions, it follows that both kinds of responsibility are essential. One should not merely serve as a backup when the other fails. Without a doubt, the way in which the existing response to crime prioritises the passive over the active should be changed. But on the Parallelist view, this does not mean that as active responsibility increases, the role of passive responsibility should diminish.

2.2.2   Active supersedes passive

Integrationists generally hold that, if an offender apologises and makes amends, there would be no justification for also imposing a state sanction. Taking responsibility is sufficient on its own. As Braithwaite puts it:

> [E]ven though an individual can reasonably be held passively responsible for a crime, if she takes active responsibility for righting the wrong, she can acquit that responsibility. … Because you have taken responsibility for making good, you will no longer be held responsible for any debt to the community. (2002a: 156, 158)

But if someone *takes* responsibility for their wrongful actions, why would it follow that they should not still be *held* responsible? The two types of responsibility are defined in terms of their distinct means of acquittal. Active responsibility can be acquitted only by 'righting the wrong'. Passive responsibility can be acquitted only by paying the 'debt to the community'. In other words, even if an offender takes responsibility for the personal harm they caused to the victim, it does not follow from the resolution of this private matter that the criminal justice system is thereby discharged of its duty to serve the public interest by upholding the rule of law.

Some may respond to this claim with the following objection: The vengeful and callous ways in which passive responsibility is so often acquitted by the criminal justice system invariably obstructs healing or brings yet more harm and hurt to all concerned. Hence, we should avoid the acquittal of passive responsibility wherever possible. Thus, if an offender acquits their active responsibility, we should count this as sufficient for the purposes of 'doing justice'. However, on the Parallelist view, this sets up a false dilemma. There is a viable alternative: reform and re-orientate the criminal justice system so that the means by which it acquits passive responsibility is humane, respectful and just.

To clarify this point, it may be worth examining an argument that might be taken to show why active responsibility, when undertaken, overrides any need to acquit passive responsibility. Dignan presents this argument in the following way:

> [T]he 'wrongfulness' of a criminal act may be determined in part by the way the offender responds to it, and the extent to which s/he is prepared to undertake appropriate reparation for it ... (for example, by participating in a restorative process that affirms the wrong done to the victim, apologising and, possibly, undertaking other forms of reparation). (2003: 153)

But if the wrongfulness of the act can be diminished or even cancelled out by the offender acquitting their active responsibility, then it follows that there would be no justification for acquitting passive responsibility in relation to that act. There would no longer be a 'wrong' for which the offender would need to be held responsible.

The problem with this argument is that it confuses an after-the-fact assessment of the offender with the act itself. Would we seriously suggest that rape is a less wrongful act when it is followed by repentance? Is it not more that, by repenting, the offender demonstrates their recognition of the wrongfulness of the act, and thus distances themselves, morally speaking, from any endorsement of that act? But this hardly warrants a reassessment of the extent to which the act in question was wrong, even 'in part'.

The argument, in short, trades upon an ambiguity in the word 'wrong'. We can say that the offender was morally wrong *in having performed the act*. This kind of wrong can be acquitted by means of active responsibility. But this does not alter the inherent wrongfulness of *the act itself*. It is this quality upon which the legal system is primarily designed to focus. When someone is found to be guilty of rape, they should be held accountable as a way of publicly demonstrating the state's official stance with respect to the wrongfulness of such an act. As I will later argue (§2.3), that is how the norm-clarifying-and-reinforcing functions of criminal justice work. No action or attitudinal change in an individual citizen – whether the victim or the offender – should be able to remove or diminish the extent to which rape is, and is considered by the polity to be, a wrongful act. Holding an offender accountable is one of the primary means by which such societal norms are upheld by the state and communicated to its citizens. That is why acquitting active responsibility cannot – and should not be allowed to – remove or override the need to acquit passive responsibility. This is reflected in the general legal principle that the resolution of a victim's civil rights and remedies should have no effect upon criminal prosecution.[23] As the *Corpus Juris Secundum* (an encyclopaedia of US law) puts it:

---

23   One might argue that victims can affect prosecution insofar as they can choose not to report the crime or not to cooperate as a witness. However, as Jeremy Andersen points out, 'this is a practical power, not a

[Since] a crime is a wrong directly or indirectly affecting the public, the fact that a person who was injured by the commission of a crime has condoned the offense or made a settlement with [the] accused or with some third person in his behalf does not relieve [the] accused or bar a prosecution by the state. (1961: §41 at 132)

2.2.3   Active mitigates passive

An Integrationist might argue that, even if active responsibility cannot supersede passive responsibility entirely, it should nevertheless function as a mitigating factor. Robinson, for instance, argues as follows:

Genuine remorse, public acknowledgement of wrongdoing, and sincere apology can all, in my view, reduce an offender's blameworthiness – and, thereby the amount of punishment deserved. (2003: 380)

To assess this argument, we first need to disambiguate the term 'blameworthiness'. An individual can indeed reduce their *moral* blameworthiness if they take active responsibility for their crime. But this does not alter the fact that they are *factually* or legally to blame for having committed the act in question. An apology will have no bearing on this second type of blameworthiness. Yet it is primarily this fact for which the offender is being held accountable by the state. So, one might assume that an offender's apology should have no impact on the judicial estimation of 'the amount of punishment deserved'.

Whether it should or not, it clearly does. Judges routinely consider remorse as a mitigating factor in accordance with widely accepted sentencing principles. For example, the *Victorian Sentencing Act* 1991 (Austl.) states that, in sentencing an offender, a court must have regard to whether 'the conduct of the offender on or in connection with the trial [was] an indication of remorse or lack of remorse on his or her part' (s.5.2C). One might argue that this is one of the ways in which the public and private dimensions of crime overlap within the criminal justice system. But there is another way of interpreting this phenomenon.

Suppose an offender publicly admits guilt and expresses genuine remorse for the harm they have caused to the victim in a court hearing. This demonstration of active responsibility is likely to mitigate their sentence. But this is not because it brings about healing or closure for the victim. Nor is it because it lifts the psychological burden of guilt from the offender. These are private matters, and the judge cannot be expected to adjust the sentence on the

---

legally vested one' (2003: 1-2, n. 2), and so does not fall under the aforementioned general legal principle.

basis of whether these subjective phenomena have occurred. Rather, the offender's demonstration of remorse in the context of a court should be mitigating *only insofar as it has a bearing on matters of public interest.*

For example, there is clearly a connection between recidivism and genuine remorse. One judge told researchers Jessica Jacobson and Mike Hough 'that "if you see a fully grown man in the dock crying" this can be seen as a clue that he will not offend again in the future' (2007: 48). If recidivism is less likely, that will have a bearing on the safety of the public. So the type or length of sentence employed may be adjusted accordingly.[24] Again, if an offender pleads guilty in court, this saves court time, costs and inconvenience to all concerned. Finally, public admissions of wrongdoing and demonstrations of remorse can serve to amplify or reinforce the societal norms that were violated by the criminal act. It is therefore in the public interest that such expressions be encouraged and rewarded.[25] These reasons alone are sufficient to warrant the offender's demonstration of active responsibility in the court as a mitigating factor. But none of these reasons fall outside the public interest domain. Parallelism does not therefore claim that active responsibility cannot have a legitimate *impact* on the extent to which an offender is held passively responsible. It only claims that active responsibility alone cannot *acquit* passive responsibility.

It might be argued that Parallelism is internally inconsistent on this matter. On the one hand, it takes a stance against Integrationism on the grounds that restorative justice – which is about enabling active responsibility – should not have any impact on the legal process. But then Parallelism also entails that active responsibility can have a legitimate impact on the severity of a sentence. This apparent inconsistency can be dispelled by distinguishing between demonstrations of active responsibility *within a restorative justice process* and demonstrations that take place *within a court*. On the Parallelist model, when an offender takes responsibility in a restorative justice process, this is a private and personal matter. Its effectiveness depends entirely upon the responses of the individuals involved. But when an offender admits wrongdoing and expresses remorse in a court, then, as we have seen, it is primarily a matter of public interest. Given this distinction, it is possible to

---

24   A mere apology in court is not always regarded as sufficient, however. Jacobson and Hough (2007) found that, 'Many of our respondents stressed that they take remorse into account only when it is demonstrated: it is not enough for a respondent simply to say "sorry". Some sentencers thus place an emphasis on defendants' letters to the court ... efforts at reparation' (p. 24), and/or 'an apparent capacity to tackle his personal problems' (p. 41).

25   If the judge perceives an absence of *genuine* remorse, this can also be taken into account. In the case of George Pell's (2018) sexual abuse conviction, for instance, fourteen Australian news outlets were charged with contempt of court for breaching a suppression order. The companies eventually pleaded guilty, apologised and paid legal costs. The judge said that 'he took the "sincere and unreserved apology" to the court into account but said the "timing" of the apology – made at trial – "did not demonstrate any significant degree of remorse and contrition". Rather, he found it was "entered to protect their individual journalist, presenter and editor employees from conviction on the contempt charges they separately faced"' (McGowan, 2021).

argue, without contradiction, *both* that restorative justice should remain independent of the judicial process *and* that if an offender demonstrates active responsibility within the court, this may have a legitimate impact on the sentence.

One might reply to this by arguing that, even if an offender demonstrates active responsibility in court as a direct consequence of participating in restorative justice, all that need be taken into account by the judge is the offender's court-based demonstration, not their participation in restorative justice. However, this restriction could occur only if the offender, in their court-based demonstration, was not permitted to speak directly about the restorative justice process, and only if the court had no knowledge that the process had taken place. But applying this kind of hermetic seal would no longer be an Integrationist approach (see §3.1, 'Principle 7').

The Integrationist may yet respond as follows: When restorative justice is used as a diversion, the facilitator will usually submit a report to the court providing evidence that the offender has demonstrated active responsibility in the restorative justice process. It might be argued that, in such cases, it is *the report* that is having a legal impact, not *the process* itself. But the report can make no impact unless it is taken to be an accurate reflection of the process. It is only the medium by which the otherwise private deliberations of the restorative justice participants can be reviewed by the court and, thus, be taken into account in its decisions. The problem here is that, if the participants know that the contents of such a report could mitigate the offender's sentence, this will invariably have a detrimental impact on the quality and effectiveness of the restorative justice process (or so I argue in §4.7.1).

Finally, an Integrationist might respond by arguing that the offender's experience of restorative justice is very likely to encourage them to demonstrate active responsibility in court. Surely this would be a productive and useful outcome, not only for both the offender and the victim but also in terms of the public interest. However, there are also significant costs, and these, I would argue, outweigh any potential benefits. Allowing the kind of private exchanges that take place in a restorative justice setting to have an impact on the legal process will *undermine* the quality and effectiveness of both criminal justice and restorative justice (or so I argue in Chapter 4). By contrast, allowing an offender's demonstration of active responsibility within the context of a court to be taken into account as a mitigating factor is likely to *increase* the quality and effectiveness of criminal justice.

2.2.4   Active secondary to passive

It may be helpful to explore the Maximalist perspective on active and passive responsibility and how it compares to the Integrationist view. Within the literature, the debate between

Maximalism and Integrationism is often depicted as a disagreement about whether restorative justice is only an *alternative to punishment* (Integrationism) or whether it can also be *an alternative punishment* (Maximalism). Maximalists generally advocate reparative definitions of punishment.[26] But Integrationists are typically keen to avoid any implication that restorative justice involves punishment, no matter how it might be redefined in theory. This is largely because their understanding of 'punishment' reflects the real-world effects of traditional criminal justice sentencing. Uppermost in their minds are the humiliation, stigmatisation, suffering and damage caused by incarceration. Other forms of penal deprivation – such as community service that is designed to humiliate or shame the offender – are not far behind in terms of their disapproval.

From a Parallelist perspective, however, this focus on punishment misconstrues the real difference between the Integrationist and the Maximalist. The distinction that is important here is between active responsibility and passive responsibility, not between punishment and non-punishment. Maximalists are just as opposed to the brutalising nature of imprisonment and other punitive measures. For example, Martin Wright, who endorses Maximalism, argues that '[n]ot only specific punitive sanctions, but punishment itself, [should] be recognised as "cruel, inhuman and degrading"' (2003: 17-18). Another Maximalist, Walgrave, writes: 'Punitive justice stigmatises, excludes, responds to violence with counter violence and does not contribute to reconciliation or the peace' (2001: 27).[27] However, a Maximalist will also argue that it is inconsistent of Integrationists to leave the criminal justice system's punitive sentencing policy intact, let alone to advocate that punishment may be used as a backup for cases that are not suitable for restorative justice. If Integrationists are so averse to retribution, then they should join the Maximalists in advocating for the replacement of traditional punishments with reparative sanctions.[28]

Integrationists might indeed be willing to support this kind of reform. But, as Integrationists, they would not be prepared to classify reparative sanctions as 'restorative justice', and the reason for this resistance is crucial. Even though a reparative sanction might not be retributive, it will not have been arrived at and agreed to in a voluntary dialogue that involves the victim, the offender and others who were directly affected by the crime. Instead, it will be entirely determined by the court. In other words, the real

---

26   *See*, for example, Duff (2003). Not all Maximalists take this view. David Boonin, for instance, defends a Maximalist account in which reparative sanctions are not conceived of as punishment – a view that he calls 'pure restitution' rather than 'restorative justice' (Boonin, 2008: 216, n. 8).

27   Walgrave, it should be noted, now prefers the term 'consequential approach to restorative justice' to 'Maximalism'. *See* Walgrave (2021). My thanks to the Series Editors for alerting me to this change.

28   Jolien Willemsens defines a 'reparative sanction' as follows: '[A]n imposition of some sort that is not deliberately (but probably is) burdensome to the offender but that is constructive and imposed with the intention to contribute to the overall achievement of restoration for the victims, offender, their communities of care and society' (Willemsens, 2003: 31).

disagreement between Integrationists and Maximalists is on whether the acquittal of passive responsibility alone can be legitimately classified as 'restorative justice'.

We need to be more precise here. The Integrationist concept of restorative justice is *process-oriented*. It takes the view that what is essential to restorative justice is the dialogue between the victim, the offender and, where relevant, their respective support persons. Without this level of interpersonal engagement, the restorative goals of moral repair and healing are far less likely to occur. Any outcome agreement that emerges from such a process will thus be a largely symbolic means of demonstrating and reinforcing the moral and relational repair that has taken place. But a reparative sanction that has been determined by a court could not function in the same way. It would not have the same meaning or value for the participants, since it has not emerged from their own self-directed journey of repair and healing. This is why an Integrationist will resist the Maximalist's view that the state's imposition of a reparative sanction can count as 'restorative justice'. As McCold (2000) puts it:

> RJ requires a cooperative approach between victims, offenders, and their communities that can be encouraged and facilitated, but cannot be forced or be accomplished on their behalf (p. 373). ... It is the coming together that allows for the possibility of healing the relational injuries among the affected parties. Maximalists propose that outcomes could be decided for the affected parties and imposed on the offender and still qualify as restorative (p. 393). ... [But d]eciding for people is fundamentally non-restorative, even when done with good intentions. ... The choice is between imposing alternate sanctions or engaging a process for finding solutions. From the perspective of the [Integrationist] model, solutions are restorative, sanctions are not. (p. 397)

Maximalists, as we have already seen (§1.1.2), usually accept that a reparative sanction is not the highest quality of restorative justice possible. Willemsens, for instance, states that 'the restorative value of these impositions is less than that of voluntarily accepted, informal methods' (2003: 31). The Maximalist would, for this reason, prioritise the use of voluntary dialogue over the court when it comes to determining a 'restorative obligation'. In this respect, Maximalists endorse the way that the Integrationist model privileges active responsibility. But they also argue that most offenders are not willing to take responsibility, and many victims are not willing to take part in a dialogue. So if the aim is to ensure that restorative values are dispersed throughout the criminal justice system, then the scope of 'restorative justice' will need to be extended so that it can include the way in which the state acquits the offender's passive responsibility. In other words, Maximalists argue that restorative justice advocates need to put just as much energy and resources towards the greater use of court-determined reparative sanctions. As Walgrave puts it:

> As long as restorative justice is presented as a model of voluntary settlement among victims, offenders and communities, based on free agreements between the parties concerned, it will be condemned to remain some kind of a 'soft ornament' in the margin of 'hard core' criminal justice. (1999: 131) The Maximalist model of restorative justice would provide a non-judicial voluntary process where it can, but require formal coercive processes for the majority of criminal cases where cooperation is not possible. (1998: 13)

The Maximalist concept of restorative justice is, for this reason, *outcome-oriented*. What matters most, in the end, are the tangible results. The fact that reparative sanctions will produce a lower quality of 'restorative justice' is, in their view, a compromise that is worth making. Put another way, the Maximalist holds that active responsibility – while superior to passive responsibility – is, in the end, of secondary importance as a 'restorative' justice mechanism. It should be made available, of course, but since it is subject to the cooperation of individual victims and offenders, it cannot be relied upon to provide the kind of uniform response that is necessary for any 'restorative' justice system. In other words, Maximalism, in effect, prioritises the acquittal of passive responsibility over active responsibility.

How would a Parallelist view this perspective? As mentioned previously, a Parallelist would support the Maximalist's endeavour to replace retributive sentencing with reparative sanctions – but without classifying them as 'restorative' justice. They would also agree that not every offender or victim will be willing or able to take part in restorative justice, and so it could never replace criminal justice. But the Parallelist will reject the view that voluntary forms of restorative justice can be legitimately used as a diversionary approach.

A Parallelist would, of course, side with the Integrationist by insisting on the voluntary nature of restorative justice. This is, after all, a non-negotiable prerequisite for the acquittal of active responsibility, which, for a Parallelist, is the primary function of restorative justice. However, a Parallelist would go on to argue that the Integrationist's commitment to voluntariness does not go far enough. Integrationism is apparently willing to make significant compromises of its own for the sake of its diversionist strategy. In other words, the Integrationist model, as I will argue in the following, creates a 'justice mechanism' that mashes together the acquittal of both active responsibility and passive responsibility, making it significantly more difficult to achieve either.

2.2.5   *Active compromised by passive*

Many traditional sentences – such as community reparation orders – are claimed to be 'voluntary', in the sense that an offender is required to give their consent. But this 'consent' is given under legal duress. If they do not agree to undertake the tasks required by the sentence or do not complete those tasks, then, typically, a more unpalatable option will be imposed by the court. This kind of consent clearly does not imply – nor does it require – active responsibility. The offender can give their consent in this context without acknowledging that their actions were wrong. They do not even need to accept that they were responsible for the crimes in question. They can consent to the sentence without expressing genuine remorse, offering an apology or anything of the kind. All that is required on the part of the offender is the ability to make a cost-benefit calculation. They need only ask themselves what the easiest, least burdensome option will be.

To say that the offender is 'choosing freely' in such a situation is like saying that an execution is 'voluntary' if the offender can choose either the electric chair or lethal injection. As Serena Olsaretti puts it, 'a choice is voluntary if and only if it is not made because there is no acceptable alternative to it' (1998: 71). The offender only chooses the injection because they have been given no other acceptable option. So their decision is not strictly voluntary. Asking consent in this context is little more than a way in which the criminal justice system can weaken the offender's resistance to the means by which they will be held responsible. If they have chosen their fate on the grounds that it is the lesser of two evils, then they are more likely to comply than if they had no choice available to them. To repeat, it does not entail – nor does it need to involve – any active responsibility.

As we have seen, the chief complaint that Integrationists make against Maximalists is that, by suggesting that 'restorative' measures can be determined by the court, the Maximalist view entails that 'restorative justice' falls squarely within the domain of passive rather than active responsibility. A court-imposed reparative sanction is a way of *holding* an offender responsible, not a way of enabling them to *take* responsibility. But what Integrationists fail to see is that their own solution is scarcely better. By employing restorative justice as a diversionary mechanism, they have created a similar Sword of Damocles situation. The offender may give their consent to participate in the process, and they may have willingly collaborated with the victim to design a suitable reparative task. But these decisions are enforced by the criminal justice system. If the offender does not agree to take part in the process or fails to complete the outcome agreement, then there is always the threat, if not the reality, that their case will revert to the normal legal consequences. As Ashworth observes, the offender may have the right to 'walk out' of a restorative justice process and 'take his or her chances in the "conventional" system'. However:

> [T]he result of doing so would usually be to propel the case into a formal criminal justice system that is perceived to be harsher in general, or that the offender may expect to be harsher on someone who has walked away from a

restorative justice process. … [Hence] it is right to remain sceptical of the reality of consent, from the offender's point of view. (2002: 587)[29]

In other words, the offender's choice is this: either they cooperate in the restorative justice process or they will be subject to the legal consequence they would otherwise have received, the precise nature and severity of which they will not be made aware until it is too late. In such a situation, offenders are essentially being asked to make a cost-benefit analysis, with most deciding that restorative justice will probably turn out to be the lesser of two evils. This is consent under legal duress and, as such, falls well within the category of passive responsibility.

2.2.6   Active subordinated to passive

An Integrationist might argue, in response, that an experienced restorative justice facilitator will ensure that this legal threat is kept in the background, so that the offender does not feel like they are being coerced into participating or that they must give the victim whatever they want. As Braithwaite argues:

When punishment is thrust into the foreground even by implied threats, other regarding deliberation is made difficult because the offender is pushed to deliberate in a self-regarding way – out of concern to protect him- or herself from punishment. This is not the way to engender empathy with the victim, internalization of the values of the law, and the values of restorative justice. (2018: 81-82)[30]

Thus, facilitator guides will rightly stipulate that participation should not be coerced in any way. However, most restorative justice schemes operate within a diversionary context.

---

29   Many others have made the same objection. For example: 'The character of making amends as an imposition cannot be avoided by pointing out that the offender's consent is required. The offender cannot choose simply to have nothing happen to him. If he refuses his consent, he will have to face whatever alternative sanctioning system awaits the non-consenting. … He may have reason to fear that those latter responses would be (at best) no less unpleasant' (von Hirsch et al., 2003: 27); '[T]he extent to which [offenders] can be said to have freely "consented" [to restorative justice outcomes] … is dubious. Consenting implies the ability to walk out of the situation without prejudice' (Shapland, 2003: 209); '[I]t is hard to pretend that, in practice, a minor has a free choice and is in no way obliged to participate [in RJ], when his unwillingness to co-operate can be sanctioned by prosecution before the juvenile court and/or a harsher punishment from the juvenile judge' (Eliaerts & Dumortier, 2002: 212-213).

30   Or again: 'The problem is that if deterrent threats cause defiance and reactance, restorative justice may be compromised by what sits above it in a dynamic pyramidal strategy of deterrence and incapacitation. … The challenge is to have the Sword of Damocles always threatening in the background but never threatened in the foreground' (Braithwaite, 1999: 63-64).

So facilitators are encouraged to manage this quandary, as Braithwaite suggests, by drawing the offender's attention away from this legal Sword of Damocles. For instance, Peter Wallis and Barbara Tudor's 'Pocket Guide to Restorative Justice' includes the following statement:

> Ensure that all parties have a genuine choice about whether to participate or not. Under no circumstances should any person be coerced into taking part in any restorative process. ... There must be no sense for the offender that there is a system pay-off for them in participating – for example that it will lead to their sentence, community reparation or punishment being reduced. They will, however, benefit personally from addressing the harm caused in a positive way, and by having reclaimed a 'clean sheet'. (2008: 22)

To give another example, Zernova discovered a promotional leaflet – designed for restorative justice participants – which focuses on the need to give their consent, but omits to mention the legal consequences for the offender if they fail to do so: 'Restorative Justice is *entirely voluntary* so if you do not want to take part you cannot be forced to' (emphasis added; 2016: 74). The problem with these attempts to keep the legal threat in the background is that facilitators cannot control what the offender thinks. The legal situation in which the offender is placed would be almost impossible for them to ignore.

But suppose a facilitator could foreground the offender's choice to opt out, thereby giving them the impression that their participation is 'entirely voluntary'. What would be the underlying rationale? What would be the purpose of doing so? We might assume that this strategy is only designed to ensure that the offender will be better able to *take* responsibility. But the diversionary context would suggest that this foregrounding tactic is also being employed to serve a quite different end. Personal healing and moral repair are not the only objectives here. The acquittal of passive responsibility must also be achieved. One key aim, then, will be to *hold* offenders responsible. But a particularly compelling, if disingenuous, way of doing so is to create a situation in which they *feel* that they are taking responsibility. It is a way of killing two birds with one stone. Offenders are held to account in such a way that they buy into it.[31] Braithwaite goes so far as to call restorative justice a kind of 'self-punishment' for offenders:

---

31   Cf. '[T]he way conferences were prepared and conducted could have masked the punitive aspects of restorative sanctions. ... Offenders may be made to believe that, despite the fact that attending a conference and apologizing was in their court order, they themselves freely chose to attend and apologize' (Zernova, 2016: 63, 76).

> The [responsive] pyramid says 'unless you punish yourself for lawbreaking
> through an agreed action plan near the base of the pyramid, we will punish
> you more severely higher up the pyramid (and we stand ready to go as high as
> we have to).' So, it is cheaper for the rational actor to self-punish (as by agreeing
> to payouts to victims or community service). (2018: 80)

Thus, far from privileging active responsibility over passive responsibility, it turns out that Integrationism instead treats active responsibility not as an end in itself, but rather as a means of securing passive responsibility. This strategy is often quite explicit, as in one report which stated that '*Holding offenders accountable* for their actions and the consequences of them for others, through *acceptance of responsibility* for the offence is a fundamental element of restorative justice' (ACT Restorative Justice Sub-Committee, 2003: 1, my emphasis).

This idea might seem, on first glance, to be an attractive prospect. But there are two serious problems with this strategy:

1. It confirms the criticism that restorative justice is, as Boyes-Watson suggests, 'an ideological mask for the continued extension of state power and control' (2004: 216). And this control can reach even beyond the offender to encompass their immediate family or support persons, who often agree to monitor the offender and ensure that they comply with the restorative justice agreement. As Zernova writes:

> Such enforcement of the plan can be very effective, and in its duration it may
> continue far beyond a court order. Thus, offenders' families may be 'empowered'
> to govern their children in such a way as to advance the agenda and goals of
> the criminal justice system. (2016: 81)

It might be argued in response that there is nothing wrong with social control per se. As John Blad argues, 'it is only a bad thing when it goes wrong, when it is counterproductive, producing exactly those things it claims to control or reduce' (2003: 199). However, the objection here is that the Integrationist model is indeed 'counterproductive' in the sense that it produces the very things that Integrationists hope to avoid, namely, involuntary participation in restorative justice and punitive mechanisms of control. In other words, Integrationism undermines its own commitment to the normative superiority of active responsibility by subordinating restorative justice to the demands of passive responsibility. As Christian Eliaerts and Els Dumortier observe:

> In RJ literature, and in European and UN documents, the voluntary acceptance
> and the voluntary commitment of the offender and the victim are stressed. RJ
> must be an opportunity for offender and victim, not an obligation. Indeed, if

parties participated in a RJ procedure because they are obliged to, the restorative philosophy and goals of mediation would be betrayed. (2002: 212)

2. If the rule of law means anything, it is that the state cannot use its coercive powers to impose or enforce a burden of any kind upon an offender without the application of well-established sentencing principles and due process. But the Integrationist fusion of active responsibility and passive responsibility entails that the state is using its coercive powers to impose or enforce key aspects of restorative justice. So it follows that, if the rule of law is to be maintained, the use of restorative justice in a diversionary setting must abide by these sentencing principles and due process. But as I argue in Chapter 4, the conditions required for the highest quality of restorative justice stand in direct opposition to this requirement. Integrating restorative justice into the criminal justice system will therefore undermine the integrity of both.

2.2.7   Passive does not imply unwilling

I have argued that, from a Parallelist perspective, the acquittals of active responsibility and passive responsibility are of equal value, and so they must both be pursued (separately) in the aftermath of a crime, to whatever extent possible. But it might be thought that this view implies that the acquittal of passive responsibility must be experienced in an entirely passive way. The offender just needs to submit to whatever sanction the state has imposed upon them, regardless of whether they agree with it or not.

In one sense this is true. As I will later argue (§4.5), the state should not violate the moral agency of offenders by demanding that they pretend to agree with the state's judicial decision or the sentence they have received. But of course the offender might still in fact agree. It is, for instance, entirely possible for an offender to view a state-imposed reparative sanction as a means by which they can meet their civic obligations and repair the harm done to the community. They could, in other words, acquit their passive responsibility willingly and for the right reasons.

To be clear, this is not to confuse or intermingle active responsibility with passive responsibility. The goal of passive responsibility is to address the public dimension of crime, not the private. In carrying out a reparative sanction, the offender would not be apologising or making amends to the victim in a private forum. In other words, even if the offender undertakes a sanction willingly, they will not have thereby fulfilled their moral obligations to the victim. A reparative sanction remains a criminal justice disposal, with all that this entails. Nevertheless, if it was willingly undertaken by an offender, with the understanding that this was a civic obligation, there would be several important implications.

First, it could radically alter how the offender sees themselves and the meaningfulness of the task in question. This would in turn be very likely to transform their experience of the sanction and how they carry it out. If all this was somehow conveyed to the victim – perhaps in a subsequent restorative justice process – it could potentially help to affirm the victim's sense of vindication and thus enhance their recovery process. Second, if the Parallelist model were to be implemented, then criminal justice sanctions would all be calibrated so as to be humane, respectful, fair and reparative. This would increase the likelihood of both victims and offenders understanding and endorsing the value and the appropriateness of any sanctions that have been imposed. Such an outcome would, in turn, have a significant impact on the legitimacy and moral standing of the criminal justice system in the eyes of the public. In short, one potential consequence of fully implementing the Parallelist model would be to maximise the probability that offenders will be motivated to acquit their passive responsibility willingly.

2.3   PUBLIC VS. PRIVATE CENSURE

2.3.1   Role of public censure

Imagine arriving in a new country, with little knowledge of its norms or moral standards. You want to establish how this country divides the line between what it takes to be social vices and what it considers a serious moral wrongdoing. For example, does domestic violence rank alongside gossip and adultery? Or is it more like theft and murder? Where would you look? How does an entire country make it known what behaviours it takes to be serious moral wrongs? How does it take a stand and register its collective disapproval? How does it signify – loudly and unambiguously – that within its national boundaries, such actions are unacceptable and will not be tolerated? How can victims of domestic violence, for instance, know that the country in which they live recognises that the acts that have been committed against them are serious wrongs? How will they know that national resources and powers will be employed to protect them and hold those who have caused them harm accountable?

The almost universal answer in the modern world has been for states to create laws against such conduct and to assume responsibility for both detecting and holding to account those who violate these laws. Moreover, states have acquired sufficient power to overrule the views of individuals or minority groups who dispute the wrongness of such violations – a power which, ideally, should be held in check by international human rights legislation and democratic accountability. In short, these processes, which are the responsibility of the criminal justice system, are the primary means by which states are able to declare, publicly and unequivocally, which acts are taken by the majority of its citizens to be serious moral wrongs.[32]

This kind of public censure can also be a powerful way of generating and upholding a consensus around certain moral standards. To criminalise behaviour is a way of exposing its wrongness in a way that would, for many, have otherwise passed beneath their ethical radar. It alerts and challenges the public conscience. It ensures that witnesses have no excuse to look the other way. It provides moral clarity and affirmation to victims who might otherwise feel neglected, abandoned or even deserving of the suffering they have endured. As Andrew von Hirsch, Andrew Ashworth and Clifford Shearing argue:

> In providing that public acknowledgement of wrongdoing, the state gives public recognition to the value of the rights involved, and makes a moral (rather than purely prudential) appeal to citizens that they should desist from the conduct. (2003: 34)

2.3.2   An integrationist critique

Advocates of the Integrationist model might concede that the criminal justice system does indeed have an important societal role in terms of signifying to the public the wrongfulness of certain acts. But they will also argue that restorative justice can offer a far superior form of denunciation. The following four points are often made in defence of this claim:

1. The court system is notorious for its inability to censure criminal acts in a way that can be heard and absorbed by individual victims and offenders. As Walgrave argues (albeit in the context of defending Maximalism):

> Good communication needs an adequate setting. This is not the case in court, where confrontation prevails over communication, and where it is the judge who will in the end decide upon the hard treatment. … The offender does not listen to the moralizing message but tries to get away with as lenient a punishment as possible. He or she does not hear the invitation to improve his or her behaviour, but merely experiences the threat. (2007: 567)

2. The aggressive and threatening mechanism of a state-imposed sanction is far more likely to produce defiance or defensiveness than a 'moral message' that can be heard. Many offenders might appear to accept the moral message conveyed by their sentence. But it is

---

32   As John Tasioulas notes, 'not all moral wrongs should be criminalized; instead, only those moral wrongs that attract the appropriate public interest are even candidates for criminalization' (Tasioulas, 2007: 508).

easy to be sceptical of this phenomenon, particularly in light of the fact that human submission is often no more than a coping mechanism. As Gresham Sykes argued:

> The phenomenon of men identifying themselves with their oppressors – of publicly proclaiming the virtues of rulers, expressing their values, or, still worse in the eyes of the inmates, obeying them all too gladly – may represent a deliberate, Machiavellian attempt to flatter those who have power in order to gain favors. (1958: 89)

3. The primary means by which the criminal justice system can communicate the wrongfulness of an act is the severity of the sentence. And yet, evidence suggests that variations in severity have no corresponding impact on deterrence. An international review found that 'sentence severity has no effect on the level of crime in society' (Doob & Webster, 2003: 143).[33]

4. The vast majority of individuals who are subjected to a criminal sentence are victims of social injustices and oppressive conditions that were caused or not adequately prevented by the state. But in that case, the state does not have the moral standing to censure their behaviour. Indeed, as Jeffrey Howard and Avid Pasternak argue, 'When the state holds victims of its own oppression accountable for their wrongful crimes, it commits a further wrong against them' (2021: 18).[34]

Integrationists will then go on to argue that restorative justice, by contrast, is remarkably good at eliciting moral disapproval for criminal acts within the hearts and minds of those individuals who were directly involved, often resulting in profound attitudinal changes and personal healing. It is, for instance, far more likely than a court to persuade an offender to accept the wrongfulness of their crime. In relation to domestic violence, for instance, Morris accepts that the criminal law does signify its wrongfulness to the public, but argues that it is not nearly so effective in communicating this to the offender:

> [T]he offender's family and friends are by far the most potent agents to achieve this objective of denunciation. In the context of men's violence against their partners, denouncing the violence in the presence of the abuser's family and

---

33   *See*, for example, 'The evidence, though limited in this area, provides no basis for making a causal connection between variations in sentence severity and differences in deterrent effects' (The Halliday Report, 2001: 129). Again, 'the evidence from the deterrence literature [indicates] that perceived and actual severity of punishment are rarely good predictors of compliance with the law, while perceived and actual certainty of detection are often useful predictors' (Braithwaite, 2018: 83). Cf. Weatherburn, Hua and Moffatt (2006).

34   Or as Antony Duff puts it, '[p]unishment is not justifiable within our present legal system; it will not be justifiable unless and until we have brought about deep and far-reaching social, political, legal, and moral changes in ourselves and our society' (Duff, 1986: 294).

friends means that the message is loud and clear for those who matter most to him. (2003: 464)

Moreover, restorative justice is not humiliating, out-casting or threatening, and so the 'moral messages' it conveys are far less likely to be met with defensiveness or defiance. As Dignan puts it, in comparison to the mechanisms available to the criminal justice system, restorative justice processes 'provide an alternative, and arguably far more effective form of normative discourse through which to convey censure without stigma' (2003: 144).

Given all the foregoing concerns, an Integrationist will argue, there would seem to be ample justification for marginalising criminal justice by diverting as many cases as possible to restorative justice. As Howard and Pasternak argue, the state should 'step back' and 'open up an institutional avenue [i.e. restorative justice] where victims of crime take center-stage in holding their perpetrators to account' (2021: 18).

2.3.3   Parallelist perspective

There is a great deal of truth in the foregoing critique. However, it ultimately turns on a false comparison. There is no single objective of denunciation, the achievement of which both criminal justice and restorative justice are competing to fulfil. Rather, there are two different kinds of denunciation required. Public censure is needed in order to communicate to the population which acts will be recognised and treated by the state as serious moral wrongs. Private censure is needed to induce moral and behavioural change in individuals. But then why would we assume that both forms of censure could be successfully communicated at the same time or in the same way? Why should we expect that what it takes to deliver private censure effectively will be identical to the best way of communicating public censure, or vice versa?

Consider the limitations of restorative justice as a form of public censure. What is needed here is a communicative medium that is capable of denouncing serious wrongdoing in an open and demonstrative fashion, accessible across the population, with no room left for doubt. It must be a powerful signifier that communicates an unwavering, proportionate and non-arbitrary condemnation of acts that the majority of citizens would take to be serious moral wrongs. It is difficult to see how a medium like restorative justice could possibly fill these shoes. The censure that it delivers is almost entirely person-specific, a private matter, and highly contingent upon a range of unpredictable variables.

Suppose we were dependent upon restorative justice as the dominant means of signifying the wrongfulness of a certain act to the polity, and of demonstrating that the public stands with its victims in condemning this act, thereby affirming their equal worth as human beings. The problem is that a great many offenders are not willing or suitable for restorative justice. To illustrate, New Zealand's Integrationist legislation would seem to be optimal for maximising the use of restorative justice. Yet the number of conferences per year is tiny compared to the number of convictions that would normally involve at least one identifiable victim. For instance, in 2015 there were 2,782 conferences, but almost 60,000 convictions that year were likely to have involved a victim.[35] In such a scenario, then, a chasm of silence would open up, with vast numbers of victims left uncertain as to whether their humanity is indeed recognised by the general public. Roche provides a good example of this by noting the reaction that many have to the use of restorative justice to address domestic violence cases:[36]

> One of the achievements of the women's movement in the 1970s and 1980s was to change public opinion so that violence against women and children is now more widely seen as a crime, and critics are concerned that restorative justice does not serve to jeopardize these hard-won achievements. (2003: 35-36)[37]

Some advocates have responded to this kind of concern by arguing that restorative justice could make its processes and outcomes accessible to the wider public. For instance, Jennifer Brown argues:

> To have general deterrent effect ... the costs associated with facing the victim would have to be publicized more, so that potential criminals would know the fate that might await them if their contemplated crime is detected. (1994: 1299)[38]

---

35   This approximation is based on the number of convictions for offences that were classified under types 1-9 in New Zealand's Justice Statistics data tables: www.justice.govt.nz/justice-sector-policy/research-data/justice-statistics/data-tables/. The conference statistic is from the Ministry of Justice (2020: 6).

36   While this kind of reaction has been especially prominent in relation to domestic violence given that it has only recently been criminalised, it is hard to see how this concern would not also apply to other crimes, although perhaps to varying degrees depending on the seriousness of the offence.

37   Elizabeth Schneider argues that there are a number of other ways in which the criminalisation of domestic violence has redefined it as a public issue. 'First, because of the availability of these legal remedies, there are more proceedings in court, and the participants, judiciary, court personnel, and public are educated about the problem of domestic violence. Public participation in these disputes may well have contributed to changing attitudes concerning the acceptability of violence against women. The media frequently focuses on court cases, so there are many articles in newspapers and programs on television about these cases. Analysis of the actual implementation of these legal remedies, and the failure of the courts to enforce these provisions, has been widely publicized in the many state gender bias reports and has further expanded an educational process within the states' (Schneider, 1991: 990).

38   Cf. 'Restorative justice does not aim at general deterrence, although there is always the fear of being caught and possibly the fear of meeting one's victim when a greater number of potential offenders are aware of [restorative justice]' (Wright & Masters, 2002: 56).

One problem with this suggestion is that restorative justice processes are, for principled reasons, meant to be private and confidential. But suppose that this objective can be waived or circumvented in some way, for example, by obtaining consent from all participants to make only the bare essentials public. Or, more plausibly, the public could be provided with the *kind* of 'costs associated with facing the victim'. But even here, how could we have any confidence in generalisations about the 'fate' that might 'await' offenders?

It is true that restorative justice can exact 'costs' that most offenders would want to avoid – such as facing the intense anger and emotional distress of the victim or the disapproval and embarrassment of their own family members. But what happens in any given restorative justice meeting will be entirely dependent on the views and attitudes of the individuals who are present. As Patrick Lenta argues, this means that the degree of censure an offender will encounter 'may or may not be commensurate with or proportional to the severity of their crimes' (2021: 23). An offender who committed a minor burglary might be faced with multiple victims who are consumed with intense anger and bitterness, while their own family members cannot hide their disapproval and acute embarrassment. Meanwhile, an offender who committed a crime of severe violence might encounter a single victim who is well into their journey of healing and simply wants to offer their forgiveness in person. As von Hirsch et al. put it:

> [I]f the procedure leaves decisions primarily to individual offenders and their victims … [w]hat will come to matter is not so much how culpable the offender was in committing his wrong, but the particulars concerning how much the victim has been hurt. (2003: 35)

Again, whatever censure an offender experiences in the restorative justice process might persuade them not to commit further offences against the victim in question. But the harm-specific focus of the censure means they may not readily apply it to the *kind* of offence they committed. At the end of one restorative justice meeting, the victim was reported to have asked the young offender: 'So do you think you'll ever steal a car again?' His reply was, 'Well, I'm definitely not going to steal *your* car again' (Roche, 2003: 12, n. 14).

In short, it would, at best, be highly misleading to broadcast generalisations about 'the costs associated with facing the victim' in a restorative justice process. Even if two offenders were equally culpable for the same type of crime, there could be no certainty about the kind or degree of censure that each of them would face. Restorative justice cannot, therefore, provide a public signifier that is consistent, proportionate and non-arbitrary in its condemnation of serious wrong, and so it cannot function as an effective form of public censure.

By contrast, this kind of public denunciation is precisely the role for which criminal justice was designed. As Keith Hawkins writes:

> Prosecution is a ceremonial restatement of norms by which people and individuals order social life. Its use sustains the moral world which the regulatory organization inhabits. One way it does this is through the satisfaction given by the prosecution of a blameworthy defendant that moral boundaries are being maintained and reinforced. … In making public those standards of conduct deemed proper, decent and desirable, prosecution can be cathartic, since it can sometimes satisfy a demand, whether from the victim, the victim's family, the media or people generally, for a public statement of the worth of the victim and the culpability of the defendant. (2003: 416, 417)

And it is important to be clear that this norm-clarifying role outweighs the fact that it has little, if any, deterrent effect. The public denunciation of serious wrongdoing is, in this sense, an end in itself. As von Hirsch et al. argue:

> It would not be necessary to try to determine whether tougher burglary sentences actually help reduce the burglary rate, because even if this did not occur it would still be a good thing for an authoritative source to express on the public's behalf the sentiment that burglary ought better to be prevented. (2003: 24, n. 4)

In other words, the rationale for criminalising certain acts, holding formal court hearings and adjusting sentence severity to fit the crime does not lie in their capacity to deliver a compelling moral message to individual offenders or even to reduce the overall offending rate. The role of such mechanisms is instead legitimised by their ability to communicate to the population the wrongfulness of certain types of conduct and, thereby, affirm and sustain key moral standards that are held by the majority. This is why it is in the public interest for offences to be dealt with openly and demonstratively by the state. As Hyman Gross puts it:

> The threats are not laid down to deter those tempted to break the rules, but rather to maintain the rules as a set of standards that compel allegiance in spite of violations by those who commit crimes. In short, the rules of conduct laid down in the criminal law are a powerful social force upon which society is dependent for its very existence, and there is punishment for violation of these rules in order to prevent the dissipation of their power that would result if they were violated with impunity. (1979: 401)

Similarly, suppose a state has lost its moral standing to censure offenders who have suffered from unjust and oppressive social-structural conditions for which it is ultimately responsible. In such a scenario, the rule of law would be more important than ever. The solution is not therefore to relinquish, marginalise or circumvent the one institution that has the power and the authority to hold wrongdoers to account without fear or favour. The criminal justice system must instead be reformed (or transformed) so that it can openly and demonstratively denounce the structural violence, social injustices and oppressive conditions that were experienced by the offender and hold those responsible to account.

It is only by ignoring the inherent differences between public and private censure that any defence of the denunciative superiority of restorative justice can get off the ground. The primary objective of criminal justice is not to persuade individual offenders to accept the wrongfulness of their actions, let alone to inspire repentance or induce moral transformation. If that were the case, it would be a miserable failure, but through no fault of its own. The only techniques of persuasion to which it has access are simply not up to the task. Likewise, the public denunciation of serious wrongdoing cannot be effectively performed by a private, highly particularised and variable process such as restorative justice. But again, this is not a failure. It is simply doing what it was designed to do. We clearly need both public and private forms of censure. But if they are to be effective, they must be carried out independently and by using separate processes that are specifically designed for the task at hand.

Herein lies the problem for the Integrationist model. When restorative justice is used as a diversionary scheme, it is effectively functioning as a criminal justice disposal. Hence, it is expected to fulfil the additional role of delivering something akin to a public denunciation of the crime. The individual victim cannot therefore simply communicate their own personal moral views about the offence, or merely focus on how it affected them as an individual. The victim must also somehow represent the moral stance of the entire polity and how a crime of this nature affects society as a whole. As Duff puts it:

> [S]ince the crime is a public wrong, the victim (and her supporters, if the [restorative justice] process includes them) must speak not just for herself, but for the community as a whole; and the offender must speak not just to her, but through her to the whole community. (2003: 56)

But as we have seen, restorative justice is inherently ill-equipped to fulfil this role. Even worse, when it attempts to do so, it undermines its own integrity and effectiveness as a means of private censure. In my own experience as a facilitator and observer of restorative justice meetings, when a victim attempts to explain how the offender's actions have not only harmed them personally but also 'society as a whole', the offender will tend to switch off or lose focus. As Suzanne Retzinger and Thomas Scheff explain:

> Generalised consequences are apt to be shrugged off by the offender as completely unrelated to him, and in so doing, he mobilises his defences. The consequences likely to have emotional effects on the offender are only those that are clearly and directly related to his own actions. (1996: 330)

Moreover, when an offender is faced with a legal Sword of Damocles, they are far less likely to be affected by any censure they might face in the meeting. Thanks to the diversionary context, their chief focus will be on doing whatever it takes to avoid a more punitive outcome – not unlike Syke's account of the prisoners who 'flatter those who have power in order to gain favors' (1958: 89). And this is not mere conjecture. To give just one example, the experience of the Thames Valley Restorative Justice service suggests that this kind of Machiavellian performance is a routine occurrence:

> Offenders invited to take part in an RJ Conference as part of a Community Sentence may express a great willingness to meet with and apologise to their victims at the Pre-Sentence Report stage. For this positive attitude of remorse and desire to make amends they may gain credit in the Pre-Sentence report. Experience in Thames Valley has shown that many such offenders tend to be reluctant or withdraw their co-operation once a Community Sentence has been imposed. By this shift in attitude they have failed to live up to their implied commitment to the court. (Thames Valley Partnership, 2013: 22)

In short, only a model that preserves the legal independence of restorative justice, such as Parallelism, can ensure that the most effective forms of both public and private denunciation are made available.

2.3.4   Possible responses

I have argued that one reason why criminal justice is a more effective means of delivering public censure is that, unlike restorative justice, its mechanisms are more likely to reflect both the culpability of the offender and the wrongfulness of the crime. But there are two key responses that an Integrationist could make.

First, they might argue that questions of culpability are indeed raised and taken seriously in restorative justice. For instance, the dialogue usually begins with a stage in which the offender is invited to explain what happened, in terms of their role in causing the harm. The victim will then have an opportunity to question the offender about their role. In other words, the process is designed to enable the participants to explore who was responsible and to what extent. And this will normally have an impact on the outcome.

Thus, suppose that three offenders are meeting with a victim. It turns out that one of them was the ringleader, while the others played only backup or lookout roles. If the victim was to request a reparative task, then it is highly likely that this difference in culpability between the participating offenders would be taken into consideration. In addition, the kind of process that is used can also reflect culpability or wrongfulness. For example, conferences and face-to-face meetings tend to be used for more serious offences, while indirect communication via a facilitator (shuttle dialogue) is often used for more minor crimes. Again, serious offences typically require a longer and more intensive preparation phase, and, if there is a meeting, they tend to be longer. Cases that involve crimes of severe violence, for instance, can take anywhere from 4 to 12 months to prepare the participants, and the meetings can last for 'up to 8 hours' (Umbreit & Armour, 2011: 223).

However, this response overlooks three severe limitations that are inherent to these features of a restorative justice process:

1. In a diversionary context, participants are unlikely to have access to independent evidence that could confirm or deny the offender's account of what happened. They are invited to ask questions of the offender in case there is a lack of clarity in their minds. But in most cases, the facilitator will intervene if the victim's questioning begins to sound like a quasi-criminal investigation.[39] This is partly because any admissions – other than what they have already conceded in order to be eligible for the process – could be self-incriminating. And in the absence of legal representation or watertight confidentiality protections, extracting additional confessions would violate their right to due process (see §4.3). But there is another even more important reason why restorative justice is not suited to the kind of interrogation that might be expected in court. Such overt scepticism about the offender's honesty, together with the conflict, inhibition and bad feeling that could ensue, is likely to undermine any progress that might otherwise have been made towards the goal of moral repair.

2. How the offender's culpability is taken into account is not prescribed in advance. There are no rules that rank reparative tasks according to the culpability of the offender. If the process is to remain voluntary, these decisions must be negotiated by those involved and must not be imposed from above. And the nature of the reparative task is typically modified more by the degree of remorse shown by the offender than the degree of their accepted culpability. Reparative tasks are typically taken as symbolic expressions of penitence, rather than as a precise reflection of the offender's culpability. This explains why a victim of a life-threatening assault may be content to receive nothing more than a

---

39   If a police officer is attending (let alone facilitating), as is often the case in a diversionary setting, then it can be considerably more difficult to prevent them from using the process to conduct this kind of investigation, with predictable results (*see* §4.7.4).

heartfelt apology, whereas a victim of a burglary might request a fairly onerous reparative task if they are in two minds about the offender's sincerity.

3. While the differences between restorative justice processes can track the level of a crime's seriousness, they are just as likely to correspond to the participants' level of preparedness for a meeting. It may just be a matter of how long they wish to talk with each other. Shuttle dialogue may be the most appropriate form of communication, even for a homicide. What process is used ultimately depends upon the needs of the participants and not upon the nature of the offence. Cases involving a crime of severe violence can take relatively little time to prepare if all the participants happen to be at a stage whereby more preparation would be unnecessary. Yet a relatively minor theft could take many months of preparation if, say, one participant has complex mental health issues. In order to ensure that a restorative justice process is most likely to be effective, in terms of meeting its own objectives, then it should not be altered for any reason other than to meet the needs of participants.

The second response that an Integrationist might make is to argue that the main signifier available to the criminal justice system is inherently defective as a medium for publicly censuring wrongdoing. Specifically, the legal criteria of guilt and the punitive sentences employed by existing criminal justice systems are not capable of reflecting important moral distinctions and judgments about objective culpability or the wrongfulness of an act. Three considerations might be put forward to support this claim:

1. The legal culpability of offenders is routinely determined in a way that fails to take into account the morally mitigating effects of poverty, systemic racial injustice, mental illness, drug addiction, brain injuries, developmental immaturity, ignorance of the law and so on – at least not in a sufficiently reliable or fine-grained way.[40] In America, the vast majority of offenders are not even given the opportunity to have their culpability assessed in a court of law, given the widespread use of plea bargaining. As Gregg Caruso writes:

> [T]he state often resorts to plea-bargaining and settling cases prior to a trial, which deprives poor and disadvantaged defendants from a proper hearing of the facts or a close examination of their moral and legal guilt. In fact, in the United States 97 percent of federal cases and 94 percent of state cases end in plea bargains, with defendants pleading guilty in exchange for a lesser sentence. The image of a criminal justice system where defendants get their fair day in court and a fair and just sentence once a trial is concluded is very different from the real, workaday world inhabited by prosecutors and defense lawyers in the United States. (2021: 139)

---

40   *See,* for example, Kelly (2018: 11) and Caruso (2021: 141).

2. The blunt instrument of prison time is notoriously subjective. Imprisonment to one prisoner will be extremely oppressive and painful. To another, it will be little more than 'time out'. As Wright observes, 'Prison is a trauma for some, an occupational hazard for others' (2003: 16). Or the conditions within one prison may be worse than another. As the then Lord Chief Justice Woolf put it:

> While consistency in sentencing is highly desirable, in practice it can never be achieved totally and the judge is always having to sentence recognising the realities on the ground in which he has to impose the sentence. Even if it was possible to achieve consistency, one prisoner will pass his sentence in much better conditions than another prisoner sentenced to the same sentence for exactly the same offence because what is on offer in different prisons is not the same. (2002: 2)

3. One might argue that the meaning of punishment, as delivered by the criminal justice system, is not whatever the recipient takes it to be. The offender is not, after all, the intended audience. What matters is how punishment is perceived by the public. But even here, the nature or extent of punishment appears to be relative to the accidental variable of the country or the moment in history in which one happens to live. As Thomas Mathiesen writes:

> The severity of punishment is bound up with and relative to the vantage-point, especially proximity. The meaning of prison time, the meaning of two months, two years, twenty years of imprisonment, is therefore morally relative and relative in terms of perspective. This fact is reflected in the great international differences which exist concerning the evaluation of the importance of prison time. If prison time were objective, various nations should converge towards the same punishment times. We know that they certainly do not converge, but show dramatic differences. (2006: 137)

A Parallelist can accept that these issues have seriously damaged the credibility and moral standing of criminal justice as a medium of public censure. But this situation does not entail that we should abandon the rule of law or give up on the constraints of due process. Many aspects of the criminal justice system are, at present, cruel, discriminatory, corrupt and dysfunctional. But it does not follow that it must be literally impossible to create a public institution that can censure criminal behaviour in a way that is humane, reliable and fair. In relation to proportionality, for instance, Parallelists would align with the Maximalists by arguing that, in terms of public censure, reparative sanctions are considerably more effective and objective than punitive sanctions. They are better able to reflect – and thus communicate – degrees of culpability and wrongdoing insofar as they seek to repair or compensate for the measurable harm for which the offender is responsible.[41] Thus, as Boonin argues, if an offender was 'only 50 percent responsible' for a criminal incident, then it would be fair to compel them to make reparations for 'only one-half of the harm' that was caused (2008: 258).

In sum, Parallelists would by no means endorse the status quo, but they also would not submit to a counsel of despair. Instead, they will join with those who seek to reform (or transform) the criminal justice system so that it can better fulfil its foundational remit, while also acknowledging how enormously challenging, complex and costly such changes would be.

---

41   Jim Dignan argues that reparation should be linked to the wrong that has been done, rather than the harm that has been caused on the grounds that 'it may be much more difficult to resist calls for the response to "equate" in some way with the harm that has actually been caused' (Dignan, 2003: 153). But this confuses the concept of retribution ('we shall pluck out your eye to *avenge* the victim whose eye you destroyed') with reparation ('we shall ensure that you *compensate* the victim for the eye you destroyed'). Any calls for reparation to 'equate' with the harm caused can be resisted by pointing out the distinction.

3 IMPLEMENTATION

This chapter presents a set of Guiding Principles that would need to be put into practice in order to implement the restorative justice arm of Parallelism. It then offers suggestions about how a Parallelist model would organise referrals to restorative justice, obtain funding for services and arrange for implementation and evaluation. Finally, it proposes that Parallelism offers a more viable vision for how restorative justice might become a mainstream response to crime.

3.1 GUIDING PRINCIPLES

3.1.1 Introduction

In Chapter 2, I defended the theoretical perspective that underpins Parallelism. But how feasible is such a model in reality? I have argued that the full Parallelist model will involve substantial reforms (or transformations) to the criminal justice system, and I have suggested the kind of changes that are likely to be required in broad terms. But to provide any further details would require several additional tomes, and in any case this groundwork has, to a great extent, already been carried out by many others. Thus, my focus in this chapter will be on how the restorative justice arm of the Parallelist model might be implemented.

As I have mentioned previously, given the variety of justice systems, let alone the differences between legal systems and cultures, it would be almost impossible to set out detailed, concrete recommendations that will be universally applicable in every jurisdiction. Thus, my approach will be to set out a list of general principles that could be used by virtually any particular jurisdiction to guide its implementation of Parallelism. These principles are derived from the theoretical foundations specified in Chapter 2, and so I take each of them to be necessary for an approach to count as 'Parallelist'. I have tried to be comprehensive, so that, if they were all implemented together, this would be enough to create a genuinely Parallelist model. But I accept that each jurisdiction may need to add or amend one or more principles so as to reflect its own distinctive terminology, culture or legal system.

Guiding Principles
1. The crime needs to be serious or complex enough to require third-party intervention.

2. The crime must involve significant wrongdoing or harm.

3. When restorative justice is used to address a crime, there must also be a criminal justice response to that offence – but not necessarily at the same time.

4. Restorative justice should not be used to enable or encourage people to evade the criminal justice system.

5. The decision about whether a criminal justice intervention would be in the public interest needs to be made by a judicial authority.

6. Confidentiality protections should not be used to undermine the legitimate enforcement of law.

7. Legal independence for restorative justice must be guaranteed, rather than optional or accidental.

8. No legal benefit should be available to an offender as a direct consequence of satisfying the eligibility criteria for restorative justice, agreeing to take part in the process or participating successfully.

9. Restorative justice should only take place after a case has actually or effectively exited the justice system.

3.1.2   Explanation

Principle 1. *The crime needs to be serious or complex enough to require third-party intervention.*

Adam Crawford notes: 'Most crimes are dealt with, put aside or managed by the public in one way or another' (2002: 108). Some aspects of this management may be consistent with restorative values, insofar as they involve relatively spontaneous or self-initiated acts of apology and reparation. But the Parallelism is, by definition, about the relationship between restorative justice services and the criminal justice system, and so this model only applies where the incident is serious or complex enough to require third-party facilitation and a certain level of organisation.

Principle 2. *The crime must involve significant wrongdoing or harm.*

This principle is designed to ensure that, whenever Parallelism is implemented, a clear distinction is made between restorative justice and other types of informal processes. To give an illustration, Gerry Johnstone makes the following suggestion:

> One [option] would be to … [provide] restorative justice services outside the criminal justice system, making them available on a purely voluntary basis,

making it clear that compliance with any agreements made is also voluntary, and refusing to employ within them any of the vocabulary of criminal justice. They would then be forums to which people involved in disputes with each other (even disputes arising from 'criminalizable events') could go (if all agreed) instead of seeking state intervention in the form of criminal justice. (2007: 607)

Insofar as the incidents to be addressed are not only 'criminalisable events' but also involve some form of wrongdoing or harm done to a victim, this kind of direct referral could be considered a potential means of implementing Parallelism (although I will raise serious concerns about this approach under 'Principle 3'). However, the way Johnstone's proposal is expressed might suggest that its purpose is to focus on the resolution of 'disputes'. Despite the widespread misappropriation of 'conflict' language by advocates,[1] restorative justice is not primarily designed to resolve disputes or conflicts. The central purpose of restorative justice is to address wrongdoing or harm, even if, in order to do so, the process may need to resolve some associated conflict.[2] As I have previously argued (§1.2.2), there are already longstanding extralegal processes that are specifically designed to focus on the resolution of conflict alone and which almost always operate 'outside the criminal justice system'. These include alternative dispute resolution, community mediation, peer mediation and so on. It is crucial that these processes are not (re)conceived of or carried out under the banner of 'restorative justice', especially within an extralegal context. This would only cause unnecessary conceptual confusion and lead to unworkable and unsafe hybrids.

Principle 3. *When restorative justice is used to address a crime, there must also be a criminal justice response to that offence – but not necessarily at the same time.*

Two important clarifications are needed here. First, a 'criminal justice response' need not involve an actual arrest or prosecution. The response might be a decision *not* to make an arrest or file charges. Second, this principle does not entail that restorative justice must be applied to *every* crime for which there is a criminal justice response. There will be criminal incidents where restorative justice is not suitable or possible.

Perhaps the most important implication of this principle is that it precludes the use of restorative justice in the absence of any criminal justice response. On the face of it, this might seem counterintuitive, given that such a use would guarantee legal independence.

---

1   To give one example, 'RJ is a conflict resolution technique not confined to incidents defined by law as criminal. It is increasingly used in school and workplace settings' (Sherman & Strang, 2007: 37).
2   For a defence of this position, *see* Brookes and McDonough (2006).

The victim and the offender could bypass the police and refer themselves directly to a restorative justice service, thereby avoiding the legal system entirely.[3] There are three other reasons why this idea might be thought to have some merit.

1. Most victims do not report the crimes they have experienced to the police. To give one example, a *New Zealand Crime and Victims Survey* estimates that, in 2020-2021, only '25% of victimisations were reported to the Police', a figure which was not significantly different from previous years (Ministry of Justice, 2022: 9). If restorative justice were to be made available to the remaining victims, this could potentially open up a vast reservoir of cases that would otherwise be neglected. As Jo-Anne Wemmers puts it, when the availability of restorative justice services 'depend on the ability of the police to apprehend the offender, only a small group of victims will ever be able to profit from restorative justice programs' (2002: 56).

2. Many unreported crimes would appear to be suitable for a restorative justice approach. For example, in the New Zealand *Survey*, the most common reasons that victims gave for not reporting crimes were, as might be expected, that the offence was 'too trivial', there was 'no loss or damage' and it was 'not worth reporting' (45% of incidents). Indeed, the *Survey* found a correlation between the perceived seriousness of a crime and whether it was reported to the police: 'those who rated the offence as very serious ... were significantly more likely to report that incident to the Police' (Ministry of Justice, 2022: 161-162). However, even if all the minor incidents were excluded, there would remain a great many unreported crimes that were not perceived to be 'trivial' by the victims. The *Survey* found that only 8% of sexual assaults and 27% of incidents involving interpersonal violence were reported to the police (2022: 158). Such cases would be well-suited for restorative justice, as well as consistent with Principle 2 above. And the referral numbers would not be insignificant.

3. The exclusive use of restorative justice would avoid the most damaging and ineffectual aspects of the criminal justice system. This is, after all, one of the main reasons why many victims do not report crimes, especially serious offences. For instance, the New Zealand *Survey* found that the reasons victims gave for not reporting serious offences were almost always linked to wanting to avoid the kind of public exposure or punitive consequences that a criminal justice intervention would invariably bring. Many victims claimed that they wanted to avoid 'shame', 'embarrassment' or 'further humiliation' or did not report due to 'fear of reprisals' or because doing so 'would make matters worse' or because they 'didn't want to get [the] offender into trouble' (Ministry of Justice, 2022: 169.). Again, victims said they did not report the incident because the 'police couldn't have done anything' and that they 'didn't have enough evidence' (2022: 167). And this kind of

---

3   This approach has been suggested by Simon Green. Victims, he writes, could 'access restorative schemes regardless of whether the offence was reported, or an offender apprehended' (Green, 2007: 186).

reason is not without merit. In Germany, for instance, 40% of the 3.25 million offences detected by police in 2013 were closed because the reported facts 'did not meet the requirements of a criminal offence or the evidence was not sufficient' (Hartmann, 2019: 135).

Given these considerations, it might be argued that Principle 3 should be amended so as to allow restorative justice to be used on its own. However, this way of achieving legal independence would effectively undermine the rule of law and, as such, would be incompatible with Parallelism – as I will argue in connection with the next guiding principle.

Principle 4. *Restorative justice should not be used to enable or encourage people to evade the criminal justice system.*

There is an important difference between a restorative justice process that evades the legal system entirely and one that is merely independent of it. If someone has experienced a serious crime, such as a homicide or sexual assault, then, as I have argued (in §2.1), the citizenry as a whole has a legitimate interest in making sure that the state does not simply ignore what has happened or dismiss it as unimportant or none of its business. Crime should not be regarded as merely a private matter. This is why a Parallelist would be opposed to the use of restorative justice as a way of bypassing the criminal justice system.

So how then would a Parallelist model address the previously mentioned problem of underreporting? It would begin by identifying the source of the problem. Victims and other witnesses are rarely supported and respected in the ways they need. The evidential bar for many crimes is often placed so unrealistically high that prosecution can be far too easily evaded. Criminal justice systems can be so drastically underfunded that they are unable to give each case the time, the resources and the attention it deserves. Many justice systems have lost their moral standing and public trust by allowing themselves to be exploited by multinational corporations, misdirected into retributive dead-ends and used as a politically expedient means of concealing entirely preventable social-structural injustice and disadvantage. Fix these systemic issues, and it is likely that the reporting rate would dramatically increase.

In sum, using restorative justice to evade the justice system will not solve the issue of serious crimes not being reported to the police. The criminal justice system must be subjected to a root and branch reform (or transformation) so that it can better fulfil its remit. Encouraging and enabling people to circumvent the system only undermines its legitimate societal role even further.

Principle 5. *The decision about whether a criminal justice intervention would be in the public interest needs to be made by a judicial authority.*

Restorative justice is clearly not equipped to detect or investigate crimes, nor should it be. But it follows that a direct referral to restorative justice could only be made if the victim already knows the offender (or, vice versa, depending on who initiates the referral). This means that self-referrals are most likely to occur where the victim and the offender are members of the same family or live in the same community or belong to the same institution – such as a school, prison, residential home, church, hospital, university, defence force, sports association, workplace and so on.

But this feature opens up a way of qualifying the scope of the principle that breaches of the criminal law should be dealt with by the justice system. Social institutions, such as schools or workplaces, frequently address criminal wrongdoing by using their own internal disciplinary mechanisms.[4] This practice is normally justified on the grounds that the public interest dimension can be properly subsumed under or scaled down to the institution's interests (or, more precisely, the interests of the institution's members). But this justification would only apply when the wrongdoing is of greater significance to the institution than it is to society as a whole.

Put another way, the institution's interests take priority only where it would be contrary to the public interest if the justice system were to intervene. This scenario might arise due to the fact that the crimes are relatively minor or there is evidence that a criminal justice response is likely to do more harm than good to all concerned. As I argued earlier (in §2.1.7), the public interest is not always best served by applying the coercive powers of the state. To give an example, when Paul Robeson High School in Chicago introduced restorative justice programmes, its rate of police notifications dropped 93% from the previous year (Alternatives, 2017: 5). The Washington-based Justice Policy Institute defended this approach on the grounds that 'Pushing kids out of school by focusing on law enforcement responses and punitive policies toward behavior ultimately results in more incarceration and reduced community well-being' (Petteruti, 2011: 1).

This approach is, of course, already happening in many schools, workplaces, universities and other institutions and on a rapidly increasing scale. Much of it now occurs under the banner of 'Restorative Practices' or 'Restorative Approaches'. Unfortunately, both of these terms usually encompass not only restorative justice processes, as defined here, but also a range of other informal approaches, such as conflict resolution techniques, mediation, circle-time, mentoring, counselling, problem-solving, democratic decision-making and

---

4   For instance, the New Zealand *Survey* found that 'victims were significantly less likely to report incidents that occurred in community settings such as schools, sports grounds, hospitals and religious buildings, with only 12% of incidents in these locations reported' (Ministry of Justice, 2022: 160).

so on. As a consequence, 'restorative justice' is itself often used as a catch-all term to describe the full gamut of these informal approaches. Nevertheless, if we can, yet again, overlook this unhelpful muddle, it would seem that restorative justice could be legitimately used as an exclusive response when the crime has occurred within an institutional setting.

Despite its initial plausibility and increasing use, there are several important challenges that can be made to this approach. To begin, who decides whether it would be contrary to the public interest for any particular criminal behaviour to be dealt with by the justice system? Who has the expertise or the authority to decide when the rule of law need not apply? And how would they determine whether, in any particular case, the institution's interests should take priority over the interests of society as a whole? There would, of course, be little controversy about excluding the most serious offences, such as homicide, manslaughter, rape or aggravated sexual assault. The significance of such harms to the polity at large will always outweigh any subsidiary institutional interests.[5] But what about crimes that are not as serious but nevertheless cause significant harm?

One problem here is that, by definition, any behaviour that violates the criminal law is a matter of public interest.[6] But then, as far as legitimate crimes are concerned, it seems clear that no school, sports association or workplace is entitled to make a decision, on its own, about whether or not it would be in the public interest to prosecute one of its members for committing a crime. Even the assistance of a qualified lawyer would not be sufficient. When the state appoints a police officer, a prosecutor or a judge, it gives these individuals the authority to represent the polity on criminal matters. They are assigned the task of making decisions, on behalf of the citizenry, as to whether the state's coercive powers should be used to address a particular crime. Judicial authorities are not, of course, infallible, and so their decisions should be independently reviewed, and any errors corrected. But if an institution fails to report a genuine crime to the police and, instead, uses an in-house restorative justice approach or some other disciplinary mechanism, then, with respect to this behaviour, they have effectively claimed for themselves, without justification, an authority that properly belongs to the justice system.

It might be thought that this situation could be avoided if institutions were to report criminal incidents *before* they arranged an in-house restorative justice process. This would not entail that institutions needed to report *every* instance of perceived misconduct or harm, let alone that they should employ campus-based police officers, as is increasingly

---

5   Once again, we can acknowledge that many such offences, even if reported, will not be prosecuted or sentenced due to an unrealistic evidential bar or the unwillingness of victims to face the ruthlessness of an adversarial court. But from a Parallelist perspective, the solution here, as always, is to change the legal system, not merely circumvent it.

6   This is why, from a Parallelist perspective, trivial harms and arguably victimless behaviours, such as illicit drug possession, should be decriminalised. To employ the state's coercive powers against such behaviours is largely counterproductive and, thus, indefensible from a public interest standpoint.

the case in schools and universities. Instead, a review system could be put in place so that both the institution and the judiciary could come to an agreement about the kind of offences that would be most likely to proceed to a prosecution, thereby preventing unnecessary arrests and administrative backlogs. There is a good example of this in Connecticut, where a review was conducted to determine the rate at which cases referred by schools were dismissed by the court, as compared to other referral sources. Collecting this data was designed to ensure that, over time, 'arrests and referrals for minor offenses, like disorderly conduct, could be prevented from entering the justice system' (Petteruti, 2011: 31).

Thus, suppose an institution implements such an arrangement and reports an incident to the police *prior* to initiating an in-house restorative justice process. But suppose that, in this case, the judicial authorities decide not to make an arrest or file charges. So the institution proceeds to address the offence, on its own, by using a restorative justice process. This would clearly not be a case in which restorative justice has been used exclusively. The institution has not bypassed the criminal justice system, nor has it usurped the judiciary's decision-making authority. So this approach would be consistent with Principles 4 and 5.

However, there is a catch. The case may not have in fact exited the system but, instead, is still pending. It depends on why the authorities made their decision not to prosecute. If, say, the offender has admitted responsibility or it is a first-time offence or it is not sufficiently serious, then, even though technically the offence could be prosecuted, they might have decided to close or dismiss the case unconditionally. But if their decision not to prosecute was due to a lack of evidence, and so the case is in fact still pending, things become more complicated. A restorative justice process may unearth crucial information that was not previously available, not least the offender's admission of responsibility. And so if this evidence found its way to the police, they might then want to proceed with a prosecution. This situation is not the kind of legal independence envisaged by the Parallelist model. To give an example, Gordon Bazemore, in his book review of *Restorative Justice on the College Campus*, describes how one of the editors, David Karp, illustrates what can happen when a university attempts to run a restorative process (in this case, an 'integrity board') while the criminal case is still 'pending':

> [Karp] describes an apparent 'double-bind' situation for defendants who may be open to a restorative process but who have been told by their attorney to say nothing to the board while their case is pending 'downtown'. While he notes that such students may be shunned by the integrity board or other restorative process, blaming the defendant facing double jeopardy for recalcitrance would not seem to do much to advance the cause of either due process or restorative justice. (Bazemore, 2006: 445)

It might be thought that this kind of issue would not arise if the restorative justice process was protected by confidentiality. But as I will now argue, this remedy is not as straightforward as it might seem.

Principle 6. *Confidentiality protections should not be used to undermine the legitimate enforcement of law.*

As we have seen, one reason why victims do not report a crime is their perception that the case would be dismissed on the grounds of insufficient evidence. But if an offender agrees to take part in restorative justice, they may, by admitting responsibility within the process and explaining what happened, thereby provide the victim with the evidence they need for a prosecution. A facilitator (or any other participants who witnessed the offender's admission) could even be subpoenaed to testify in court.

The standard solution to this possibility is to ensure that any admissions or information about the incident in question presented in the restorative justice process cannot be used in any subsequent criminal or civil proceeding. But how could the participants be assured that this kind of confidentiality would be maintained? There are two possibilities here.

1. Participants could be required to sign a confidentiality agreement. This agreement would not be legally enforceable, but it would at least provide clarity about the risks involved. It would also give everyone the opportunity to state openly that they intend to participate in good faith and in a way that is consistent with the values and objectives of restorative justice. A good example of this approach can be found in the *Guidebook* of Reed College (Oregon, USA). The 'Agreement to Dialogue', which all participants must sign, includes the following:

> If I decide to pursue other judicial processes, either at Reed or externally, I will not use the information disclosed in this process within those cases. In addition, I will not subpoena the Facilitators to testify or produce records at any hearing. I understand there are exceptions to confidentiality, which will be enumerated at the beginning of the Restorative Conference. (Reed College, 2019: Supporting Document II).

However, there is a well-known problem with this kind of agreement. The exceptions to confidentiality include, as might be expected: 'Information about abuse or neglect of a child or vulnerable adult' and 'Credible threats of physical harm to self or others'. But the confidentiality agreement also excludes: 'Cases in which the College has received a lawful subpoena or is required to provide information pursuant to a court order' (Reed College, 2019: §6.3). Suppose, then, that both the victim and the offender are participating in good faith and so intend to keep their agreement. If the incident is brought to the attention of the police, as it should be if it is a crime, then this confidentiality agreement could easily be overridden by a court order or a lawful subpoena. With such a flimsy protection, any attorney would be highly negligent if they did not advise their client to 'say nothing' while their court case is still pending.

2. Another option would be to institute legislation that prohibits even a court of law from accessing any information conveyed in a restorative justice process.[7] For instance, Tennessee's statute relating to the use of victim-offender mediation rules out the disclosure of any written materials or communications made within the restorative justice service in any subsequent judicial or administrative proceeding. But even here, there is a significant exclusion. If the court decides that a participant has tried to exploit this legislation by submitting certain materials or facts in the restorative justice process so as to keep them out of the hands of lawyers as they prepare for trial, then the court will no longer deem these materials to be confidential or privileged (*Tennessee Code*, §16-20-103, eff. 2021). This exclusion seems an entirely reasonable precaution, but it is not difficult to see how it might be readily used by lawyers to get around the prohibition on disclosure.

There are, of course, ways to close this loophole without allowing participants to hide evidence. For instance, suppose that all communications and materials conveyed within a restorative justice process (relating to the offence in question) were completely privileged. This appears to be the case in the legislation covering the Community Dispute Resolution Center programme in New York.[8] Indeed, this statute is so strong that, as Mary Reimund notes, even in a murder case, where the prosecutor subpoenaed records of a prior mediation between the victim and the offender, 'the court upheld the validity of confidentiality' (2004: 417). However, even confidentiality protections that are this robust often do not preclude such information from being used in a trial if it is independently discoverable outside of the restorative justice process.[9] And it would be of no small assistance to a prosecutor's investigation to know from the outset that the offender is, by

---

7   Many Integrationist schemes already employ this kind of legislation, but it is not universal. In her survey of US legislation, for instance, Thalia González found that '[T]here is a noticeable absence of court rules, administrative guidelines, or legislative provisions specifically addressing confidentiality or admissibility of statements made before (intake) or during restorative justice practices' (González, 2020: 1051).

8   'Any communication relating to the subject matter of the resolution made during the mediation process by a participant, mediator, or any other person at the dispute resolution shall be a confidential communication.' *New York Judiciary Law*, §849-B.6 (eff. 2021).

9   *See*, for example, the legislation covering alternative dispute resolution in Texas and Minnesota: 'An oral communication or written material used in or made a part of an alternative dispute resolution procedure is admissible or discoverable if it is admissible or discoverable independent of the procedure.' *Texas Civil Practice and Remedies Code*, §154.073(c) (eff. 2021). Cf. 'Any communication relating to the subject matter of the dispute by any participant during dispute resolution shall not be used as evidence against a participant in a judicial or administrative proceeding. This shall not preclude the use of evidence obtained by other independent investigation.' *Minnesota Statutes*, §494.02 (eff. 2021).

their own (inadmissible) words, guilty of the crime. Hence, it is difficult not to agree with Eliaerts and Dumortier's realism on this matter:

> [W]e wonder if it would not be more logical to state that offenders who participate waive their right to be presumed innocent (of course only for the facts they acknowledge). (2002: 218)

But there is a critical issue that all these attempts to protect the confidentiality of a restorative justice process are missing. Suppose an offender admits to having committed a crime in a restorative justice process and presents evidence in that forum that would be sufficient to warrant their prosecution in a court of law. Why should this information not simply be handed over to the court? Does not this kind of confidentiality protection merely subvert the rule of law? As Peter Thompson puts it, 'the interest in privacy in mediations should give way to the legitimate interest of law enforcement' (1997: 365).

There are also significant risks to the victim that must be taken into account. Suppose there is a confidentiality statute in place which covers all that is said within a restorative justice process. Once they are out of legal earshot, offenders might use the opportunity to try and persuade victims to drop their case or change their witness statement. Victims might, in turn, feel unduly pressured to do so. Jennifer Brown has suggested that such an eventuality could be avoided if the prosecutor took the victim's testimony (or deposition) prior to the restorative justice process so as to ensure that it did not change as a result. But she then goes on to enumerate the severe risks this would pose for the victim:

> If the victim were deposed prior to the mediation, she would have to commit to a version of the events without knowing how cooperative or remorseful the offender might be. If the victim successfully mediated a satisfying agreement with the offender and then sought to make her testimony more favorable to the offender, prosecutors could use the premediation deposition to impeach this altered testimony. … Indeed, the state might even prosecute [the victim] for perjury. (Brown, 1994: 1304-1305, n. 223)

Then there would be the strain and potential unfairness of requiring total confidentiality. What if the victim felt that justice would not be served if certain additional facts – mitigating or aggravating – revealed to them by the offender were omitted from a subsequent trial? This is no doubt why Victim Support UK has argued that victims who attend a restorative justice process should not be prohibited from 'offering evidence of confession if they believe it is appropriate to do so' (2003: 4). After all, what is the alternative? As put so succinctly by Eliaerts and Dumortier, 'shall we punish victims who reveal confidential information?' (2002: 217).[10]

Then again, suppose that, in cases that are still pending, all confidentiality protections were removed from the process (or could be overruled by a court). This might enable victims to use any admissions as evidence in any subsequent trial. But it also opens up the possibility that offenders could do the same in return. As Shailly Agnihotri and Cassie Veach note:

> [N]o legislation can extinguish the accused's right to cross-examine witnesses against them in a criminal trial, and [so] … a defense attorney could use a diversionary restorative process to gather information, return to the adversarial process, and use information to the benefit of the accused. (2017: 340)

And this is not merely hypothetical. Reimund cites a case in which two young people were charged with throwing rocks in a vandalism case.[11] The incident was initially diverted to mediation. However:

> During the mediation, the victim admitted that he did not see the person who threw the rocks. The youths then subpoenaed the victim's testimony for their juvenile delinquency hearing so they could impeach the victim for prior inconsistent testimony. In this case, the court held the juveniles' constitutional right to confrontation trumped the public policy providing confidentiality in mediation. (2004: 219)

In sum, I have argued that institutions – such as schools, universities and workplaces – should report any criminal behaviour that occurs within its jurisdiction, subject to a review system so as to prevent unnecessary arrests. But it follows that if an institution commences a restorative justice process while the case is still pending, then it will not be sufficiently independent. Not even a strong confidentiality statute can fully protect the process, and there are, in any case, good reasons to think that it should not prohibit legitimate law enforcement. So the workings of the legal system will invariably influence the restorative justice process and vice versa. But then, the best way to secure complete independence, and so avoid such problems, is to wait until *after* the case is no longer in the system.

---

10 It should be noted that some jurisdictions appear to be willing to do so. For instance, Ireland's *Children Act 2001* states that anyone who discloses 'confidential information obtained by him or her while participating (or as a result of having participated) as a member of a conference … shall be guilty of an offence and shall be liable on summary conviction to a fine not exceeding £1,500.' Part 4, §32.7-8.

11 *Rinaker*, 74 Cal. Rptr. 2d 464 (Cal. Ct. App. 1998).

There is one related point that is worth making in this context, even though it falls outside the topic of how restorative justice should relate to criminal justice. Most schools and other institutions use restorative justice as an alternative to exclusion, suspension, detention and other in-house disciplinary methods – and, in many cases, with considerable effectiveness. April Mustian, Henry Cervantes and Robert Lee found that 'School-based RJ implementation has been shown to decrease office disciplinary referrals ... and suspensions across multiple public-school settings' (2021: 54).[12]

But it is not difficult to see how this approach might create the same kind of tensions and compromises that accompany the integration of restorative justice into the criminal justice system. For example, students are just as likely to be suspected of faking remorse in order to avoid suspension as offenders are to escape prosecution. Corralling a student into uttering a surly and resentful 'sorry' is just as unethical and ineffective as a parole board's extraction of a grovelling apology from a prisoner. Likewise, teachers, parents and the school community in general may not have been individually affected by an incident, but they all have an interest in seeing harmful behaviour dealt with in a consistent, transparent, fair and proportionate manner. In other words, there is still a public dimension to wrongdoing, even if this is confined to the boundaries of the institution.

The problem is that, just like many Integrationists, advocates working in schools frequently promote restorative justice as substantially superior to traditional disciplinary processes. Hence, their overt strategy has, for the most part, been to advance restorative justice as the preferred approach, even to the extent that, over time, it will eventually replace most, if not all, of the more formal disciplinary procedures. For instance, Miles Davison, Andrew Penner and Emily Penner argued:

> RJ is most likely to achieve its transformative potential when implemented as a replacement to the traditional ethos and practice of discipline, rather than as ... an alternative disciplinary track ... [where] it is still possible for students to be referred back into the traditional disciplinary system at each step of the restorative process. (2022: 703, 707)

But since it is formal discipline that tends to reflect the public interest dimension of wrongdoing within institutions, this has created a win-lose scenario. As a Parallelist would argue, both restorative justice and formal discipline are necessary because there are public and private dimensions to institutional wrongdoing.

It might be argued that this view does not take into account the dominance of retributivist values in schools and other institutions and the resistance that this generates towards restorative justice. To give one example, Gregory Paul and Ian Borton write:

---

12   Citing the research found in Anyon et al. (2016), Armour (2015) and Davis (2014).

The punitive model is powerful, long-standing, entrenched and appeals to a certain subset of school community members, parents, and politicians. When schools are deeply steeped in the punitive philosophy of discipline, which also communicates values of centralized authority, hierarchy, and impersonality, their focus toward (and willingness to consider) a practice, which relies less on control, reduced coercive force, and non-violence is significantly diminished. (2021: 63)

But this is not necessarily the source of resistance, or at least not the only source. It may be that many teachers, parents, co-workers, managers and head teachers have a legitimate concern that restorative justice is incapable of adequately addressing the public dimension of institutional wrongdoing. For instance, in a review of local teacher union surveys, Max Eden found:

In Philadelphia, more than 80 percent of teachers believe that suspensions are valuable for maintaining safety, removing disruptions so other students can learn, sending a signal to parents about their child's behavior, and helping to ensure that other students follow the rules. (Eden, 2018)

It might be argued that these teachers are simply mistaken in supposing that suspension is needed to address these issues. But we do not need to endorse the use (or overuse) of suspensions to note how the *rationale* here largely appeals to the public interest dimension.

There is little doubt that many forms of institutional discipline could be more reparative, constructive, non-exclusionary, fair, respectful, non-discriminatory, rehabilitative and less frequently used as a first resort than they are at present. But these reforms, if required, are entirely feasible as a complement to the implementation of restorative justice.[13] And a Parallelist approach would, of course, strongly support such an approach, given that the quality and effectiveness of restorative justice can easily be damaged or infected by coexisting disciplinary policies and methods that remain unfair or discriminatory. For example, Mustian. et al. found:

[S]tudents who were Black, low [socio-economic status], and/or had disabilities, remained more likely than their white counterparts to be suspended in the second semester following RJ participation during the first

---

13   Richard Olshak, for instance, disputes the view that disciplinary systems used on college and university campuses are 'generally focused on punishing offenders for their misconduct'. There is good evidence, he argues, that disciplinary sanctions 'imposed for misconduct are generally designed to be both educational and developmental' (2006: 6). Even if this is not the case for many campuses, Olshak's view shows that a non-retributive disciplinary system is not inconceivable.

semester despite similar rates of RJ participation across groups. Implementation of RJ, in the absence of any critical, systemic examination of policies and practices that harm students and are antithetical to RJ's core, resulted in a distorted and inauthentic version of RJ. (2021: 55)[14]

In sum, a Parallelist approach in relation to this matter would involve the following strategy: (1) If required, reform (or transform) existing disciplinary mechanisms and policies so that they operate as a more effective and fitting counterpart to restorative justice. (2) Any restorative justice process should occur independently of a disciplinary process. (3) This separation is most likely to be attained if restorative justice takes place after the formal discipline.

Principle 7. *Legal independence for restorative justice must be guaranteed, rather than optional or accidental.*

There are some jurisdictions that claim to be using a 'parallel' approach to restorative justice, even when they are in fact operating a diversionary scheme. Their reasons for doing so highlight the importance of Principle 7 as a requirement for implementing genuine Parallelism, as I have construed it. One such example can be found in the Australian Capital Territory's (ACT) *Crimes (Restorative Justice) Act* 2004, which explicitly claims to have been designed as a 'parallel' approach. As the *First Phase Review of Restorative Justice* in the ACT stated:

> The *Act* is constructed so that restorative justice 'augments' the criminal justice system without replacing criminal justice. In this sense, restorative justice processes in the ACT may run parallel with the existing criminal justice processes. (2006: 8)

And the *Act* itself states:

> [The object of this *Act* is] to enable access to restorative justice at every stage of the criminal justice process without substituting for the criminal justice system or *changing the normal process* of criminal justice. (s.6.d, my emphasis)

---

14   Citing the research of Anyon et al. (2016) – the use of RJ 'was not successful in transforming the underlying racial logics of punishment and anti-Blackness that place Black students at heightened risk of experiencing exclusionary discipline' (Davison et al., 2022: 708).

More specifically, it states:

> [I]f an offence is referred for restorative justice, the referral is to have *no effect* on any other action or proposed action in relation to the offence or the offender by the referring entity. (s.7.2, my emphasis)

And it gives the following example:

> Sían is arrested and charged with an offence. The chief police officer refers the offence for restorative justice. The referral of the offence does not prevent Sían being required to attend court to answer the charge. (s.7.2)

On the face of it, this looks like it should establish a Parallelist approach. A referral to restorative justice is to have no influence or bearing on any subsequent legal process. However, in practice, this does not appear to be how the *Act* is being interpreted. Referrals to restorative justice *are* having an effect on the legal process. They *do* 'change' the 'normal process of criminal justice'. For example, the *First Phase Review* states the following: 'In many cases that have been referred to [restorative justice], young people are being given the opportunity to be spared a criminal conviction by participating in restorative justice' (2006: 31). And one of the 'common' reasons young people gave for participating was 'to demonstrate to the court that they have taken responsibility for the offence' (p. 34). In another section, the *Review* reports:

> A number of young people said that by participating it would help with their court case. Others said they participated 'more or less to avoid having to go to court'. (p. 34)

While the court may not be *required* to take account of what happens in a conference, participants are clearly being led to understand that they are very likely to do so.

Perhaps there is a principled explanation for this apparent inconsistency between the *Act* and its interpretation. The *Act* seems to have been primarily designed to make sure that the offender is no worse off, legally speaking, as a consequence of restorative justice. This is best exemplified by the *Act* allowing the offender to plead not guilty to a charge at court even if they have taken responsibility for that same crime within a restorative justice setting.[15] For instance, to achieve its 'parallelist' goal, the *Act* sets out two safeguards:

---

15   Whether the *Act* does in fact succeed in protecting offenders from legal disadvantage is a question that I will address in the following.

[1] An offender may accept responsibility for an offence without affecting his or her capacity to plead not guilty to the offence at a later court hearing. [2] Even if the offender pleads, or is found guilty, the court is not compelled to take account of what happens in any conference that may be held. (*First Phase Review*, 2006: 8-9)

Yet these safeguards are not, in themselves, sufficient to create a Parallelist system. Take the second safeguard, for example. A Parallelist approach would compel the court to *refrain from* taking account of what happened in the conference. Or again, another section of the *Act* explicitly states that a court, in sentencing the offender, is:

not required to reduce the severity of any sentence it may impose on an offender ... because the court is aware [that the offender] accepts responsibility for the commission of the offence. (s.20.2, s.19.1.b.i)

But this is very different from saying that a court is required *not* to reduce the severity in such circumstances. Similarly, the *Act* states that in sentencing the offender, a court 'must not consider whether the offender has chosen not to take part, or not to continue to take part, in restorative justice' (s.53.e.i). However, this, again, is not the same as stipulating that a court must also not consider whether the offender *has* chosen to take part, or continue to take part, in restorative justice. Finally, referrals to restorative justice, as stated in the *Act*, may arise from a court, and, if so, 'may be in the form of a court referral order or sentence-related order, or as a condition of a bail order' (s.23.2.b). As a consequence, the *First Phase Review* states, 'it is possible for restorative justice agreements to be encompassed in Court or Parole Orders, effectively giving certain referring agencies the power to enforce agreements' (2006: 12). So if the agreements are breached, then there will be legal consequences.

In other words, so far as the *Act* is concerned, the court is permitted – and perhaps encouraged – to consider the offender's successful participation in a restorative justice process as grounds for 'changing' the 'normal process of criminal justice'. The court can, and usually will, ensure that such offenders are better off than they would otherwise have been from a legal standpoint. This is consistent with a key principle that seems to have motivated the *Act*, namely, that restorative justice should be 'a recourse of first preference throughout the criminal justice process' (ACT Restorative Justice Sub-Committee, 2003: 4). However, if the *Act* was intended to set up a truly Parallelist model, then the overarching principle would instead be that restorative justice should supplement the criminal justice process but without taking precedence over it. The possibility of legal consequences should be guaranteed, rather than left up to the discretion of the judiciary. In other words, the *Act* is clearly designed to implement an Integrationist approach.[16]

There is another way in which a system might initially appear to be implementing a Parallelist framework. Within an Integrationist model, a large number of cases will turn out, quite fortuitously, to have had no impact upon the legal process. In their evaluation of one restorative justice pilot, Shapland et al. reported that only 41% of offenders in pre-sentence trials thought that their participation in restorative justice had affected the legal outcome (2007: 30). They were probably right. In another study, Sherman and Strang compared pre-sentence cases that were randomly assigned to restorative justice with cases that were not. They found 'no difference in the length of sentence' imposed by the court (2007: 42). But this was not necessarily the result of principled decision-making. As Sherman and Strang note, it turned out that 'almost half of the judges to whom these reports had been sent could not recall having seen one' (2007: 42).

One might think that this kind of 'accidental independence' shows that a Parallelist approach in a diversionary context is technically possible after all. However, having no actual legal impact may be necessary, but it is not sufficient. On the Integrationist model, properly informed participants in restorative justice will generally believe, in advance, that the process *may* have an impact on the legal outcome of their case. Independence needs to be guaranteed, not just as a result of mere chance – even if the probabilities are high.

As I later argue (in §4.5 and 4.6), this is one of the most important differences between the two models, primarily because this expectation can have such a profound effect on the incentives of the offender and on how the victim perceives this motivation. The kinds of cases recorded above, in which the absence of legal impact is either a matter of chance or relatively rare, do not remove this difference. The initial expectations of the participants would have remained Integrationist regardless. The offenders would still have assumed that participating would be in their legal self-interest, and victims would still have had good reason to suspect them of doing so. In other words, cases that are accidentally independent lack one of the most important benefits of Parallelism. So they can hardly count as evidence that Parallelism is feasible in a diversionary context.

For a Parallelist approach to occur when the case is still pending, even the fact that a restorative justice process had taken place – along with whatever happened within that process – would need, in effect, to be hermetically sealed so that it could not influence the legal process. Neither the existence, the content nor the outcome of a restorative justice process could be accessed by the prosecutor prior to their decision or by the judge prior to

---

16 This is not in any way intended to impugn the quality of the ACT's Restorative Justice Unit, the professionalism and expertise of its staff, or its long record of positive outcomes. *See*, for example, the findings of a ten-year evaluation (2006-2016) of the ACT's Restorative Justice Unit: 'Overall results indicate very high levels of satisfaction with the conference process, consistent across all participant groups' (Broadhurst, Morgan, Payne & Maller, 2018: 9).

their sentencing. But we have already seen how such draconian confidentiality restrictions are unlikely to be bulletproof.

So imagine, instead, that new legislation is created which states that the court is *not* permitted to consider whether the offender has chosen to take part, or continue to take part, in restorative justice, or how successful the process was, or whether any agreement was fulfilled. The statute could also stipulate that, even if the offender participates successfully in a restorative justice process, the prosecutor is *not* permitted to dismiss the case, and the judge is *not* permitted to amend or reduce the severity of any sentence they impose on the offender. Would these prohibitions not create the required independence?

The answer, as I will suggest in the following, is still 'no'. But even if these prohibitions *were* sufficient, we need to remember that this is a diversionary context. Restorative justice would be taking place *prior* to a final ruling. The cases in question would still be pending. But why would any prosecutor or judge, operating under such restrictions, take the trouble to divert the case to restorative justice and then wait for the facilitator to report back? They might as well save time and proceed directly to make whatever ruling they think is most suitable. After all, the restorative justice process cannot influence their decision either way.[17] Indeed, taking this shortcut would be the most prudent option. If a prosecutor or judge were to wait for the report, this could make it considerably harder to claim that their decision had not been influenced in any way.

In sum, it would appear that using restorative justice in a diversionary setting is not a viable Parallelist option. To be clear, if it *was* possible to create an innovative legal framework or set of policies which could guarantee legal independence in this context – free from any legal Sword of Damocles, without any impact on due process and so on – then a Parallelist would be the first in line to embrace such an approach. Parallelism, to reiterate, is not defined by such contingencies. Its claim is only that full legal independence – *however this might be secured* – is the optimal relationship between restorative justice and criminal justice. Put another way, Parallelism per se would not be refuted if some way could be found of using restorative justice as a legally independent diversionary approach. But this independence would need to be guaranteed *and* the judicial authorities would need to be willing and able to divert cases under such a condition. Until then, a Parallelist will continue to work towards implementing whatever options remain.

Principle 8. *No legal benefit should be available to an offender as a direct consequence of satisfying the eligibility criteria for restorative justice, agreeing to take part in the process or participating successfully.*

This principle will need several clarifications.

---

17   The possibility of using restorative justice as an 'unconditional diversion' is discussed under Principle 8.

1. A 'legal benefit' generally refers to the avoidance of a negative legal outcome that would otherwise have been imposed – such as an arrest, charges being filed, a criminal record, the sentence that would otherwise have been imposed, a harsher sentence and so on.[18]

2. For a legal benefit to be 'available' does not mean it is guaranteed or automatic, only that it is not prohibited, and so *could* be given to the offender. As argued in relation to Principle 7, even the potential for some legal advantage is enough to create a Sword of Damocles situation.

3. There is good evidence that participating in restorative justice can bring about important changes in an offender's attitudes and behaviour. This result could have legal benefits, insofar as they do not reoffend or if their newly altered behaviour is taken into account by judicial authorities, for instance, by a parole board. But this kind of legal benefit is not conditional upon the offender's participation in restorative justice. Any such changes in the offender's perspective or behaviour, no matter what the cause might have been, would have received the same benefit. Put another way, these benefits are not a 'direct consequence' of restorative justice.

4. The term 'participating successfully' is intended to cover both how offenders conduct themselves in the process and whether they fulfil any outcome agreement. What counts as 'successful' would, if legal benefits were available, be a matter that lawmakers and judicial authorities would need to determine – which, I will later suggest, is itself of serious concern (see §4.7.1).

5. One final clarification. This principle stipulates that an offender cannot access any legal benefits just by virtue of 'satisfying the eligibility criteria for restorative justice'. What does this mean? In the Integrationist model, an offender will only be considered eligible for a diversion to restorative justice if they admit (or decline to deny) responsibility for the charges as specified.[19] If the diversion is offered in the context of a deferred (or adjourned) sentence, then they must also plead guilty in court.[20] The problem is that this kind of eligibility criterion is, in effect, not dissimilar to a plea bargain, which, as we shall see (§4.5), is deeply problematic, especially from a Parallelist perspective. It places the offender in a Sword of Damocles situation. If the offender satisfies this pre-condition, they will be diverted to a restorative justice programme instead of facing the normal legal consequences. This would not be acceptable under a Parallelist model.

---

18   Removing any legal benefits does not necessarily mean there will be no legal risks for an offender who takes part in restorative justice. *See* §5.2.2 for a discussion on the potential risks of appeals and litigation.

19   For instance, the *Crimes (Restorative Justice) Act 2004* states: 'An offender who commits an offence is eligible for restorative justice if … (b) the offender – (i) either – (A) accepts responsibility for the commission of the offence; or (B) if the offender is a young offender and the offence is a less serious offence – does not deny responsibility for the commission of the offence' (s.19.1).

20   *See*, for example, New Zealand's *Sentencing Act* 2002: 'Adjournment for restorative justice process in certain cases … applies if … the offender has pleaded guilty to the offence' (Part 1, s.24A.1.b).

It is important to be clear about what is required here. As a matter of *best practice*, an offender will only be eligible for a restorative justice process if they can demonstrate to a facilitator beforehand that they are willing to take responsibility for the harm they have caused to the victim. This is no doubt one of the main reasons why the admission of responsibility or a guilty plea has become a *legal prerequisite* for any diversion to restorative justice. There is little point in referring the offender to this kind of programme if they would not be suitable for it. But being eligible for *restorative justice* is not the same as being eligible for *diversion* to restorative justice. The latter may have legal benefits, while the former, understood in its own terms, does not.

For example, suppose a prosecutor explains to an offender that they will dismiss the charges unconditionally and close the case, as long as the offender admits responsibility for the crime. If a restorative justice process is subsequently arranged, then this scenario would be compatible with Parallelism. Once the offender's case has been dismissed, they can decide not to take part in restorative justice without any adverse legal consequences. Put another way, there would be no legal benefits available to them if, at that point, they decided to take part in restorative justice. But if the prosecutor tells the offender that they must admit responsibility *in order to be eligible for a diversion to restorative justice*, then this would not be a Parallelist approach. If the offender refuses to admit responsibility, they will thereby forgo the potential legal benefits of diversion.

This would even be true if the diversion is 'unconditional' – that is to say, when the case is effectively closed once the referral to restorative justice has been made. For example, Ireland's *Children Act 2001* provides for a 'Diversion Programme', the purpose of which is 'to divert any child who accepts responsibility for his or her criminal or anti-social behaviour from committing further offences or engaging in further anti-social behaviour' (Part 4, s.19). This Programme is, as one might expect, 'mainly for first-time and less serious juvenile offenders' (O'Dwyer, 2005: 65). Indeed, the *Children Act 2001* stipulates that some offences may be excluded from the Programme due to their 'serious nature' (s.47), 'unless the Director of Public Prosecutions directs otherwise' (s.23.3). Even so, under this legislation, children (aged 10 to 18) who admit to having committed an eligible criminal offence may be offered, as a voluntary measure, the opportunity to participate in a restorative caution or conference, to which the victim may be invited.

What is perhaps unique about this Programme is that, even after the decision has been made to divert the case, the child can choose not to participate in the restorative justice process. And if one is arranged, the child is free to leave at any time. There are, of course, strategies in place designed to enhance the prospects of the process succeeding. For instance, a conference will only be offered if it is considered to be in the best interests of all concerned, and their consent to attend has been obtained (s.30-31). Again, a follow-up conference will be held to review the child's compliance with the action plan. If the child has failed to honour the agreements made, those present at the reconvened conference 'shall encourage the child to comply with the plan or any amended version of it that they may agree upon' (s.39.12).

But crucially, there are no legal repercussions or formal sanctions imposed on the child if they fail to participate or comply with the agreement. The child cannot, for instance, be prosecuted for the crime in respect of which they were admitted to the Programme (s.49.1). And the *Act* also stipulates that no admissions of responsibility for the crime by the child, or any other information that was disclosed only in the conference, can be admitted as evidence in any civil or criminal court (s.48, 50). The only 'consequence' available for noncompliance is that the period or level of the child's supervision by a juvenile liaison officer could be altered (s.41). In short, once the child admits responsibility, and a decision is made to divert the child from prosecution is made, then, no matter what the outcome might be, the child will not be subject to any further criminal justice proceedings or sanction with respect to the crime in question. This scheme is, in effect, an 'unconditional diversion', where an offender is diverted without being required to meet any conditions in order for the case to be closed. At first glance, it looks as if there is no legal Sword of Damocles hanging over the offender. Hence, it would seem very close indeed to a Parallelist approach.

But there is a fly in the ointment. As mentioned, one eligibility criterion for the Diversion Programme is that the child must admit responsibility for the crime. Otherwise, they will be considered unsuitable – in which case they may be prosecuted in the usual manner. In other words, *access* to the Programme involves a Sword of Damocles for offenders. This is sufficient to make their participation in restorative justice legally conditional, and so the Programme is not a genuine example of Parallelism. It is certainly true that Ireland's approach is more voluntary than most other Integrationist schemes.[21] But a clear and unambiguous separation between restorative justice and the legal system is critical if the advantages of Parallelism are to be realised. As we shall see, there must be no confusion or scepticism in the minds of the participants as to whether the justice system is effectively compelling the offender to take part. This doubt would surely be present in the minds of those who take part in Ireland's Diversion Programme, given its preconditions.[22]

---

21 Kieran O'Dwyer describes some of the advantages to the level of voluntariness available in the Diversion Programme. For instance, it 'increases the chances of a successful outcome for both offender and victim. An agreement is more likely as is compliance with its terms' (O'Dwyer, 2005: 54).

22 These doubts are likely to increase even in the restorative justice process itself, not due to any legislated benefits, but simply because the *Act* allows police officers to serve as facilitators (s.31.4.b) or as attendees (32.3.e). This could easily give participants the impression that the process is not as voluntary or legally independent as it purports to be (*see* §4.7.4).

Principle 9. *Restorative justice should only take place after a case has actually or effectively exited the justice system.*

An offence can be said to have *actually* exited the system when it has been closed or dismissed unconditionally, with no further threat of prosecution for the offence in question or a change in the sentence. This might occur when the charges are dropped, the case is unconditionally dismissed, or a prison sentence has been completed and the case is closed. The legal conditions or the terminology here will depend on the justice system in question, but whenever or however the exit occurs, the crucial requirement is that, so far as the justice system is concerned, no further legal benefits can be attached to any subsequent restorative justice process.

This principle raises several important questions. To begin, most cases that exit the system prior to sentencing will not usually be most suitable for a restorative justice approach since they are lower-end offences. But this is not necessarily the case. There may be offences that have caused significant harm to a victim, and yet the prosecutor decides that the public interest would not be best served by employing the coercive powers of the state. As suggested previously, this approach is perhaps most likely to occur when the offender and the victim are known to each other or they are members of the same family or where the case was reported to the police by an institution, such as a school, college or workplace. It may also be considered more appropriate for first-time or young offenders. Even so, if such a decision were to be made, it would provide a good opportunity to hold a legally independent restorative justice process, without undermining the legitimate authority of the judiciary. What distinguishes this use of restorative justice from any Integrationist approach is that it would be a genuinely private and voluntary undertaking. Once the benefits of this approach are more widely understood and accepted, it is not inconceivable that cases which exit the system in a pre-sentence context might then be referred to restorative justice more frequently, especially for young people, first-time offenders and less serious crimes.

What would it mean for a case to *effectively* exit the system? In a post-sentence situation, a case will have actually exited the system only when the sentence has been completed, including any period of parole. But if this were the only option available in a Parallelist model, then it would face a serious challenge. Take the prison context. If restorative justice was not permitted until a case has actually exited the system, this would unfairly deny restorative justice to many people. There are cases in which it would not be feasible or optimal to wait until the offender has been released from prison or ended their parole. The participants may not feel safe enough to meet outside of a prison context or without parole supervision. The offender's release date may be years away, and the participants might feel they cannot wait until then.[23] The offender may be on death row or serving a life sentence. Mark Umbreit, for instance, argues:

> [Excluding] death penalty cases will strip those most directly affected by the horror of the crime of the opportunity to find some degree of meaning, healing and closure: a fundamental pillar of restorative justice (2000b: 95).[24]

And yet, including pre-release cases would face its own challenges.[25] In Chapter 4 of this book, I will argue that one key objection that can be made against the Integrationist model is that situating restorative justice in a diversionary context will inevitably give rise to actual or suspected ulterior motives. That is, the offender may be – or may be perceived by the victim as – participating in restorative justice primarily to avoid a harsher outcome. To that extent, their participation will be – or will be suspected by the victim as being – disingenuous. As I will argue (in §4.5 and 4.6), there is good evidence to suggest that this is very likely to cause serious damage to the process. Most importantly, the offender's lack – or perceived lack – of authenticity could potentially revictimise the victim. But it might be argued that situating Parallelism within a pre-release context is also subject to this kind of problem, but for different reasons.

Suppose that a restorative justice process was held as a voluntary (non-enforceable) adjunct to an offender's prison sentence or during their parole period. On its own, this would be very unlikely to lead to a reduced sentence or parole period for the offender. These decisions have more to do with the assessment of a wide range of risk factors, including the offender's mental health, their overall behaviour in prison, their participation in drug and alcohol or other rehabilitation programmes and so on. Their participation in

---

23 A similar objection can be raised against insisting on a Parallelist approach in cases where a court hearing or trial is significantly delayed, which, in some cases, can extend to many years. This concern is addressed in §5.1.2.

24 Cf. 'Implementation of victim-offender mediation programs in capital cases should be promoted and encouraged as an option after sentencing, as restoring affected parties is a necessary element of justice' (Rossi, 2008: 210). Any criminal justice system that includes the death penalty would not, of course, be a fitting counterpart to restorative justice, and so it would be excluded from any full-blown Parallelist model. Thus, the use of restorative justice in this context would be considered by the Parallelist as an interim practice.

25 The pre-release setting does not include institutional practices such as restorative justice processes used to address in-prison offences or standalone victim awareness programmes or reparative activities directed towards the general community. I am referring only to processes that are designed to facilitate a dialogue between a prisoner and the victim of the crime for which they are serving a sentence. This is not to exclude the possibility that they might be linked in some way. A victim-awareness programme can, for instance, motivate, or be used to prepare for a dialogue, but this appears to be rare. As William Wood and Masahiro Suzuki note, 'Since the late 1990s numerous "restorative" prison programs have been implemented within English-speaking countries. With few exceptions, however, such programs do not include the use of conferencing between victims and offenders' (Wood & Suzuki, 2016: 151).

restorative justice could potentially play a small role in the overall assessment, but it is very unlikely to count as a deciding factor. Nevertheless, it would be naïve to suppose that the offender's decision to participate will not have been influenced by the thought that doing so *might* lead to a reduced sentence or parole period. Victims would therefore not be unreasonable if they were to suspect the offender's authenticity.

There is, however, a good option here, should it become available. If the relevant agencies could establish a formal policy to the effect that the decision to reduce or not reduce an offender's sentence or parole period *cannot* be made a direct consequence of their participation or nonparticipation in restorative justice, this would remove the problem altogether.[26] A good example of this practice can be found in a post-sentence restorative justice programme run in the state of Delaware, in which, as Miller describes it, 'no tangible benefit was offered to the offenders for participation' (2011: 184). Thus, one offender who took part in the programme, for instance, 'tried to use his participation … to his advantage at a parole hearing and was reprimanded for that attempt' (p. 252, n. 9). This is precisely what is meant by a case *effectively* exiting the justice system. Under these conditions, the restorative justice process might as well be occurring after the offender has actually exited the system, since it cannot have an impact on their sentence or parole period (Figure 3.1).

Figure 3.1 Parallelism in a post-sentence context

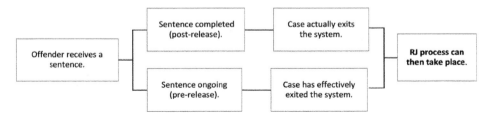

It might be argued here that if a Parallelist can allow that a formal policy such as this is sufficient to exclude ulterior motives, why could the Integrationist not employ a similar approach in a diversionary setting? For instance, restorative justice could be offered not *as* (or even part of) a diversionary programme, but rather as a voluntary adjunct that occurs *alongside* a non-restorative justice (non-RJ) diversionary scheme. This would, after all, be

---

26   Again, this kind of policy would not preclude decision-makers from taking into account an offender's *change in attitude or behaviour* that resulted from their participation in restorative justice. But any such changes could justify amending a sentence or parole period, regardless of whether they were due to restorative justice. In other words, the amendments would be an *indirect* consequence of restorative justice.

analogous to the way that a pre-release restorative justice process is not part of the sentence but merely runs alongside it.

However, this option does not appear to be feasible. In any (conditional) diversionary programme, the case is still pending. This makes it crucially different from a post-sentence setting. Even though the offender has been diverted, the crime could still be prosecuted, or a traditional sentence could still be imposed. This means that all the risks identified earlier would come into play. For instance, the victim could be pressured by the offender to drop the charges or change their testimony. Confidentiality protections, even when legislated, are far from unassailable, so any admissions or other evidence that turn up in the restorative justice process could potentially be used in any subsequent hearing or trial, whether directly or indirectly. In short, not even a formal policy could prevent the restorative justice process from succumbing to a Sword of Damocles scenario.

There are, however, two possible Parallelist solutions here, both of which are compatible with Principle 9.

1. In cases where a non-RJ diversionary programme is being used, then, once the programme has been successfully completed and either the case has actually or effectively exited the system, then a restorative justice process could at that point be offered. A case could *actually* exit the system where the programme operates as a diversion from prosecution. It would *effectively* exit the system where the programme only results in an amended sentence, and so restorative justice would then be offered in a post-sentence context. (If the offender does not complete the non-RJ programme successfully, then the offer of restorative justice would of course need to wait until the next point at which the case has actually or effectively exited the system.)

2. Restorative justice could be undertaken while the offender is engaged in a non-RJ *unconditional* diversionary programme.[27] But this offer should only be made if waiting until the programme has been completed (and the case has exited the system) would be unreasonable or unfair – for instance, where the programme extends over many months, such as might be the case for a substance misuse scheme. Since unconditional diversion is not widely used, this second approach is likely to be rare, or at least limited to minor or first-time offences. Even so, once a case has been referred to an unconditional diversionary programme, it has *effectively* exited the system. So situating restorative justice alongside such a programme is nevertheless an option that would be consistent with Principle 9 (Figure 3.2).

---

27   Restorative justice should not be used *as any part of* an unconditional diversionary programme, since, as we have seen, such programmes typically require the offender to admit (or decline to deny) guilt as a legal prerequisite, which is incompatible with Principle 8.

Figure 3.2 Parallelism in a diversionary context

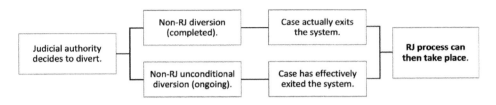

There is an important challenge that could be made to both of these suggestions, and so I will address this more thoroughly in §5.3.2. But it may be useful to present my response briefly here. The challenge is this: In this book, I present a series of objections against using restorative justice as a diversionary approach. But these objections could, to varying degrees, apply to *any* form of diversion. I agree, but with one qualification. When restorative justice is employed as a diversion, it is, on balance, *more susceptible* to these objections than existing non-RJ diversionary schemes. Nevertheless, these issues remain, so a Parallelist would advocate that diversionary approaches should either be eliminated or transformed so as to avoid these problems. (I suggest how this could be done in §5.3.2.) In the meantime, I take it that holding restorative justice after a non-RJ diversion or alongside a non-RJ unconditional diversion is an acceptable compromise. This is not unlike the interim solution of holding restorative justice within existing prisons, given that one key reform advocated by Parallelism would be to abolish or radically transform the prison system.

A second objection that might be raised against the foregoing proposal is that an offender who attends *both* a non-RJ diversionary programme *and* a restorative justice process is effectively being punished twice for the same crime.[28] However, restorative justice is not, as we will see (§4.2.4), properly construed as a 'punishment', or at least not as many would understand the term. This is especially the case in a Parallelist context, given that it would be entirely voluntary rather than a state-imposed sanction. Moreover, as I argue in §5.2.5, this approach does not involve any overkill or redundancy. An offender who commits a crime thereby acquires both civic obligations (towards the community) and moral obligations (towards the victim). The offender can acquit their civic obligations by completing the diversionary programme and changing their subsequent behaviour. But to address their moral obligations, they need to work towards repairing the moral harm they have caused to the victim, which is precisely the role of restorative justice. Indeed, the offender's prior work in the diversionary programme is very likely to be viewed by the

---

28   Theo Gavrielides, for instance, argues that a Parallelist approach will 'create a risk of double punishment for offenders' (Gavrielides, 2022: 82).

victim in a positive way and could easily be taken into account in any outcome plan. Each approach, then, is distinctive, just as each is essential to bring about 'justice' in the fullest sense.

3.2   LOGISTICS

3.2.1   Victim-initiated referrals

In a Parallelist model, most referrals to restorative justice would begin by securing the offender's willingness to participate. The reason for this practice is that victims are more likely to have confidence in the process if they are approached with the information that the offender wishes to apologise and make amends for the harm done, an assumption that has been confirmed by empirical studies. For instance, researchers Ken-Ichi Ohbuchi, Masuyo Kameda and Nariyuki Agarie found:

> [W]hen the harm-doer apologized for her wrongdoing, in contrast to when she did not, the subjects generally had more favorable impressions of her, felt more pleasant and refrained from severe aggression toward her. (1989: 222)

Even more importantly, if the offender turns out to be unsuitable or unwilling, then the person harmed is not revictimised by having their expectations let down. As Mark Umbreit writes:

> Mediators/facilitators will usually need to meet first with the offender, prior to contacting the victim. Then if the offender is willing to participate in a victim-offender conference, the victim can be contacted and a meeting arranged. If the mediator/facilitator meets first with victims, however, gaining their consent to participate, and then later discovers that the offender will not participate, victims may feel revictimized, having gotten their hopes up for some resolution to the crime, only to be denied that opportunity. (2000a: 19)[29]

---

29   Cf. 'As a courtesy to victims, facilitators should first contact offenders and ensure their willingness to participate in a conference. This will save victims any disappointment should offenders decline' (O'Connell, Wachtel & Wachtel, 1999: 37). Also, '[I]t is preferable to talk first with the offender and, if they agree to participate, contact the victim. If the offender does not agree, or, if after talking to the offender it is decided the case should not proceed for some reason, the victim's expectations do not have to be dashed' (Amstutz & Zehr, 1998: 61). Furthermore, 'This practice is based on a desire not to bother crime victims with the emotional work of deciding whether or not to communicate with the offender – unless the offender is willing to communicate and appropriately takes responsibility' (Sherman & Strang, 2007: 37).

The only exception to this practice would be crimes involving repeated victimisation or severe violence. The reason for this policy is that, if the offender initiated a process in such cases, they could potentially re-traumatise the victim or reinforce the severe power imbalance implicated in such offences.[30] But even here, the victim will often be responding to some indication that the offender has admitted responsibility and demonstrated remorse, for instance in the court trial or a subsequent letter of apology (as discussed later). In any case, a facilitator would not proceed with the process if, in their initial assessment of the offender or in the preparation phase, they discovered that their display of remorse was in fact insincere or that they refused to acknowledge their culpability for central aspects of the crime.

In such cases, the victim could initiate a referral by registering their interest with a restorative justice service that is equipped to facilitate such cases. The victim would need to be informed from the outset that a restorative justice process can only take place once the case has actually or effectively exited the system and the reasons for this policy. If they are willing to proceed, a specialist facilitator from the service would work with the victim over a period of time so as to ensure that this kind of process is likely to meet their needs. If so, the facilitator would then make contact with the offender to determine whether they are eligible and willing to take part.

Given the nature of the offences in this category, it is likely that the majority of victim-initiated cases will take place in a post-sentence context. If the offender is still serving their sentence in a prison setting, then the facilitator will also need to confirm that the prison is willing and equipped to provide the necessary cooperation and support. This would include providing the prisoner with access to an internal psychologist or social worker throughout the process; ensuring that the prisoner is given the time and a private meeting space for regular preparation meetings with the facilitators; and giving permission for the victim and any support persons to come into the prison for the purpose of attending a restorative justice process in a private room with the prisoner. A victim-initiated process could, of course, be held outside of a prison context. The offender's case may have been closed or unconditionally dismissed prior to sentence or they might be undertaking a non-prison-based sentence, or they could have been released. In such cases, both participants should have access to additional support from relevant community-based agencies or services.

Even though crimes involving repeated victimisation or severe violence will be victim-initiated, offenders who have yet to be contacted could still lodge their interest with the restorative justice service just in case the victim should make enquiries. One way of implementing this kind of approach is to set up what has been called an 'Apology Letter

---

30 Cf. 'Victim sensitive offender dialogue in crimes of severe violence should be victim initiated' (Umbreit, Vos, Coates & Armour, 2006: 47).

Bank'. This scheme was developed by the Delaware-based 'Victims Voices Heard' (VVH) post-sentence restorative justice programme. Miller describes this approach as follows: Offenders are able to write letters of apology to the victim, which they can then send to the programme. Each letter is first 'screened for appropriateness' so as to exclude letters that offer excuses for the offence or that ask the victim to forgive them (2011: 254, n. 13). Accepted letters are then kept on file, in case the victim should contact the programme:

> Victims can find out by word of mouth or on the VVH website about the Apology Letter Bank. They are then able to contact VVH and ask whether their offender has deposited a letter, and they can choose whether to receive it. Offenders will never know if the victim receives the letter they have placed in the bank unless the victim chooses for them to know. If no letter has yet been deposited, the victim's information remains on file so that they can be contacted should a letter become available. (2011: 196)[31]

Another approach Miller suggests would be for specialist restorative justice services to provide victims of severe violence or repeated victimisation with a pamphlet or website address 'at the time the case is assigned to a prosecutor' in case they might wish to use the service once a final ruling has been made. A victim's readiness to participate in a face-to-face meeting may only eventuate after many years, if at all. But if the case has actually or effectively exited the system, then they could nevertheless access other restorative elements as and when the need arises, such as getting answers to their questions from the offender. For this kind of arrangement to become routine, however, there would need to be sufficient resources, procedural safeguards and close cooperation with the relevant criminal justice agencies (Miller, 2011: 197-198).

3.2.2 Offender-initiated referrals

Where a crime does not involve severe violence or repeated victimisation, a victim should still be able to initiate a referral if they wish. However, given the best practice issues mentioned previously, the standard approach for less serious crimes would be to secure the offender's willingness to participate before contacting the victim. In such cases, there would be two possible referral pathways.

1. *Self-referrals*. If the offender is still undergoing a sentence, for instance in a prison context, then they could contact a restorative justice service directly. Again, this would

---

31 A similar process is used in a number of other jurisdictions, such as the Minnesota Department of Corrections. Umbreit and Armour (2010: 220).

require the support and assistance of the relevant prison facility. If the self-referral occurs after the case has fully exited the justice system, then the offender should be supported by a community-based agency, preferably one with which they are already involved. These direct referrals may be small in number at first, but with enough education and support, they could easily grow over time.

2. *Third-party referrals.* With the offender's consent, a referral could be made to a restorative justice service on their behalf by a relevant agency or organisation. In a pre-release context, this might include a prison-based service, such as social work or the chaplaincy. In a post-release setting, it could involve a parole agency or a community-based service. If the case has exited the system prior to any sentence, then it could be referred by a community service or a criminal justice agency, such as youth justice, the police or a prosecutor. In either case, the referral would involve the referring body providing the restorative justice service with the contact details for the offender, as well as the basic information that any service would need to initiate a case: the crime, the sentence, known risk factors and so on.

When any criminal justice personnel or agencies are involved in making referrals, great care will need to be taken to ensure that *restorative justice is not – and is not perceived by offenders as being – legally beneficial in any way*. For instance, if the police or prosecutors are making referrals, then their decision not to make an arrest or file charges must not be made *on condition that* the offender agrees to take part in restorative justice. In such a circumstance, there would be a legal benefit attached to restorative justice, and so it would not be a Parallelist referral. To ensure that this level of independence is clear to everyone concerned, a judicial authority should only offer the offender the opportunity to be referred to a restorative justice service *after* they have already made and communicated their decision to close or unconditionally dismiss the case.

Establishing an embedded and consistent impetus for making such referrals will be crucial. If there are individual professionals working within the referring organisation who are persuaded about the benefits of a Parallelist approach to restorative justice, and so are committed to making appropriate referrals, then this discretionary approach may be sufficient. However, it is also highly vulnerable to personnel turnover as well as unexpected alterations to policies and procedures. A more secure pathway would involve creating a standing agreement with the referrer – parole agency, community-based service, police or prosecutor – that any offender of a less serious crime who meets the basic eligibility criteria (as specified later) will, once the case has actually or effectively exited the system, be offered the opportunity to speak with a facilitator about the possibility of taking part in a restorative justice process. If the offender is interested, then, with their consent, the referrer would forward their details to the restorative justice service.

It is crucial that no information regarding the referral is recorded in the offender's criminal case file. This includes: (a) the offender's decision to accept or decline the opportunity to be referred to restorative justice, (b) the outcome of any referral and (c) the 'success' or otherwise of any subsequent restorative justice process. (This would not preclude the collection of anonymised data for statistical purposes.) It is equally important that offenders are informed about this policy. Otherwise, they could easily suspect – perhaps not unreasonably – that how they respond to the offer of restorative justice might have an impact on how the authorities view other crimes that are still pending or any future alleged offences.

Once the restorative justice service has received a referral, it would then contact the offender to conduct a suitability assessment. If the assessment is positive, the service would then request the victim's contact details from an appropriate source. This might be the referring criminal justice agency, a victim support service and so on. If the referral is made when the offender is in prison, then the decision about whether to conduct the process in a pre- or post-release context will be made with the consent of all those concerned: the agency, the offender, the victim(s) and any support services.

For offender-initiated referrals to work, victims will need to consent to their contact information being forwarded to the restorative justice service. As long as they are provided with accurate information about the service and its voluntary nature, this should not be a significant obstacle. However, in some jurisdictions, there may be legal or policy barriers that prevent victim details from being provided to a restorative justice service. In such cases, the agency that holds those details will need to contact the victim to obtain their consent for the restorative justice service to contact them. This is not always ideal since the relevant staff member at the agency may not have the training or the willingness to convey the nature of restorative justice to the victim in an accurate or credible way. Thus, it is recommended that either the legislation or policy be changed or appropriate staff members be identified and trained to make this initial contact with the victim. Victims should always be informed at this stage that no legal benefits will be available to the offender should they choose to participate in restorative justice.

Regardless of the pathway, a restorative justice service should only accept a referral if it meets the following basic criteria: (1) The case must have actually or effectively exited the justice system. (2) The offender must accept responsibility for committing the offence. (3) The offence must have caused significant harm to an identifiable person or persons. (4) If the offence involved severe violence (such as sexual assault, attempted murder, or murder) or repeated victimisation (such as domestic or family violence[32]), then the facilitator must be specifically trained and have expertise in the relevant area, specialist

---

32 In my view, widely used restorative justice processes – such as conferencing – are unlikely to be sufficiently safe or effective in cases of domestic violence *as these processes are standardly designed and practiced*. If restorative justice is to be used in such cases, then new specialist processes will need to be co-designed with key stakeholders to ensure they embody not only restorative justice principles but also feminist theory and the concept of transformative justice. *See* Brookes (2019b).

case supervision and independent therapeutic support must be available to all those involved, and any appropriate modifications to the standard restorative justice processes must be made.

3.2.3   Funding

One important logistical question that a Parallelist model will need to face is the source of funding for restorative justice services. On the Integrationist model, if the protocols for restorative justice have become official government policy or written into law, then the funding will generally be provided by whatever government department or agency has been assigned the task of overseeing or delivering the service – for instance, the police, corrections, social services, youth justice, victim services and so on. In addition, when restorative justice is supported by legislation, it is more likely to result in government funding that is uniform and consistent across every local jurisdiction.

This raises a potential problem for the Parallelist model. As we have seen, on this approach, restorative justice services are unlikely to require legislated protections or protocols. But if Parallelism operates outside of a legislative framework, many communities could be disadvantaged by not having a service at all, or at least not one that is adequately funded. Any solution to this quandary will, as always, depend upon local conditions. But there are several general points that can be made by way of response:

1. While Parallelism may not *require* a legal framework, it is not inconceivable that legislation could be developed to provide for the availability of post-sentence restorative justice. For instance, the Australian Capital Territory's *Crimes (Restorative Justice) Act 2004*, although predominantly focused on pre-sentence protocols, includes the following provision for post-sentence restorative justice:

> (1) A post-sentence referring entity may refer an offence for restorative justice if – (a) the entity is satisfied there is an eligible victim or eligible parent in relation to the offence; and (b) the offender – (i) was at least 10 years old when the offence was committed; and (ii) is in the post-sentence stage in relation to the offence … for which the offender is found guilty, [that is] (a) after a court has made a sentence-related order for the offender; and (b) before the end of the term of the sentence-related order or the sentence (if any) of which it forms part (whichever is later). (s.28A.1, 3)

Thus, it is at least theoretically possible that a government that wished to support a Parallelist approach could put in place this kind of legislation (i.e. without any Integrationist elements), thus making funding, as well as equal access, more likely.

2. Even if Parallelism was not supported by legislation, this would not necessarily make it more financially unstable. Integrationist services are also subject to the ever-changing winds of political favour. Many such services operate without a legislative framework that requires the state to provide ring-fenced funding for restorative justice. So if the government of the day has other priorities that outweigh equitable distribution or financial security for restorative justice services, then the Integrationist approach will find itself facing virtually the same concern raised above about the Parallelist model. For instance, in a 2016 review of restorative justice in the UK, 'the Office of the Sussex Police and Crime Commissioner advocated ring-fenced funding for restorative justice in order to prevent the "post-code lottery" nature of the current system' (Justice Committee, 2016: 12). But the relevant minister at the time, Mike Penning, disagreed, arguing that:

> overall the funding [allocated to victim-initiated RJ] was used to commission services to support victims of crime to cope and recover. RJ is only one of the services aimed at achieving this, but restorative justice is unique in that it requires the voluntary participation of the offender as well. It is therefore difficult to accurately predict victim take-up and 'success rates' of any RJ scheme put in place, and similarly difficult to accurately allocate indicative budgets. (Penning, 2016: 2)

Even where there is legislation, governments need only amend or withdraw the relevant Act if, for whatever reason, they do not wish to be bound by law to continue allocating funds to restorative justice. Relying on government funding for long-term certainty is never a failsafe solution.

3. The Parallelist model would sit far more comfortably within the community-based or charity sector, at least compared to Integrationism. Financial sources might therefore include relevant community grant foundations. In-kind contributions could be sourced from nongovernment rehabilitation agencies, victim support services, social justice charities and community-based services. This might include offering low-cost meeting rooms or office space, for instance. Restorative justice might even operate under the umbrella of such services, with existing staff taking on managerial, administrative and facilitator roles, thereby significantly reducing overall costs.

Indeed, as I later argue (§4.8), such partnerships could potentially result in other important nonmonetary benefits. For instance, they could provide a 'safe space' in which participants feel free to extend their conversations and activities to include the social-structural injustices that gave rise to or contextualise the harmful behaviour. As Zernova writes:

> Forming alliances with [grassroots social movements] could benefit restorative justice by significantly widening its agenda and escaping the present situation where the application of restorative justice is limited to wrongs, harms and injustices which fall within the legal definitions of crime. (2016: 114)

By contrast, Integrationist services, many of which are run by state-based agencies or departments, rely almost exclusively on government funding. If, for whatever reason, the government withdraws its support, these services almost invariably collapse or, at best, are forced to limit severely the number of referrals they can accept. Since the Parallelist model is more likely to attract and depend upon a more diverse range of income streams, this may, in the end, give Parallelist services a better chance of financial stability and potential for growth. This approach would also mirror the distinctive benefits that restorative justice can bring to both individuals and society as a whole.

4. It could be argued that, without centralised government funding, equal access across all jurisdictions will be more difficult to achieve. But 'difficulty' is not impossibility. Restorative justice advocates, in my experience, tend to be persistent, strongly committed and highly entrepreneurial, and so I have little doubt that, over time, this kind of obstacle could be resolved. In a similar vein, it might be argued that, if restorative justice services are not funded and managed by a central government agency, the practices, protocols and quality of service will lack consistency, thus, once again, leading to inequity for participants. This kind of fragmentation is an important concern, but there are alternatives to centralisation. The various services could organise a cooperative, in which they meet periodically and work together to form agreements on protocols and best practices. They might also share training events and coordinate external evaluation studies. It is worth noting that centralisation and government controls can introduce excessive uniformity, resulting in practices that are unsuited to the particularities of each situation, the needs of a local community or the culture in question. (An example of this issue is explored in §4.9 in relation to First Nations communities.)

5. A final cautionary note is needed here. If restorative justice services working within a Parallelist model are unable to obtain the security of on-going external funding, they might be tempted to take up a user-pays approach. This is especially of concern in jurisdictions that are already seeing the privatisation of previously government-funded services, such as medical care, disability services and so on – many of which are now provided on a user-pays basis. It would be a tragedy if restorative justice became accessible only to those with sufficient wealth. Yet this is precisely what has happened to key aspects of criminal justice. Many jurisdictions are even charging prisoners for their incarceration, whether explicitly or by virtue of being required to work for very low or non-existent wages or by charging exorbitant prices for essentials, such as food, clothing or medical care (Trounstine, 2018). Even the due process constraints that should be available to all

citizens – such as legal representation and a fair trial – are, in many jurisdictions, beyond the reach of all but a small minority. As Kali Holloway writes:

> Justice in [America] has always been for the privileged. The nation's criminal courts are particularly punitive toward those who are too poor to afford bail, represented by overworked public defenders or simply not rich enough to mount an 'affluenza' defense. From arrest to conviction, wealth and whiteness are precious assets for any defendant in a system that favors both. Numerous jurisdictions profit off fines and fees that nickel and dime the poor into debtors' prisons. And then there are Southern California's 'pay-to-stay' jails, which offer more monied inmates nicer accommodations in exchange for cash. (Holloway, 2018)

There are also clear warning signs in the professionalisation of informal conflict resolution processes, such as mediation or arbitration. As Braithwaite has found:

> When the legal profession could not fight off competition from more accessible informal justice practices, it reappropriated them as expensive and professionalized mediation services. Large fees had to be paid to accredited mediation professionals to learn the craft. (2019: 2)

However, there are also grounds for thinking that Parallelism comes with a built-in resistance to a user-pays approach. First, unlike most cases of mediation or arbitration, restorative justice would not be offered as an *alternative* to a legal proceeding. Hence, services could not rely upon users having this kind of incentive to pay for a restorative justice process. Second, as I later argue (§4.2.4), a restorative justice process is not a 'cheap civil court' in which the main point is to extract as much restitution or compensation as possible from the offender. If an agreement contains any reparative element, this is largely a symbolic gesture. It is primarily intended to demonstrate the sincerity of the offender's remorse and, hence, may not come close to restoring the victim's financial or material losses. In any case, on Parallelism, there would be no legal consequences for the offender if they failed to pay up as agreed. Thus, once again, services could not depend upon this kind of user-pays incentive.[33]

Third, a Parallelist model would be focused entirely on realising the kind of benefits that restorative justice is uniquely designed to deliver. This would include providing the

---

33   It might be argued here that if an offender fails to pay the restitution amount agreed to in a Parallelist restorative justice process, one recourse that might be available to victims would be to exercise their right to bring civil proceedings against the offender. I consider this issue in §5.2.2.

victim with an opportunity to receive answers to questions about the crime, hearing the offender admit responsibility, receiving a genuine apology and so on. It is hard to imagine how any service could, in good conscience, charge a victim to gain access to such goods, let alone find any victim willing to pay. But in any case, how would such a scheme work? Would the victim be entitled to a refund if they were not entirely convinced about the offender's sincerity? Would facilitators be expected to make sure the offender 'performs' as expected so that the victim can 'get their money's worth'? One can imagine facilitators advising offenders to 'just tell the victim what they want to hear'. In short, in a Parallelist context, a victim-pays approach would invariably undermine the very rationale for holding a restorative justice process in the first place.

Could offenders pay for the process? Unlike the victim-pays model, it is hard to see how giving offenders the opportunity to make a voluntary contribution towards costs would damage the process of moral repair. It might even enhance it by the offender demonstrating to the victim their commitment to repairing the harm. Even so, very few offenders would have the capacity to cover all of the relevant costs, or even a significant fraction of them. Many could perhaps make a contribution, but this would be largely symbolic. Hence, no service could operate sustainably on an offender-pays principle. In any case, no restorative justice service worthy of the name would refuse to work with an offender merely on the grounds that they could not afford it.

Thus, there are good reasons to think that Parallelism will be inherently resistant to a user-pays approach. However, the most effective safeguard would be to ensure that no such business model could survive due to the abundance and superior quality of free restorative justice services.

In sum, the Integrationist model has, in general, seemed to most advocates of restorative justice to be the only model worth pursuing. As a consequence, while advocates may have started out by engaging in grassroots community organising and campaigning, they have, as the movement has grown, poured more of their time and energy into trying to persuade governments to change criminal justice policy, amend legislation and provide dedicated funding. But suppose advocates were to shift their focus to setting up a Parallelist model. In that case, they would not need to depend so entirely upon convincing the government of the day. Their resources could instead be redirected towards identifying a diverse range of income streams, establishing networks or cooperatives of practitioners, collaborating with NGOs and community groups, and making sure that every local jurisdiction was equipped to deliver a restorative justice service of the highest quality, while at the same time joining forces to work towards the long-term goal of reforming (or transforming) the criminal justice system.

3.2.4   Implementation and evaluation

Any change is likely to be met with resistance, and a Parallelist approach to restorative justice is a new idea that will, at least initially, go against the grain. While there are a few thriving post-sentence schemes, the Integrationist model has dominated the field so far. There exists a hard-won legacy of political campaigning, theoretical work, policy development, referral protocols, funding agreements and legislative innovation – none of which will be easily relinquished. As Suzuki and Wood put it, 'RJ is now firmly ensconced in state justice practices' (2017: 287). It may therefore be worth offering a brief suggestion about how the restorative justice component of a Parallelist model might be implemented and tested in such a context.

As I mentioned in the Preface, one of the main advantages of Parallelism is that restorative justice services could initially be implemented not as a replacement, but rather as an addition to the way in which restorative justice is currently applied. Suppose, for example, that a system offers restorative justice in the context of diversion from prosecution or a deferred sentence. Suppose also that it is deemed too complex, too late or too politically controversial to remove the Integrationist protocols, at least not immediately and certainly not without further evidence. Yet suppose, in light of the substantive concerns about Integrationism, there is also a desire to test the comparative effectiveness of Parallelism. Since, on the Parallelist model, restorative justice is only offered when a case has actually or effectively exited the justice system, the solution is relatively straightforward. Keep the Integrationist protocols intact but introduce (or increase any existing) Parallelist protocols in a way that ensures complete legal independence. Once the referral numbers are sufficiently large, Integrationist and Parallelist approaches could then be compared, with timing and context being the chief variables. If, over time, the evidence tends to confirm the higher quality and effectiveness of Parallelism, then the Integrationist protocols could be phased out.

It is worth emphasising here that this proposal only concerns the restorative justice arm of Parallelism. Implementing the complete model will, in most cases, require extensive systemic reforms to – if not a wholesale transformation of – the criminal justice system, along the lines suggested earlier. Only once these changes are in place can it be legitimately claimed that the Parallelist model has been implemented in full, and so any evaluations of the model would need to take this into account.

3.3   MAINSTREAMING

3.3.1   *Potential for expansion*

One objection that might be raised against the Parallelist model is that, by contrast with Integrationism, it would radically diminish the use of restorative justice to address criminal matters. Hence, implementing Parallelism would remove even the possibility of restorative justice ever becoming a mainstream option. Here is an argument to that effect:

Suppose the policy makers in a particular jurisdiction are convinced about the reasons for preferring Parallelism over Integrationism. After an experimental trial, this view is confirmed by empirical evidence. So they set about implementing the Parallelist model across the board. In doing so, however, they would be very unlikely to retain any existing Integrationist approach. In other words, if they are adhering to the Guiding Principles for implementing Parallelism suggested in §3.1, then any pre-sentence use of restorative justice would, eventually, be removed.

But take a different scenario. Suppose these same policy makers are not convinced about Parallelism and so decide to retain the existing Integrationist model. In this case, it is very unlikely that they would have any principled objections to setting up legally independent referral routes as an *additional* option. In other words, while the Parallelist model would exclude any Integrationist approach on principle, the converse is not true. And this is not merely hypothetical. Most jurisdictions, at present, include a combination of diversionary and post-sentence approaches. Of course, the focus has largely been on expanding the diversionary schemes. Hence, the post-sentence approach has, at best, remained ad hoc and underdeveloped, with comparatively low case numbers as a consequence. However, these jurisdictions could, in theory, develop and expand the Parallelist referral routes. Such a jurisdiction would then be employing both Integrationist and Parallelist approaches. And this combination could easily increase the use of restorative justice far beyond the capacity of Parallelism on its own. So it follows that implementing the Parallelist model would decrease the use of restorative justice in comparison to Integrationism.

But there is a fatal flaw in this argument. The Parallelist model would only exclude the use of restorative justice to address cases that are *still inside the system, pending a final judicial outcome*. It does not exclude such cases forever. Once they have actually or effectively exited the justice system then, on the Parallelist model, these cases will become eligible for restorative justice. Put another way, the objection assumes that, under Parallelism, an Integrationist approach will still be available. If that were true, then any cases that were already referred to restorative justice as a diversion would not be available for a Parallelist approach. But as noted earlier, any jurisdiction that is persuaded to adopt the Parallelist model would, for principled reasons, make sure that it was applied exclusively. So these cases would not be 'lost' to a diversionary approach, since no such approach would exist. Every case that would have been diverted in an Integrationist system would instead be referred to restorative justice after it had actually or effectively exited the system. Hence, Parallelism on its own could potentially result in just as many cases as the Integrationist model, even when it is combined with Parallelist referral routes.

It might, of course, be argued in response that many offenders will not agree to take part in restorative justice unless it helps them to avoid prosecution or reduce their sentence. Since no such legal benefit would be available in a Parallelist setting, these offenders would not agree to participate – in which case many cases *would* be 'lost' in a Parallelist model.

But there is a crucial problem with this argument. It assumes that offenders who have this kind of ulterior motive would still be suitable for restorative justice, and, from a Parallelist perspective, this view is deeply problematic (see §4.5). Put another way, the number of cases that take place under Parallelism could well turn out to be significantly lower than they would have been in an Integrationist model. But if this decrease is due to the fact that the only offenders who are agreeing to take part are doing so for the right reasons, then the higher case numbers available under an Integrationist approach will need to be weighed against the substantial increase in quality and effectiveness that is likely to result from using a Parallelist model.

3.3.2   Requirements for mainstreaming

The foregoing objection to Parallelism not only argued that this model would result in lower case numbers but that this would also make it impossible for restorative justice to become a mainstream option. I have suggested that the first prong of this objection was flawed. But even if Parallelism did reduce case numbers overall, would it follow that restorative justice would thereby lose any chance of being a mainstream response to crime?

The concept of 'mainstreaming' is often confused with expansion or permanence, but these are different goals. Of course, there is likely to be a correlation, if not a causal link. However, a service can be widely used, and yet, it could still operate as a discretionary adjunct to a mainstream institution. It could even have the assurance of ring-fenced funding and a legislative framework and yet have become co-opted by or subordinated to the needs and priorities of the institution to which it is attached. In other words, for a service to be genuinely mainstream, it must be able to function *autonomously*, or on its own terms, answerable to its own values and objectives, and it must be seen as performing an *essential* societal role, one that would not be easily overlooked or overridden by other priorities.

These two characteristics are, I suggest, what it would take for restorative justice to become a truly mainstream response to crime. So, which model – Parallelism or Integrationism – is most likely to produce such a result? To answer this question, we would need to look at the societal role that restorative justice plays within each model, as well as the nature of its relationship to the criminal justice system. Much more will be said about these issues throughout the book. But a few salient points can be made here.

3.3.2.1   Autonomous

To what extent is restorative justice, under the Integrationist model, able to function on its own terms? Given that Integrationism is restricted to using a diversionary approach, it is hard to see how restorative justice, on this model, could ever play anything other than a subordinate role in relation to criminal justice. For instance, a diversionary process can only take place within the time frame set by the court's priorities, rather than in accordance with the needs of the participants. Again, the judiciary decides, using their own legal criteria, whether an offender (or any other participant) is eligible for restorative justice. And any outcome agreement is usually reviewed by the court to ensure it is appropriate, as measured by its own standards of proportionality. In New Zealand, even the 'genuineness' of the offender's apology must be taken into account in the court's sentencing decision.[34] This kind of legal framework and judicial scrutiny, as we shall see, cannot help but have a significant impact on how the participants think about the purpose of restorative justice, the kind of agreement they are expected to make, and on how the offender's underlying motivations are perceived by the victim.

To make this point more vivid, it may be helpful to use a concrete example from Scotland. (No doubt there will be somewhat different criteria in certain jurisdictions, but this example appears to be broadly similar to the majority.) Thus, I will set out in the following the standard reasons why a case would be deemed suitable for restorative justice, according to the values and objectives of restorative justice alone. Then I will show why Scotland's public prosecutors – called 'Procurator Fiscals' – are likely to be prevented by their own Prosecution Code from diverting *precisely such cases* from prosecution.[35] My

---

34   'In sentencing or otherwise dealing with an offender the court must take into account [1] ... any measures taken or proposed to be taken by the offender to ... apologise to any victim of the offending ... [2.d.ii] ... [and] whether or not it was genuine [2.a]' (*Sentencing Act* 2002 (NZ), s.10).

35   It is worth noting that in 2019 the Scottish Government made a commitment 'to have RJ services widely available across Scotland by 2023'. However, it appears that the 'availability' of restorative justice for victims of crime is very likely to be curtailed by the Prosecution Code in the ways described as follows, given that the Scottish Government has also stipulated the following in advance: 'risk assessments [for the use of RJ] ... will take full cognisance of the role of The Crown Office and Procurator Fiscal Service (COPFS) as the independent public prosecution service for Scotland. In that respect, RJ will not impinge on any ongoing

purpose is to illustrate how restorative justice, in an Integrationist context, cannot function on its own terms. It will always be subordinated to legal priorities, many of which are directly opposed to the principles of restorative justice.

1. The evidence suggests that restorative justice provides greater benefits for victims when it is applied to serious crimes. As Joanna Shapland, Gwen Robinson and Angela Sorsby report, 'victims of more serious offences ... were significantly more likely than victims of less serious offences to say that the restorative justice [process] had helped them' (2011: 184).[36] Again, as many researchers have found, the reconviction rates after a restorative justice process are significantly lower for more serious crimes and repeat offenders. For this reason, Strang, Sherman, Mayo-Wilson, Woods and Ariel argue as follows:

> [B]anishing [restorative justice conferencing] to low-seriousness crimes is a wasted opportunity. If governments wish to fund RJ at all, this evidence suggests that the best return on investment will be with violent crimes, and also with offenders convicted after long prior histories of convictions. (2013: 48)[37]

However, Scotland's Prosecution Code advises against diversion from prosecution in precisely such circumstances:

> In general, the more serious the offence the more likely it is that the public interest will require a prosecution. ... Where an offence results in significant injury or impairment, significant financial loss, distress or psychological consequences for the victim or any other witness it is likely that the public interest will be best served by prosecution. (Crown Office and Procurator Fiscal Service, 2001: 6)

2. There are no theoretical limits on how many restorative justice processes an offender may undertake. Each offence is likely to have involved a different victim, and so their needs must also be taken into consideration. Nor is there any reason to prohibit someone who has a history of offending from participating. What matters is that they are assessed

---

criminal proceedings. Decisions relating to the prosecution or diversion of a case from prosecution are matters solely for COPFS' (The Scottish Government, 2019: 3, 5).

36 *See also* Sherman and Strang (2007: 8) and Miers et al. (2001: x).

37 In a similar vein, Carolyn Hoyle writes, 'It is not worth ... making a commitment to the spread of restorative justice practices to help the police deal only with shop theft or minor incidents of disorder' (Hoyle, 2010: 72). It is important to note that the researchers quoted here are not claiming that restorative justice should not be used for less serious crimes or first-time offenders or that it is wholly ineffective in such cases.

as willing and suitable to address the harm caused by the offence in question. The Prosecution Code, however, states that 'previous convictions' would count as a reason *not* to divert a case from prosecution:

> The public interest is more likely to require prosecution where the accused has a significant history of recent previous convictions, particularly where they include convictions for similar crimes. (2001: 7)

3. The victim should not be required to decide between restorative justice and prosecution. The two approaches meet different needs or interests, so they are complementary rather than mutually exclusive. But the Prosecution Code implies that, if the victim's view is that prosecution is 'appropriate', then this will count as a reason to prosecute *rather than* seek an 'alternative' such as restorative justice – thus ruling out the possibility that the victim might want both:

> [T]he prosecutor must take into account any available information indicating the views of the alleged victim about whether prosecution or alternative action is appropriate. (2001: 7)

4. The offender's motive for committing the crime does not determine their suitability for restorative justice. The only requirement is that they have been assessed as both willing and able to take full responsibility for their actions in a safe and constructive manner. However, the Prosecution Code does take motive into account in relation to whether a diversionary approach would be suitable:

> The public interest is likely to require prosecution where criminal behaviour was sexually motivated or motivated by any form of discrimination against the victim's ethnic or national origin or religious beliefs. It may also be relevant to consider whether the behaviour of the accused was spontaneous or planned in advance and whether it was part of a course of criminal conduct by the accused. (2001: 7)

An Integrationist might argue, in response, that the criteria listed above only conflict with the use of restorative justice as a diversion from prosecution. Jurisdictions could simply elect to prosecute cases in accordance with such criteria, but then refer offenders to restorative justice in the context of a deferred sentence. However, even here, there are often legal restrictions that would rule out otherwise suitable cases, most of which are not dissimilar, in effect, to Scotland's Prosecution Code. For instance, the UK's *Sentencing Act*

2020 specifies that a 'deferment order' – which can include a referral to restorative justice – can only be made if:

> the court is satisfied, having regard to the nature of the offence and the character and circumstances of the offender, that it would be in the interests of justice to make the order. (Part 2. Ch. 2, s.2.d)

But an Integrationist might argue that, while these restrictions exist in some jurisdictions, they are not required by the Integrationist model as such. And this can be confirmed by counterexamples. For instance, New Zealand's amended *Sentencing Act* 2002 stipulates that, if certain criteria are met, a District court 'must adjourn the proceedings' prior to sentencing 'to determine whether a restorative justice process is appropriate ... taking into account the wishes of the victims' (s.24A.2.a). But the *Act* does not require the court to take into account the seriousness of the offence and the offender's motive, character or history of recidivism. Its eligibility criteria are simply as follows:

> (a) an offender appears before a District Court at any time before sentencing; and (b) the offender has pleaded guilty to the offence; and (c) there are 1 or more victims of the offence; and (d) no restorative justice process has previously occurred in relation to the offending; and (e) the Registrar has informed the court that an appropriate restorative justice process can be accessed. (s.24A.1.a-e)

It follows that, at least with respect to the criteria for diversion, the Integrationist model does not *necessarily* entail that restorative justice is subordinated to irrelevant legal priorities.

But there is a problem with this example. As we might expect, New Zealand's virtually unrestricted approach has opened the door to a vastly greater number of referrals. In the year after the introduction of this amendment to the *Act* in 2014, New Zealand's Ministry of Justice reported:

> a 200% increase in the number of restorative justice referrals [from 3,998 referrals in 2014 to 12,123 referrals in 2015] and a 51% increase in the number of restorative justice conferences [from 1,838 to 2,782]. (2020: 2, 3, 6)

Yet, in terms of case numbers, restorative justice still plays a very limited role in New Zealand's adult justice system. Only a small fraction (23%) of the eligible cases led to a conference in 2015, and since then the percentage appears to have 'decreased further' (2020: 6). Why is this?

The Ministry of Justice explains the discrepancy in terms of 'the offender and/or the victim not wanting to participate, or the service provider assessing the case as unsuitable for a restorative justice process' (2020: 3, n. 2). However, Sarah Pfander spoke with New Zealand practitioners and found that the main reason, from their perspective, was 'a shortage of willing victim participants' (2020: 180). This could, Pfander suggests, be due to certain cultural constraints:

> [T]he number of cases that are appropriate for victim participation *and* have victims willing to participate has a natural plateau, which may mean that the mechanism cannot grow into a primary justice response without substantial cultural changes in how victims view their role in the justice process. (2020: 182)

However, an international survey found that 'between 40% and 50%' of victims would be interested in a restorative meeting with the offender, which is a significantly larger percentage than the 'plateau' emerging in the New Zealand criminal justice system (Wemmers & Canuto, 2002: 35). So I would suggest that there are more plausible explanations available. For instance, given the fact that the offender's participation is likely to reduce their sentence, victims would have good reason to be sceptical about the offender's sincerity (see §4.6). Or again, a conference is only offered within a time frame that suits the court process, rather than the victim's needs (see §4.7.2). These obstacles have nothing to do with restorative justice values or objectives. They are instead due entirely to the way that, in an Integrationist context, restorative justice is subordinated to the priorities and constraints of the criminal justice system.

It might be argued here that the Parallelist model is itself subject to obstacles and restrictions that are caused by the criminal justice system. For instance, a review by Shapland et al. found that only 12-15% of potentially eligible pre-release cases proceeded to a conference. The reasons for this low uptake included difficulties in recruiting facilitators, making contact with victims or obtaining their contact details, setting up conferences within a reasonable timeframe and so on (2004: 31). No doubt many of these issues were due to the kind of administrative obstructions that can arise in a correctional context. But it is important to note that these are entirely logistical problems. It is conceivable that such issues could be overcome if more energy and resources were devoted to a pre-release setting. These are not, in other words, comparable to the built-in obstacles that are found in the Integrationist model, such as legislated criteria for the use of a diversionary approach, time frame restrictions, the legal Sword of Damocles and so on.

In sum, Integrationism invariably leads to restorative justice becoming subject to and co-opted by criminal justice objectives and priorities. This subsidiary role is clearly exhibited in the following (mostly Integrationist-oriented) recommendation offered by Shapland et al.:

> [W]e would argue that the key stages [in which a restorative justice should be held] are pre-sentence and pre-release from prison, because it is at these stages that *criminal justice would itself benefit most* from the outcomes and process of restorative justice. Pre-sentence, restorative justice can create individualised outcome agreements which meet victim needs and also *suggest helpful possibilities for sentence*. Pre-release, restorative justice can help to create agreements which will minimise the possibility of revictimisation or unhelpful encounters after release. However, immediately post-sentence it is difficult to see how participants in restorative justice can create the best solutions, given that *the parameters of the sentence will already have been set*, so that there are few possibilities for offenders to undertake additional activities, nor for restitution. (2011: 187, my emphases)

By contrast, on the Parallelist model, the role of restorative justice is not to provide a source of 'helpful possibilities' from which the court can draw when determining a sentence. Participants should not be conscripted to produce 'outcomes' from which 'criminal justice would itself benefit most'. Their only focus should be on finding ways to address the personal harm that the offender has caused to the victim, not on creating 'the best solutions' for a sentence. The chief purpose of criminal justice is to serve the public interest, not the private needs of the participants. Trying to combine these two distinct objectives into a single mechanism might seem more efficient, but it will only distort and compromise the value and meaningfulness of both. The criminal justice system should be focused on fulfilling its remit to deliver a fair, humane and proportionate response to crime, without fear or favour. The victim and offender should *then* be given an opportunity – after the case has actually or effectively exited the system – to take part in a private process in which the offender can fulfil their moral obligations towards the victim, including any 'additional activities' this might entail.

3.3.2.2   Essential

To what extent is restorative justice seen as performing an indispensable role in society under the Integrationist model? In New Zealand, the court is, as we have seen, required by law to take a restorative justice process into account in its sentencing decision. But in most other jurisdictions, the court can simply ignore the outcome of a restorative justice process altogether. For instance, the UK's *Sentencing Act* 2020 states:

[F]ollowing [a] deferment order … [t]he court may deal with the offender for the offence in any way in which the original court could have dealt with the offender for the offence if it had not made a deferment order. (Part 2, Ch. 2, s.11.2)

In other words, the court is effectively permitted to treat a restorative justice process *as if it had never occurred*. In practice, this might be rare. But even so, it is difficult not to see this statute as a pronouncement about the nonessential status of restorative justice in the eyes of the state legislators. Is it possible to imagine the court being allowed to deal with the offender as if their criminal trial had not taken place?

It might be argued that, even if the court has this kind of discretionary power, restorative justice could still come to be regarded as playing an essential role in how society responds to crime. As the practice of diverting cases to restorative justice is more consistently deployed, it could, at some point, usurp the dominant position currently held by traditional punitive sanctions. This is, indeed, the Integrationist vision for mainstreaming restorative justice. As Zernova and Wright observe:

Proponents believe that as more and more cases are diverted from the traditional procedure to restorative justice programmes … the restorative way of dealing with offences would [eventually] become the norm and traditional punishment an exception. (2007: 92)

But there are several key problems with this aspiration. First, it assumes that restorative justice is in a zero-sum contest with criminal justice. Why else would the ultimate aim be to create a permanent and consistently used way of evading it? But as we have seen, criminal justice is not inherently at odds with restorative justice. These two approaches only clash when they try to merge in the way that Integrationism demands. Granted, the criminal justice system in its current form is, in certain respects, doing more harm than good. But if we believe that a functioning democracy cannot exist without an institution that can uphold the rule of law, then we need to focus on *solving* the problems that plague the criminal justice system, rather than on simply finding a way to circumvent them. Changing the criminal justice system will only be achieved by the usual methods of political influence and social change: persistent lobbying, public protests, sustained research and so on. As Boyes-Watson puts it:

Reform of the criminal legal system requires more than programmatic add-ons – it needs significant political movements for sentencing reform, police, prosecutorial and judicial accountability and justice reinvestment along with shifts in cultural mindsets, political power, resources and priorities. (2019: 15)

Second, restorative justice is, in any case, not the Trojan Horse that Integrationists imagine it to be. When it is bolted onto the existing system as a diversionary approach, it is, as we have seen, far more likely to be co-opted and constrained by criminal justice priorities. The Integrationist strategy for mainstreaming restorative justice, even at its most successful, can only produce a contorted hybrid. Even if diverting cases to restorative justice became 'the norm', the quality and effectiveness of the process itself will still be undermined by the legal system to which it is subordinate. Thus, under such conditions, restorative justice would in fact be prevented from reaching its full potential as a distinctive and vital response to crime.

In other words, the two characteristics required for mainstreaming stand or fall together. Restorative justice cannot play its essential role in society to maximum effect unless it is able to function autonomously, answerable only to its own objectives and values. And this requires complete independence from the criminal justice system. Once restorative justice is no longer operating as a discretionary appendage, it can start to live up to its true potential. There would be no built-in structural barriers to the highest quality that it is capable of achieving. Restorative justice could become a service that is available to anyone who has caused harm or who has been harmed by criminal behaviour, not only to those who manage to squeeze past the bottleneck of criminal justice priorities and legal restrictions.[38]

It could eventually become common knowledge that 'doing justice' in the aftermath of a crime does not only involve serving the public interest. It also requires providing those who were harmed by a crime with the opportunity to find the kind of healing that can emerge in a safe and voluntary dialogue with the person who caused that harm. Over time, most citizens would come to understand that, while the criminal justice system's response to crime is necessary and legitimate, it does not relieve offenders of their moral obligation to repair the personal harm they have caused. That requires an entirely separate response called 'restorative justice'.

This vision, in my view, is what gives Parallelism the edge over Integrationism as a pathway to mainstreaming restorative justice. The Parallelist model is better able to protect and enhance the quality and effectiveness of both restorative justice and criminal justice and is therefore more likely to result in restorative justice becoming widely regarded as an equally essential response to crime.

---

38   In §5.1.2, I address the concern that, on the Parallelist model, a protracted investigation or court process may, in some cases, result in a considerable delay before the opportunity to hold a restorative justice process arises – thus preventing those involved from communicating in a time-frame that best suits their wishes and needs.

4 ADVANTAGES

In this chapter, it is argued that Parallelism offers significant advantages over Integrationism insofar as it avoids the multiple ways in which Integrationism can detract from the quality and effectiveness of both criminal justice and restorative justice. The first four sections focus on the former and the remaining sections on the latter, although, due to the 'tug of war' nature of these issues, there are inevitably a number of overlaps.

4.1 EQUALITY

4.1.1 Equality for offenders

One of the principles that underpin the criminal justice system is equality before the law. This means, in part, that, once accidental or irrelevant variables are taken out, the opportunity to evade or have access to the relevant legal processes should be the same for any citizen. But in an Integrationist framework, violations of this principle of equality would be extremely difficult to avoid.

Suppose two offenders, call them 'Ari' and 'Blake', commit exactly the same type of crime. Suppose that Ari is, through no fault of his, not offered diversionary restorative justice. For example, there is no restorative justice service available in the relevant location; or the caseload capacity of the service has been exceeded; or the court does not have the time or resources to make a referral to the service; or the service protocols insist that a diversionary process can only be made available to the offender if the victim agrees to participate in restorative justice, and, even though Ari is willing and suitable, the victim refuses to take part or cannot be contacted or is unavailable due to other commitments; or Ari is genuinely remorseful, but is not referred because he is well known to the criminal justice system as a repeat offender or a member of an ethnic minority group or too poor to make a restitution payment.[1]

---

1   These latter possibilities are not merely hypothetical. For instance, in Western and South Australia in the mid-90s, the comparatively low referral rates of First Nations young people to restorative justice programmes as an alternative to court suggested that police were discriminating against them on racial grounds (Cunneen, 1997: 297-298). Again, some restorative justice programmes in America 'allow offenders to participate only if they are likely to be able to make restitution payments to the victim' (Brown, 1994: 1285). Finally, 'people already well-known to the system and who are most vulnerable to imprisonment because of criminal records, may be systematically excluded from participation' (La Prairie, 1999: 146). These sources were identified by Roche (2003: 39).

Alternatively, suppose that Ari is offered the opportunity, but turns it down on grounds that are not entirely blameworthy. For example, Ari has been assessed by a psychologist as being unsuitable for such a challenging and demanding process; or Ari's family are, for whatever reason, strongly opposed to his meeting with the victim; or Ari feels that he ought to be punished and does not want to mislead the victim into thinking that he is trying to avoid what he deserves; or Ari sincerely believes that someone else was to blame for what happened and so would find it impossible to offer a genuine apology; or Ari has good reason to be worried that the victim may take what he says in the meeting and use it against him in court or in a civil case.

Meanwhile, suppose that Blake is not afflicted by any of these obstacles and so is offered the opportunity and agrees to participate in restorative justice. As a result, Ari is prosecuted or sentenced in the usual way, while Blake is not. This kind of situation may occur routinely in the criminal justice system, whether the referral is made to restorative justice or some other diversionary scheme. But it is clearly unfair, particularly given that being prosecuted or receiving a traditional sentence is likely to be a more severe outcome than merely participating in restorative justice.[2] In the Parallelist model, problems of this kind could not even arise since restorative justice is only available after a case has actually or effectively exited the system. Yet it is very difficult to imagine how these situations could be avoided in the Integrationist model.

To give a concrete example, the research design for evaluating the English restorative justice pilot schemes involved setting up control groups of offenders who did not participate in a conference. The research report by Shapland et al., states that 'the senior members of the judiciary and prison authorities' assured the schemes 'that control group offenders would not suffer detriment from being randomised out of the possibility of attending a conference' (2007: 15, n. 14). In other words, offenders would be randomised out only after they had agreed to participate. In accordance with the Court of Appeal ruling, 'agreeing to participate in restorative justice was itself mitigating, irrespective of whether a conference took place'. However, this does not take into account the fact that what might happen within a restorative justice process could result in *further* mitigating factors for participating offenders. As the report states, '[i]t is likely that aspects of outcome agreements would be seen as mitigating (such as apologising, paying compensation, undertaking programmes)' (2007: 15, n. 15).

---

2   Many jurisdictions follow the UN Basic Principle: 'Failure to implement [a restorative justice] agreement ... should not be used as justification for a more severe sentence in subsequent criminal justice proceedings' (The Economic and Social Council, 2002: 4-5 (III. 16)). But even if the sentence imposed as a result of their failure to implement the agreement is *exactly* the one they would ordinarily have received, it will still be 'more severe' for the offender than having the sentence waived or reduced on the grounds that they successfully participated in a restorative justice process.

But offenders who had been randomised out would not, of course, have had access to these additional mitigating factors. They were therefore potentially disadvantaged from a legal standpoint.[3] One might respond to this, as the then Lord Chief Justice Woolf did, by arguing that offenders cannot claim to have been treated unfairly if they have not received an advantage to which they were not entitled:

> The fact that an offender wants to participate in the project but for one reason or another cannot do so is not a matter of which the offender can legitimately complain. He has no entitlement to be involved in the project. The position is exactly the same as a situation where some particular form of disposal is not available, for example, a drug treatment project. The sentencer has to sentence in the way that he considers are appropriate in the circumstances which actually exist. The judge may still be satisfied that the offender is genuinely remorseful and the court can give such credit for that as it considers appropriate. (2002: 1)

There are several problems with this response. First, suppose that a team of ten lawyers are gathered around the office Christmas tree, awaiting their annual gifts from the Head of the Firm. The Head, however, announces that, due to a miscount, there are only seven gifts and that the lawyers will need to draw their names from a hat to receive one. The lawyers start to protest, but the Head dismisses their objections by arguing that none of them are entitled to a gift, otherwise it would not be a 'gift'. So the three who miss out will have no legitimate cause for complaint. This argument is unlikely to win the hearts and minds of the team, and for good reason. Even if the miscount was unintended, and even if they were not entitled to a gift, the unequal distribution was unfair – just as the unequal availability of restorative justice would be. The principle that *like cases should be treated alike* is a touchstone of the rule of law, and it applies regardless of entitlement.

A second problem with Woolf's response is this: Many offenders are more than willing to participate in a drug treatment programme but cannot for reasons that are beyond their control. For example, they happen to have been sent to a prison in which the current programme is understaffed, and so all the places are full. Do offenders in such a predicament have no legitimate complaint, particularly when their early release or parole could depend on attending such a programme? In other words, to say that the unequal availability of restorative justice would be no different from other disposals, such as drug

---

3   There were also disadvantages from a restorative justice perspective. One offender who had been randomised out stated: 'Very disappointed, because [victim] was the first person that I felt guilty about because [I] got clean a week after theft. Very, very disappointed haven't had chance to meet [v] and tell her I'm sorry, feel this would help me to move on with my life, can't move on. (Northumbria offender)' (Shapland et al., 2007: 30, 31).

treatment programmes, hardly renders the situation fair. An injustice that is commonplace remains an injustice. Dame Sian Elias, as the then Chief Justice of New Zealand, makes a similar point:

> Even those who are supportive of the goals of restorative justice ... express concern that those who do not have access to such programmes are disadvantaged by geography or by the attitude of the particular victim. Although in sentencing in New Zealand judges must consider restorative justice outcomes[4], the availability of access to such programmes is in practice limited by financial and practical considerations. The use of 'pilot' programmes in particular areas without attempt to set up universal access is inevitably discriminatory. (2018: 129-130)

Finally, Woolf suggests an alternative recourse for offenders who have not been able to access a restorative justice process: If they display genuine remorse before the judge, then 'the court can give such credit for that as it considers appropriate'.[5] But, as argued previously, a display of remorse in court would clearly not be given *equivalent* credit to attending a restorative justice process. It would be similar to the difference between an offender who merely informs the judge that they are willing to attend a 12-week drug treatment programme and one who has actually completed the programme. Thus, Woolf's alternative does not rectify the situation for offenders who, through no fault of their own, do not have access to restorative justice. They remain unfairly disadvantaged from a legal point of view.

4.1.2   Equality for victims

It might be argued that most victims who take part in restorative justice within an Integrationist setting report that they are 'satisfied' with the process and its outcomes. But not all victims are so amenable to restorative justice. As Martin Wright and Guy Masters note:

> We do need to bear in mind ... that the reason so many researchers have found victims to be sympathetic may be that the unsympathetic ones are screened out. What does restorative justice offer the vengeful victim? Some may become

---

4   *Sentencing Act* 2002 (NZ), s 8(j) and 10.

5   Cf. Hoyle suggests a similar solution in cases where the model stipulates that offenders can only access restorative justice if the victim agrees to participate: 'A "retributive sentence" discount could be given for willingness to participate in a conference, even if it later becomes clear that it cannot proceed. ... Whilst such offenders might not receive a fully reduced tariff – as would those who participated in a conference – they would get some credit' (Hoyle, 2010: 60).

less vengeful after the passage of time, and perhaps after having discussions with [restorative justice] workers; for others, there remains the still-retributive criminal justice system. (2002: 59-60)

Most restorative justice advocates would agree that victims who have vengeful feelings – or who, for whatever other reason, are 'unsympathetic' to restorative justice – should not be judged, or pressured into participating or receive any kind of prejudicial treatment.[6] Yet in the Integrationist model it is not necessarily the case that a punitive disposal will, in fact, remain available to victims who, for whatever reason, are unwilling to participate in restorative justice.

For example, most Integrationist protocols will stipulate that if the offender decides to participate but the victim does not, then the offender may instead attend a conference without the victim present or engage in a victim awareness programme or undertake a reparative task for the community. The problem with this protocol is that it offers nothing to the 'unsympathetic' victim. Once the judicial decision has been made to divert the case, and the offender agrees to participate, then the victim's decisions are thereby limited to the following: (1) they can either participate in restorative justice or (2) they can decline and hope that the court ignores the outcome of the offender's participation in restorative justice and prosecutes anyway or delivers what would have otherwise been the normal sentence for a crime of this nature – neither of which is likely. In Scotland, for example, the procurator fiscal's right not to prosecute is, as Sheehan and Dickson write, 'almost unchallengeable':

> The views of the alleged victim are considered by, but are in no way binding upon, the procurator fiscal. Anyone aggrieved by the decision may raise the matter with the Lord Advocate, who may instruct a report from the procurator fiscal. Where further evidence comes to light the decision not to proceed may be reviewed. (2003: 86)

In other words, if the victim is 'unsympathetic' to restorative justice, then the Integrationist model is unlikely to offer them the usual criminal justice response. Again, this kind of situation may occur routinely in the criminal justice system whenever a diversionary approach is employed. But implicit in the Integrationist model is that restorative justice should be mainstreamed. What this means in practice is that there should be a presumption

---

6   In a similar vein, Wright and Masters elsewhere argue that victims who feel unable to forgive their offender should not be blamed or pressured to do so: '[T]he process of victim/offender communication *may* enable victims to forgive; they are fortunate if they can do so, but in no way to be reproached if they cannot' (Wright & Masters, 2002: 57).

in favour of diverting offenders so that restorative justice can be pursued. In other words, their aim is to substantially increase the use of restorative justice as a diversionary approach. But it follows that, in such a system, the numbers of victims who feel disenfranchised, simply because they happen to be 'unsympathetic' to restorative justice, will also increase. This is clearly unfair. Yet, once again, it is not at all easy to see how it can be avoided in the Integrationist model.

There is, however, a possible response that an Integrationist might give to this objection. The Integrationist model could change its protocols so that the offender was allowed to participate in restorative justice only if the victim also agreed to do so.[7] But this would effectively hand over to the victim the decision as to whether to prosecute or sentence the offender, which would introduce a subjective variable into the legal proceedings that is patently unfair to the offender. As Jakob Holtermann notes:

> [I]t is definitely possible to imagine a case where a remorseful offender with her mind set to fully restore values meets a revengeful victim that stubbornly rejects any other outcome than the one that equals the hardest punishment available under law. If disagreement automatically refers the case to traditional criminal court it appears that the vengeful victim de facto gets dictatorial powers to decide the case her way. (2009a: 77, n. 14)

It would also impose a decision-making power on victims that they may not wish to exercise. Many victims simply want to be left alone so that they can get on with their lives. As Brown notes, in one study of restorative justice participants, many victims reported that 'the amount of time required to participate in [the process] was a point of some dissatisfaction'. One victim stated: '[I]t's like being hit by a car and having to get out and help the other driver when all you were doing was minding your own business' (1994: 1281).[8] Yet if they are told that their decision to opt out could mean that the offender will face the full force of the law, they could easily feel considerable pressure to agree. As Richard Delgado puts it, in an Integrationist context, restorative justice 'casts the victim in the role of sentencer ... determining the fate of an often young and malleable offender. Not every victim will welcome this responsibility' (2000: 762-763). Again, Wright found that the average sentence for offenders referred to restorative justice was 38 days, versus 212 for those who were not. He concluded that '*victims* may feel a burden of decision because if

---

7   Obtaining consent from the victim is a requirement for a diversionary approach in some jurisdictions. For example, in the UK, the *Sentencing Act* 2020 states that a 'restorative justice requirement may not be imposed as a deferment requirement without the consent of every person who would be a participant in the activity ... where the participants consist of, or include, the offender and one or more of the victims' (Part 1. Ch.2. s7.1a, 2).

8   Quoting from the report by Coates and Gehm (1985: 9).

they refuse to participate ... they may bear some responsibility for a *heavier sentence* imposed on the offender' (1996a: 114, 183).

Finally, the victim could agree to participate merely to avoid any reprisals from the offender, should their non-participation result in the offender being prosecuted or receiving a harsher sentence. This is not a good reason to participate in restorative justice. Victims should participate in the expectation that doing so is likely to bring them positive benefits, not in order to avoid negative repercussions. As noted in the following guidance by Victim Support UK:

> [A] decision to divert the case from prosecution should not be overturned because the victim declines to take part in restorative justice, nor should a lenient sentence be increased because the victim declines to take part. To do so puts undue pressure on the victim and in some cases could put the victim at risk of retaliation. (2003: 2)

4.1.3   Inequality in maximalism

It is worth noting that these equality before the law problems also plague the Maximalist's expanded definition of 'restorative justice'. Their view appears to be that, if, for whatever reason, a diversionary restorative justice process does not come up with a suitable reparative outcome agreement, then an involuntary 'restorative justice' process can be used. That is to say, the state should impose its own reparative sanction on the offender, such as compensation, community service or reparation for the victim. Within Dignan's Maximalist proposal, for instance:

> [R]ecourse to the courts would not normally be allowed unless either the accused denied guilt, the victim was unwilling to participate, the parties were unable to reach agreement on the subject of reparation or the offender refused to make reparation as agreed. (2003: 147)

The Maximalist view here is that, because the outcome of this scenario is still 'restorative', the objections regarding equality made previously either do not apply or are less of a concern. As Wright puts it:

> [T]he human rights implications are less serious when it is a question of how much good a person should be required to do, rather than how much pain he or she should be required to suffer. (1996b: 236)

But why should the type of sanction imposed by the state diminish or nullify the offender's right to equality before the law? Whether the sanction is reparative or punitive, there is still a need for due process. Yet because the Maximalist approach employs an Integrationist framework for voluntary forms of restorative justice, the state could still end up imposing a sanction on one citizen rather than another for reasons that have nothing to do with their culpability, the extent of the harm done or the seriousness of their wrongdoing. Instead, the reasons could include the fact that, when the diversionary approach was tried, the victim could not be contacted, or they were demanding an unreasonable or humiliating reparative agreement or any one of the other irrelevant reasons previously listed. In short, even in the Maximalist model, cases will arise in which offenders and victims will not be treated equally before the law.

4.2   PROPORTIONALITY

One of the essential features of restorative justice is that outcome agreements cannot be specified in advance. They need to be worked out by the individual participants. All those involved must agree that a certain kind of task or commitment is sufficient as a way of making amends for the harm that was caused. However, in an Integrationist context, this can leave the door wide open to a situation in which the state is enforcing agreements that the judiciary would otherwise have regarded as disproportionate. Early research in Australia, for instance, showed:

> [F]or property cases, offenders were agreeing to harsher outcomes than they would have received in court. This [was] certainly the case for a 13-year-old girl who completed 40 hours of community service for the theft of one candy bar. (McCold & Wachtel, 1998: 95)

Advocates of Integrationism have responded to this problem by arguing that various proportionality constraints can be put in place. But the kind of restrictions that have been employed, while not wholly ineffective, give rise to significant concerns.

4.2.1   Reasonableness

One proposal has been to stipulate that restorative justice outcomes must not be 'excessive' or 'unreasonable'. This means that any burden which the agreement places on the offender must match up with a sound assessment of both the seriousness of the crime and the culpability of the offender. As the Council of Europe Committee of Ministers put it:

> [Agreements] should contain only reasonable and proportionate obligations … [This requirement] means that, within rather wide limits, there should be correspondence between the burden on the offender and the seriousness of the offence; for instance, compensation should not be excessive. (1999: 9, 33-V.4, 31)[9]

But who decides what is 'unreasonable' or 'excessive'? It may be problematic if this judgement is left up to the participants themselves. The offender could easily feel that they have little option but to consent to whatever reparative task or compensation the victim requests, even if it is excessive or unreasonable in their view. As Patrick Gerkin found in his research:

> [V]ictims hold too much power in the agreement-writing stages. They can effectively impose their will on the offenders by individually creating the agreement and including stipulations that extend beyond the scope of the harm created by the offenders' actions. (2009: 239)

4.2.2   Punitive Limits

One way of addressing such a 'danger' would be to identify a more objective standard of proportionality. Thus, it has been proposed that restorative justice agreements should be no more burdensome than the sentence that would have been handed down by the courts. As Braithwaite puts it, '[r]estorative justice processes must be prohibited from ever imposing punishments which exceed the maximum punishment the courts would impose for that offence' (2002c: 567). However, participants are unlikely to know in advance exactly what the upper punitive limit would have been for the offence in question. Hence, in practice, this constraint is usually applied by subjecting restorative justice agreements to a subsequent judicial review. If the court then deems that the agreement exceeds 'the maximum punishment' that it would have imposed, it can overrule the agreement and reduce the burden accordingly.

This might initially seem like a viable safeguard. Within an Integrationist context, the judicial authorities are ultimately responsible for overseeing the process and monitoring its outcomes in any case. But a court-imposed upper limit is a slippery slope. This kind of proportionality constraint cannot help but lead to additional court-imposed requirements, thus severely impacting the restorative quality of the process.

---

9   Cf. 'Proportionality constraints [in restorative justice] may come mainly to constrain proposed dispositions which involve manifestly unreasonable views of the wrongfulness of the conduct' (von Hirsch et al. 2003: 38).

For instance, suppose two offenders have committed the same type of crime and are roughly equivalent in culpability, and both are referred to restorative justice. The judicial review might ensure that, in the ensuing agreements, one does not receive a *greater* burden than the other. But why stop there? Why should one offender be let off with a *lesser* burden than the other simply because, say, their victims were more forgiving or were content to receive nothing more than a written apology? If it is the court's responsibility to ensure that each agreement is proportionate, as measured by its own punitive benchmarks, then the court should also be required to reject or modify an agreement on the grounds that it would 'impose a punishment which fell short of the *minimum* punishment the courts would impose for that offence' (to modify Braithwaite's words). Thus, the upper limits solution will invariably result in the courts requiring that agreements also satisfy its *lower* punitive limits.

Indeed, this is precisely what has happened. There are several well-known cases in which a judge has chosen to overrule a restorative justice outcome as being insufficiently punitive. For instance, in 1998 the District Court of Auckland (New Zealand) sentenced an offender to two years' imprisonment (suspended), reparation and community service, after taking into account the decisions made in a restorative justice conference. However, the New Zealand Court of Appeal substituted this sentence for a custodial sentence of three years and $5,000 reparation on the following grounds:

> [A] wider dimension must come into the sentencing exercise than simply the position as between victim and offender. The public interest in ... deterrence of others are [sic] factors of major importance.[10]

And this kind of overruling is not an anomaly. The evidence suggests that when judicial authorities modify restorative justice agreements they will tend to increase, rather than reduce, their punitiveness. As Braithwaite has noted:

> [T]he empirical experience of the courts intervening to overturn the decisions of restorative justice processes, which has now been considerable, particularly in New Zealand and Canada, has been overwhelmingly in the direction of the courts increasing the punitiveness of agreements reached between victims, offenders and other stakeholders. (2002a: 150)

Integrationists might protest that this is an example of 'retributive thinking undermining the restorative ideal' (Wright & Masters, 2002: 56). And they would be right. But there

---

10   *R v Clotworthy* 1998 15 CRNZ 651, 661 (CA): note 5 at 659. For a discussion of the case and critique of the Court of Appeal's decision, *see* Bowen and Thompson (1999).

does not seem to be sufficient awareness or concern about how this kind of 'retributive thinking' cannot help but infect – and so undermine – the restorative justice process itself. The participants will ordinarily be made aware that the court will overrule their agreement if it is not sufficiently punitive. But if so, they will almost certainly feel pressured to construct an agreement that is harsher or more burdensome than they might otherwise have preferred.

It might be argued here that well-trained facilitators could prevent any such pressure from undermining the restorative aims of the process. Wallis and Tudor, for instance, offer the following guidance to facilitators:

> If the offender is required as a condition of their [court] order to undertake a fixed number of hours of reparation or community punishment, don't subvert the restorative process to fit this requirement. Direct reparation, if requested, could be just part of the total hours. Reparation is only restorative if it reflects the victim's wishes. (2008: 67-68)

But if the participants know that the court has required a fixed number of hours, then they also know that it will not simply ratify an agreement that only covers a portion of those hours. The court will need to impose an additional form of reparation so as to make up the remaining hours. But since this court-imposed addition does not 'reflect the victim's wishes', the final outcome will, as Wallis and Tudor acknowledge, not count as fully 'restorative'. It will instead be a confused hybrid, with criminal justice subverting the values of restorative justice in order to meet its own objectives.

In sum, when restorative justice is undermined in this way, it is not due to the retributive orientation of the court's sentencing principles. It is instead a direct consequence of the way restorative justice has been integrated into the criminal justice system. As we have seen (§2.1), a restorative justice process is designed to address only the private dimension of crime. However, if it is being deployed as a diversionary approach, then it is effectively functioning as a criminal justice disposal, and so it must somehow also address the public dimension. But since it does not have the capacity to do so, the court must step in and, where necessary, ratchet up the level of punitiveness so as to ensure that the level of censure applied is proportionate to the culpability of the offender and the wrongfulness of the crime. As Eliaerts and Dumortier put it:

> On the one hand, young offenders will have to fulfil restorative efforts during the RJ process towards the victim. On the other hand, the juvenile judge can still impose sanctions or punishments in order to restore the damage caused to society. (2002: 217)

4.2.3   Disparity between the limits

We have seen that the Integrationist solution to the problem of excessive or unreasonable agreements has been to allow the court to impose its own upper punitive limits as the benchmark for proportionality. We have also seen how, as a matter of consistency, this strategy has resulted in the court also imposing lower punitive limits. But what is striking about this situation is that the court is required to retreat when it comes to measuring the proportionality of *whatever falls in between these limits*. The only possible rationale for this restriction is that the participants need at least some room to negotiate the content of the agreement for themselves; otherwise, from an Integrationist perspective, the process could not legitimately be classified as 'restorative justice'. Roche, for instance, argues that judges should ensure that restorative justice agreements comply with both 'upper limits based on human rights' and 'lower limits based on public safety [while at the same time] *allowing room for the variation and creativity of democratic deliberation'* (2003: 220-221, my emphasis).[11]

How is this 'in between limits' solution likely to be perceived by the legal profession? Roche has argued that they should view this kind of hybrid as a positive innovation. It 'encourages us to see accountability in less rigid, formal terms than it is often seen' (2003: 5). This does not, however, imply that the participants should be given carte blanche. Their decision-making freedom – even if restricted to 'in between the punitive limits' – must, he argues, be closely monitored by the court. But in doing so, judges will need to put aside their standard punitive benchmarks for proportionality. They should instead measure the acceptability of the agreement in terms of 'the quality of the decision-making process'. Specifically, judges will need to satisfy themselves that all those invited to the meeting were able to 'participate effectively' and that 'their deliberations reflect[ed] the range of affected interests' (2003: 4).

> When a judge finds that an agreement … is the product of a faulty decision-making process, that agreement should be quashed and participants invited to make the decision afresh, perhaps with some input from the judge. Only when this invitation is declined would a judge be entitled to substitute his or her own decision for that of the restorative justice meeting. (2003: 5)

---

11   Eliaerts and Dumortier likewise argue that there should be 'a retributive minimum and a retributive maximum … within which victims and offenders can agree on forms of reparation' (p. 210). However, they also acknowledge that a '(legal) "default setting" with a retributive minimum and maximum could limit discretion in the RJ process … as well as in the traditional juvenile-justice procedure following' (Eliaerts & Dumortier, 2002: 21).

There is a crucial problem with this suggestion. It hinges entirely on the assumption that the judge is *entitled* to ignore the legal system's benchmarks for proportionality. Without this assumption, a judge will almost invariably need to 'quash' such agreements. Suppose the court sets the lower punitive limit for an offence at 20 hours of reparative work and the upper limit at 50 hours. The participants then agree on 22 hours and decline to reconsider their decision. So long as the decision-making process was not 'faulty', the judge, according to Roche, would not be entitled to overrule the agreement and increase the hours. But then, suppose there is another restorative justice case. This time, the offender has committed the same type of crime, under almost identical circumstances, and so the court's upper and lower limits would be the same. In this case, the participants decide that the offender should complete 48 hours of reparation. Again, the judge cannot fault the decision-making process and so would not be entitled to overrule. Yet would not such an agreement be manifestly unjust in view of the former case?

The possibility of this kind of scenario has been of serious concern to legal professionals, and for good reason. In a 2001 lecture, Dame Sian Elias expressed support for the aims of restorative justice but simultaneously raised a concern that 'consistency of treatment of like cases' may be jeopardised in diversionary restorative justice schemes. As she noted, offenders who have engaged in the same kind of criminal conduct should receive roughly the same sanction. 'Without such consistency', she stated, 'corrosive unfairness can result' (2001: 3).[12] And yet it is difficult to see how the principle of treating like cases alike can possibly be maintained if the court is not permitted to overrule an agreement where (a) it cannot find fault with the decision-making process, and (b) the agreement falls within the upper and lower limits. Different participants discussing what should happen in the aftermath of the same type of offence will invariably produce different outcomes simply because of their focus on the specifics of their own experience and the lack of any comparison. As Delgado notes:

> [J]udges, prosecutors, and defense attorneys are repeat players who tend to see cases in categorical terms (e.g., a car accident: pedestrian versus driver) rather than in terms of ascribed qualities of the participants (e.g., black driver, white pedestrian). However, [in restorative justice] … the victim and the offender will most likely be in their situation for the first time [and so] different victims and offenders may decide similar cases differently, leading to inconsistency. (2000: 759-760)[13]

---

12   Quoted in Schmid (2003: 130-131).
13   Cf. 'When the response to crime is thus privatised, what will tend to matter is the *parties'* sense of the degree of wrongfulness of the behaviour, and of the disposition appropriate thereto; and if different negotiating pairs perceive these matters differently, so be it' (von Hirsch et al., 2003: 38). Again, 'restorative justice aims

Given their duty to uphold the rule of law, judicial authorities who divert cases to restorative justice are thereby placing themselves in a very uncomfortable position. The court is only able to preserve a semblance of consistency by determining penal sanctions in accordance with established sentencing principles, rather than the private views and interests of the individuals involved (von Hirsch, 1993: Ch. 2). Yet if the court is prohibited from applying this approach to the space that lies in between upper and lower limits, it thereby gives free rein to all the hazards of subjective variability that sentencing principles are designed to avoid. As Ashworth states:

> The principle of proportionality goes against victim involvement in sentencing decisions because the views of victims vary. Some victims will be forgiving, others will be vindictive; some will be interested in new forms of sentence, others will not; some shops will have one policy in relation to thieves, others may have a different policy. If victim satisfaction is one of the aims of circles and conferences, then proportionate sentencing cannot be assured ... (2002: 586)

In response to this concern, it might be argued that there has always been inconsistency in sentencing, so this is evidently not a judicial priority. But Dame Elias would not have raised this concern if outcome parity was not foundational to the rule of law, even if it can be extraordinarily difficult to achieve in practice.[14] Why would a court want to make it even harder for itself by diverting cases to restorative justice when this approach is *inherently* incapable of preserving such a core principle? A Parallelist model would avoid this problem entirely.

4.2.4   Incommensurability

There is an even more fundamental problem with the Integrationist's 'in between limits' solution. Sentencing principles are, in part, designed to ensure that different levels of punishment are assigned to different degrees of seriousness and culpability. This is usually

---

to reach a conclusion which is satisfactory to a particular victim and offender, which need bear no relation to what is appropriate for any others who may appear similarly placed' (Wright & Masters, 2002: 55).

14   As Michael Tonry notes: 'In a perfect system of criminal justice, like cases would be treated alike and different cases differently according to established principles for the distribution of punishment. No real-world system can do that, partly because human beings must operate it. ... Judges vary in personalities, socialisation, beliefs, and life experience. Their assessments of information and normative judgements occur within different cognitive frames.' Even so, Tonry suggests that these 'interpersonal differences can be reduced by making sentencing policies detailed and clear and sentencing processes transparent' (Tonry, 2014: 161).

done by using penalties that are quantifiable – which generally means time, frequency or money.[15] We have already touched on some objections to the feasibility of this kind of measure. For instance, degrees of harshness are unavoidably subjective. But two other problems are relevant here: Restorative justice agreements are neither quantitative nor punitive. I take each in turn.

1. The quantitative approach to proportionality cannot sensibly apply to the agreements that are typically made in a restorative justice context. The aim of an agreement is not (or should not be) to recompense the victim in a way that matches up as closely as possible to the exact amount or degree of harm that was done. Such an approach would quickly undermine any good will and degrade the process into a cheap civil court, with consequences that are far from restorative.

For instance, if a quantitative approach was routinely applied, then agreements would be far more likely to contain a financial component. In that case, since the court already uses a quantitative method to calculate just deserts, it could more easily assess whether the agreement fell within its upper and lower punitive limits. One likely effect of this convenience, however, is that the judicial authorities would tend to divert wealthier offenders to restorative justice. For example, if a well-off offender is faced with the prospect of a certain length of time in prison, the court might be more willing to divert them to restorative justice on the grounds that the victim could still impose a cost on the offender that would, according to its own punitive calculus, serve as suitably proportionate. The only difference would be that the quantitative measure of proportionality would be money, rather than prison time. Kent Roach cites an actual case in which this occurred:

> The Supreme Court has indicated that a $10,000 payment made by a 'successful entrepreneur' convicted of assaulting and sexually assaulting an employee 'weighed in favour of restorative objectives' (R. (A.) 2000). Although the court held that the need to deter and denounce serious crimes justified a sentence of one year imprisonment in that case, the case indicates the advantage that offenders who can make payments to victims may experience under restorative approaches to sentencing. (2006: 185)

Offenders who are economically disadvantaged, on the other hand, are more likely to be excluded, thus making the process unavailable to their victims. And if disadvantaged offenders *are* referred to such a process, they will find themselves humiliated by their

---

15   John Castiglione defines 'quantitative proportionality' as 'the proportionality, under any theory, between the crime committed (or the culpability of the offender, or both) and the length or frequency of the sentence imposed [such as] the length of the custodial sentence [or] the number of lashings imposed' (Castiglione, 2010: 89).

inability to make the required restitution payments – thus potentially triggering the kind of shame-reactions that may have contributed to their offending in the first place (see Brookes, 2019a: Ch 3ff.).

It is for such reasons that restorative justice agreements usually consist of largely symbolic tasks. They are designed to give the offender a tangible opportunity to demonstrate to the victim the sincerity of their remorse and their desire to make amends. They should not be humiliating or retaliatory in any way. Rather, they should be crafted so as to create experiences that are meaningful and constructive for both the offender and the victim. At their best, they should help to build the participants' sense of human dignity and personal self-esteem. They might even begin to set the offender 'on the right path' by giving them opportunities to develop new or enhanced skills or by introducing them to a non-offending peer group. But there is no standard menu of options from which participants must choose.[16] This is why restorative justice theorists tend to define 'fairness' not in terms of consistency or quantitative measures of proportionality but in terms of whatever outcome is agreed on by those involved as meeting their harm-related needs. As Skelton notes, 'restorative justice's fluid, victim-centred process … values resolution and restoration of relationships over proportionality and equitable outcomes' (2019: 36).

Restorative justice agreements, then, should be tailored to the highly specific circumstances and needs of the participants. And when this is allowed to occur, the agreements can be surprisingly inventive. Indeed, they often include astonishingly thoughtful and generous contributions from the victim, such as an agreement to have the offender do some paid work for them or participate in a community project alongside them.[17] In many cases, the victim will feel that a reparative task is unnecessary. Or they might prefer a written commitment by the offender not to reoffend or to engage in a programme or activity that might help them in this respect. Miller, for instance, describes the kind of agreements made in the post-sentence programme 'Victims' Voices Heard' (VVH):

---

16   Or at least, there should not be. Fernanda Rosenblatt's research on Youth offender panels in the UK found that '[W]hen reparation was recommended, it stemmed not from deliberation at the panel meeting, but was picked from a "set menu" of reparation activities from which the panel or the young people could choose. Regardless of the crime committed or the harms caused, reparation activities tended to be chosen from "a one-size-fits-all" list of reparation programmes available to the YOT [Youth Offending Team] – with litter-picking, painting, and carpentry among the most popular' (Hoyle & Rosenblatt, 2016: 37). The explanation given by YOT workers was that a 'menu' ensured that agreements would be 'workable/relevant' and meet 'health and safety concerns' (Rosenblatt, 2015: 112). But this is clearly a time-saving strategy. More creative and tailored agreements will typically require post-meeting risk assessments and then potential adjustments and renegotiations with the participants. This process is entirely feasible, but not if the timescales are tightly constrained, as they usually are in an Integrationist model (see §4.7.2).

17   Many examples of this can be found in Liebmann (2007).

> Affirmation agreements developed between victims and offenders are voluntary and not legally binding, nor are they subject to any punitive response if offenders fail to carry through on their promises. By not having VVH participation tied to coercive control, victims felt more free and creative in their admonitions or requests to the offenders, such as asking an offender not to give up hope or to be more respectful to his grandmother or asking an offender to take advantage of every program offered in the prison so that she could contribute something positive to the world since the victim's son no longer could (2011: 184)

But this means that even where an agreement includes a reparative task with a time limit or a symbolic restitution payment, the proportionality of these measures cannot be plausibly assessed in terms of the punitive quantities employed by courts. As von Hirsch et al. argue:

> In this kind of negotiated disposition ... it would not seem feasible to impose the kind of rigorous ordinal-proportionality requirements that a desert model envisions for criminal punishments. ... This is because considerable leeway would be needed for the parties to choose a disposition that they feel conveys regret in a satisfactory manner. (2003: 31)

2. In most jurisdictions, sentencing will typically have objectives in addition to punishment, such as rehabilitation and community safety. But the hard treatment that a sentence inflicts on the offender is generally intended by the judicial authorities to be painful, since it is the punitiveness of the treatment that is taken to communicate or embody the state's denunciation of the criminal act.[18] A restorative justice agreement may be uncomfortable and involve hard work on the part of the offender. But this is a by-product or side-effect of the agreement, not the main point. Restorative justice does not censure the criminal act or communicate moral disapproval by intentionally inflicting pain or hardship on the offender. It does not trade in the currency of punitiveness. Rather, it delivers moral censure by using a quite different coinage: First, the victim will affirm the wrongfulness of the act by giving voice to the personal harm that it has caused them. Second, the offender will then show that they now share this moral assessment by demonstrating that they no longer stand by or endorse what they did. This is achieved by expressing remorse, offering a sincere apology to the victim and then willingly doing what they can to make amends for or repair the harm they caused.

---

18   For a defence of this definition of 'punishment', *see* Boonin (2008: 1-28).

In other words, it is not the *painfulness* of the offender's experience that is doing the censorial work here. It is rather the *collective moral stance* that the participants have taken against the criminal act, as expressed in their emotions, their words and in any subsequent reparative activities or commitments. This means that a restorative justice agreement cannot be sensibly translated into or cashed out in terms of punitive quantities, at least not without ignoring or expunging everything that makes it restorative. But, then, how can the participants possibly know if their agreement falls safely within the punitive limits required by the court?

One response might be to argue that this is a good thing. If the participants uphold the values of restorative justice in their agreement, then it will not contain anything that could be construed as 'punitive'. And in that case, the penal benchmark of upper and lower limits could not, by definition, be violated. As Holtermann argues,

> [I]t could actually be a fairly easy matter for restorative justice conferences not to exceed legally specific upper limits on punishment. The only thing to remember when deciding on an outcome would be to stay out of the penal currency traditionally dealt with in the courts. And as long as this is done, there are no limits to the agreements of the conference. (2009b: 200)

The problem here is that, in an Integrationist context, a diversionary restorative justice process *cannot* 'stay out of the penal currency'. The way that it is attached to the system means that it effectively functions as a criminal justice sanction. The participants may, in good faith, try to design an agreement that is entirely restorative in its orientation. But, as we have seen, if the court which oversees the process does not think that the agreement is proportionate – which it will invariably measure in terms of its own penal currency – then it can override the agreement and impose a punitive sanction in its place. What this means is that, within an Integrationist context, if a restorative justice agreement lacks any qualities that can be plausibly construed as 'punitive', then it is unlikely to survive the judicial review. Participants will know this and so will feel compelled to design an agreement that is compatible with the punitive currency of the court, thus, once again, compromising the restorative objectives of the process.

A Maximalist might want to argue that this issue would not affect their model, since criminal justice sanctions would be entirely reparative, rather than retributive. In that case, it would at least be theoretically possible for certain aspects of an agreement – such as requested tasks or material recompense – to be translated into a 'reparative currency'. But even a Maximalist model would require proportionality. Duff, for instance, defends a Maximalist approach, and argues that voluntary agreements must 'communicate an adequate conception of the [seriousness of the] crime, which is marked by the onerousness of the reparation'. And so 'the reparation must not be disproportionate in its severity to the seriousness of the crime' (2003: 57). But since it is unlikely that participants would have the capacity to make this kind of calculation on their own, the court would need to stipulate the relevant upper and lower reparative limits and review the agreement to make sure it complied. But then it follows that the Maximalist framework would not, in the end, avoid the problems that beset the use of restorative justice in a diversionary context. The inclusion of court-imposed reparative limits would invariably undermine or severely constrain the flexibility, autonomy and creativity that any restorative justice dialogue requires if it is to reach its full potential.

4.3   DUE PROCESS

4.3.1   Legal representation

Most Integrationists accept that some due process safeguards should be allowed. For this reason, many jurisdictions have created legislation that is designed, in large part, to ensure that such safeguards are in place. For instance, offenders will be granted access to legal advice prior to and after a restorative justice process. In some cases, the offender can even be accompanied by a lawyer, but only on condition that they do not speak unless the offender is at legal risk. And, as we have seen, the referring court is typically required to ensure that any agreement observes upper and lower proportionality constraints, which includes giving the court the right to alter or overrule the agreement if necessary.

But no legislation will ever require the offender to have access to a lawyer to *represent* them – in the sense of speaking on their behalf – within a restorative justice meeting. For example, the Australian Capitol Territory's *Crimes (Restorative Justice) Act* 2004 permits an offender to 'seek independent legal advice about taking part in restorative justice' (s.25.c). But the *Act* prohibits legal representation within a restorative justice process:

> If a participant in a restorative justice conference is represented by someone acting for the participant in a professional capacity [e.g. as their lawyer], the representative may not take part in the conference in that capacity. (s.44.3)

Why is this? Is it that legal representation is thought to be surplus to requirements? Or is it rather that allowing this additional safeguard would dominate the process and effectively silence the participants, just as it typically does in court, and thus break the back of an already much diluted and co-opted form of restorative justice? As Inge Vanfraechem writes, in Belgium, 'a lawyer can be present at conferences', but 'they are not there to speak for the young offenders and thus *should not take over the conference*' (2003: 322, my emphasis).

In response, it might be argued that the main purpose of a defence lawyer is, as Morris puts it, to 'minimize the offender's responsibility or to get the most lenient sanction possible' (2003: 462) – an objective that would conflict with the restorative justice priorities of supporting and encouraging the offender to take full responsibility for their actions and make amends for the harm they have caused. There is, however, another side to this. A clever defence lawyer can certainly evade the truth and thereby achieve a lighter sentence for the offender. But 'unsafe verdicts' cut both ways. It misrepresents the role of defence lawyers to say that 'helping offenders to cheat the system' is their primary objective. In an adversarial system, the offender's lawyer is not the only voice in the arena. They will be combating attempts by the prosecution to maximise the offender's culpability so as to achieve the most severe sanction possible.

Thus, the objection would only apply where the prosecution's accusation against the offender has assigned the correct degree of culpability and where the court has imposed the most proportionate sanction available. But what if they are wrong? And what if the offender is unaware of this or unable to defend themselves against a false accusation? This could easily happen in a restorative justice meeting, particularly where the victim dominates the proceedings or where the offender is a child. As Eliaerts and Dumortier note:

> [M]inors can be put under enormous pressure by their parents and extended family, by the victim, by a police officer, by a judicial actor, etc. As contrasted with adults, minors might be more in need of [legal] assistance during the process than we assume. (2002: 214)[19]

Problems can also arise for adult offenders who lack legal representation. Researchers Andrew Goldsmith, Mark Halsey and David Bamford reported a case from South Australia, where a police prosecutor was in attendance at a conference:

> [D]ue to administrative error in a matter involving multiple victims, during the course of the conference it became apparent that the offender had not pleaded guilty to the offences relating to some of the victims and was claiming he had not committed those offences. However these victims were present and had heard considerable information from the offender and other victims when they were potential witnesses in future trials. The swift intervention of the police prosecutor stopping the conference and suggesting that those victims

---

19   Cf. '[C]hildren are highly suggestible and are more likely to be coerced into making false admissions to avoid "more trouble"' (Skelton, 2019: 36).

leave the conference before any significantly prejudicial information was disclosed avoided the potential difficulty that could arise. (2005: 22-23)

In other words, without the quick thinking of the police prosecutor, the 'offender's legal position could have been jeopardised'. Yet the prosecutor's professional role is not to defend or represent the offender's rights or interests. That is the business of the defence counsel. But in this scheme, the defence lawyer was excluded on the grounds that 'they might attempt to speak for their client or at least mediate on the communication process and possibly distort the conference dynamic' (2005: 18).

In sum, it is no doubt true that legal representatives acting within their professional role could easily undermine restorative justice priorities. But why are these priorities taken to override the right of the offender to due process? If there is a conflict between the two, then, from the perspective of the legal system, the rule of law should always take precedence.

We can acknowledge that the court system is susceptible to abuse by lawyers more interested in winning their case than the cause of justice. And, as already mentioned, due to the prevalence of plea bargaining and other cost-saving measures, most offenders are not legally represented or afforded due process even within the standard legal process. There is abundant evidence of the criminal justice system's failure to live up to its own standards and objectives. As Morris argues, 'It is quite farcical for critics of restorative justice to imply that, in contrast, conventional criminal justice systems adequately protect offenders' legal rights' (2003: 462). But is the Integrationist model so sacrosanct that, in our desire to defend it, we are willing to give up on the principle of due process or the right to an impartial trial? Do we really want to put ourselves in the same camp as those who wish to abandon or erode basic human rights that have taken centuries to achieve recognition?

There is solid justification for the principle that if an offender is being sanctioned by the state – as they effectively are in the Integrationist model – then they have a right to a defence lawyer. And it is not sufficient for a lawyer to attend in a merely 'supportive' or 'advisory' capacity, since it is unclear how this would allow them to protect the offender's rights as required. If this *was* possible, then why do we not find defence lawyers routinely playing a merely 'supportive' role in the court room?

Nor is it sufficient for their role to be limited to advising the offender prior to or following the restorative meeting. Recall the 'in between limits' solution to proportionality mentioned in the previous section. In this view, the court would only be permitted to reject or modify an agreement if (a) the decision-making process was faulty, or (b) the agreement fell outside the upper and lower limits. If the court cannot object on these grounds, then it must ratify the agreement. So even if a defence lawyer was able to represent the offender post conference (during the court's review), there is nothing to which they could appeal to alter the agreement.

It might be thought that if the defence lawyer merely attended the conference, then they could, if need be, challenge the agreement before the court on the grounds that the decision-making process was faulty. But it is not clear how the lawyer could present evidence to this effect without impinging on the restorativeness of the process. The judge is unlikely to rely on the (invariably partisan) observations of the defence lawyer, especially if the victim also had their own legal counsel in attendance and they were prepared to argue to the contrary. One solution would be to transcribe or video every restorative justice meeting so that, in such an eventuality, the judge would be able to make an independent assessment. But this option, as we shall see (§4.7.1.4), is very likely to deter participants from engaging in an open and emotionally authentic conversation, knowing that every word or gesture will be scrutinised by an absent judge.

And yet, at the same time, the risk to due process is real. The participants are responsible for devising a sanction that will be enforced by the state. This means that if the state is to exercise its power in accordance with the rule of law, it must be assured that the participants' decision-making process was at least as fair and as equitable as the process by which a (properly functioning) court would have determined its own sanction. We have already seen how the victim holds 'too much power in the agreement-writing stages' (Gerkin, 2009: 239). But there can also be other significant power imbalances between the participants, such as a difference in wealth, education, gender, age, and so on. Hence, even if the agreement is within the punitive limits, this kind of inequality could easily pressure either the offender or the victim into accepting an agreement that they believe is unreasonable – for instance, because it falls towards the extreme end of either the upper or the lower limit.

The only viable alternative, it seems, would be to demand that restorative justice processes include all the legal protections and formal procedures of an 'independent and impartial tribunal', as stipulated, for instance, by Article 6.1 of the European Convention on Human Rights (Ashworth, 2002: 586). In other words, defence counsel must not only attend any proceeding in which a state-enforced sanction could be decided on, but also speak on the offender's behalf so as to ensure that (a) the offender is not disadvantaged by any educational, socio-economic or other inequality they bring with them; (b) the offender is protected from self-incrimination or revealing prejudicial information; (c) any accusations of criminal wrongdoing made against the offender are accurate and evidence-based; and (d) the sanction agreed on is proportionate, as defined by official sentencing guidelines, with relevant mitigating factors taken into account. Victims, likewise, must be given equivalent access to their own lawyers to ensure that their rights and interests are equally protected.

In short, if an Integrationist approach is to be used, then legal representation should be provided to all concerned. If the power of the state is involved, then the protection of rights needs to be strengthened, not weakened or dispensed with altogether. This approach would, of course, be extremely unappealing to restorative justice advocates, since it would effectively remove the last vestiges of voluntary deliberation. It would also effectively turn the process into a quasi-court of law – in which case, the full potential of restorative justice is far less likely to be achieved, if at all. And yet, the 'in between limits' solution will remain equally unpalatable to legal professionals. Given the centuries of struggle and incremental refinement it has taken to create a legal system that is designed to uphold due process protections, why would the judiciary want anything to do with such an intrinsically flawed alternative?

Thus, it appears that Integrationists are prepared to make some concessions to the quality of restorative justice in order to make it available as a diversionary option. But it does look as if they are, in the process, asking the criminal justice system to make significant compromises of its own. In the meantime, the victim and the offender are caught in the middle, short-changed either way. They receive neither the highest quality of restorative justice available nor the independent and impartial tribunal to which they are entitled. This is precisely why the Parallelist argues that restorative justice should be entirely divorced from the legal system. In this model, individuals who take part in restorative justice could not *thereby* become subject to an unwarranted imposition of state power, and so the protection afforded by legal representation would not be required.

4.3.2   Presumption of innocence

Where Integrationist systems have been introduced, a great deal of attention has been focused on protecting the offender from any disadvantage with respect to the presumption of innocence within a court of law.[20] But it is not clear that the legal safeguards that have been implemented are sufficient. Here is the main concern: Suppose an offender has not yet entered a plea but is diverted from prosecution in order to take part in restorative justice and admits responsibility for the criminal act within that process. But then they are unexpectedly returned to court. This might be because the offender opted out of the process, or breached the agreement, or no agreement was possible and so on. In such cases, the offender would have been 'caught on the hop'. Having admitted the offence in

---

20   This issue does not arise in the context of a deferred sentence. Most jurisdictions will not defer sentencing for restorative justice (or anything else) without a plea of guilty. So offenders in this situation cannot both participate in restorative justice and plead not guilty. *See e.g.* New Zealand's *Sentencing Act* 2002: 'Adjournment for restorative justice process in certain cases ... applies if ... the offender has pleaded guilty to the offence' (Part 1., s24A.1.b).

the restorative justice process, they would now find themselves at a serious legal disadvantage. Their earlier admission could be raised in court and so make it impossible to uphold their right to be presumed innocent.

The standard solution to this concern has been to construct legislation that prevents any admission of responsibility made in the course of a restorative justice process (convened under the relevant Act) from being admissible in other legal proceedings. For instance, the *UN Basic Principles for the use of Restorative Justice in Criminal Matters* states that '[p]articipation of the offender shall not be used as evidence of admission of guilt in subsequent legal proceedings' (The Economic and Social Council, 2002: II, 8.). And this principle is reflected in most legislative frameworks. For example, the *Crimes (Restorative Justice) Act* 2004 (ACT) states:

> [I]f the offender has not entered a plea for the offence [then] the offender is not prevented from pleading not guilty only because [they have accepted responsibility for the commission of the offence for the purpose of restorative justice]. (s.53.d)

How much protection would this kind of legislation, in fact, give the offender? As always, a firm answer to this question must await the moment when the legislation is tested in a court. But there is at least one loophole that does seem almost impossible to close in a diversionary context. Suppose an offender admits responsibility in a restorative justice process, is unexpectedly returned to court and decides to plead not guilty. How likely is it that the court would be inflicted with collective amnesia? Would it not instead view the plea as nothing more than an obstructionist, time-wasting legal fiction, with no moral or factual credibility? Could we seriously imagine the court, in such a case, finding the defendant not guilty? As the cognitive scientist Steven Pinker writes, 'Juries are forbidden to see inadmissible evidence from hearsay, forced confessions, or warrantless searches – "the tainted fruit of the poisoned tree" – because human minds are incapable of ignoring it' (2021: 57-58).

Thus, even if there is legislation in place that allows the offender to plead not guilty in court, this will, at best, merely prevent the prosecution from having an easy ride to a guilty verdict. But any legal professional worth their salt would soon find a way around this evidential obstacle. After all, it is not unheard of for a prosecutor to find evidence that proves guilt in the absence of a confession. And as we have already seen (§3.1), most confidentiality statutes do not prevent prosecutors from using evidence related to the offence that they discovered outside of the restorative justice process.

4.4   BOUNDARIES

The Integrationist model, as we have seen, includes the criminal justice system as a stakeholder within the restorative justice process. Its role is to make referrals, monitor the process, review any outcome agreements and enforce their compliance. In many jurisdictions, the judicial authorities and other criminal justice employees can even facilitate the process. However, as I will argue in this section, these functions require the state to become involved in private matters about which it is not entitled to have an interest, to use its powers in areas where it has no legitimate authority to do so, and to increase the number of citizens over which it can exercise control or amplify the control it already has over them, both without adequate justification. Integrationism, in short, is inherently liable to result in state overreach. This is clearly not in the public interest, and so, in these respects, the Integrationist model will diminish the quality and effectiveness of the criminal justice system. By contrast, the Parallelist model operates outside the purview and involvement of the state, and so these boundary issues do not arise.

4.4.1   Privacy

In the Integrationist model, the offender is effectively compelled by the state to participate in a restorative justice process. I have argued that the state's use of its coercive powers in this way is, in fact, unjustified (see §2.1.7). But if there *were* any justification available, it could only be the fact that the offender committed a crime. The state would, in that case, have no right to intrude into or expose any other aspect of the offender's life, thoughts, feelings or circumstances. Yet in most Integrationist models, there are state representatives involved in the process itself – such as state-employed facilitators, police officers and social workers. In addition, a report of the process will usually be made available to the court, which, as we will see later (§4.7.1.4), could potentially include a video or a full transcript of the dialogue. Thus, if the restorative justice process takes place in an Integrationist context, then, to avoid this kind of state intrusion, it should concentrate exclusively on matters such as the impact of the crime, a proximate explanation for why it was committed, and how best the harm might be repaired. As Duff argues:

> Restorative theorists sometimes take it to be a merit of 'informal justice' that it allows a wider, unconstrained discussion of whatever problems exist in the offender's relationships with others, or in her life as a whole: but this is not something in which offenders should be required to participate. What justifies [integrated restorative justice], and the demand that the offender take part in it, is her crime. A community that is to respect the privacy of its citizens must

respect certain limits on how far it seeks to intrude into their lives or thoughts – which, in this context, means that it should inquire only into the crime, her reasons for it, and its implications: that is their business, but other aspects of her life are not. (2003: 56-57)

Yet if the process were governed by restorative justice priorities, then such restrictions would not apply. Many offenders report that the reason they participated was not merely to make amends but also to explain their actions and to find ways of ensuring that they did not repeat the same behaviour. Many victims have, in turn, claimed that they participated in order to help the offender find solutions to the underlying factors that gave rise to their offending behaviour. Some of the most effective restorative justice processes are those in which the victim comes to understand the reality of the offender's life history, family relationships, current living and employment circumstances, and so on. This, in itself, can contribute powerfully to the recovery process for a victim. Hence, to restrict the discussion to the facts of the crime and the reparation owed would make it impossible for participants to satisfy these expectations and needs. As Shapland observes:

> [R]estorative justice, by its nature, does not limit itself to discussion of the instant offence, bounded as strictly as the evidential rules of formal criminal justice would ensure. Simply because ordinary people do not see the offence as a time-limited slice of action carved from ongoing social interaction, participants at restorative justice sessions will not just discuss the offence alone. They will raise the circumstances round the offence, previous incidents, previous interaction between offender and victim and matters which have occurred since the offence. Nor, given the purposes of restorative justice, will they be wrong to do so. It is not possible to have a problem-solving, forward-looking orientation to the session and omit all these other circumstances. (2003: 205)

In sum, if a restorative justice process is operating within the Integrationist model, then, to avoid state overreach, the judicial system would be right to insist on precisely the kind of privacy protections suggested by Duff, and for the reasons that he gives. Parallelism, by contrast, would require no such restrictions.

4.4.2   Conceptions of the good

One of the chief functions of a liberal state is to protect the freedom and equality of its citizens. It is this broad conception of the good that authorises and justifies the coercive powers of the criminal justice system. There are, however, narrower conceptions of the good about which the state is not entitled to exercise its coercive powers. These are goods about which citizens can have a reasonable disagreement, in the sense that it is possible for them to disagree without thereby violating the freedom and equality of other citizens. In most liberal states, this will include religious beliefs, sexual orientation, body piercing, aesthetic taste, university curricula, and the like.

The criminal law, by contrast, is (or should be) designed to reflect conceptions of the good about which it is not possible to have a reasonable disagreement, in this sense. The behaviours that fall into each category can, of course, change over time within any state and be quite different between states. For instance, most liberal states now criminalise domestic violence and intramarital rape but no longer regard adultery and homosexuality as crimes.[21] As Linda Radzik argues:

> Meaningful liberty requires the freedom of individuals to develop and pursue their own conceptions of the good, at least within reasonable limits. To the extent that a criminal justice system tries to enforce a particular, contestable conception of the good on citizens, it is illiberal. ... While the liberal state values neutrality among reasonable conceptions of the good, the values of freedom and equality define the bounds of the reasonable. (2009: 161, 162)

The problem here is that this restriction on *which* conceptions of the good the state may enforce is undermined by the Integrationist model. When the participants form an agreement in a restorative justice process, it is up to them, as private individuals, to decide what tasks or activities the offender should undertake in order to make amends. However, in the Integrationist model, the state enforces agreements by threatening the offender with legal consequences should they fail to complete them. But since the state is not entitled to enforce behaviours about which it is possible for citizens to have a reasonable disagreement, this entails that the court must ensure there is nothing in the agreement that falls into this category. But this places a considerable constraint on the restorative justice process. Agreements can, and should, be highly individualised. As Radzik argues:

> [T]he state might find itself monitoring and enforcing an offender's regular attendance of a certain church service or religious education class, if such attendance was part of the sentencing agreement. ... In [such a] case, it would

---

21   As Antony Duff writes, 'Adultery is still criminal, and occasionally prosecuted, in some American states; but to liberals it is *clearly* a private matter. ... [T]o argue that we should criminalise adultery would ... require arguing that it is a wrong that cannot be left to the individuals concerned to deal with (or to ignore), but that *must* be publicly condemned and sanctioned' (Duff, 2007: 144).

be required to enforce a conception of the good that, while reasonable, is also outside the scope of the state's legitimate interest. (2009: 162, 166)

This example is not just theoretical. Miller describes a post-sentence restorative justice programme in which 'two different victims asked their offenders to study Christian teachings so they might follow a stronger moral compass upon release' (2011: 184). If the offenders agree to such a request, then, as Radzik puts it, 'who is the state to disagree?' (2009: 166). The good of religious education is, after all, a matter about which citizens can hold a reasonable disagreement. So the state would be overstepping its authority if it were to enforce such an agreement.

By contrast, in a Parallelist model, no such restriction would apply. The dialogue is strictly a private matter. In such a context, the offender and the victim are perfectly free to agree to whatever they feel will contribute to the goal of moral repair, so long as it is not degrading or unlawful. In an Integrationist setting, an offender could feel that it would be safer to go along with whatever the victim asks, given the possibility of being returned to court or prosecuted if no agreement can be made. In the Parallelist model, the offender is free to say that they cannot, in good conscience, comply with a request, even if this means that the process cannot continue.

4.4.3   Net widening

The Integrationist model has often been charged with widening the criminal justice net on the grounds that it focuses on minor offenders who are unlikely to reoffend. As a consequence, cases that would previously have been seen as not warranting any penal intervention are drawn into the net. As Kerry Clamp notes:

> A wide range of empirical studies investigating police decision making in referrals to independent restorative justice schemes have demonstrated that they have widened the net rather than reducing it. (2019: 184)[22]

One way in which advocates of Integrationism have responded is to argue that, in this model, restorative justice is only used as a diversion: it draws offenders away from the

---

22   Cf. '[B]oth in Belgium and abroad, the [restorative justice] procedure appears to have given rise to a net-widening effect. In other words, the public prosecutor's office seems to select cases that would have been dismissed under the older system' (Eliaerts & Dumortier, 2002: 215). It should be noted that net-widening does not seem to occur in every jurisdiction or restorative justice scheme. Jeremy Prichard, for instance, found that in Tasmania between 1991 and 2002 the diversionary use of police cautions and restorative justice conferences did not result in an increase in 'the total number of youth matters' over the period (Prichard, 2010: 119).

criminal justice system, rather than towards it. Thus, if a case is referred to restorative justice, then it has fallen into a net that does not in itself cause any harm, and that could potentially do much good.

The trouble with this response is that the Integrationist application of restorative justice, as we have seen, effectively functions as a penal intervention, albeit one that is an alternative to the norm. The cooperation of the offender and the outcome agreement are overseen and enforced by the state. As Johnstone argues, restorative justice processes might be 'less formal and regarded as more benign' than 'professionally administered penal sanctions'. But since restorative justice is being used for 'cases which previously would not have given rise to penal interventions', it still follows that 'the reach of the system of penal control will be extended rather than cut back' (2007: 609).

Another response Integrationists might offer is to argue that their schemes need not be confined to minor offences. They are able to accept more serious crimes, and in such cases the net would not be widened. However, this response, if taken seriously, may lead to an unpalatable outcome for Integrationism. In most jurisdictions, the use of restorative justice for serious crime is only feasible in a deferred sentencing context, not as a diversion from prosecution. As the Prosecution Code in Scotland states, 'In general, the more serious the offence the more likely it is that the public interest will require a prosecution' (Crown Office and Procurator Fiscal Service, 2001: 6). But it is only the most minor offences that would not previously have resulted in a penal intervention. So if Integrationists are serious about the net widening concern, then they would need to focus on expanding the use of restorative justice to a deferred sentencing context and severely restricting, if not ruling out diversion from prosecution altogether.[23]

Some Integrationists might warm to this strategy, given the evidence that restorative justice is most effective when used to address serious crimes. But there is also likely to be considerable resistance, given that, in many jurisdictions, the use of restorative justice as a deferment option is not yet available, or subject to serious administrative obstacles, or not widely used by the courts and so on. Hence, this option, in such areas, could easily result in a significant decrease, perhaps even a collapse in referrals to restorative justice.

4.4.4   Net tightening

There is another type of net widening – often called 'net tightening' – that can occur where the Integrationist model is employed. In this case, the potential effect of using restorative

---

23   It might be argued that the diversion from prosecution pathway could be limited to serious offences that warrant prosecution, but, owing to, say, a lack of evidence, are diverted to restorative justice on the grounds that a successful prosecution would be unlikely. See §5.3.4 for a critique of this approach from a Parallelist perspective.

justice as a diversionary approach is not so much to draw people into the criminal justice system, but rather to absorb them further into the system. In the absence of legislation to prevent it,[24] the failure to comply with a restorative justice agreement could potentially result in a sanction that is harsher than the maximum penalty due to the original offence. For example, in many jurisdictions restorative justice is being increasingly used as a condition of probation. But this means that offenders may be incarcerated not as a punishment for their original offence but simply because they failed to comply with the restorative justice agreement – a result that would dismay advocates who embraced the Integrationist model as a strategy to reduce the prison population. As Sharon Levrant, Francis Cullen, Betsy Fulton and John Wozniak write:

> [A]s conditions of probation expand through restorative justice programs, the potential that offenders will not meet these conditions also increase. This higher level of noncompliance, combined with heightened public scrutiny and a demand for offender accountability, will likely result in the revocation of more offenders. ... Thus restorative justice programs may not only increase social control within the community but may also result in more offenders being sent to prison because they fail to comply with the additional sanctions imposed within the restorative justice framework. (2003: 418-419)

Net tightening is even more likely to occur when *repeat* offenders fail to successfully participate in a restorative justice programme, since they are already liable to be given increasingly severe sanctions. As von Hirsch et al. argue:

> [U]ncooperative offenders – multiple recidivists especially – tend to be especially resented. Even within sentencing systems that purport to follow a proportionalist sentencing rationale, the temptation to escalate sanctions for recidivists has not been easy to resist. (2003: 36)[25]

---

24 For instance, the Australian Capital Territory's *Crimes (Sentencing) Act* 2005 states that 'a court must not increase the severity of the sentence it would otherwise have imposed because ... the offender chose not to take part, or chose not to continue to take part, in restorative justice for the offence under the *Crimes (Restorative Justice) Act 2004*' (s.34.1.h).

25 Cf. 'To guard against the risk of rational actors who might be tempted to pursue a "free-loading" strategy by making a deceitful pretence at participating in a restorative justice negotiation ... Braithwaite envisages an enforcement strategy based on the principle of "active deterrence". The latter involves the strategic use of *escalating* threats in response to recalcitrance on the part of the offender, and could result in custodial incapacitation. ... [T]here is a danger that this ... approach could readily lend itself to an escalation in the level of punitive responses towards repeat and recalcitrant offenders' (Dignan, 2003: 146).

Even worse, the Integrationist model does not, as we have seen, provide the kind of due process protections that should be in place when conditions of probation are set. So offenders who take part in restorative justice within this framework could easily feel compelled to agree to tasks or conditions that are, in their minds, unreasonable or degrading, and so these agreements are more likely to be breached.

To be clear, instances of net tightening may turn out to be relatively rare, but, unless legal safeguards are put in place, it remains a significant risk that is built into the Integrationist model. Parallelism would not face such problems. Restorative justice would only be offered in an extralegal context, and so it would not carry any risk of widening or tightening the net.[26]

4.5   SINCERITY

The Integrationist model, as we have seen, places offenders in a Sword of Damocles situation. There are two ways in which the 'wrong choice' could result in a legal sanction: first, if an offender decides not to accept the option of participating in restorative justice and, second, if they fail to fulfil whatever outcome agreement was made in that process. In this section, I will argue that enforcing the offender's participation in this way will diminish the quality and effectiveness of restorative justice. There are two fundamental reasons for this: it is unethical, and it is, in any case, unlikely to work as intended.

Before doing so, however, I need to make one point clear. It may, at first glance, seem that my critique is directed against facilitators who are insufficiently skilled, poorly trained or simply unwilling to adhere to the values and standards of best practice in restorative justice. This is not the case. While these issues may be true in some instances, the problems that I am concerned with here are caused primarily by the Integrationist framework. Facilitators who are required to operate in such a context are, in general, highly skilled and strongly committed to the values of restorative justice and to achieving best practice. But no amount of training, proficiency or good will can overcome the restrictions and compromises that are necessitated by the Integrationist model. In other words, structural problems upstream are resulting in less-than-optimal practices downstream.

4.5.1   Violation of moral agency

The ethical issues associated with enforced participation are frequently underestimated by advocates of the Integrationist model. But this is a profoundly serious concern, especially

---

26   In §5.3.3, I address the concern that although Parallelism may not *expand* penal control, it is nevertheless at a disadvantage compared with Integrationism insofar as it cannot *reduce* it.

in light of the relational values that restorative justice is supposed to embody. An offender who participates in a diversionary context will, at best, have mixed motives, one of which will be virtually inevitable. Like most of us, offenders will want to avoid the most burdensome or painful outcome, and so they will, in general, opt for restorative justice. But this is no ordinary escape route.

To take part in restorative justice as an offender effectively means subjecting your private thoughts and feelings to the moral scrutiny of others – some of whom will, for good reason, be extremely hurt and angry over what you have done. You will need to accept personal responsibility for causing them harm. They will want you to explain your motives and the circumstances that led to your committing the crime. You will be expected to display remorse and offer them a sincere apology. They will then want you to discuss with them how you can make amends for what you did. After the meeting, you will need to carry out whatever was agreed to in good faith.

But what happens if, for whatever reason, you are not, in fact, willing or able to respond to the victim in these ways? This means that, in order to avoid a state sanction, you will have to convey thoughts, attitudes and feelings that are not your own. You must express emotions you do not feel, say what you do not believe to be true, and carry out actions under the guise of motives you do not have. In other words, to escape the threat of punitive consequences imposed by the state, you are effectively compelled to conceal who you really are.

What is so wrong with this? Why would it be unethical to place an offender in this situation? Perhaps the best way to answer this is to unearth the underlying messages that we would be conveying to an offender when we force them to choose between restorative justice and the usual legal sanction. To begin with, we are telling them, however implicitly, that we cannot trust them to do the right thing for the right reasons. We think they are incapable of choosing to act in a way that is morally responsible *just* because it is the morally responsible thing to do. This is why we must corner them into doing the right thing, irrespective of what they think or feel about it. We are also sending them the message that they must conform to the will of those who are more powerful than them *merely* because they are more powerful.

When we want someone to do the right thing, there are two options: moral persuasion or enforcement. We can either offer them good reasons to do what is right or we can threaten them with pain or hard treatment should they fail to comply. But what happens if we try to do both at the same time? What if we use moral persuasion but then back it up with a threat should they fail to be persuaded? Given the nature of human beings, it is highly likely that the emotion of fear will dominate. So our back-up threat will invariably push its way into the foreground, if not cancel out the good reasons entirely. But in that case, the one message that the offender will hear – snarling loudly over all the rest – is that 'might makes right'. Or, more directly: 'Do what you're told! Whether you agree with it or not.' This alone is more than likely to undermine the full potential of restorative justice as a means of moral persuasion.

It is important to note here that when the state enforces participation in restorative justice, this is not the same as enforcing the speed limit or threatening to penalise tax cheats. Neither of these interventions violates the sanctity of our own private thoughts and feelings. We are not placed in a situation in which the only way that we can avoid a speeding ticket is to pretend that we agree with the speed limit. The state does not care what we think about the road laws; it only requires that we obey them. We do not need to conceal the fact that we would prefer not to pay taxes. So far as the state is concerned, we are free to publish entire books against taxation, so long as we pay our tax bill on time. The reason for this is that the criminal law is designed to deal with the public dimension of crime, not the private. Integrationism blurs the boundaries, creating a hybrid species that cannot help but result in the state regulating the kind of thoughts and feelings we are free to express. As Vincent Geeraets puts it:

> The criminal law is primarily concerned with the offender's conduct, far less with how he experiences the world, i.e., what he feels, how engaged he is in what he says, and so on. By contrast, no such limit exists within the restorative enterprise. (2016: 280)

Placing offenders in this situation is a violation of their inherent right to self-determination. It is an assault on their very humanity. It tells them that their views and their feelings do not count. It is patronising, degrading and humiliating, since it fails to respect their moral agency and thus their inherent dignity as human beings.[27] As John Tasioulas argues:

> This sort of intrusion into [the] innermost self [of an offender] fails to respect his status as a responsible moral agent: it is an attempt coercively to manipulate his deepest moral feelings and convictions, pre-empting his own decision-making about how it is best for him to live. If the process succeeds, the resultant condition will have been achieved heteronymously and, as in indoctrination or domination, the offender's rational capacities will have been overborne. If it fails, then the offender will at best have been forced to make certain insincere

---

27   Cf. '[Someone] fails to treat me with respect if she makes no effort to hide her disinterest in, or contempt for, my feelings. When she treats me this way, she implies that my concerns, my feelings, my point of view do not matter, that is, that I have no intrinsic value, after all' (Buss, 1999: 804). Again, '[I]t is deeply demeaning to be compelled to express views or attitudes that are at variance with those one actually holds' (von Hirsch et al., 2003: 33).

protestations of guilt and repentance that he will inevitably find demeaning. But either way, his status as a responsible moral agent is violated. (2007: 509)[28]

4.5.2 Moral corrosiveness

This consequence of enforced participation is not only wrong in itself; it is also likely to have a corrosive impact on the offender's moral character. There are two ways in which this can occur.

1. We might suppose that even if an offender is forced to apologise, the humiliation of that experience will 'teach them a lesson they won't easily forget'. But shame does not work in this way. If it is demeaning and degrading – as it would be if we are forced to apologise against our will – we are far more likely to resent what was done to us. We will rebel against those who have humiliated us. And we will find the social support and affirmation we need from another group – which, in this case, is likely to consist of other law-defying outcasts. Far from learning a moral lesson, we will simply change tribes as a way of recovering our self-respect.[29] As Harry Blagg vividly describes it:

> For the [young offenders] I interviewed, the apology fulfilled their expectations; they were punished by an authority figure, they were powerless to prevent the process, they acquiesced; they then, in order to retain peer-group status and keep their egos intact retrospectively recreated the encounter as one in which sullen obeisance was transformed into heroic resistance. (1985: 272)

2. Many offenders feel genuine remorse for the harm they have caused, and they want to do the right thing by the victim. They are keen to participate in restorative justice, and for the right reasons. But in a diversionary context, they will also be aware of the legal sanctions they are likely to face if they do not take up the option of restorative justice. No one would be immune to wanting to avoid such sanctions. So this would invariably become a motivating factor in their decision.

The problem is that this kind of offender will now have mixed motives. They want to participate, but they also feel as if they have no choice. So are they doing the right thing for the right reasons, after all? A doubt will have been placed in their minds, and it can be very difficult to know which motive is playing the greater part. Are they morally virtuous, or

---

28 Cf. '[A]ny contrition or self-criticism expressed by the [offender] must – if his moral agency is to be respected – reflect his own views' (von Hirsch, 1993: 83-84). Again, 'One of the unfortunate aspects of concentrating on the personal dimension of crime and attempting to repair the emotional harm suffered by a victim is that offenders may be put under considerable pressure to respond in a grovelling, self-abasing fashion' (Roche, 2003: 35).

29 For an extended explanation of shame-reactions, see Brookes (2019a).

are they just 'gaming the system'? When they come to offer their apology, there will be a part of them that wonders if they really mean it. And these inner doubts are likely to be reinforced by the victim, who, being aware of the diversionary context, will have good reason to be sceptical of their sincerity. All of this cannot help but eat away at the offender's sense of their own moral integrity. As Robert Grant writes:

> Excessive regulation destroys virtue, since, even if the subject is otherwise disposed to it, the penalties for disobedience make him unsure whether he is really choosing freely. They call his virtue into question where it is most important, in his own eyes. (1992: 163-164)

4.5.3   *Taking ethics seriously*

The diversionary approach therefore suffers from substantial ethical problems. But it is crucial to note that these issues only arise when restorative justice is integrated into the criminal justice system. It is not inherent to restorative justice per se. If restorative justice services were completely independent of the legal process, as they would be in a Parallelist model, offenders would not face this kind of Sword of Damocles situation. As von Hirsch et al. argue:

> The more the offender's failure to participate in the RJ process would involve risk of deterrent or incapacitative sanctions, the more offenders will feel compelled to participate in RJ on purely cautionary grounds and the less genuine any purported efforts at making amends are likely to be. (2003: 36)

Unfortunately, the prevalence of Integrationism across most jurisdictions suggests that this ethical issue is not taken seriously. Here are three examples of how it has been dismissed, obscured or minimised:

1. Enforced participation is sometimes defended on the grounds that it is, in key respects, equivalent to plea bargaining. In many jurisdictions, offenders can plead guilty to avoid being charged with a more serious offence or receiving a harsher penalty. This is not dissimilar to what happens when offenders agree to take part in restorative justice. They are effectively engaging in the same kind of 'bargain'. Skelton, for instance, writes that an offender who opts to take part in restorative justice is thereby:

> voluntarily relinquishing [their rights to the presumption of innocence and the right to silence] in order to benefit from the restorative justice option and

does the same in the criminal justice system when opting to plead guilty or enter a plea bargain. (2019: 35-36, my emphasis)

This kind of comparison is revealing. Plea bargaining may be ubiquitous, but that does not mean it is morally justified. The practice is frequently critiqued for the way that it effectively coerces offenders to confess. As John Langbeinm puts it:

[W]e have duplicated the central experience of medieval European criminal procedure. ... We coerce the accused against whom we find probable cause to confess his guilt. To be sure, our means are much politer; we use no rack, no thumbscrew, no Spanish boot to mash his legs. But like the Europeans of distant centuries who did employ those machines, we make it terribly costly for an accused to claim his right to the constitutional safeguard of trial. We threaten him with a materially increased sanction if he avails himself of his right and is thereafter convicted. This sentencing differential is what makes plea bargaining coercive. (1978: 12-13)

When restorative justice is situated within an Integrationist context, it is, in principle, equally coercive. Offenders are threatened with the strong likelihood of a 'materially increased sanction' if they do not take up the offer of restorative justice and comply with any agreements made therein. This level of coercion is not, of course, equivalent to torture, but the difference is, as Langbeinm would say, only one of degree, not of kind (1978: 13).[30]

2. It is often argued that virtually every restorative justice programme that operates within an Integrationist context includes safeguards that are designed to ensure that the offender's participation is voluntary. For instance, facilitators are trained not to be threatening, manipulative or intimidating; offenders are often required to sign a consent form; they can opt out of the process at any time, and so on. In addition, there are internationally recognised principles and legislative frameworks which stipulate that, within an Integrationist setting, participation in restorative justice must be 'voluntary' and not the result of 'coercion'. The *UN Basic Principles on the use of Restorative Justice in Criminal Matters* (2002) states that:

---

30   Adriaan Lanni argues that 'pre-arraignment restorative diversion and plea bargaining differ in one important respect: where the defendant retains the ability to return to the criminal process without prejudice, these programs offer a potential benefit without requiring the defendant to plead guilty or give up the right to a jury trial. For this reason, restorative diversion programs seem to be less coercive than programs that require a guilty plea' (Lanni, 2020: 17). However, as I have argued (§4.3.2), it is unlikely that a defendant will be found not guilty when the prosecutor and the judge know that they have admitted responsibility in a restorative justice setting. Hence, even if the legal threat might be somewhat diminished in pre-arraignment cases, it is certainly not removed.

> Restorative processes should be used only ... with the free and voluntary consent of the victim and the offender. The victim and the offender should be able to withdraw such consent at any time during the process. Agreements should be arrived at voluntarily ... Neither the victim nor the offender should be coerced, or induced by unfair means, to participate in restorative processes or to accept restorative outcomes. (Principles 7 and 13c)

The problem with such 'safeguards' is that none of them can cancel out or override the primary source of coercion: specifically, the threat of being prosecuted or sentenced in the usual way. To bring out the ethical seriousness of this point, it will be instructive to draw, once again, on the underlying similarity between plea bargains and torture. Langbeinm writes:

> [Medieval] European law attempted to devise safeguards for the use of torture that proved illusory; these measures bear an eerie resemblance to the supposed safeguards of the American law of plea bargaining. Foremost among the illusory safeguards of both systems is the doctrinal preoccupation with characterizing the induced waivers as voluntary. The Europeans made the torture victim repeat his confession 'voluntarily', but under the threat of being tortured anew if he recanted. The American counterpart is Rule 11(d) of the Federal Rules of Criminal Procedure, which forbids the court from accepting a guilty plea without first 'addressing the defendant personally in open court, determining that the plea is voluntary and not the result of force or threats or of promises apart from a plea agreement.' Of course, the plea agreement is the source of the coercion and already embodies the involuntariness. (1978: 14)

In the case of Integrationism, it is standardly supposed that restorative justice can be characterised as 'voluntary' so long as the offender's decision not to participate or their failure to fulfil their outcome agreement is not used to justify a more severe sanction than would otherwise have been imposed.[31] But this 'safeguard' is, as Langbeinm puts it, an 'illusion'. It does not remove the source of the coercion that is embedded within Integrationism. If an offender decides not to participate or fails to implement their agreement, they cannot simply walk away from the legal system. They will instead be subject to the sanction that they would have ordinarily received. This threat cannot be

---

31   For instance, '[f]ailure to implement an agreement, other than a judicial decision or judgement, should not be used as justification for a more severe sentence in subsequent criminal justice proceedings' (The Economic and Social Council, 2002: Principle 17). Or, again, 'a court, in sentencing the offender ... must not consider whether the offender has chosen not to take part, or not to continue to take part, in restorative justice' (*Crimes (Restorative Justice) Act* 2004 (ACT) s25.f.2 (Austl.)).

removed from the Integrationist model, and it is on its own sufficient for coercion. As Agnihotri and Veach put it, 'most practitioners and courts know that the result of any guilty plea is the result of many coercive, systematic pressures toward the least injurious resolution of a case' (2017: 342). This built-in involuntariness should be openly acknowledged and taken seriously, rather than dismissed as 'equivalent to a plea bargain', or reframed as an 'incentive', or masked by get-out clauses which effectively permit the use of coercion so long as it is not by 'unfair means' (UN Principle 13c).

3. Advocates of Integrationism will often argue that one of the major benefits of this model is that it gives offenders the chance to avoid a punitive outcome. But then it is easy to slip into thinking that an offender should *therefore* be allowed to take part in restorative justice – even when this is their primary, if not their sole, motivation. An early review of one pilot restorative justice programme put it in the following terms:

> A number of young people said that by participating it would help with their court case. Others said they participated 'more or less to avoid having to go to court.' These reasons are quite acceptable. Young people are not excluded from participating because they believe they will avoid a criminal record by doing so. It is in their best interests to allow them to participate for those reasons. (ACT Department of Justice and Community Safety, 2006: 34)

What is astonishing is that, only a few lines later, the same review reported several young people saying that 'they felt pressured to participate' for these very same reasons: that is, (a) 'because if they didn't they may be charged with the offence and have to go to court', and (b) 'because the court had referred their case to restorative justice and it was in their interest to participate' (2006: 34). Zernova gives another example from her research:

> [A] number of offenders said in interviews that their attending a conference was court-ordered, and a refusal to attend would lead them back to court for re-sentencing. Most of these offenders did not seem very enthusiastic about attending. It appeared that their attendance was motivated by fear of returning to court and being punished for breach of a court order. (2016: 74)

As we have seen, placing offenders in this kind of Sword of Damocles situation is not, in fact, 'acceptable' for a variety of ethical reasons. Much less is it in the 'best interests' of the offender, given its morally corrosive effects. Little wonder that researchers for another restorative justice pilot found that some offenders would have preferred a Parallelist approach:

[M]ore than one offender remarked that conducting the conference post-sentence would help to remove some of the underlying skepticism regarding offenders' motivation for attending which pervaded the conferences (all but one was conducted prior to sentencing). (Goldsmith et al., 2005: 36)

Indeed, in one case, an offender evidently realised that the only way he could ensure that his sincerity would be accepted was to request that the process be held in a post-sentence context:

At least two offenders (according to the conference reports) stated clearly in the course of the conference that they did not expect a sentence reduction, and that their participation in RJ had other motivations. ... One offender chose to make this point even more explicit by requesting that the conference be conducted *after* he was sentenced; a request which was followed through by the project. (Kirby & Jacobson, 2015: 33-34)

4.5.4   *Possible responses*

It will be worth looking at some of the responses that might be given to the foregoing concerns.

1. It might be argued that, in an Integrationist model, there is an inherent uncertainty about whether, or to what extent, restorative justice will have an impact on the legal process. This is because the court generally retains the discretionary option of ignoring the outcome of a restorative justice process. For instance, the 2014 UK Ministry of Justice guidance for pre-sentence restorative justice states:

At the sentencing hearing the court may have regard to the report and the offender's participation, willingness or lack of willingness to participate in a RJ activity and any outcome agreement. However, these considerations, together with considerations of other factors of the case remain entirely a matter for the courts to interpret and come to a sentencing decision about. (2014: 11. 2.33)

The offender would no doubt take account of this uncertainty, and so their motivation is unlikely to be *entirely* self-interested. In other words, they probably would not participate unless they felt that it would still be worth doing, even if it had no impact on the legal outcome. But then it follows that Integrationism does not necessarily lead to the ethical concerns noted previously.

There are several problems with this response. First, things are not as uncertain as they might appear. Should an offender decide to participate in restorative justice and comply with their outcome agreement, then, if these facts are made known to the court, they will almost certainly be taken into account in its decision-making, rather than ignored or dismissed as irrelevant. And even though the court may have discretion as to how it interprets or responds to such facts, it is hard to imagine that it would not see them in a positive light and so reduce or amend the sentence accordingly. This is precisely why the offender's legal adviser or the facilitator will usually consider it their duty to remind the offender of this as they are mulling over whether to participate or if they show any resistance to completing their outcome agreement.

Second, the offender may be uncertain about the precise nature of the legal sanctions with which they are being threatened. But they will be certain that restorative justice is a way – perhaps the only way – of escaping or minimising that threat. If you were given the opportunity to avoid a penal sanction, would you not take the chance? And would you not, for that reason, jump through whatever hoops were set out for you? In other words, even without an iron-clad guarantee, the perception that participating successfully in restorative justice *could* reduce or avoid the punitive outcome they would otherwise have received will be sufficient for most offenders. Even if the odds are slim, this will invariably become a dominant factor in their decision-making. As Jeremy Andersen argues:

> Sometimes, offenders have been adjudicated (whether by a trial or plea-bargaining) as being guilty, but the judge offers the offender the option of entering a VOM [victim-offender mediation] program *instead of* facing 'traditional' sentencing. Given the unknown 'traditional' sentence, and given that usually judges seem to drastically reduce sentences when using VOM programs, it seems that the 'choice' offered the offender is particularly coercive. If this is true, then the offender (striving to successfully complete the VOM program) seems particularly likely to feign repentance and fake his or her way through the mediation program. (2003: 17)

2. It might be argued that this Sword of Damocles can be kept in the background of an offender's consciousness by not making the threat explicit *to them individually*. Instead, as soon as the system starts to use restorative justice as a diversionary option, it should openly communicate *to the general public* its policy that participation in restorative justice will be enforced with possible penal consequences. As Braithwaite puts it:

> How then can police and judges be threatening in the background without making threats? One way is by being transparent for the first time that the pyramid is the new policy that precedes escalation. ... Law enforcers [could

communicate] openly with society about the design policy of the pyramid. …
The ideal is to communicate the inexorability of deterrence in this way rather
than by making threats in specific cases. (2018: 94)

But the system cannot control when an offender comes to learn about or respond to such
a policy. It is highly likely that the first time they encounter or understand this policy will
be just at that point when they are required to decide whether to take part in restorative
justice. How would this be different, in effect, from 'making threats in specific cases'? The
avoidance of penal sanctions will almost always take centre stage as a motivating factor, no
matter how much we try to keep this threat in the wings.

Again, Skelton argues that '[i]mproving the manner in which the options are put to the
suspect can reduce the risk of coercion, and proper training is necessary'. And yet this
recommendation is immediately followed by this:

> [F]or restorative justice to be respectful of an offender's rights to autonomy,
> participation must be voluntary – and in principle this is correct. However, to
> some extent, there is often some element of coercion in restorative justice
> because the criminal justice system is a looming alternative. (2019: 36)

But it would seem to follow that, in order for a facilitator to reduce the 'risk' that the
offender might feel coerced into participating, they must be 'trained' to put 'the options' to
the offender in a way that somehow minimises or keeps in the background the fact that
'the criminal justice system is a looming alternative' and that their participation is therefore
not voluntary, even 'in principle'. Thus, even if a facilitator could succeed in momentarily
drawing the offender's attention away from this legal Sword of Damocles, it is hard to see
how doing so would be 'respectful of an offender's rights to autonomy'.

3. One common argument is that most offenders will not opt to take part in restorative
justice unless there is some element of coercion. Thus, enforced participation can be
justified on the grounds that it makes the potential benefits of restorative justice available
to far more offenders and victims.[32] As Braithwaite argues:

> Very few criminal offenders who participate in a restorative justice process
> would be sitting in the room absent a certain amount of coercion. Without
> their detection and/or arrest, without the specter of the alternative of a criminal
> trial, they simply would not cooperate with a process that puts their behavior

---

32   As one judge described it, '[a] lot of defendants will simply see this as a way of trying to manipulate their
     sentence … but even if this is the case it could have a beneficial effect' (Kirby & Jacobson, 2015: 42).

under public scrutiny. No coercion, no restorative justice (in most cases). (2002b: 34)

There are four problems with this defence. First, the end does not justify the means. As we have seen, enforced participation can violate an offender's moral agency and have a morally corrosive impact on their character. These ethical concerns need to be taken seriously, not swept under the carpet of expediency. Second, the means make it far less likely that the end will be achieved. This Sword of Damocles situation cannot help but constitute a formidable obstacle to realising the benefits of restorative justice. Third, as we shall see (in §4.6), this defence entirely overlooks the victim's needs. Enforced participation means that victims will have good reason to feel sceptical about the offender's motives. With this cloud hanging over the entire process, it will become far more difficult for them to experience the maximum benefits of restorative justice.

4. It might be argued that facilitators should be skilled and experienced enough to identify an offender who is participating mainly in order to avoid a penal sanction. They would never knowingly allow a victim to be faced with a largely unrepentant, calculating 'player of the system'. The referral would be returned without hesitation.

But a diversionary system, by its very nature, will give the facilitator reasonable grounds to doubt the offender's true motives, no matter how remorseful they might actually be. As we have seen, even if an offender is genuinely repentant, their fear of a punitive outcome will tend to play a central role in their behaviour and decision-making. Thus, if offenders were to be excluded on the grounds of acting primarily out of legal self-interest, then almost none of them would be eligible for restorative justice. As Malini Laxminarayan found in her interviews with victims and offenders from five European countries:

> For the offenders, a dominant theme regarding reasons to participate was the impact participation would have on the legal outcome of the case. ... [As one offender stated:] *'If it meant not going to prison I was open to it ... it meant a chance I wouldn't do time. So I was open to looking at it.'* Offender 3, Ireland. (2014: 144)

5. It might be argued that it is legitimate for the state to use restorative justice as a form of moral education. Criminal behaviour is, in no small part, due to the character or moral views of the offender. Hence, if the liberal state is to protect the freedom and equality of its citizens, then it has a responsibility to try to change the offender's character or moral views. It follows that the state would be justified in using the instruments available to the criminal justice system – such as restorative justice – as a means of moral education.

However, even those who advocate this kind of argument will acknowledge that there is an important caveat here. The liberal state cannot, as a matter of principle, seek to change an offender's character or moral views in a way that overrides or undermines their freedom or equality. This kind of 'education' would violate their moral agency. As Radzik argues:

> Brainwashing, for instance, is out of bounds since it would itself violate the principle of respecting freedom. Liberal moral education, then, must be education that approaches its subjects as free and equal persons, which suggests that such education may not be based on coercion. (2009: 163)

But then it follows that an Integrationist cannot justify the use of restorative justice as a way of changing an offender's character or moral views, given that, in this context, restorative justice is effectively coercive. As Radzik herself notes:

> [C]riminal justice systems, even those based on restorative justice models, are inherently coercive. How, then, could it be permissible for the liberal state to use the criminal justice system as a means of education? (2009: 163)

One possibility, Radzik suggests, is to borrow from Jean Hampton's moral education theory of punishment (1984). According to this view, the offender is not coerced by the state into changing their moral views or character. Rather, they are coerced into receiving a punishment which communicates to them the moral message that their behaviour is wrong and to a degree that matches the severity of their punishment. But the offender is not thereby forced to change. They may choose not to listen to the message, or they may choose to reject it. Their moral agency is thus preserved, even though the state has acted to do what it can to change their character and moral views.

The way in which the state uses restorative justice, Radzik argues, might be conceived of in a similar way. The state may effectively coerce an offender into taking part in the process. But it does not thereby force them to accept the moral messages that are conveyed by the facilitator, the victim or any other participant. As Radzik puts it:

> [R]estorative justice systems allow the offender ample opportunity to pointedly reject those [moral] messages. He can disagree with the alleged victim, voice his own interpretation and evaluation of his actions, refuse to agree to a particular restitution, and even opt out of the restorative process altogether. ... Restorative justice procedures, which make offender participation optional and allow the wrongdoer the opportunity to voice his own views, appear to be

consistent with [the offender's right to form his own conception of the good].
(2009: 164)

But there is a problem with this solution. What would it mean for an offender to 'reject' the moral messages of a restorative justice process in the way that Radzik suggests? To disagree with the moral views of the 'alleged victim', for instance, could include denying responsibility for causing them harm, or minimising or justifying the harm that was caused. To refuse to agree with the morality of a restitution proposal could involve rejecting the entire notion of making amends or that the offender had any obligation to provide reparation. Such an offender should have been assessed as ineligible for restorative justice. But assuming that safeguard is not in place, if the offender presented such views in the process itself, they would (or should) be assessed by the facilitator as unsuitable and returned to court.

In other words, in an Integrationist context, restorative justice would not, in fact, 'allow' the offender to obtain the legal benefits of completing the process while overtly refusing to accept its moral messages. And offenders are fully aware of this situation. That is precisely why, if they do disagree with these messages, they will invariably pretend otherwise. Put another way, in the Integrationist model, the moral education that restorative justice purportedly offers does not treat its subjects 'as free and equal persons'. By placing a legal Sword of Damocles over the offender's head, what the offender hears is that restorative justice cares little for their 'freedom of conscience' or their 'right to form his own conception of the good'. It cares only that they perform as expected. Or else.

4.6   TRUST

4.6.1   Justifiable scepticism

Victims who are offered restorative justice in a diversionary context will be aware that the avoidance of a punitive outcome is likely to be uppermost in the offender's decision to participate. As Goldsmith et al. found in their evaluation of a restorative justice pilot:

> [V]ictims were attuned to the possibility that offenders might not be sincere in their attempts to own their offending behaviour – that taking responsibility was another hurdle which offenders knew (explicitly or intuitively) that they must jump in order for their contributions to the conference to be seen as successful by authorities. (2005: 33)

But the mere possibility of insincerity raises a serious difficulty. Why would a victim want to take part in a process if the offender could, for all the victim knows, 'play them for a fool', simply in order to avoid a punitive sanction? This issue is not merely hypothetical. Researchers who evaluated seven restorative justice schemes across England found that:

> [Many victims] were willing to be conciliatory, but were equally concerned that they should not be taken in by the offender's disingenuous behaviour, the aim of which was to secure a favourable sentence. (Miers et al., 2001: 33)

And these concerns, the researchers noted, were 'well-founded'. In one case, a victim had participated in a restorative justice process after experiencing a burglary and damage to her home:

> [B]eing more concerned for the welfare of the imprisoned offender, she had written a reassuring reply to a 'genuine' letter of apology she had received from him. She described her anger upon discovering the subsequent use of her letter during a court hearing in the offender's defence. (2001: 33)

Of course, some victims may decide to proceed regardless of the Integrationist setting, perhaps because they still need answers to certain questions about the crime or want to express how they feel about what happened.[33] But in doing so, they are very likely to bring along a healthy dose of scepticism about the offender's sincerity. As Grant argues:

> [C]ompulsion also destroys trust; that is, the disposition to believe in another's truth or honesty. The more numerous the possibilities of non-compliance, and the more dangerous its consequences, the less trust there must be. (1992: 163-164)

What this means is that the offender might tell the truth and display genuine empathy and deep remorse, and yet, because of the diversionary context, the suspicion of insincerity could easily remain at the back of the victim's mind. As Lenta argues, an 'amnesty conditioned upon verbal apology ... devalues the currency of apology generally by increasing the likelihood that even sincere apologies will be viewed as expediently fabricated' (2021: 18). Thus, the victim will have good reason to keep their guard up, and so they will be less open to hearing the messages of genuine respect and remorse that are being conveyed. Even if the process meets some of the victim's needs, this situation will

---

33   I discuss later (§4.6.3) the facilitator's duty of care to all participants in cases where the victim is not interested in moral repair per se.

constitute a significant obstacle to moral repair, and so it is likely to prevent the victim from progressing further along their journey to recovery and healing. In short, the lack of trust generated by an Integrationist setting is liable to have a significant impact on the potential benefits that a victim might gain from restorative justice.

4.6.2   Pedagogical props

A second related impact that the offender's enforced participation can have on victims is more subtle but no less damaging. The diversionary context, as we have seen, cannot help but implant an inappropriate incentive in offenders, even if they might also be, in part, motivated for the right reasons. What this means in practice is that facilitators cannot simply screen out offenders who exhibit this kind of ulterior motive – even if it appears to dominate their decision-making. Virtually no offender would be eligible if they did. But as a result, facilitators are far more likely to accept offenders into the programme who would, on any measure of best practice, be regarded as unsuitable for restorative justice. These are the kind of offenders who admit to the crime, but display little, if any, genuine remorse for the harm they have caused. Instead, the prospect of avoiding or reducing the expected punitive sanction is uppermost in their minds.

The question is, what is the likely impact of this practice on victims, and how do its advocates justify it? A useful place to begin is by noting how Integrationists will often counter the suggestion that the lack of suitable screening is 'bad practice'. One of the main weapons in their artillery will be positive anecdotes. There are numerous stories in which reluctant and unremorseful offenders were pressured to attend a meeting with a victim. Yet the outcome was one in which their attitudes – and sometimes their lives – were transformed by hearing firsthand the effects of their actions. Marian Liebmann presents a quote that perfectly illustrates this kind of anecdote:

> Some of the most powerful meetings I have been involved in with victims and offenders have taken place when the offenders were very, very, reluctant, and their families refuse to take part – only when pressure was exerted did they attend. I have strong misgivings about this, but these meetings appear to have restored the victim, who at least had their voice given back about the offence, and for the most part the offender did accept responsibility. Interestingly, the parents of the offenders were the most affected – seeing their child confronted with the person whose life had been turned upside down by their child, stopped them in their tracks, preventing any more denial. (2007: 325)[34]

---

34   This quote was a personal communication to Liebmann by L. Cross made in 2006.

There are several responses that can be made to this kind of defence. First, a constant refrain heard from both victim groups and restorative justice advocates alike is that it is profoundly unethical to use victims as a kind of prop to 'educate' or rehabilitate offenders. Yet this is precisely what is happening when a victim is invited to participate in a meeting where, due to the constraints of an Integrationist setting, the facilitator has not conducted a proper assessment of the offender's suitability. In such cases, facilitators cannot be reasonably assured that the offender will accept responsibility for their part in what happened, let alone express remorse or offer a sincere apology. As the preceding quote suggests, there are restorative justice meetings that take place even when it is known in advance that the offender denies responsibility and has no intention of apologising – a practice that would be inconceivable in a Parallelist context.

Victims, in such cases, are then required to debate the facts of the case or to persuade the offender that what they have done was wrong and that it caused serious harm. The victim's very personal accounts of pain and suffering are used to elicit feelings of remorse or an acknowledgement of wrongdoing that would otherwise have remained absent. Such cases are not as rare as one might think. Daly, for instance, found that:

> [J]ust over 40 per cent of the [youth offender] subset apologised spontaneously to the victim at the conference, but for 28 per cent, the apology had to be drawn out. (2003: 224)

But extracting an apology from the offender should not be the role of the victim. There are, of course, examples of victims who happen to be articulate, forceful and assertive – so much so that the offender eventually caves in and apologises for the harm they have caused. But why should any victim be placed in a situation where they have to defend themselves or argue their case? Why should it be their role to convince the offender to do the right thing?

Restorative justice should not be set up so that it can only accommodate the most confident and persuasive of victims. Victims should be invited to participate only if the offender has agreed to take part so that they can fully admit their role in the harm that was caused, offer a sincere apology and make amends as best they can. The sense of remorse that the offender will feel is likely to increase or deepen as a consequence of a dialogue with the victim. But if no genuine remorse or acceptance of responsibility emerges *prior* to any such dialogue, then the offender should be assessed as ineligible. Why, after all, would a victim want to take the risk of meeting an offender who, for all the facilitator knows, could lace their account of what happened with justifications, minimisations, half-denials and excuses? Why would a victim want to take their chances and potentially face an offender who cannot even find it in themselves to say the word 'sorry'?[35]

There is a sound theoretical reason behind this. When we offer an apology, we are telling the person we have harmed that we no longer stand by what we did to them. We are, in effect, withdrawing the disrespect that our actions conveyed. An offender who refuses to offer a sincere apology is therefore sending the implicit message that they continue to hold the victim in contempt.[36] As Jeffrie Murphy argues:

> [Repentance] is surely the clearest way in which a wrongdoer can sever himself from his past wrong. In having a sincere change of heart, he is withdrawing his endorsement from his own immoral past behavior; he is saying, 'I no longer stand behind the wrongdoing, and I want to be separated from it. I stand with you in condemning it.' Of such a person it cannot be said that he is *now* conveying the message that he holds me in contempt. (1988: 26)

Thus, Umbreit is quite right to say that 'the offender's attitude or insincerity may constitute an additional offense in the eyes of the victim' (2001: 27 n. 5). A genuine apology is intrinsic to what it means to take responsibility. This is precisely why we can predict that an unremorseful offender will be more likely to miss or turn up late at a planned restorative justice meeting, or to resist attempts to negotiate a satisfactory outcome agreement, or breach any agreement that is made or reoffend. As Allison Morris and Gabrielle Maxwell found, 'those offenders who failed to apologize to victims were more likely to be reconvicted than those who had apologized' (1998).

If repentance is therefore so important to a restorative justice process, why is it that the number of unapologetic offenders is so high? In one South Australian pilot, only 27% of victims felt that the apologies they received from offenders were sincere (Daly, 2003: 224). Sherman and Strang found that a Canberra pilot produced a significantly higher percentage (77%) of victims who reported that the apologies were sincere (2007: 63). Even so, they admit that '[c]onfronting the (fortunately rare) unremorseful offender in a RJ conference … may appear to be a significant risk for victims' (p. 62). But one key explanation for this astounding situation is that, within an Integrationist framework, facilitators know that screening for remorse would be virtually impossible. Every single offender in this context will have a powerful incentive to jump through the restorative justice hoop, whether they are sincere or not. Zernova gives a striking example of this:

---

35 This is not to suggest that uttering the word 'sorry' is the *only* way in which remorse can be expressed. For example, '[t]here are no words in Maori language that equate to the English language expressions, "sorry" … Rather it is practical demonstrations of reciprocity, rebalancing and processes of restoration across a number of dimensions that rule Maori processes' (Love, 2002: 47, n. 52).

36 For more detail, *see* Brookes (2021a, 2021b).

> In one case study, in order to avoid a trial, the offender pleaded guilty to something he claimed in the [researcher's] interview he did not do. The court ordered him to attend a family group conference and apologize to victims, which he did. If this offender indeed did not commit the crime, he offered a false apology. (2016: 78)

In sum, voluntariness and sincerity are essential to optimising the quality and effectiveness of a restorative justice process for victims. Yet given the ever-present risk of punitive consequences in an Integrationist context, these two features are almost impossible to implement.[37] By contrast, the Parallelist model is designed to maximise the possibility of both. Researchers Goldsmith et al. came to the same conclusion:

> Victims seemed to take into account in deciding upon the genuineness of offenders' apologies or expressions of remorse whether they could detect any self-serving element behind the offender's actions. While, in process or performance terms, no one factor is likely to ensure the presence or absence of trust in a particular conference, post-sentencing conferences (of which we observed only one) seemed to have a natural advantage in this respect. (2005: 38)

These same researchers go on to say that, in making this observation, they are not suggesting that 'pre-sentence conferences are inappropriate'. Instead, the implication they draw is that 'the work needed to establish trust in particular conferences at the pre-sentence stage may be greater in view of this difference' (2005: 38). Likewise, it would be a mistake for any Parallelist to argue that establishing trust is *impossible* in a pre-sentence context. The evidence clearly shows otherwise. Many victims feel that the apology they received was sincere, even though it was offered under legal duress. But, again, the case for Parallelism does not rest on a zero-sum assessment. The advantage that Parallelism claims to have over Integrationism is that, by removing a potent cause for suspicion, the Parallelist model makes it considerably easier for participants to trust each other. And as a consequence, they are more likely to access the full benefits of restorative justice. Tasioulas makes a similar case for a Parallelist approach in the following:

---

37   There is some experimental evidence to support this claim. Researchers Alana Saulnier and Diane Sivasubramaniam, for instance, designed a 'deceptive, live paradigm' to test the impact of coercion on the quality of an apology. Subjects were threatened with punitive consequences unless they apologised for a transgression, while the control group were simply asked to apologise (p. 4). They found that coerced apologies conveyed 'less remorse, guilt, and potential for dispute resolution than apologies that were not coerced (with large effect sizes)' and thus concluded that 'coercion to apologize has clear and robust negative effects on the quality of apologies that offenders offer' (Saulnier & Sivasubramaniam, 2015: 7).

[S]ome of the repentance rituals that advocates of restorative justice have suggested as alternatives to punishment might, instead, be supported as supplements to the punitive process. It is plausible to think, for example, that a repentance conference involving the offender, the victim and other interested parties that is conducted *after* the offender has been sentenced, or even served a significant part of his sentence, would be more likely to induce forgiveness and reconciliation than one clouded by the suspicion that the offender is insincerely mouthing apologies in the hope of getting off lightly. (2007: 520-521)

4.6.3   Possible responses

There are a range of responses that advocates of Integrationism have made to this criticism of how victims are impacted by the enforced participation of offenders. So we will need to address them in turn.

1. Sherman and Strang report that many restorative justice services do not 'require evidence of "remorse" as a precondition for RJ', and they offer the following justification for this practice:

> Many offenders agree to restorative justice in a matter-of-fact way, in a one-on-one meeting with a facilitator. It is when they get into a RJ process that they may become quite emotional and make apparently sincere expressions of remorse and apology. As facilitators often say, 'RJ doesn't screen for remorse; it aims to *achieve* remorse.' This basis of the *facilitator's* consent to have an offender participate has resulted in no documented cases (to our knowledge) of offenders verbally abusing victims, let alone behaving violently, in any RJ process in the UK. (2007: 37)

This justification does not hold water. First, the purpose of 'screening for remorse' is not to select out offenders who might 'verbally abuse victims' or 'behave violently' within the conference. There are other risk assessments that can provide that type of screening. Rather, the aim is to ensure that the offender is suitable for a meeting in which their expression of remorse plays a central role.

Second, restorative justice should not aim to 'achieve remorse'. That would be an entirely offender-oriented ambition, leaving the victim to take their chances as to whether the offender will, in the end, agree to take responsibility for their actions and apologise accordingly. Restorative justice should aim to enable an *already* remorseful offender to communicate these feelings in a safe, meaningful and constructive way so that both the victim and the offender can receive the maximum benefit from their encounter. As researchers Jung Choi and Margaret Severson found:

> Teaching the offender specific skills to deliver an effective apology, for example, and helping victims understand the anxieties experienced by the offender in framing, composing and delivering the apology is likely to end in a meaningful experience for both. (2009: 819)

To be clear, this does not mean that offenders who show insufficient remorse in their initial assessment interview should be automatically ruled out. If they accept that they were responsible for the crime, then they should, if they are willing, be allowed to hold a series of discussions with a facilitator, perhaps extending over a long period if necessary. If at some point the offender comes to express remorse in a genuine and stable way, then – and only then – should they be considered suitable for a dialogue with a victim.

In sum, the catchphrase 'let them fake it till they make it' may be necessitated by the Integrationist model, but in terms of best practice, it should be repudiated in the strongest terms. However, this position entails that the chief source of the problem – the legal Sword of Damocles – be removed, and this can only be done by shifting to a Parallelist model.

2. One justification that is often made for not requiring offenders to be screened for remorse is that apologies should be made 'spontaneously or not at all' (Bowen, Boyack & Hooper, 2000: 93). It might be thought that this view is justified by the principle that the offender should not be coerced or pressured into apologising. However, the recommendation that an apology should be allowed to 'arise spontaneously or not at all' does not follow. An apology is such an essential element in a meeting that it cannot be left to chance. Indeed, there is evidence that facilitators who agree with the centrality of an apology, but have been schooled into taking the spontaneous-or-nothing approach will, when the need arises, switch to a spontaneous-or-extract policy. The results are entirely predictable. In a 2002 UK study, Carolyn Hoyle and Fernanda Rosenblatt found:

> [P]olice officers tended to view a restorative caution as successful when the offender apologized at the meeting (when the victim was present) or agreed to send a letter of apology to an absent victim. Hence, when apologies did not flow naturally from the process, facilitators often 'extracted' apologies from offenders in a fairly coercive way. In such cases participants typically felt that the apology was not genuine. (2016: 36)[38]

---

38   Citing Hoyle, Young and Hill (2002).

Most would agree that this is bad practice, but it would be a mistake to lay all of the blame on the facilitators. They are, after all, working in a context where it would be impossible to exclude any offender who is trying to escape a punitive sanction. Within an Integrationist setting, this ulterior motive will be virtually universal. But then it is hardly surprising if facilitators come to regard 'screening for remorse' as a pointless exercise, hoping instead that the offender's self-interest will at some point become so overwhelmed by the pedagogical potency of the victim's story that, in the heat of the moment, they will instinctively spurt out a 'spontaneous' apology. If not, then an 'extracted' version will have to do. In other words, the source of this practice lies upstream with the Integrationist model, not downstream with the facilitator, who is simply trying to make the best of a less-than-optimal situation.

Offenders need the opportunity to prepare what it is that they want to say in their apology. It is too easy for an offender to throw out the word 'sorry', without giving a thought to what that word means or what exactly it is that they are sorry *for*. It is equally easy to deliver a victim-blaming apology, such as 'I'm sorry you feel that way'. Offenders need to have the opportunity to think these matters through in advance. Speaking within a restorative justice meeting is not easy, and offenders need to be able to prepare themselves as best they can. Only then will all those involved gain maximum benefit from the process. As Daly puts it:

> Because there is little to go on, except their experience in a previous conference, many young people and their parents do not know what is expected of them. The potential for restorativeness is greater when participants, and especially offenders, have taken time in advance to think about what they want to say. Yet, as we learned from the interviews [in the South Australian evaluation], over half the YPs hadn't *at all* thought about what they'd say to the victim. ... Most did not think in terms of what they might *offer victims*, but rather what they would be *made to do by others*. (2003: 232-233)

Likewise, facilitators need to be reasonably assured that the offender will not do more harm than good by delivering a careless or distorted apology. None of this preparatory work will make the apology any less sincere or heartfelt, just as an orchestra's rehearsal of a piece will not make the players any less passionate and inspired when they come to perform the music. The quality and sincerity of the apology, when it is delivered, will be far higher than if it were 'spontaneous' or off the cuff. The offender will have thought hard about what they want to say and how best to communicate their feelings effectively. And there is nothing to prevent them, at any point in a meeting, from changing their mind, altering or adding to the content of their apology in accordance with how they are feeling at the time or what they have heard from the victim. None of this is likely to diminish or threaten the sincerity of what they say.

A good example of the importance of this preparation work can be found in Daly's evaluation of how victims in the South Australian programme *perceived* the apologies they received.

> The main reasons victims gave for why the [Young Person] said sorry were the YP thought they would get off easier (30 per cent) and the YP was pushed into it (25 per cent). *Just 27 percent believed that the main reason that YP apologised was because s/he really was sorry.* It is not surprising, then, that half the victims said the YP's apology did not at all help to repair the harm. (2003: 225)

When the researchers asked the young offenders why they decided to say sorry, the picture that emerged was somewhat more complicated:

> 27 per cent said they didn't feel sorry but thought they would get off easier, 39 per cent said to make their family feel better, and a similar percentage said they felt pushed into it [by the coordinator, police officer, or both; the 'whole situation'; and a family member]. However, when asked what was the *main reason* for saying sorry, most (61 per cent) said they were really sorry. (2003: 224)

It is not at all surprising that, with virtually no screening or preparation, over a third (39%) of the young offenders, even when pressed, claimed that they did not feel sorry *at all*. Nor is it surprising that, given the Integrationist setting, so many had ulterior motives for apologising. But if it is true that 61% really were sorry, then it is not inconceivable that, in a legally independent setting with adequate preparation, more of these young people might have been able to work out how to communicate their feelings in a way that could be heard. Instead, a mere 27% of victims believed that the apology they received was sincere.

In sum, the suggestion that apologies must be 'spontaneous' could only get off the ground in an Integrationist context, where little is to be gained from screening offenders for signs of genuine remorse. Even if this highly tendentious practice might 'work' in many cases, it effectively requires the victim to perform as a pedagogical prop, which, as we have seen, is profoundly unethical and potentially revictimising. In a Parallelist model, such an approach would be entirely unnecessary.

3. Some victims may know that, given the legal context, the offender is unlikely to be genuinely remorseful but still want to meet with them in any case. Advocates of Integrationism might argue that their wishes should be honoured, and in certain cases this

will be appropriate. But it is not always respectful or honouring to give people what they want. If the risk to a victim's well-being is significant, then the facilitator has the right and the duty to refrain from arranging such a meeting.

The facilitator must also take into account the impact of such a meeting on the offender. For instance, if the victim shows little concern about whether or not the offender is likely to take responsibility, apologise and make amends, then the facilitator will need to be extremely cautious about the victim's ulterior motives. Some victims may just want the chance to attack, degrade and humiliate the offender. This kind of 'revenge-fest' should never proceed, even if the offender appears 'willing' to take it. Miller and Hefner present an example of what appears to be this kind of approach in an interview with one facilitator:

> I went to [a conference] where the offender had [committed] – I think it was a murder or manslaughter … The victim's wife just basically met with the offender … but, she just screamed at him for two hours … I think he sort of decided he was going to go there to be a punching bag – whatever it took – and that's what he wanted out of it. (Miller & Hefner, 2015: 157)[39]

Not only would it violate the facilitator's duty of care to the offender but such a process would be diametrically opposed to the values and objectives of restorative justice. If best practice principles were being employed, this kind of scenario would never arise.

In short, the practice of 'honouring' a victim's decision to meet with a potentially insincere or unrepentant offender could only be considered acceptable in a context where this scenario was not only routine but virtually unavoidable – namely, the Integrationist framework.

4. Previously I quoted Sherman and Strang acknowledging that victims who agree to take part in a restorative justice process take a 'significant risk' that they will end up confronting an 'unremorseful offender'. But they go on to suggest that, in taking such a risk, 'the payoff' for a victim would nevertheless be 'substantial when the encounter results in a sincere expression of apology' (2007: 62). But again, why should victims be placed in a situation where they have little choice but to take such a risk? It is not as if there is no alternative. The gamble that victims are required to take is not due to the nature of restorative justice as such. It arises as a direct consequence of the involuntariness that is

---

39 A UK-based report found similar cases: 'One [offender reported] that the victim yelled at him continually; "it was a terrible experience, [the victim] kept talking about prison and trying to scare you". One offender who had taken part in a restorative conference said she felt "picked on", that the victim's mother yelled at her and that she continues to be "wound up" by the victim since the conference. The offender … felt that it had simply subjugated her to the victim and, in doing so, had exacerbated the ongoing hostility between them' (Miers et al., 2001: 40).

structurally locked into the Integrationist model. A Parallelist framework would eliminate this kind of risk entirely.

5. Carolyn Hoyle argues that, in an 'ideal world', coercing offenders to take part in restorative justice would be used 'sparingly'. There are cases, however, in which she believes it would be justified. Suppose an offender is 'resistant' or 'unwilling' to participate. The problem, Hoyle argues, is that, if we allowed this preference to 'take precedence', then we would, as a consequence, 'deny' the victim the opportunity to take part in 'a process that might bring them some relief'. However, if it is clear that the offender is 'determined to revictimise' the victim, then, Hoyle suggests, they should be excluded and face the criminal sanction they would otherwise have received.

> [W]here it is genuinely believed that an unwilling offender would use the restorative encounter to intimidate or in another way further harm the victim, coercion should be avoided and the retributive 'sentence discount' lost. (Hoyle, 2010: 58)

But what is overlooked or at least minimised here is the risk posed to the victim merely by virtue of the offender's 'resistance' or 'unwillingness'. An offender need not abuse or intimidate the victim in order to revictimise them. As we have seen, all it takes is a refusal to admit responsibility for their actions or show genuine remorse. But then the rationale for allowing coercion collapses. If the interests and needs of victims take precedence, then the last thing we should do is use a legal threat to compel an unwilling offender to meet with them. Far from bringing them 'some relief', such an encounter is only liable to cause them 'further harm'.

Once again, the practice of coercing unwilling offenders into meeting a victim would only ever be considered acceptable in an Integrationist framework. As Hoyle acknowledges, 'if restorative justice and criminal justice are to coexist it will be necessary to coerce offenders in some cases' (p. 58). In a Parallelist model, such an option would never arise.

6. It might be argued that, while the enforced participation of offenders may 'not present the best possible starting position for restorative encounters', it nevertheless appears to 'deliver more satisfying outcomes than traditional court proceedings' (Walgrave, 2003: 571). For instance, victims have a far better chance of receiving a sincere apology in a restorative justice process than they do in court. Sherman and Strang found that 86% of victims who experienced a restorative justice conference 'said their offender had apologised', compared with only 19% of victims who were assigned to court. Moreover, 77% of the conference-assigned victims 'felt the apologies they received were sincere', in contrast to only 41% of the court-assigned victims (2007: 62).

But this comparison trades on a false equivalence. Courts, as we have seen, are not designed to address this kind of private emotional need. The priorities of the court in many ways preclude such an objective. It is like arguing that the court system is superior to restorative justice because it allows defence lawyers to speak on behalf of offenders. But, then, since the comparison is fallacious, it cannot, in itself, serve to justify the enforced participation of offenders in restorative justice.

7. Another response might be to argue that most victims appear to be 'satisfied' with their experience of restorative justice *regardless* of whether or not they participate in a Parallelist setting. Van Camp and Wemmers, for instance, conducted interviews in Canada and Belgium with 28 victims of serious crime, half of whom took part in a restorative justice process prior to sentencing and the other half in a post-sentencing setting. While these two contexts did give rise to significant differences, the researchers report that, overall, the respondents' 'satisfaction with the restorative approach' in the pre-sentence group was 'as positive' as that in the post-sentence group (2011: 187, my translation).[40]

But there are serious problems with using this kind of small-scale study to defend the practice of enforced participation.[41] Most victims will not have had any prior experience of restorative justice, so they have no point of comparison. Perhaps one day sufficient numbers will allow for a statistically meaningful side-by-side comparison of these two models from the victim's perspective. In the meantime, a question that victims could be asked is whether their experience of restorative justice might have been *more* satisfactory if there had been no legal incentive for the offender to take part in the process.[42] It is, for instance, worth noting that, in a subsequent article reporting on the same data, Van Camp and Wemmers mention one 'cause for frustration' among victims that could only have arisen in a non-Parallelist context and which therefore appears to confirm the issue at hand:

> Trust can also be translated in terms of the respondent's assessment of the offender's sincerity in engaging in the restorative intervention … For example, an ulterior motive for participation (such as obtaining a lenient sentence) on the part of the offender was cause for frustration. (2013: 125)

---

40   To clarify, the majority of respondents in the pre-sentence group were involved in Belgium's pre-trial VOM scheme, which differs from diversionary approaches insofar as (a) referrals do not depend on a prosecutor or a judge's decision to divert a case but can instead be requested by the victim or the offender; and (b) VOM participants can choose not to share any outcome agreement with the court. Nevertheless, the scheme is not strictly Parallelist, since the court *can*, if it wishes, take any (shared) agreement into account in its decision-making (*see* §5.1.1 for more details).

41   This is not to suggest that Van Camp and Wemmers used their findings for this purpose.

42   Although it is important to note the limitations of this kind of hypothetical question: '[I]t is well established that people find it difficult to anticipate how they would in reality respond to actually experiencing a specific event or stimulus' (Allan et al., 2021: 604).

Second, this kind of response fails to take into account the casualties. Victims can feel worse or more fearful as a result of their encounter, largely because of the insincerity of the offender. Umbreit, for instance, reports a study in which some victims did not find the restorative justice process 'helpful', due to 'the negative, non-repentant attitude of their specific offender. "I felt he wasn't owning up to it." "He just slouched all the way down and just sat and half-heartedly gave answers"' (1990: 56).

8. It might be argued that a victim could still find some value in an offender's apology, even if they have good reason to suspect it lacks authenticity. What matters to them is that it was offered, not whether it is heartfelt. Duff, for instance, argues that:

> [I]n the more distant relationships in which we stand to each other simply as fellow citizens we can often make peace with each other by going through the ritual motions of making and accepting an apology without inquiring into its sincerity. (2003: 53)

However, for this response to succeed, it would need to show not merely that an insincere apology can bring about peace-making in *some* situations but rather that it could be sufficient for the purposes of restorative justice.

There are two situations in which going through the 'ritual motions' of an apology could potentially 'make peace'. The first would be where the disrespect conveyed by the act is minimal. We apologise for bumping into someone on the train. The waiter apologises for the delay in service. In such cases, expressions of heartfelt remorse or questions about sincerity would be out of place. Indeed, overt attempts to demonstrate sincerity would be more likely to arouse suspicion. The second kind of situation would be where those involved need to work together or live in peace, and this priority overrides the temptation to inquire into sincerity. If, in such cases, an apology is made and accepted, this ritual will invariably be quick or superficial. But any such 'peace' or 'reconciliation' will be little more than a pallid 'at-least-we-are-not-at-war' imitation, rather than the full-blooded reality. These are not the kind of cases that would be most suitable for a restorative justice encounter. Nor, one could argue, do either of these two situations resemble the kind of moral breach that results from serious crime.

9. It might be thought that the Maximalist model has a solution to the foregoing problem. If an offender is assessed as insincere, they would be excluded from taking part in a diversionary restorative justice process and would instead receive a reparative sanction – which, in the Maximalist view, still counts as 'restorative justice'. The proceeding would be court-based, and so victims could be involved in the usual way, for instance as witnesses or by giving a victim-impact statement. But there would be no expectation or requirement that victims receive a personal apology in this context. So the kind of secondary harm that can occur in a diversionary context would be avoided. It follows that, in the Maximalist

model, a sincere apology is not required for every form of 'restorative justice'. But this solution depends entirely on the Maximalist view that the term 'restorative justice' can include *both* voluntary *and* court-imposed sanctions, and, as I argued earlier (§1.1.5), this kind of taxonomic extension is both unnecessary and unhelpful.

4.7 INTEGRITY

If restorative justice is to be integrated into the criminal justice system, it will inevitably need to adapt to the priorities of that system – which, as I have argued, are determined by public interest considerations and the rule of law. In this section, I explore the compromises that are routinely made to restorative justice when it is subject to the court's criteria for what constitutes a successful outcome, its timescale restrictions, caseload pressures and its duty to ensure that the process is guided and overseen by someone who can speak with the authority of the law – none of which would be applicable in the Parallelist model.

4.7.1 Criteria for success

In the Integrationist model, the success or failure of a restorative justice process will normally be taken into account by the judiciary. For example, if the court finds that an offender has failed to participate as required, then it will usually impose the sanction they would ordinarily have received. The problem is that the criteria for success used by the court may not coincide with what is (or should be) considered successful from a restorative justice perspective. This is largely because the court, as we have seen, is primarily interested in making decisions that satisfy at least three requirements: they must be objective or evidence-based, they must be fair in the sense of treating like cases alike, and they must be proportionate, as measured by the court's own punitive calculus. Hence, when legislators or the judiciary are considering how a diversionary process should be assessed, they will tend to select benchmarks for success that can be reliably verified, that involve only the most essential features of the process, and that include a quantifiable burden or hardship for the offender.

However, such benchmarks are particularly difficult to find or assess when it comes to a highly variable, subjective and repair-oriented process like restorative justice. So, as might be expected, a diversionary restorative justice scheme can easily end up compromising its own values and objectives in order to provide the court with the evidence it requires. We have already seen how this can occur when the court sets punitive limits as its benchmark for assessing the proportionality of a restorative justice agreement (§4.2). But, as I shall argue, there are a number of other ways in which the court's criteria for success can eat away at the integrity of a restorative justice process.

4.7.1.1   Completed agreement

One feature of a restorative justice process that can be easily verified is whether or not an offender completes the activities or tasks agreed to by the participants. Moreover, the court would have good reason to suppose that this is an essential component of restorative justice. The formulation of an outcome agreement is virtually always included in the standard formats. And since the agreement can involve the offender giving up their time or money, this will, in the court's eyes, constitute a quantifiable burden or hardship for the offender. It is largely for these reasons that, where restorative justice operates within an Integrationist context, most courts will use the offender's compliance with the agreement as a primary indicator of success.[43]

However, it is not at all clear that this feature can serve as a benchmark for success from a restorative justice perspective. To give one example, suppose the task was agreed to by all in good faith, but it turned out to be impossible to complete for justifiable reasons. A hypothetical example of this is given in the *Crimes (Restorative Justice) Act* 2004 (ACT):

> After taking part in a restorative justice conference, Sam and Bella sign a restorative justice agreement under which Sam agrees to work in Bella's garden every Saturday for 6 months. However, 4 months after the start of the agreement, the company Sam works for moves its head office from Canberra to Brisbane, and Sam is required to move there before the 6 months is over to keep his job. Sam has until then complied fully with the agreement. The convenor may consider, because of Sam's history of compliance with the agreement, and the change in Sam's situation, there is a change in Sam's situation that would justify an amendment to the agreement to reduce its term so that it will end when Sam has to move to Brisbane. (s.55)

The *Act* allows the conference convenor to amend the agreement only if they have first 'consulted each required participant in the conference', which includes the victim (s.55.3). But suppose the victim does not accept the justification provided or does not agree to the proposed alterations? In such a scenario, it is very likely that the convenor would make the extenuating circumstances known to the court. If the court then agreed that the alteration was justified, and the offender complied with the revised agreement, then, all else being equal, the court would judge this to be a successful outcome.

---

43   For instance, the *Crimes (Restorative Justice) Act* 2004 (ACT) states: 'A restorative justice conference has as a primary object the formation of an agreement under this division (a restorative justice agreement) between each required participant in the conference' (s.50). And 'If the [conference convenor] is satisfied on reasonable grounds that there has been a significant failure to comply with the restorative justice agreement, the [convenor] must report the noncompliance to the referring entity' (s.57.2).

But it is hard to see how this result could be considered successful from a restorative justice perspective. If the victim's views about the revised agreement are simply overruled by the court, this would ordinarily damage any progress that had been made towards the goal of moral repair. And yet, from the court's perspective, its decision would have been fully in accord with its own guiding principles. A different offender in the same circumstances could easily have had a victim who agreed to the alteration. Hence, in order to fulfil its remit of treating like cases alike, the court would have had little option but to ignore this particular victim's views on the matter.

It might be argued that this concern is inconsistent with the evidence, presented earlier (§2.1.2), that many victims do not wish to carry the burden of deciding the legal outcome of their case. They might also (rightly) feel that, as private citizens, they lack the authority or expertise to decide on such matters. As Jo-Anne Wemmers and Marisa Canuto found, 'Victims support many of the elements of restorative justice; they want notification and restitution. However, they do not seem to want to usurp the power of the courts' (2002: 5).[44] So if a court were to overrule the restorative justice agreement and impose a sentence of its own making, or even just amend the agreement, then, for such victims, this outcome need not necessarily damage the preceding restorative justice process. Indeed, it might enhance their experience since they would know in advance that they will not be required to take on this formal decision-making role. They can instead focus on meeting their own private harm-related needs. As Van Camp found in her interviews with victims:

> It appears that when accessing restorative justice before adjudication, a judicial decision is anticipated by the victim-participant, rather than being absent. Victims wanted a judge to have the final word. This exempted them from the burden of decision control and the necessity to reach an agreement with the offender. They argued that the informal outcome of the restorative intervention needed to be complemented with a formal judicial decision. … It is exactly the idea that victims are involved without being burdened with decision-making power that adds to their satisfaction with the restorative offer. It is also consistent with their expectations towards the criminal justice system, to which they turn for a societal and formal recognition of their victimization and of the offender's accountability for it. (Van Camp, 2014: 160)

---

44 This does not entail that victims do not want a greater voice and more control in relation to the judicial process. Therapeutic jurisprudence would be a good solution, but even here the public interest orientation of criminal justice means that there will always be limitations. This is one of the reasons why restorative justice can play such a powerful role in enabling a victim to regain their sense of autonomy and control after a crime.

But the foregoing objection is not that victims who take part in restorative justice lose control over *the legal decision*. This is not a decision-making power that is rightfully theirs, nor is it one that most victims want – as the study above indicates. The concern being raised here is that, in an Integrationist context, victims lose control over *their own private agreement*. In this setting, the restorative justice agreement is not 'complemented with' the court's decision but is instead subjugated by that decision. The legal decision is not made in addition to and separate from the restorative justice agreement. It takes over that agreement. The court treats it as a legally conditional disposal, whereby punitive consequences could be imposed should the offender fail to complete it. Where necessary, the court can even reshape the agreement so that it will better accord with its own judicial priorities. It could even remove aspects of the agreement that, even though important to the participants, could not be plausibly construed as serving the public interest.[45]

It is this judicial commandeering of the restorative justice agreement that is so disconcerting. It would only make sense in a situation where restorative justice values have become subordinated to criminal justice priorities. If restorative justice is to function in accordance with its own values and objectives, then victims should be free to make their own decisions about what happens in the restorative justice process and how it is conducted. This should include any decision about whether to form an agreement and, if so, what it should contain. There should be no expectation that this agreement will then be appropriated and then potentially revised or overruled by the court to serve its own, quite different purposes. The restorative justice outcome and the legal outcome must, in other words, be kept entirely separate and independent, as they would be under a Parallelist model.

4.7.1.2   Genuine remorse

There are other elements of a restorative justice process that, when used by the court as a benchmark of success, are equally, if not more, problematic. For example, the court might wish to know whether the offender expressed genuine remorse to the victim. This is not an unlikely request, given that, as we have seen (§2.2.3), the presence of remorse is often regarded by courts as a mitigating factor.

We have already seen how the Sword of Damocles situation created by Integrationism is likely to give the offender an ulterior motive to participate. And if the offender discovers, as they surely will, that the court will regard genuine remorse as a criterion of success, then this is just as likely to undermine any chance of authenticity. In other words, there is already good reason to think that, in such a context, any display of remorse will either be

---

45   To give one example, researchers found that when 'the courts' reviewed agreements made in family group conferences (in Manitoba, Canada), they 'largely ignored the families' recommendations regarding cultural components, community service, and other programs' (Longclaws, Galaway & Barkwell, 1996: 195).

completely feigned or less sincere than it could have been, since it is likely to be driven by mixed motives. For this reason alone, providing the court with reliable evidence of genuine remorse will therefore be especially challenging.

But putting this issue aside, establishing the genuineness of remorse is, in itself, an extremely subtle and complex matter. It would hardly be sufficient to report back to the court that the words 'I am sorry' were uttered by the offender. Non-verbal gestures and tone of voice are equally important. A verbal apology can be uttered with sullen resentment or mocking derision, effectively cancelling out the meaning of the words. Again, an offender might, in their expression of remorse, avoid eye contact with the victim. But this gesture is highly ambiguous. In certain contexts, it can be a way of displaying contempt or a lack of concern. But in others, it can be a sign of deference, especially in certain cultures (Goldsmith et al., 2005: 31-32).

So who, then, would have sufficient expertise to conduct a reliable assessment of an offender's level of remorse and then report back their findings to the court? If this role is left to the facilitator, as it usually is, then this puts them in a very difficult position. Facilitators are often highly skilled at reading emotions. But presenting evidence with regard to their presence or authenticity for the purposes of a court of law is a different matter altogether. A facilitator could easily misread or even fail to notice an offender's display of remorse. But if they subsequently report the absence of a genuine apology, the offender could face adverse legal consequences as a result. This might be rare in practice, but the risk remains.

Or again, suppose the victim feels that the offender's apology was insincere, but the facilitator – who has worked with the offender privately, perhaps over a long period of time – disagrees. How should the facilitator's report be written? If the facilitator rejects the views of the victim and reports the offender's apology as 'authentic', how would this be perceived by the victim? Or again, what if the victim was the only participant who felt that the offender was insincere? Suppose the facilitator included this fact in their report. How would the court interpret such a mixed result? How should they take account of this outcome in their legal decision? Whose perspective should they believe: the victim's or the other participants'?

Either way, someone is likely to feel disadvantaged by the process. The victim, for instance, will be hoping that the judge will deem the offender's participation a failure on account of their insincerity, while the offender would be hoping that their attempt to convey genuine remorse might have the opposite effect. The facilitator would have little choice but to report this disagreement, which itself could suggest to the court that the offender's participation was unsuccessful. And this type of scenario is not merely hypothetical. Goldsmith et al. describe one conference they observed as follows:

[M]ost of the participants thought the offender was genuine in his remorse, but the victim, for a variety of reasons, thought otherwise. As a result the outcome of the conference was not particularly successful but a distorted picture could have been presented if the report had simply reported the lack of the outcome or the victim's perspective. (2005: 19-20)

4.7.1.3   Forgiveness

Given these complexities, it might be thought that the court should instead only require evidence that the victim accepted the offender's apology or explicitly offered forgiveness. But are judges likely to incorporate such a subjective factor into their decision-making? Jacobson and Hough surveyed judges in the UK and found that, in certain cases, their sentencing would be affected by the victim's (or their family's) support for and/or forgiveness of the offender. 'Unlike a lot of judges,' said one, 'I attach real importance to what the victim or victim's family want.' Another said:

This mitigation is important 'in a discreet way' – you must not sentence according to what the victim wants, but this makes it easier not to send [the offender] to prison. (2007: 30)

Jacobson and Hough suggest that the reason for this range of views reflects 'the ambiguity of the relevant legal guidance' and that, as a consequence, 'the courts have, in spite of the principle of no involvement, allowed the forgiveness of the victim to have an effect on the sentencing of the offender' (p. 31).[46]

Similarly, in a study on the use of restorative justice processes in China, Yan Zhang and Yiwei Xia found that 'receiving forgiveness from the victims reduces sentence length by 22.4%' and that 'offenders who received forgiveness have 2.5 times the chance of getting probation rather than imprisonment' (2021: 1483, 1484). In New Zealand, the courts are required by law to take account of whether the victim 'accepts' the offender's apology or remedial action 'as expiating or mitigating the wrong', although the legislation does not specify the kind of evidence the court would need to form a reliable judgment about such matters (*Sentencing Act* 2002 (NZ) s.10.1-2). Finally, to give a concrete example from the UK, Amy Kirby and Jessica Jacobson report a case in which the victim's views about the

---

46   Quoting Currie (2005: 21). Cf. '[T]he courts of England and Wales [only provide a direct role for victims in the determination of a sentence] to cases where the suffering of the victims is increased by the sentence set by the courts, or where the forgiveness of the victim indicates that he or she is less negatively affected than might be expected. This approach has, however, only led to a reduction in the custodial sentences imposed in the relevant matters, and not a replacement of the custodial sentence with a non-custodial one' (Van der Merwe & Skelton, 2015: 372).

offender's participation appear to have contributed to the judge's decision to deliver a harsher sentence.

> A project manager ... described a case in which the defence counsel had made much, in the plea in mitigation, of how grateful the victim had been to take part in RJ; but the judge, from reading the conference report, knew that this was a misrepresentation of what had happened and told the barrister as much. The offender was given a significant sentence and returned to prison telling other prisoners not to bother with 'bloody RJ'. (2015: 33)

It goes without saying that this practice conflicts with the principle that sentences should reflect the objective seriousness of the offence and the offender's culpability, rather than the victim's wishes. As Ashworth puts it:

> Just because a person commits an offence against me ... that does not privilege my voice above that of the court (acting 'in the general public interest') in the matter of the offender's punishment. (2002: 585)

Still, the fact that such a practice exists means that the presence or otherwise of the victim's acceptance of the apology or an offer of forgiveness should be contained in any restorative justice report, given that it could have a significant effect on any judicial review of the process. But this requirement would only increase the problems faced by the facilitator, in terms of needing to provide the court with reliable evidence for the occurrence of complex psychological phenomena.

Perhaps there is a way around this. It could be stipulated in relevant legislation that if an apology is given in a restorative justice process, then this should be noted in the agreement. The *Crimes (Restorative Justice) Act* 2004 (ACT), for instance, states that:

> (1) A restorative justice agreement in relation to an offence must include measures intended to repair the harm caused by the offence. (2) The agreement may include 1 or more of the following: (a) an apology by the offender to any victim or parent of a victim (s.51.1-2.a)

The court may then take it that if the victim signs the agreement – as they are usually required to do[47] – then this would suggest that they accepted the apology and perhaps even that they forgave the offender.

---

47 *See, e.g.*: 'A restorative justice agreement must be – (a) in writing; and (b) signed by each required participant in the conference' (*Crimes (Restorative Justice) Act* 2004 (ACT) s.52.(1) (Austl.)).

But there are problems with this solution. A victim can acknowledge that an apology was given and yet deny that they took it to be sincere, or that they accepted it or that they experienced forgiveness. Most victims are willing to acknowledge an apology in a minimal, courteous and almost automatic way. As Braithwaite and Stephen Mugford put it:

> Most English-speaking people find it normal to cancel grudges at the moment of a physical act of compensating wrongdoing by uttering the word 'sorry'. Faced with such an utterance, only unusual victims resist the imperative to return a word of forgiveness, to 'let bygones be bygones', or at least to show acceptance, thanks, or understanding. (1994: 154)

However, conforming to this social imperative is unlikely, on its own, to indicate the experience of forgiveness, especially when the wrongdoing is a serious crime. Likewise, the mere fact that a victim has signed the agreement is not sufficient evidence.

One might conclude that facilitators should report any verbal or non-verbal signs of forgiveness. But even if such a report were possible, it would clearly be detrimental from a restorative justice perspective. Suppose the victim was somehow made aware that their forgiveness of the offender would count as a criterion of success in any judicial review. It is easy to see how this knowledge would significantly distort the emotional dynamics of the process and place an unwelcome pressure upon the victim. As Martha Minow writes:

> Forgiveness is a power held by the victimized, not a right to be claimed. The ability to dispense, but also to withhold, forgiveness is an ennobling capacity and part of the dignity to be reclaimed by those who survive the wrongdoing. (1998: 17)

So here is the dilemma: If the principles of restorative justice are the priority, then it would be wrong to include the victim's forgiveness as a criterion of success. But if the court's assessment of the process is the priority, then whether or not the victim has displayed signs of forgiveness may be precisely the kind of substantive evidence that it needs. How else can the court decide whether the process did, in fact, produce the relevant mitigating factors?

4.7.1.4   Reporting issues
An Integrationist might argue that there is a way of avoiding the two horns of this dilemma, one that avoids all of the problems associated with reporting on the offender's level of remorse or the presence of forgiveness: the court should only be informed about the bare facts of who participated and the outcome. Wright and Masters, for instance, propose that, in cases where an agreement is not made, restorative justice facilitators:

should observe both neutrality and confidentiality, not judging whether either part was unreasonable, and telling the court only that agreement was not reached, without disclosing the content of the discussion. (2002: 57)

There are two problems with this approach. First, there is good reason to be sceptical about whether the judge will remain ignorant of the real reasons for the lack of agreement. Even if the facilitator maintains confidentiality, there are other informal ways in which such information might come to light, such as through attending police officers or social workers who are in regular contact with the judge. As Eliaerts and Dumortier found:

Within the Belgian experiment on family group conferences, ... the attendance of a social worker from the social youth services might be implemented. However, these social workers are often in close (informal) contact with the juvenile judge. (2002: 217)

Second, even if confidentiality could be protected, the very fact that the process failed to produce an agreement is likely to be interpreted as a negative outcome and may thus influence the judge's sentencing decisions. Hence, it would be unfair to withhold information that would be relevant. For example, the offender may have been willing to negotiate a reasonable and proportionate agreement, but the victim insisted that the offender carry out tasks that were excessive or demeaning. As Eliaerts and Dumortier argue:

[I]s it fair that information on the RJ process is not communicated to the judge in cases where the offender does co-operate entirely, but is being confronted by the victim's unwillingness to do the same? (2002: 217)

Or, again, the failure to produce a written agreement may have been the result of a victim being satisfied with the demonstration of remorse that took place in the meeting. No additional reparative tasks or commitments, in their eyes, were needed. In short, a judicial decision cannot be properly made merely on the grounds that no agreement was reached. Fairness requires that the reasons for that failure also be taken into account.

But how should this information be recorded? We have seen the problems that facilitators face, in terms of identifying and assessing intricate, subtle and yet highly significant elements of the interaction. Perhaps videos should be made of the proceeding so that the judiciary can assess the interaction for themselves. Given the weight that it might carry in terms of the offender's legal situation, this is not an unreasonable suggestion. There are indeed cases in which videos have been presented to the court as evidence of the offender's cooperation and contrition.[48] At the very least, a full transcript of the proceedings should be made available so as to enable the court to make an independent decision where necessary. This would serve as a more credible source of evidence than a facilitator's post hoc summary. The evaluators of one adult restorative justice pilot, for instance, mentioned 'one offender who felt that the conference report did not fully capture the conference' insofar as 'the contributions of the support person had not been given sufficient weight nor adequately reported'. And so it was suggested that 'the conference should be transcribed and the transcript made available to the sentencing magistrate' (Goldsmith et al., 2005: 20).

This approach would, however, need to overcome a number of practical obstacles. Very few judges or magistrates would have the time (or the inclination) to read a full transcript of a typical conference, even if it is made available to them with sufficient notice. In one English pilot, for instance, it was noted that such reports may not have an impact since judges fail to read them in any case. Sherman and Strang write:

> A survey of Crown Court judges … found that almost half of the judges to whom these reports had been sent could not recall having seen one. While judges may be flooded with paperwork in making sentencing decisions, it is also true that the delivery of paperwork to a judge's office does not guarantee that it will find its way, in time, into the case file. (2007: 42)

As Sherman and Strang go on to note, this issue raises a serious question about whether the rule of law can be maintained under such conditions:

> Since RJ has been accepted by the High Court in relation to the law of mitigating harm as a sentencing criterion, it would seem to be essential for counsel to make any RJ known to the court before sentencing. The fact that this does not always happen does not mean that RJ, per se, violates the rule of law. It does, however, raise one more item for a long list of matters that could be tidied up by a sustained institutional commitment to developing RJ as an enhancement to the rule of law. (2007: 42)

We have already seen how the use of restorative justice in an Integrationist framework is far more likely to dilute the rule of law than 'enhance' it, and here is just one further example. But what would happen if, as Sherman and Strang envisage, criminal justice priorities win this particular 'tug of war'? What would be the effect if there was a 'sustained institutional commitment' to ensure that the court received and reviewed a full transcript

---

48   For example, *see* the video 'Burning Bridges' (Wachtel & Mirsky, 2005).

or even a video recording of the process? From the perspective of restorative justice priorities, this would invariably have a considerable impact on how the dialogue is perceived by the participants. Scepticism as to the authenticity of what is said or how it is said by the offender would be omnipresent. As we have seen, guidance material routinely stipulates that there should be no compulsion or duress applied to any participant within the process itself. Yet with cameras rolling and microphones attached, how could participants not feel pressured to perform for the absent judge?

Perhaps, then, a summary report should be written up after the event by the presiding facilitator, after all. However, aside from the problems already identified, this would have an immediate impact on the facilitator's standing in the eyes of the participants. The facilitator would be seen as having the power to decide on the success or failure of the offender's participation. Their perspective on the process could directly influence the court's decision regarding prosecution or sentencing. But how might this affect the participants? Would not an offender – with an eye on their legal situation – be more guarded, circumspect and compliant, voicing only what they think the facilitator might want to hear, rather than their honest views and feelings? Any defence counsel who did not advise them to take such a precaution would surely be failing to meet their obligations towards the offender.

Offenders perhaps have less reason to be concerned than the victims. Facilitators naturally hope for a successful outcome to their casework. There is nothing intrinsically untoward about this. However, if restorative justice is linked to the legal process, then matters become more complicated. Facilitators will commonly have a value-base that is contrary to the punitive orientation that underpins the criminal justice system. They will therefore be even more strongly motivated to ensure that there is a successful outcome. In such a context, it would not be unreasonable to suspect that the facilitator's report might be biased in favour of the offender. In other words, there would be reason to question whether facilitators are prone to overlooking or softening any evidence that the offender was unsuitable or uncooperative, even if they did so unconsciously. The problem here is that facilitators might be entirely above board, scrupulously professional and objective in their assessments. But there is clearly a potential conflict of interest. So it is natural that both the victim and the judiciary will remain, to some degree, suspicious or at least cautious.

Ensuring that the facilitator's report is seen by the participants, and even signed off by them, may be a good legal solution. Yet, as Shapland et al. discovered after reviewing one pilot service, 'participants were not always sure what [the facilitator reports] contained or whether everything had been conveyed accurately' (2007: 4, 34).[49] Unsurprisingly, this

---

49 Cf. 'The participants do receive copies of the report, and while the sentencing process does formally provide an opportunity for an offender to make comments on or object to the report, it is not clear that offenders

lack of transparency was reported as one of the 'factors which tended to lead to dissatisfaction' in the restorative justice processes they evaluated:

> [Where] the victim or offender were unaware of the content of any reports that the scheme produced for criminal justice practitioners or were not shown such reports … [this] tended to cause suspicion about the scheme's objectives and some distrust of scheme personnel. (2007: 47)

But even if such reviews were routine, it remains the case that the facilitator's report entails a potential legal risk. And it is not difficult to see how this, on its own, might damage the quality of the restorative justice process, in terms of diminishing the participants' level of trust or sense of safety. This is not a position into which either facilitators or the participants should be placed.

In sum, this issue is yet another reason why the restorative justice process should be placed entirely outside the judicial system, as in the Parallelist model. On this alternative, the phenomena of forgiveness and remorse take their proper place as private matters. Participants need not fear or question how their slightest gestures or emotional displays will be interpreted by the facilitator or used in a court of law. There is no audience, no external arbiter of their sincerity and no critique of their performance. They can offer or withhold what seems honest and authentic to them, and to them alone.

4.7.2   Timescales

If a referral is made to restorative justice as a diversionary option, then the court will be waiting for the outcome of that process in order to make a decision. However, there are normally strict timescales within which the judiciary is required to come to a decision. Keeping to these timescales is a matter of fairness to all those involved, not to mention the practicalities of processing a large number of cases. However, these timescales place a restriction on the restorative justice process that is fundamentally at odds with its raison d'être.

The process of addressing personal harm, particularly for more serious cases, cannot be tied to a prescribed timetable. The offender may have so many personal and behavioural issues that, for the process to be maximally safe and effective, it requires a great deal more preparation than usual. Again, the victim may not be at a place in their journey of recovery where they feel it would be helpful to speak with the person who has caused them harm. But they might take up the opportunity to participate at a later date. If the focus of the

---

are aware that this opportunity exists' (Goldsmith et al., 2005: 20).

process is, as it should be, to address or repair harm, then the participants must be allowed to take whatever time or preparation suits their harm-related needs. Miller, for instance, highlights the importance of this feature in describing a post-sentence restorative justice programme based in Delaware:

> There is no set time for a victim to finish the preparatory process and meet the offender; facilitators recognize that every victim has different needs and follows a different timetable and path to get to the point of meeting the offender face to face. (2011: 174)

However, if restorative justice is shoehorned into timescales set down by the judicial system, then this primary objective will invariably be thwarted. To give one example, a referral order in the UK has a standard time frame of 20 days between the initial panel meeting and the sentence (Crawford & Newburn, 2003: 115). As Green notes, this 'suggests an administrative priority that does not sit well with a restorative process designed to be responsible to the needs and demands of victims'. As a consequence, 'the principles of restorative justice are diluted as they are absorbed into a criminal justice system that operates on a different set of priorities' (2007: 182).

Kirby and Jacobson provide a good illustration of this in their report of a scheme which, in an effort to be 'victim-led', had been contacting victims to offer them the possibility of restorative justice 'at or shortly after the point of charge, prior to any contact being made with the defendant'. The scheme's facilitators soon realised that this approach was 'potentially upsetting to victims who expressed an interest in RJ, but were not able to proceed with it' because the offender did not admit guilt, or was considered unsuitable or opted not to participate. So the scheme decided to revert to the usual practice of only contacting victims *after* the offender had been assessed as able and willing to proceed. As one facilitator put it, 'you cannot justify upsetting people in this way'. And yet, in the end, this practice was not implemented by the scheme because it might conflict with the time framework of the judicial system:

> [There were] concerns that it would lead to adjournments in cases that did not proceed to RJ on account of victims' unwillingness to participate, leading to unnecessary delays to the court process. (2015: 39-40)

An Integrationist might argue, in response to this issue, that setting down a window of time before the system escalates its responses will tend to concentrate the offender's mind, as well as provide a powerful incentive for them 'to co-operate with the process and accept responsibility for their crimes' (Sherman & Strang, 2007: 37).[50] But as we have seen, far from being an advantage, this threat constitutes one of the core problems with Integrationism. Their motives for participating will be dominated by legal self-interest, with negative consequences for all concerned. In sum, given that these judicial time constraints would be entirely absent from a Parallelist model, it would, in this respect, appear to be the optimal approach.

4.7.3   *Caseload pressures*

What would happen if the use of restorative justice within an Integrationist framework were to overtake traditional sentencing and become the dominant response to crime? The enormous increase in caseload, accompanied by inevitable resource constraints, would have two negative effects – both of which will be very familiar to professionals who work within the existing criminal justice system. Restorative justice would not only have to battle with the gravitational pull towards routinisation, but it would also be required to process cases within a highly restrictive timescale, simply to keep up with the number of referrals. As von Hirsch et al. ask:

> [W]ith large caseloads, will it be feasible to provide restorative hearings lasting between one to one-and-a-half hours? And if calendar pressures shrink the time available down to the ten to twenty minutes with which courts must make do, would that suffice for adequate restorative processes? (2003: 37)

This problem has already been experienced in restorative justice programmes that are required to process a large number of cases. Shapland et al., for instance, found that one restorative justice service did not usually show participants the facilitator's report for the following reason:

> [The service] felt that all parties needed to agree a report before it could be shown and time pressures did not always allow further contact after the report had been written and prior to the court hearing. (2007: 34)

Again, Tränkle reports a 'victim-offender mediation' case in which the mediator's high caseload meant that the time allocated to the meeting was so restricted that the participants were unable to come to any agreement.

---

50   The only downside Sherman and Strang mention is that 'the CJ officials with primary control of the case can use the deadlines to foreclose the possibility of RJ' (Sherman & Strang, 2007: 37).

> Considering that the whole process – including two preparatory meetings and one mediation session – took only 32 minutes, the working principle of process orientation has not been respected either. This is not only due to the mediator's interaction style, but also to the fact that the mediator is obliged to complete a high number of cases in a short time. Consequently, the participants do not get into the working principle of active and autonomous participation and the mediator is not successful in getting the participants involved in a communication process about the conflict and its aftermath. It is not a surprise that an agreement could not be reached. (2007: 405)

It is perhaps theoretically possible that the financial and staffing resources provided to both the criminal justice system and any diversionary restorative justice scheme might be so magnanimous that this kind of problem would never (or very rarely) eventuate. But given how most criminal justice systems struggle to keep on top of their own case work, starved of resources as they typically are, this utopian vision is unlikely to be taken seriously as an argument for expanding the diversionary use of restorative justice, let alone making it the dominant response to crime. Indeed, the caseload pressures placed on the legal system already play a significant role in restricting the number of cases that are referred to restorative justice. As Shapland et al. note:

> If magistrates thought that they might fall foul of criminal justice time targets for processing cases by adjourning a case for restorative justice, they tended not to adjourn but to pass sentence immediately. If they thought imprisonment might be merited, they tended to pass an immediate sentence rather than to see what the restorative justice outcome agreement might suggest. ... All of these are not actions which indicate animosity towards restorative justice – they were symptomatic of the managerial values which tend to dominate criminal justice, which are to get through the maximum number of cases as quickly as possible without breaching legal rules. (2011: 192)[51]

In sum, the procedural routinisation and restrictions required to fit in with these external pressures will only diminish the quality and effectiveness of restorative justice. These are all burdens that would be absent from the Parallelist model.[52]

---

51   Cf. '[P]rosecutors reported that restorative justice policies were challenging to implement given the pace and workload of their positions: "Slowing down the process is aching to a prosecutor who's got three, four, five hundred cases or more going on at a time"' (Sliva, Shaw & Han, 2020: 539).

52   In §5.3.1, I respond to the concern that mainstreaming Parallelism would also create caseload pressures.

4.7.4   Authority

In the Integrationist model, the role of all those involved in a restorative justice process, particularly that of the facilitator, must be conceived of in a way that takes account of the public interest. Duff presents a persuasive portrayal of the requirements this would entail:

> If victim and offender agree to [restorative justice], the court has a role both as protector of each party's rights (protecting each against exploitation or bullying), and as guardian of the public interest ... This role is best discharged by a court-appointed [facilitator], who can speak with the voice and authority of the law and of the polity whose law it is. (2003: 56)

In a number of jurisdictions, this approach is played out, in part, by the use of police officers as facilitators, the rationale for which is strikingly similar to Duff's.[53] Indeed, a substantial number of restorative justice programmes are organised and facilitated by the police, typically at the warning or cautioning stage. There are many stories of positive outcomes achieved in such programmes, and the arguments that follow are not intended to detract from these results. Nor is any disparagement intended with respect to the professional qualities and expertise of the police officers who facilitate restorative justice processes.

However, as various commentators have suggested, allowing the police to run or even attend restorative justice processes within an Integrationist context is deeply problematic. For instance, it gives them a largely unmonitored role in the delivery of a punitive sanction. As Blagg notes, restorative justice schemes for young offenders are 'giving police a very direct and overt (as opposed to simply indirect and covert) role in the deployment of punishments' (1997: 483). It also removes the ability of the court to examine the conduct of police and to exclude any evidence that was illegally or inappropriately obtained. As Roche argues:

> [B]y taking cases out of court where judges can scrutinize police conduct, [restorative justice] programmes remove a source of accountability over existing police discretion ... While judges or magistrates may exclude evidence and criticize police where scrutiny of their actions show that they have acted unlawfully or improperly, in practice this offers only a weak form of accountability, particularly when many (and in some countries, most)

---

53   In Mainland China, it appears that judges and prosecutors are taking on the facilitator's role, which, as Dennis Wong and Wendy Lui suggest, 'may lead to public concerns about the government's interference in managing disputes, as well as lack of impartiality during the conferencing process' (2019: 308).

> defendants end up pleading guilty. Nevertheless, some critics are concerned that any illegalities and improprieties are even less apparent when cases are dealt with by a restorative justice meeting. (2003: 40)

But the concern I wish to focus on here is the way in which the presence of police officers affects the quality of the restorative justice process itself. As might be expected, there is good evidence that police who act as facilitators or who attend as participants typically conduct quasi-criminal investigations, lecture and reprimand the offender for their actions, threaten them with punitive consequences should they fail to cooperate, and so on. For instance, Hoyle and Rosenblatt report a study which found that police officers dominated the discussion, often asking questions that 'took the form of judgmental statements or moral lectures'. They also 'saw instances of [police] facilitators reinvestigating the offense, seeking admissions to prior offending, and asking questions that appeared to be attempts to gather useful criminal intelligence' (2016: 42).[54]

Police officers who behave otherwise do so only by sticking slavishly to a prescribed script, or by momentarily taking off their police hat, which is often symbolically achieved by changing into civilian clothes. But when they do act in their police role, it is not difficult to see how their behaviour might transform the restorative justice process into a quite different proceeding. Just as the court environment is powerfully inhibiting, a restorative justice conference facilitated by a police officer – acting *as* a police officer – is not likely to be a place in which deep, honest and raw feelings come easily. Indeed, Daly has argued that, given what 'actually happens' in restorative processes, restorative justice should be thought of as a kind of punishment (2002: 59ff). But Daly based this view largely on the evidence gleaned from conferences in South Australia – all of which were attended by police officers. Case studies of these conferences suggest that they were, to a significant extent, punitive in orientation, just as one would expect. But what follows from this is not that restorative justice *as such* should be conceived of as a form of punishment but rather that the conferences Daly investigated, no doubt due to the presence of police officers coupled with an Integrationist framework, took on punitive objectives and motives.

This is not to suggest that police officers who act in these ways have somehow misunderstood or misused their role *as police officers*. Since the process is operating within an Integrationist framework, such behaviours, for the most part, are, in fact, consistent with their function as 'the voice and authority of the law'. But what this means is that when restorative justice processes are subject to public interest concerns and the rule of law – as they should be in an Integrationist framework – this is likely to diminish their quality and effectiveness from a restorative justice perspective.

---

54   Citing research from Young and Hoyle (2003).

It might be argued here that if policing as such were to become fully aligned with restorative values and objectives, then the behaviour described previously *would* be incompatible with the role of a police officer. Clamp, for instance, describes such a transformation as follows:

> Instead of viewing restorative justice as a *tool* for achieving the functions of policing (i.e. upholding and enforcing the law, promoting and preserving public order, protecting the public and preventing crimes), restorative policing should be perceived as an entirely different *framework* through which officers can develop an effective partnership *with* the community. Through such an approach, restorative policing can ultimately result in a way to transform the way we view crime, our responses to it and to reduce social distance. (2019: 188)

We can grant that this kind of change would almost certainly tone down some of the less-than-restorative police behaviours, such as dominating the conference. However, even the most 'restorative' police officer cannot simply put aside their duty to fulfil 'the functions of policing', or their position as 'the voice and authority of the law'. And this will invariably affect how they see their role as a facilitator and thus how they conduct themselves – as indeed it should. In any case, the participants would be very unlikely to forget that the facilitator is also a police officer and so wields the power and authority of the law. So no matter how the officer behaves, their presence alone cannot help but have an inhibiting effect on the process.

It might also be argued that the use of police officers as facilitators has been more effective in terms of victim attendance rates and recidivism. As Sherman and Strang, for instance, report:

> There is no evidence to suggest ... that [not using police-facilitators] can even attract substantial numbers of crime victims, let alone produce powerful reductions in offending or victim harm. The New Zealand system of social workers leading RJ conferences, for example, has a much lower victim attendance rate than the police-led programmes evaluated elsewhere (Maxwell and Morris, 1993). The best evidence for large-scale delivery of RJ, at present, is associated with police-organised and -led conferences. (2007: 24)

However, there are two problems with this response:[55]

1. The question at hand is whether Integrationism or Parallelism is optimal. Showing that, within the Integrationist model, the use of police officers as facilitators is more effective than non-police facilitators does not entail that this would also be true in a Parallelist setting. As I have suggested, within an Integrationist framework, the presence of some kind of legal authority or representation is entirely justified (see §4.3.1). So it would not be surprising if most victims preferred the legal safeguards and authoritative voice that a police officer could provide. Victims, in this context, will also understand that the restorative justice process is, in effect, a criminal justice disposal and that it is therefore likely to be the only chance they will have to ensure that their own legal rights and interests are protected and taken into account.

Similarly, they will be aware that any outcome agreement will be reviewed by the court, and so it would be reasonable for them to want a legal voice present to give them some guidance on whether the agreement is likely to breach the court's requirements. Of course, a police officer cannot provide legal representation, and so relying on their presence for legal protection and guidance is far from adequate. But it is at least a step up from nothing. By contrast, it is not at all clear why a victim would want a legal authority to attend, let alone facilitate, a process that takes place entirely outside the legal system.[56]

2. A victim's decision to attend occurs *prior* to the restorative justice process, and the offender's desistance from offending is *subsequent* to it. Hence, evidence of higher levels of victim attendance or lower recidivism rates tells us nothing about the extent to which the presence of a police officer affects *the process itself*. The mere fact that a victim has attended a conference – even if they claim to have been 'satisfied' with the outcome – hardly entails that the process was all that it could have been from a restorative justice perspective.

More precisely, to make a fair comparison between Integrationism and Parallelism, the evidence would need to measure the quality and effectiveness of the process in terms of its capacity to uphold restorative justice values and objectives, rather than criminal justice priorities. And I would submit, for the foregoing reasons, that, all else being equal, a restorative justice process that takes place within a Parallelist context and does not involve the presence of a legal authority – either as facilitator, support person or observer – is more likely to result in a higher score, when measured in this way, than the alternative.

---

55 This is not to suggest that Sherman and Strang are using (or would use) this evidence as an objection to the case I am making for the optimality of Parallelism.

56 It might be argued that the absence of police officers in a Parallelist setting could raise concerns for victims about their physical safety, especially if the crime involved severe violence or repeated victimisation. I address this issue in §5.1.3.

4.8   Inclusiveness

We have thus far discussed a number of factors that can prevent restorative justice from realising its full potential. Most of these obstacles have involved external procedures, legal requirements or institutional settings that make it considerably more difficult for restorative justice participants to engage or communicate in a way that is authentic and meaningful for them. But we have yet to look at the damage that can be caused by discrimination against actual or potential restorative justice participants. Individuals can, in the context of a restorative justice process, be stigmatised, demeaned, excluded and treated unfairly merely on account of their ethnicity, race, disability, gender, sexual orientation, poverty, mental health, educational background, old age[57] and so on. The question, in this context, is whether Integrationism or Parallelism is more likely to minimise and address discrimination and thus which of the two would be the optimal model in this respect.

4.8.1   *Institutional contagion*

It is important to be clear, from the outset, that neither Integrationism nor Parallelism can completely remove all traces of discrimination. Regardless of which model is used, every referral source, facilitator and participant will bring with them their own prejudices, ignorance and biases. Some of these will be overt and easy to detect, but many will be more subtle and insidious. This can be due to individuals who are adept at concealing their prejudices, perhaps even from themselves. But discrimination can also go unnoticed – or at least unchallenged – when it is commonly permitted within the institution to which a restorative justice service is attached. It is this latter kind of discrimination that is most relevant here.

It is difficult enough to ensure that the prejudices of individual participants or those within society at large do not inhibit or damage the process. But if restorative justice is situated within or linked to an institution that contains systemic or entrenched discriminatory attitudes or practices, then this will almost invariably infect the process – especially if the service is funded, managed, staffed or reviewed by that institution. The restorative justice facilitator and the participants can easily find themselves complicit in or subject to these institutionally embedded forms of prejudice and unequal treatment.

---

57   Hila Avieli, Tova Winterstein and Tali Gal make a compelling case for the view that eligible older adult victims may often be excluded from participating in restorative justice on the 'agist' grounds that 'older people are less able to withstand [such] processes than younger people', thus 'denying older adults the right to self-determination' (Avieli, Winterstein & Gal, 2021: 1456).

But if this is the case, then Integrationism, in this respect, faces a serious objection. Criminal justice systems are generally plagued by widespread and persistent forms of discrimination – and to an even higher degree than the societal culture in which they are located. Delgado writes about the American system, but his characterisation could be true of almost any other nation state:

> The criminal justice system, then, may be the lone institution in American society where formal values and practices are worse – more racist, more inegalitarian – than the informal ones that most citizens share. (2000: 772)

It might be supposed that the informality of a restorative justice process and its inclusion of ordinary citizens would give it sufficient distance from the system. Hence, even if the process was conducted within an Integrationist context, it should be able to challenge or at least mitigate any institutional discrimination with which it might have been infected. Indeed, there are many jurisdictions in which a member of a minority group is likely to be treated more respectfully and fairly in a diversionary restorative justice programme than in a court of law or a prison. As Delgado admits, 'members of stigmatized groups today are apt to receive harsher treatment from U.S. police, judges, and juries than they might get, with luck, at a mediation table' (2000: 772).

The problem, however, is that while such a result, in an Integrationist framework, is not impossible, the odds are not good. It is highly implausible to suppose that a 'bit player', such as restorative justice, could resist the prevailing discriminatory undercurrents of a criminal justice system, let alone turn the ship around.[58] As Mara Schiff puts it (and again, this could apply to almost any country),

> Given the nature of the United States' socially unjust, structurally violent criminal justice, juvenile justice and education enterprises, is it possible for restorative justice to survive and transform such systems to produce socially just results, or is restorative justice more likely to get compromised and co-opted by the overwhelming dominant cultural ethos (and corresponding power structures) of the organizations it seeks to transform? (2013: 156)

One of the obstacles faced by integrated restorative justice services is that they are more deeply embedded within the system than they might like to admit:

1. There are many ways in which a diversionary restorative justice programme cannot help but replicate – and thus reinforce – the kind of discrimination that routinely occurs

---

58　The source of this characterisation was the following statement: '[S]tates have generally decided to keep restorative justice at arm's length, as a bit player' (Shapland, 2003: 213).

within the criminal justice system. How likely is it that an offender will challenge the racial biases of a facilitator if that individual is a police officer or when they know that the facilitator will report back to the judge on the offender's level of cooperativeness and compliance? Or, again, a restorative justice service is generally not in a position to challenge the legal authorities – let alone refuse to take a referral – on the grounds that the arrest or the charges laid are contaminated by discrimination against a particular minority group. Even if the issue was raised in a conference, it is very likely that the facilitator would feel obliged to curtail the discussion. After all, in that context, the process is effectively a criminal justice disposal, and so its purpose is to apply the court's adjudicatory decisions, not to question them. Even if the facilitator permitted such a challenge, it would almost certainly fail to make it into the outcome agreement, given that it will be reviewed by the court.

2. In many jurisdictions, the legal authorities are typically drawn from the dominant or ruling class, while those subjected to the law are mostly from minority or disadvantaged groups. In such cases, the power imbalance and inequality are on the table for all to see. Tokenistic changes are sometimes made, but the disparity is rarely, if ever, rectified in a systemic way.[59]

Restorative justice, however, purports to offer a moral world that stands in opposition to precisely this kind of social injustice. So one might expect that integrated restorative justice services would do their utmost to avoid replicating these kinds of social-structural flaws. But such services are inherently dependent on the criminal justice system for their continued existence, whether for case referrals, operational funding, staff, legislative support or research evaluations. Hence, there is a significant pressure to avoid arousing any uneasiness or suspicion in the powers that be, the effect of which is very likely to be an unquestioning conformity with institutional norms. It is of little surprise, then, when Theo Gavrielides reports that:

> [I]n the search for evidence of race equality and equality within the restorative justice movement, practice and organisational structures, I found nothing but the same issues mirroring the fallacies of the current criminal justice system. Senior positions in restorative justice and organisational hierarchies … are far from being representative of those whose justice experience gets to be affected the most by inequality. (2022: 110)

---

59 To be clear, I am not arguing here that this kind of imbalance, even though stubbornly enduring, is a locked-in feature of the criminal justice system. A political movement with sufficient resources and democratic support could, in theory, radically transform how criminal justice is done – including by whom and to whom.

This might help to explain why there is evidence that offenders from disadvantaged backgrounds and racial minorities are less likely to be referred by judicial authorities to restorative justice – a practice in which the relevant services appear to have acquiesced. To give one example, Nancy Rodriguez's analysis of a juvenile justice database in Maricopa County, Arizona, found that '[b]oth black and Hispanic/Latino juveniles were less likely than were white offenders to be selected for placement in a restorative justice program' (2005: 119).

3. When discrimination occurs in an Integrationist context, there can be serious legal consequences. Researchers Roxana Willis and Carolyn Hoyle analysed a series of police-facilitated restorative justice conferences and found that offenders from socio-economically disadvantaged backgrounds tended to communicate or behave in ways that were more likely to be unfairly judged by both the victims and the facilitators as insincere or as indicating that they were more likely to reoffend. This kind of discrimination can easily place a disadvantaged offender at far more risk of 'disproportionate interventions'. For instance, victims who are sceptical about the offender's sincerity could insist on 'more onerous restorative justice reparation agreements' (2022: 133). This would be unfair in itself, but it also means that the agreement is less likely to be completed. But then it follows that a socio-economically disadvantaged offender is at greater risk of being assessed as 'uncooperative' by the court and thus of being prosecuted or receiving a sanction they would otherwise have avoided. As Chris Cunneen puts it:

> Those who are most marginalised as victims and offenders (such as those who are homeless, suffer mental illness or have intellectual disabilities, those with serious drug and alcohol problems – in other words, those who fill our courts and prisons on a daily basis) are least likely to engage in an articulate process designed to extract remorse and remedy an individual harm. (2010: 134)

So would a Parallelist model do any better? Once again, it is important to observe that Parallelism would not be immune from cultural or institutional pressures of various kinds. However, its independence from the criminal justice system is, in at least four respects, clearly an advantage:

1. Unlike Integrationism, it would not be constrained by or subject to such a formidable source of discrimination. For instance, it would be considerably easier for an offender to challenge the racial prejudices of a facilitator who is not reporting back to a judge. A conference could be regarded as a 'safe place' in which participants can feel free to call out any racialising assumptions or the discriminatory way in which the behaviour was dealt with by the state. The participants could even discuss whether the state had the moral standing to hold the offender accountable. As Howard and Pasternak note:

[A]n oppressed offender might fully accept that he has perpetrated a serious wrong without justification or excuse [and that he should be accountable to the victims]; and yet he may nevertheless deny that the state has the standing to call him to account for what he has done [on the grounds that it has subjected him to serious social injustices]. (2021: 2, 3)[60]

2. A Parallelist model would not be constrained by timescales, quotas, standardisation and other inflexible requirements imposed by criminal justice priorities. This would, in itself, make it considerably easier to ensure that all participants have an equal opportunity to achieve the full potential of restorative justice. For instance, it would be possible to take the time to re-imagine radically different ways of realising restorative justice values and objectives. This might involve negotiating carefully with all participants prior to initiating the process and then redesigning the procedures so as to meet their needs, enhance their ability to fully participate and safeguard the process from prejudice or discrimination. These preliminary discussions could be used to find ways of accommodating any participant with a disability, mental illness or substance misuse issues, or where participants have differing ethnic or socio-economic backgrounds, cultural and religious differences, communication concerns, differences in gender or sexual orientation, logistical obstacles or financial pressures that might prevent them from taking part, and so on.

To give one example, Jane Bolitho conducted research on a 'Victim Offender Conferencing' (VOC) post-sentence programme in Australia, focusing on whether participants with a disability were able to obtain 'fair access' to the process. She found that, in most cases (94%), adjustments were made that seemed to be 'consensual, specific and effective' (2019: 172). These adjustments included:

[T]he use of other professionals (primarily psychologists and psychiatrists) in the assessment, lead-up and actual VOC process, and extra time in the preparation of cases. … [S]trategies used in preparation (and the VOC) related to language, rehearsal, having contingency plans, spending more time developing trust and having behavioural contracts … [as well as providing participants with] education around what disability means … so that a genuine lack of knowledge or experience of disability does not cloud the process. (2019: 171, 172)[61]

---

60   Cf. '[W]here the state has failed to meet the basic needs of girls who break the law there is a compelling argument that the state does not have the right to intervene in their lives' (Hodgson, 2022: 199).

61   Bolitho notes that similar recommendations are made in Burnett and Thorsborne (2015), in relation to restorative practices for young people with special needs in a school setting.

Bolitho acknowledged, however, that such adjustments may not be 'routinely present' in diversionary restorative justice programmes, since they are often 'constrained by time, the use of less skilled/experienced facilitators and/or a lack of resources' (p. 173).

3. As we have seen (§3.2.3), restorative justice services in a Parallelist model are more likely to be aligned with, funded by and embedded within community organisations that are focused on upholding the rights and interests of the marginalised and the disadvantaged. This quite different set of dependencies is far more likely – even if not guaranteed – to result in an equitable distribution of power and status within their organisational structures.

4. The legal autonomy of a Parallelist model means that any discrimination against a victim or offender that does occur in a restorative justice process will not result in negative legal repercussions for that participant.

All of these are considerable advantages – not least in terms of enhancing the credibility of restorative justice itself. As Wood and Suzuki argue:

> RJ must ... contend with and be able to speak meaningfully in practice and theory to problems of bifurcated justice, particularly along racial, ethnic, and indigenous lines ... [I]ts viability and relevance as an 'alternative' justice practice [that is] predicated on the recognition and restoration of 'harms' will lessen if it continues to ignore the social stratification of justice ... in its own practices, in ways it can possibly confront these problems, and in ways in which it may be unwittingly reproducing these social relations. (2016: 164)

4.8.2   Potential for transformative justice

Restorative justice has often been criticised for assuming that 'justice' can be achieved simply by returning things to the way they were before the crime or wrongdoing.[62] For many victims and offenders, 'the way things were' was unjust to begin with. The victim might have been subject to a history of domestic violence and abuse from the same offender prior to the criminal charge. Or the offender may have been homeless, suffering from mental health issues and routinely charged for minor infractions that would have gone unnoticed had they not been from an ethnic minority. In such cases, merely restoring

---

62   Cf. '[T]he idea of restoring justice implied we had had justice, and lost it. In fact, distributive injustice abounds everywhere, and most offenders are, more than the average person is, victims of distributive injustice. Do we want to restore offenders to the marginalized, enraged, disempowered condition most were in just before the offence' (Morris, 2000: 19)? Again, 'For some Indigenous young people [in Australia] who live in communities characterised by high levels of economic and social disadvantage ... there are concerns to what these young people are being restored to' (Little, Stewart & Ryan, 2018: 4083).

participants to their pre-crime state could hardly result in a 'just' outcome. As Cunneen puts it:

> A critical question is whether restorative justice actually challenges the racializing practices of the criminal justice system or simply reconfirms the power of a bifurcated and discriminatory justice system. ... Is restorative justice about the restoration of the status quo complete with inequalities, with racism, sexism and exploitation? Or does it aspire to be *politically transformative*? (2002: 36, 37)

There is a good deal of truth to this concern, but clarity is important here. The primary and distinctive function of restorative justice is not to restore everything to its pre-crime state. This would be impossible in any case: what was done cannot be undone. Nor is its purpose to restore equality per se: no meeting or conference could, on its own, equalise the material or social-structural disparities between a victim and offender, for instance. The goal that a restorative justice process is primarily designed to achieve is the restoration of *moral* equality: that is, its primary remit is to repair the moral breach that has arisen between the victim and the offender as a result of the wrongdoing.

In committing the offence, the offender failed to acknowledge and respect the victim as having equal and intrinsic worth as a human being. The offender treated the victim as a mere means to their end, rather than as an end in themselves. The implicit message that was thereby communicated to the victim is that, in the eyes of the offender, they are 'inferior', 'worthless' or 'less than fully human'. Accepting responsibility, demonstrating remorse, offering an apology and making amends are, together, a way in which the offender can communicate to the victim that they no longer stand by these false and contemptible messages and that they now stand with the victim in denouncing the crime as wrong and inexcusable. They are, in other words, affirming the equal intrinsic worth of the victim. If the victim accepts the offender's remorse as sincere, then the moral breach that opened up between them as a result of this particular wrongdoing will have been repaired.[63] The fact that a restorative justice process is capable of facilitating the work of moral repair is precisely what makes it both unique and so immensely valuable to human society.

---

[63]   It is crucial to note the limitations of moral repair in a restorative justice context. First, restorative justice generally focuses on a particular offence. So it does not follow that the offender's moral slate has been *entirely* 'wiped clean'. There may be a host of other wrongs for which they have yet to take responsibility – even historical wrongs against the same victim. Second, moral repair is not identical to, nor does it automatically lead to interpersonal reconciliation. Moral equality can be restored without the victim and offender wanting or needing to enter into any further communication, or continue with any prior relationship. *See* Brookes (2019a, 2021a, 2021b).

Having said that, it does not follow that a restorative justice process is incapable of, let alone adverse to, addressing wider social justice issues – especially given that, in many cases, they will have a direct bearing on the process of authentic moral repair. In the following, I give two key examples of how restorative justice is inherently capable of being extended in this way, but I also show how this potential is likely to be thwarted in an Integrationist context.

1. Any restorative justice process, whether held in an Integrationist or a Parallelist framework, will be focused on behaviour that the criminal justice system has categorised as a 'crime'. Likewise, it will involve participants that the legal system has identified as 'the victim' and 'the offender' – but only if those who have been labelled in this way accept that these terms accurately reflect, even if only in part, the moral reality of what happened. The person who has been identified by the legal system as the 'victim' must self-identify as someone who was wrongfully harmed, and the person placed in the legal category of 'offender' must accept that they were responsible for causing that harm. Otherwise, they would not be eligible or willing to participate in a restorative justice process.

In other words, it is not (or should not be) the legal labels that matter in a restorative justice process but rather the participants' independently formed moral judgements and honest self-assessments. But this means that the participants are (or should be) free to challenge the discriminatory assumptions, the systemic biases and even the individualising or unfair characterisations of culpability and victimhood that might have been imposed or exacerbated by the criminal justice process. As Roger Matthews writes:

> [V]ictims and offenders [are] often presented as if they constitute two quite distinct groups. However, as criminologists are discovering there is a significant overlap between victims and offenders, with many of those who are victims today being offenders tomorrow and vice versa. (2006: 249)

Unfortunately, this kind of flexibility is not always encouraged or allowed. This is especially the case in an Integrationist context where the person designated as the 'offender' has a powerful legal incentive to ensure that the 'victim' is satisfied with the process. As Agnihotri and Veach put it:

> It is hard to conceive of a situation where a person facing a criminal conviction would participate in an RJ circle and feel free to point out how the behavior of the identified victim mitigates the defendant's own actions or may have even provoked the situation. ... The person designated as a victim is in a place of extreme protection and privilege in the court-based model. (2017: 434-444)

The impact of this kind of power imbalance can be highly detrimental. Jodie Hodgson, for instance, conducted research involving girls who took part in restorative justice in an Integrationist setting. She found that many were reluctant to be 'viewed solely as an offender', given the harm they had suffered themselves leading up to or within the same incident. And when their perspective was not heard or taken seriously, they felt victimised by the process itself.

> A number of the girls contested the circumstances surrounding the offence and contextualised their feelings of victimisation as resulting from being assaulted first or being provoked by the victim. Additionally, two of the girls conceptualised their experiences of participating in the RJ conference as leading to feelings of victimisation. (2022: 91)

As a result, the rigid 'victim-offender binary' imposed on them by the legal system, and then perpetuated by the restorative justice process served to 'subjugate' their own 'narratives' and 'their experiences of injustice and powerlessness' (2022: 93). Even if the girls had taken genuine responsibility for *their part* in what happened, it is hard to see how such a process could have resulted in authentic moral repair.

Yet this kind of 'subjugation' is not an inherent feature of restorative justice as such. But ensuring that it does not occur is likely to require a very different orientation and practice. For instance, participants will undoubtedly require more time to prepare for any meeting. They will need to be invited to consider the wider social and cultural issues that might help to explain or contextualise the harmful behaviour, without excusing it. They might reach out to include others in the process whose voice needs to be heard but who were excluded from the criminal justice process. They could then together search for ways to acknowledge and try to address the power imbalances, the social stratification, the contributions that each person made to what happened, the various harms that had occurred on all sides, the cultural differences, and the histories of injustice that they had each experienced, as well as those that they saw in the criminal justice system and in the community around them. But, once again, this kind of orientation is more likely when restorative justice is not employed in a diversionary context.

2. The vast majority of offenders are themselves victims of socio-economic injustices. And yet, because the primary focus of restorative justice is on addressing the harm caused to the victim, the offender's own experiences of oppression and injustice can be easily overlooked or dismissed as irrelevant. This kind of narrow focus can become even more glaring when the victim is from a more privileged background or social class. Gavrielides, for instance, reports an interview with one victim who stated:

> For me, as a White, middle class professional with two degrees, getting a poor, Black kid to say sorry, seems an insult to justice and the injury that was caused. (2022: 162-163)

But it is not inconceivable that a restorative justice process might involve a victim acknowledging and expressing remorse for their own contribution, however unintended, to the unjust social conditions experienced by the offender. As Howard and Pasternak argue:

> RJ is a *deliberative* forum, which means that the compromised standing of the victim is an issue that can be recognized and considered in thinking about the appropriate way to restore this rupture in the relationship. For example, the victim might be expected to express regret for being part of an unjust structure. (2021: 16)

Yet this kind of issue could only be raised and dealt with openly in the restorative justice process if it was held in a context that allowed and encouraged an unrestricted conversation about social-structural injustices. Such a process may take far longer than – and require a quite different format from – a typical restorative justice conference. It may involve drawing on the expertise and resources of grassroots organisations and programmes to help identify and address the social justice-related needs of participants. This could include financial assistance, housing, medical or therapeutic services, access to drug and alcohol programmes, and so on. These conversations and connections might in turn lead to the original participants initiating, joining up with or feeding their stories into community-based activities and movements that are focused on tackling social-structural issues at a more systemic or political level. As Anna Eriksson writes:

> Restorative justice can be a vehicle for transformative justice in situations where the processes of restorative justice are actively used not only to transform the relationship between participants, but also to change … the underlying structural injustices that often are the root causes of crime and broader conflicts. (2009: 320)[64]

---

64   Justin Smith, for instance, reports how 'formerly incarcerated people are engaging in advocacy and activism through helping others and civic engagement in political actions' in part as a pathway to 'redemption and destigmatization' (Smith, 2021: 60). The activities that Smith describes were not undertaken as a result of a dialogue with victims, but they illustrate the potential for this kind of outcome.

It is important to note here that it would be possible to apply this kind of wide-angle lens in both an Integrationist and a Parallelist context. However, it seems clear that this broader perspective, with all the concrete benefits it could generate, would be considerably more likely within a Parallelist framework. Restorative justice processes would be freed from the Integrationist shackles of court-dictated time constraints, the narrowly focused expectations of a judicial review, the cautionary advice of legal counsel, the Sword of Damocles threat, the need to comply with legislative requirements, the rigid procedural standardisations, and so on. These cannot help but place inhibiting and constrictive barriers around what can be discussed in a restorative justice process.

Zernova, for instance, gives empirical evidence of criminalised incidents which, in reality, had 'social-structural roots – classism, economic inequalities and social prejudices' – all of which were effectively 'neutralised' and 'expunged' in the restorative justice process. However, she goes on to argue that this kind of outcome is *more likely* to occur when restorative justice processes 'occur under the aegis of the criminal justice system and are facilitated by system-oriented practitioners' (2016: 108, 109).[65] Or again, as Hodgson found in her research on the experience of girls who participated in a diversionary restorative justice programme:

> [O]nly state defined harms and meanings of restoration become the focus of RJ. Therefore, the various layers of harm girls are subject to as a result of shame, stigma, processes of muting, discourses of ideal femininity, social control and the exercise of patriarchal state power are excluded from institutionalised RJ practice. … Not only does RJ conferencing intensify such harms girls are subject to, but they also make restoration incredibly difficult, if not impossible, to achieve. (2022: 196)

In sum, employing restorative justice as a diversionary option is likely to block or severely diminish its capacity to move beyond the immediate harm that was caused and begin to address the wider context – including the participants' lived experience of systemic discrimination or social-structural injustices. By contrast, a Parallelist model would not be thus inhibited and so would offer far more scope for restorative justice to become a 'politically transformative' process. To that extent, it is therefore more likely to achieve the full potential of restorative justice.[66]

---

65   Delgado reports a similar finding: 'No advocate of [victim-offender mediation], to my knowledge, suggests that the middle-class mediator, the victim, or society at large should feel shame or remorse over the conditions that led to the offender's predicament' (Delgado, 2000: 767).

66   I am not suggesting here that restorative justice is identical to what has been called 'transformative justice'. Addressing socio-economic needs or advocating for social-structural justice may not include working towards the goal of moral repair (for instance, in cases of domestic violence). Likewise, a restorative justice

4.9   SELF-DETERMINATION

In line with the work of many First Nations scholars and critics, this section will argue that whenever the Integrationist model is implemented in settler-colonialist nations – such as Australia, Canada, America and New Zealand – restorative justice will be complicit in an ongoing colonialist agenda to subjugate and assimilate First Nations peoples.

To be clear, First Nations peoples are also routinely discriminated against on the grounds of race, mental health issues, poverty, disability, and so on – almost all of which is causally connected to and amplified by the ongoing impact of colonialism. But the fact that situating restorative justice within an Integrationist framework cannot help but curtail and undermine the sovereign right of First Nations participants to self-determination is sufficient on its own to block a fully authentic and meaningful engagement in restorative justice.

Moreover, this is a locked-in structural feature of Integrationism. Restorative justice, even within an Integrationist context, is not *inherently* incapable of addressing and challenging prejudices and practices that discriminate against racial minorities, people with a disability, and the like. With sufficient political pressure from advocacy groups and human rights organisations, even the criminal justice system could, in theory, be reformed (or transformed) in this respect. Indeed, the possibility of such a change is one of the underlying premises of Parallelism. The criminal justice system will not be a fitting counterpart to restorative justice unless it is operating in accordance with the rule of law and due process, which means that it must be free from systemic discrimination and prejudice.

However, the problem of colonisation is of an entirely different order. Settler-colonialist states still claim to hold juridical authority over First Nations peoples, even though their sovereignty has never been ceded. But since, on Integrationism, restorative justice effectively functions as an extension of the criminal justice system, this model, when implemented in such states, cannot help but reinforce their colonialist agenda. By contrast, the Parallelist model, I will suggest, can be applied in such a way as to remove this kind of structurally embedded obstacle.

4.9.1   Circle sentencing

Over the past few decades, settler-colonial states have been attempting to establish justice mechanisms that are 'culturally appropriate' for First Nations peoples. The most commonly

---

process can still lead to some degree of moral repair even when the underlying social injustices are not addressed by the participants. Thus, on this account, restorative and transformative justice partially overlap, rather than coalesce. For a useful overview of transformative justice, *see* Nocella (2011).

stated rationale is to ensure that First Nations communities are not disadvantaged by a legal system that is culturally alienating and meaningless to them.[67] This move towards 'cultural accommodation', however, is generally regarded not (or not merely) as an end in itself but rather as a means of reducing the overrepresentation of First Nations peoples in the criminal justice system. As Val Napoleon and Hadley Friedland put it:

> [S]elect aspects of certain Indigenous legal traditions have been adopted as pan-Indigenous 'traditional' or 'culturally appropriate' responses to crime, and subsumed within specific parts of the states' criminal justice processes, almost always in the sentencing phase. ... In Canada, the argument for the inclusion of these select aspects is not a jurisdictional one. Rather, it is explicitly ameliorative, based first on the statistics on overrepresentation of Indigenous offenders and, secondly, on the premise that this overrepresentation is the result of cultural differences between Indigenous people and the rest of Canada. (2014: 234-235)[68]

In some cases, these governments have created specialist sentencing venues and procedures that are designed to be culturally meaningful and impactful to First Nations offenders, while remaining consistent with the mainstream legal framework and sentencing guidelines. Examples of this approach include 'Circle Sentencing' in both Canada and NSW (Australia) and in 'Koori Courts' in Victoria (Australia). In such cases, the sentencing venues will tend to include culturally significant symbols, such as First Nations flags and paintings, alongside the traditional icons of the justice system. The procedure will also involve the participation of elders or representatives from the relevant First Nations communities, along with legal representatives.[69]

However, as with any other court, it is the presiding judge or magistrate who holds ultimate power over the proceedings and its outcomes. As Heino Lilles, a Territorial Judge in Canada, explains:

---

67   Cf. 'The Koori Court Division must take steps to ensure that, so far as practicable, any proceeding before it is conducted in a way which it considers will make it comprehensible to – (a) the defendant; and (b) a family member of the defendant; and (c) any member of the Aboriginal community who is present in court' (*Magistrates' Court (Koori Court) Act* 2002 (Vic) s.6.5 (Austl.)).

68   Cf. 'Witness, for example, the dozen or so commissions of inquiry cited by the Department of Justice itself, all affirming that Indigenous people were ill-served by a foreign system and that there should be a place for Indigenous justice controlled by Indigenous peoples' (McGuire & Palys, 2020: 74).

69   For instance, the legislated 'objective' of the Koori Court is to ensure 'greater participation of the Aboriginal community in the sentencing process of the Magistrates' Court through the role to be played in that process by the Aboriginal elder or respected person and others' (*Magistrates' Court (Koori Court) Act* 2002 (Vic) s.1 (Austl.)).

> [C]ircle sentencing has not been authorized by statute but exists solely as a result of judicial discretion. Nevertheless, it is still a sentencing hearing and … [so] must conform to the rules of natural justice and other legal requirements imposed by statute or common law. (Lilles, 2002)

This means that the decisions made in a sentencing circle are subject to the judicial appeal process. Indeed, there are examples of such decisions being 'overturned' by the Courts of Appeal, even though the judges in question were 'following the suggestions of a circle' (Rudin, 2005: 98).[70]

The main role of the First Nations elders or representatives, then, is to hold an informal discussion with the offender so as to discover the underlying causes of their offending. This enables the participants collectively to identify and agree on effective solutions. These agreements are submitted as recommendations to the judge or magistrate, who may, if they concur, include them in the sentence.[71] As a consequence, many of the sentences are rehabilitative and reparative, rather than primarily punitive. Moreover, since the elders or representatives are usually held in esteem by the offender, they are also able to apply the techniques of 'reintegrative shaming', which can have an impact on the offender's desistance. As Bridget McAsey found in her study of Koori Courts in Victoria (Australia),

> [M]any [participants] speak of the role the Elders play in 'shaming' the Offender as being much more effective than a prison term. This is reflected in comments by Elders: 'when you look at them in [Koori] Court they know and they listen', and Offenders: 'one of the Elders was disgusted by my record and she had always thought highly of me … she didn't think I was this bad. It made me think' … Without stereotyping the nature of Aboriginal communities, it is arguable that a Koori community has the necessary characteristics for reintegrative shaming to be effective. (2005: 664, 665)

There is indeed some evidence that circle sentencing is comparatively effective in terms of reducing the rates of incarceration and recidivism among First Nations peoples. Steve Yeong and Elizabeth Moore's study of the NSW Circle Sentencing (Australia) programme found:

---

70 Rubin gives as an example: *R v. Morin 101 CCC* (3d) 124 (1995).
71 In NSW, the legislation that relates to circle sentencing states: 'The court that referred the offender may, if it agrees with the consensus of the circle sentencing group on the issue, impose a sentence on the offender in the terms recommended by the group following the conclusion of the circle' (*Criminal Procedure Amendment (Circle Sentencing Intervention Program) Regulation* 2003 (NSW) s.2.h (Austl.)).

> [O]ffenders participating in [Circle Sentencing] are 9.3 percentage points less likely to receive a prison sentence [or a reduction of 51.7 per cent relative to the incarceration rate for offenders who undergo a traditional sentence] … 3.9 percentage points less likely to reoffend (9.6% in relative terms) … [and they] take 55 days longer to reoffend when they do commit a new offence (a relative increase of 10.3%). (2020: 11)[72]

In some cases, victims and their support persons are invited to attend and participate in the circle discussions, so as to enable them, if they wish, to convey the impact of the offence on their lives.[73] One explicit aim of this is to increase the offender's awareness of how their actions have affected others.[74] Thus, the process is designed to restore some measure of social control over First Nations peoples, as well as repair the offender's relations with the victim, their family group and the First Nation's community. The possibility of some form of reparation is also not ruled out in the legislation.

Hence, it could be argued that the diversionary option of circle sentencing embodies many of the core values and objectives of restorative justice. And so it is often thought that circle sentencing is a way of using restorative justice to meet the cultural needs of First Nations peoples. However, this view faces a serious objection.

4.9.2   Deep colonising

Any government of a settler-colonialist state will be fully aware that the First Nations peoples did not cede their sovereignty, and never have. Their land and their right to self-determination as a people was acquired by conquest and theft, not by forming a legally binding treaty or social contract. This injustice is built into the foundations of every settler-colonial state. In May 2017, over 250 Aboriginal and Torres Strait Islander Delegates in Australia signed the 'Uluru Statement from the Heart', which calls for 'a new relationship between First Nations peoples and the Australian nation based on justice and self-determination'. The Statement includes the following:

---

72   The researchers acknowledge that 'selection bias may be responsible for our results' (p. 14). For instance, 'remorse and connectedness to the local community are explicitly considered … when assessing an offender's suitability [for Circle Sentencing] … [and] these factors are also likely to be associated with lower levels of recidivism' (Yeong & Moore, 2020: 11).

73   Such as the NSW Circle Sentencing programme: 'If a victim agrees to participate in a circle sentencing group, the victim must be given an opportunity to express his or her views about the offender and the nature of the offence committed against the victim' (*Criminal Procedure Amendment Regulation* 2003 (NSW) s.14 (Austl.)).

74   One objective of the NSW Circle Sentencing programme, for instance, is 'to increase the awareness of Aboriginal offenders of the consequences of their offences on their victims and the Aboriginal communities to which they belong' (*Criminal Procedure Amendment Regulation* 2003 (NSW) s.7.g (Austl.)).

> Our Aboriginal and Torres Strait Islander tribes were the first sovereign
> Nations of the Australian continent and its adjacent islands, and possessed it
> under our own laws and customs. … This sovereignty … has never been ceded
> or extinguished, and co-exists with the sovereignty of the Crown.
> (ulurustatement.org, 2022)[75]

Even where treaties were made, they have been ignored or reinterpreted so as to deny the
original and ongoing sovereignty of First Nations peoples. As Catherine Love, for instance,
writes:

> In the ongoing debates around the interpretation of the Treaty of Waitangi [in
> New Zealand] … Maori see the guarantee of tino rangatiratanga as [implying]
> absolute sovereign authority and, in effect, the status of independent nation
> states for hapu and iwi groups. … The Crown and non-Maori public tend to
> take the view that the Treaty of Waitangi effected a ceding of sovereignty by
> Maori to the Crown. (2002: 12)

But a settler-colonialist state cannot recognise and rectify this continuing wrong while at
the same time maintaining the rightfulness of its claim to sovereignty over the land it has
occupied and its rule over the people it has conquered. As Love puts it:

> The Crown is particularly averse to acknowledging more than one source of
> sovereignty in the land. The principle of a single source of sovereignty … is
> fundamental to the ongoing colonial endeavor. (2002: 12)

What this means is that any challenge to the single sovereignty of the colonialist state must
be crushed. To this end, brute force is essential, but it is not sufficient. A First Nations
people who maintain their own rightful sovereignty and thus aspire to autonomy and self-
determination will resist the colonial powers in whatever way they can. Hence, the ideal
goal, from the perspective of a colonial state, is to destroy their independent identity and
dignity, break their will and conform it to their own. First Nations peoples must come to
accept that their conquest and assimilation is 'for their own good' or at least that it is
'inevitable' and 'irrevocable'. They must come to think of themselves not as equals but

---

75   Cf. 'Our sovereignty was never surrendered to a Canadian state that has come to believe its own declaration
     of sovereignty superseded our rights, settled on our territories and imposed its systems of governance on
     those of us who have survived' (McGuire & Palys, 2020: 73).

rather as 'subjects of a colonial master' who has 'saved them from themselves'.[76] As Glen Coulthard, following Frantz Fanon, argues:

> [T]he long-term stability of a colonial system of governance relies as much on the 'internalization' of the forms of racist recognition imposed or bestowed on the Indigenous population by the colonial state and society as it does on brute force. In this sense, the longevity of a colonial social formation depends, to a significant degree, on its capacity to transform the colonized population into subjects of imperial rule. (2007: 443)

It follows that genuine decolonisation will not be effectively realised merely by enacting structural or institutional changes. First Nations peoples may acquire the right to become legal citizens, the right to vote and the right to due process in any legal matter. A settler-colonial state may even issue a formal recognition or acknowledgement of their status as a 'First Nations people'. But all of these changes, as significant as they might be, still keep in place and indeed reinforce the settler-colonial state's claim to be 'the rightful sovereign and ruler'.

First, such changes cannot simply be *claimed* or *asserted* by First Nations peoples. Instead, as Coulthard argues, they must be 'granted', 'sanctioned' or 'recognised' by the colonial state (2007: 442). Second, this collection of 'bestowed' rights and identities has little, if anything, to do with the customs or laws of First Nations peoples. They are 'defined solely in relation to the colonial state and its legal apparatus' (p. 452), and in ways that the state 'deems to be appropriate' (p. 450). But then it follows that such outward gestures towards decolonisation do not alter the 'background legal, political and economic framework of the colonial relationship itself' (p. 451). As Coulthard puts it:

> [O]ver the last 30 years the Supreme Court of Canada ... has secured an unprecedented degree of protection for certain 'cultural' practices within the state, [but] it has nonetheless repeatedly refused to challenge the racist origin of Canada's assumed sovereign authority over Indigenous peoples and their territories. (2007: 451)

No settler-colonial state would want to make this refusal explicit, even though it openly acknowledges that the continuing impact of colonisation lies at the heart of issues such as

---

76   Cf. '[C]olonialism is not simply content to impose its rule upon the present and the future of a dominated country. ... [I]t turns to the past of the oppressed people, and distorts, disfigures, and destroys it. ... The effect consciously sought by colonialism was to drive into the natives' heads the idea that if the settlers were to leave, they would at once fall back into barbarism, degradation, and bestiality' (Fanon, 1968: 211-212).

the overrepresentation of First Nations peoples in the criminal justice system. So, instead, the state engages in the more concealed strategy that Deborah Bird Rose has called 'deep colonising' (1996: 6). The ultimate goal is still to maintain its sole sovereignty by conquest and the elimination of any threat. But the methods it uses are buried underneath a kind of Orwellian 'doublethink'. Alison Whittaker has described this strategy as follows:

> These colonising practices manifest in instruments constructed to reverse the consequences of colonisation, reinforcing the consequences they would otherwise mitigate, all the while incentivising their adoption by Indigenous persons seeking racialised legal redress or relief. ... [They are ways of] turning Aboriginality upon itself to investigate itself through legal constructs disguised as decolonial methodologies. (2017: 11.)

In other words, no matter how 'culturally accommodating' a sentencing process might be, the fact that it remains integrated within – and so ultimately under the power of – the mainstream legal system will only reinforce the colonialist subjugation of First Nations peoples. As Blagg argues:

> [W]hile indigenous peoples may wish to develop alternative justice structures as a means of retrieving lost cultures and as an alternative to the dominant system's colonizing tendencies, ... [what is happening instead is] a process whereby elements of indigenous tradition are reconstructed to increase neo-colonial forms of control. (1997: 490)[77]

Even worse, it does so in a way that is underhanded and exploitative, using cultural practices and the good will and compassion of First Nations elders and representatives to perpetuate the colonialist agenda. As Michaela McGuire and Ted Palys put it:

> Sentencing circles are a prime example of this push [to assimilate First Nations people, but in a way that is more subtle and devious]. The colonial system will only accommodate or indigenize at a level that is convenient. (2020: 64)

It is for this reason that First Nations critics of circle sentencing, and the like, have argued that First Nations peoples must have independent legal authority over matters that concern them. This is the only way that their right to self-determination will be effectively realised.

---

77   Cf. 'The lack of statutory authority for indigenous decision-making has allowed tokenism to flourish. Indeed, some of the changes, while represented as an increase in indigenous community involvement, may represent further extensions of state power into indigenous communities' (Cunneen, 2002: 45).

First Nations peoples should, in other words, reclaim their statutory authority to deal with 'criminal offences' that directly involve members of their own community. As Mattias Ahren states in relation to the Saami people:

> An integral part of the right to self-determination is the right to have their own legal system recognized and applied, because legal norms constitute a central part of the system through which a people govern its society. ... Acceptance of the Saami people's customary legal system [as equal to the non-Saami legal system] is an essential element in finally adequately addressing Saami's colonial past, and putting an end to cultural hierarchy policies. (2004: 108, 109)[78]

To be clear, the strategy of deep colonising does not depend on the presence of state officials who hold discriminatory attitudes. It does not even rely on systemic prejudice. The initiative to include circle sentencing as a diversionary option may arise from the best of intentions and a transparent commitment to racial equality. However, the project of colonisation is in the DNA of a settler state. Defending its sovereignty – especially over the claims of First Nations peoples – is built into its very nature. State officials may be trying to soften the blow or blur the edges in good faith, and it would be hard to deny that some of these efforts have been marginally better than traditional criminal justice processes. But these innovations remain an integral part of the colonial state's judicial system and so cannot help but reinforce its claim to be the sole sovereign authority.

This is not to suggest that state officials bear no moral accountability for the situation. It is hardly a secret that the historic and ongoing failure to recognise the sovereignty of First Nations peoples or their right to self-determination is the primary cause of their overrepresentation in the criminal justice system, among many other social injustices and disadvantages. Jonathan Rudin, for instance, writes that in 1996 a Canadian Royal Commission 'concluded that Aboriginal nations currently have the constitutional right to establish and administer their own distinct justice systems'. And yet 'there have been no significant steps taken, to date, to vest control over justice matters in any comprehensive manner to any Aboriginal community or nation' (2005: 96).

Nor is there any suggestion here that state officials who engage with First Nations peoples are *always* acting in good faith. To give one illustration, the First Nations Canadian lawyer Bruce McIvor describes how he was in a café preparing for a Treaty 3 meeting between his First Nation clients and government officials. He happened to be seated close

---

78   Cf. 'If the justice programme is not rooted in the community and if the individuals the programme is meant to serve do not take away from the process that the Aboriginal community is directing the enterprise, then the colonial message that Aboriginal people are not capable of determining their own lives is reinforced' (Rudin, 2005: 96).

to the officials who were also preparing and overheard their conversation. They were, he writes, 'rehearsing the various ways they intend to say no to my clients'. They were also laughing:

> Laughing at their own well worn obstructionist tactics. Laughing at my clients' positions and expectations. Laughing at the ultimate meaninglessness of the consultation process they [had] invited my clients to join. (2018: 150)

McIvor then concludes:

> [U]ntil Indigenous people are confident that the bureaucrats they meet on a daily basis sincerely believe that their responsibility is to work with, not against, Indigenous people, none of us will be free of Canada's colonial past. (2018: 151)

4.9.3   Conferencing

We have looked at how settler-colonial states have been attempting to create 'culturally appropriate' sentencing venues and procedures as a diversionary option, most of which appear to have a restorative justice orientation. But these states have also been trying to put in place 'culturally appropriate' forms of restorative justice that take place outside of a sentencing hearing and that typically involve a standardised conferencing format. These diversionary schemes are, once again, usually advanced as a solution to the disadvantage and overrepresentation of First Nations peoples by increasing the scope of their decision-making power in relation to justice matters. For example, the Children's Commissioner in New Zealand states:

> The [Family Group Conference] is a legislative model designed to delegate state decision-making to whānau and encourage the involvement of hapū and iwi to collectively make decisions for their own children and young people. (2017: 25)

At first glance, one might think that this kind of diversionary option could indeed be a viable alternative to circle sentencing. After all, it is at least somewhat further removed from state control. A conference can influence a judge's subsequent decision, but the process is not itself a sentencing hearing. The judge does not attend or preside over the conference. And any agreement is not legally equivalent to a sentence, since it must first be reviewed and ratified by the court. So there is considerably more space for the participants to discuss the matter in ways that will suit their cultural needs. Moreover, as almost every introduction to restorative justice will claim, the conferencing format has a communitarian orientation that can be traced back to the conflict resolution procedures originally used by traditional First Nation cultures. Hence, 'cultural accommodation' is, as it were, virtually built into this restorative justice practice.

As might be anticipated, there are serious problems with these claims. Take the 'origins story', for instance. This was no doubt intended, at some level, to lend credibility to the newly emerging 'restorative justice' brand, and to conferencing in particular. If this practice could be promoted as having an ancient pedigree, then it might be more widely accepted as a universally effective justice mechanism. But it also meant that conferencing could be more effectively sold to settler-colonial states as a way of addressing the overrepresentation of First Nations peoples in their criminal justice systems. As Paora Moyle and Juan Tauri argue:

> [O]ne of the key marketing strategies deployed by the restorative justice industry and policy entrepreneurs, especially in settler colonial contexts, is the persistent, mythological representation of key interventions like the [family group conference] forum as founded on Indigenous cultural principles and practices. (2016: 89)

While there may be aspects of conferencing that were derived from or inspired by First Nations traditions, this standardised format was developed only a few decades ago by Western non-Indigenous practitioners for the specific purpose of providing criminal justice systems with an alternative method of 'crime-handling'. As Tauri puts it, conferencing is a largely 'Eurocentric' justice process that employs 'fragments of Indigenous cultural practice, but does little to empower us' (2015: 187).

In other words, this is yet another instance of the colonialist state explicitly claiming to offer a decolonised justice mechanism that devolves decision-making power to First Nations peoples. But it is, in fact, using these mechanisms as a means of reinforcing the state's sovereignty over their lives. We have seen how circle sentencing applies this kind of 'deep colonising' strategy, but it is even more flagrant in the use of conferencing as a diversionary option. To demonstrate this, I will set out four ways in which this sleight of hand works:

1. We have already mentioned how the 'origins story' of conferencing influenced colonialist governments to use this practice as a way of countering the problem of overrepresentation. As a consequence, however, when diversionary conferencing schemes were set up, governments mandated the use of these standardised practices across the board, as if they would be automatically and universally fit for purpose. But this decision

was clearly made with little, if any, regard for the highly varied cultural needs and traditions of distinctive First Nations communities. As Cunneen puts it:

> [I]ndigenous processes for maintaining social order and resolving disputes are diverse and complex. The United Nations estimates there are 300 million indigenous peoples globally, living in 70 nations spread over all continents. One might think that this basic fact should caution against claims of universalism made about indigenous restorative justice practices. (2010: 115)

Thus, a First Nations process for addressing social harm might embody many of the same restorative justice values and objectives that can be found in conferencing. Yet it will do so in a way that involves quite different conceptual categories, belief systems, procedures, rituals, terminologies, as well as a set of goals that extend beyond moral repair. Hence, when the state sets up a diversionary programme that demands, in legislation no less, the exclusive use of conferencing, this will automatically undermine a First Nations community's capacity to realise the values and objectives of restorative justice in their own way, assuming that is the approach they wish to employ. As Roach argues:

> A procedural definition of restorative justice that requires facilitated meetings between offenders and victims may … inhibit the ability of Aboriginal communities to decide for themselves the most appropriate means to deal with crime and could frustrate initiatives that could achieve positive outcomes for offenders and perhaps for victims and communities. (2006: 182)[79]

By way of an example, there are likely to be key differences in how the work of moral repair is carried out or demonstrated in any particular First Nations community. We have seen how the offer of a verbal or written apology is widely regarded as central in standard restorative justice processes. However, as Love writes:

> There are no words in Maori language that equate to the English language expressions, 'sorry' or 'thank you'. Rather it is practical demonstrations of reciprocity, rebalancing and processes of restoration across a number of dimensions that rule Maori processes. (2002: 47, n. 52)

---

79   Cf. '[E]quating restorative justice with victim-offender reconciliation does a great disservice to the range and scope of restorative justice programmes, particularly in [Canadian] Aboriginal communities' (Rudin, 2005: 109).

Again, there may be First Nations belief systems, customs or traditions that are intrinsic to how they conceive of restorative justice values and objectives. They are not an optional extra that can be added if and when there is sufficient time or resources. Yet a key reason why the standardised conferencing format has been so widely endorsed by liberal states is undoubtedly that it does *not* embody a conception of the good that is specific to any particular cultural group or religion (see §4.4.2). This would help to explain why the so-called 'culturally appropriate' qualities of conferencing are largely unrecognisable as such by First Nations communities. Restorative justice services may – if they have access to more resources than usual – try to embellish the standard format with more culturally specific elements. But, as Reza Barmaki argues, the results are rarely sufficient:

> [T]he religious beliefs of Canada's Aboriginal people is basic to their understanding of RJ. As such, their view of RJ is fundamentally incompatible with western approaches, which are essentially secular. (2021: 25)

Shelly McGrath likewise reports on how the standardised conferencing format deployed and 'endorsed' by the state was 'absolutely' incompatible with the culture, customs and traditions of Stó:lō peoples:

> [I]n 1999, Stó:lō criminologist Dr. Wenona Victor was hired to facilitate the government-endorsed 'alternative justice' programs, but after three days of training for Family Group Conferencing, Victor concluded 'there was absolutely nothing Indigenous about this model of justice whatsoever' ... Instead, guided by Stó:lō Elders, Victor began to develop a new program that would be based on three guiding principles: Stó:lō culture, customs and traditions; Stó:lō communities; and Stó:lō people ... The result was the Stó:lō First Nation *Qwi:qwelstóm Justice Program* (Qwi:qwelstóm), a self-determining framework that continues to support Stó:lō communities in Canada today. (2020: 7-8, referencing Palys & Victor, 2008: 17)

2. Whenever restorative justice is implemented as a diversionary option, it must be compatible with pre-existing legal categories and normative assumptions. For instance, the process will need to separate out the status of participants: there must be at least one individual who falls into the legal category of 'offender', and this individual must self-identify as the person who was responsible for causing harm to one or more other individuals, namely those who are legally classified as the 'victims'.

However, many critics have argued that First Nations peoples do not experience or conceptualise either the nature of self, the locus of responsibility or the impact of harmful behaviour in this way. For instance, Andrew Becroft, the Children's Commissioner in New Zealand, writes:

> Māori custom and law is based on the idea of collective rather than individual responsibility. Alleged offending by a child or young person therefore requires a collective response, as it is seen as a collective problem. (2017: B)[80]

And, as Blagg writes, this has significant implications for how the term 'restorative' is understood:

> [T]he dominant reading is one of *restoring* relations between victims and offenders, while the contrapuntal reading is one of *restoring* Maori systems of social control and restoring the child to its *whānau*. (1997: 484, n. 6)

It might be thought that the communitarian nature of conferencing would alleviate this kind of individualisation. However, within a diversionary context, there will always be a tension between the collectivist lens of a conference and the individualising lens of the legal system. The participants will be fully aware of the legal context. The court has decided that diverting the case to restorative justice is likely to be the best way of holding the 'offender' individually responsible. They also know that any agreement they come up with will be assessed by the court on this basis. This context cannot help but affect how the conference participants perceive the aim of the process and the extent to which they feel that they can (or should) retain a sense of collective responsibility.

3. In an Integrationist context, the training of facilitators and the management and regulation of how conferences are delivered will typically be carried out under the auspices of a government agency, using facilitators that are employees of the state and often holding the meetings in government venues.[81] John Boersig, writing about the NSW context in Australia, observes:

---

80 Catherine Love articulates this perspective in more detail: 'Maori conceptions of self may be described as 'ensembled' ... [That is]: a fluid self-other boundary (maintaining distinctions between self and other is not vital to identity), an inclusive definition of self (the region defined as self may include a number of people, living and dead, and elements of the environment), and a field control orientation (power and control are located in a field of influences that may include but are not confined to self). ... This position accommodates perspectives based on notions of shared (group) responsibility and accountability, and the indivisibility of self from whanau, hapu, and iwi that characterizes Maori views, systems and processes' (2002: 17-18). Cf. 'What it is to be a "victim" or an "offender" is often understood as uncomplicated and homogeneous categories of self. There are no ontological complexities and the globalizing assumption is that we all subjectively experience these categories in identical or, at least, similar ways' (Cunneen, 2002: 34).

81 *See, e.g.*: '[S]ome years ago, up to 70% of youth justice FGCs were held in CYF offices, which was certainly not the original intention: use of community, not government venues was the goal' (Becroft, 2017: D).

[N]o solution [to Indigenous overrepresentation] offered by the state ultimately countenances the handing over of the state's authority and power. All solutions remain tied to the field of state governance as articulated, for example, in juvenile justice policy that promotes indigenisation of state bureaucracy and diversion systems (such as youth conferencing). (2005: 123)

Even where the facilitators themselves are members of a First Nations community, they are still bound by statutory requirements and must conform to government standards and objectives. They are effectively functioning as an extended arm of the colonial state.[82] As Love notes:

Maori workers are employed for their Maori knowledge and standing, but pressured into conforming to institutional mores that are in conflict with tikanga Maori. ... This position also leaves Maori workers exposed to being individually demonized and labeled by institutional representatives as incompetent or unprofessional, if we do not conform to institutional mores. On the other hand, Maori workers perceived as conforming to the norms within statutory welfare systems may be viewed by their whanau, hapu, iwi and communities as brown faces doing the dirty work that was previously done by white social workers. (2002: 31)

These factors cannot help but have a cultural impact on the conferencing process, as well as how it is perceived by First Nations participants. Research into the Family Group Conferencing programme in New Zealand by Moyle (2013, 2014) and Moyle and Tauri (2016) has shown that 'practitioners and participants alike, expressed disquiet at what they often described as a tokenistic approach to Māori cultural philosophy and practice'. One participant stated:

The family group conference is about as restorative as it is culturally sensitive ... [I]n the same way Pakeha [European] social workers believe they are competent enough to work with our people ... Pakeha think they're the natural ordinary community against which all other ethnicities are measured. (Tauri, 2019: 352)

Again, a review by the Children's Commissioner in New Zealand found that some 'facilitators did not believe in or practice whānau-led decision-making' (Office of the Children's Commissioner, 2017: 7).

82   Cf. '[T]he power of facilitators [in a diversionary context] ... [is] used to reinforce the authority of criminal law and to promote the agenda and values of the criminal justice system' (Zernova, 2016: 122).

It might be argued, as Tauri once suggested, that, if a 'full set of Maori designed standards' for restorative justice processes was created 'separate from the state's standardisation process', then, if these standards were applied within New Zealand's Integrationist framework, the result would be significantly better than persisting with the pre-existing 'Eurocentric' standards. This might be true. However, this approach would not avoid the multiple problems associated with trying to operate under the governance of a colonialist state. Indeed, Tauri was himself sceptical of whether such an alternative would succeed, for this same reason:

> [F]or this process to have meaning, state officials will have to be both willing and capable of engaging respectfully with Maori. In my experience, this will require a significant change in attitude and engagement methodology on the part of state officials. (2009: 18)

In other words, a restorative justice process which has been specifically designed by a First Nations community is not sufficient. It must, as Boersig puts it, also be 'an initiative embraced and controlled by Indigenous people' (2005: 127).

4. As we have already seen, restorative justice processes within an Integrationist framework are constrained by the priorities of the criminal justice system. This includes ensuring that the process is completed before the court is scheduled to review the outcomes. We have also seen how this impacts on the quality and effectiveness of the process in terms of the values and objectives of restorative justice (§4.7.2). But the same issue also affects the capacity of restorative justice to include culturally essential practices.[83] Moyle and Tauri's study of participants in New Zealand's FGC programme gives an example of an interviewee who stated:

> For me the FGC process does not begin until we've had our *whakamoemiti* [words of praise] ... for us (Māori), it would not be appropriate to do so ... But often the rush of the FGC diminishes the importance of the *karakia* [prayer] and other *tikanga* [rules of proper conduct] processes ... I've heard some *whānau* say no to the *karakia* because they know it is unappreciated. (Moyle & Tauri, 2016: 98)

---

83 This issue, among others, appears to have led to a decrease in the use of circle sentencing in Canadian Courts: 'A sentencing that might be done in 10 to 20 minutes if done in the traditional court manner might take half a day or longer if done through a sentencing circle. Although the result of the process may well be better for all, institutional pressures, particularly in busy urban courts or in remote fly-in courts where the court party might arrive for a day every two or three months, make reliance on sentencing circles problematic' (Rudin, 2005: 98).

Compressed timescales also have an effect on whether family networks and significant community members are able to be identified and invited – both of which are essential from a First Nations perspective. The Children's Commissioner's review in New Zealand states:

> Without hapū and iwi involvement [in the decision-making], FGCs too easily revert to a process involving minimal family, often only a mother in the case of youth justice FGCs, with a majority of those attending being officials employed by the state. (2017: 25)

And yet the Commissioner's review found:

> [A]t the two youth justice sites, hui-a-whānau and whakapapa searching were not being used at all. [We know from national office that this is the case for most other youth justice sites.] This is partially due to the short timeframes, given in s249 of the Oranga Tamariki Act 1989, for completing youth justice FGC. (2017: 7, 15)

The Commissioner then offers a solution that appears to take advantage of a loophole in the existing legislation: 'youth justice coordinators [could] use s249(6) … more frequently. This allows for extension of the [statutory] timeframes where there are special reasons' (2017: 16). However, even here, the inclusion of an essential cultural practice is only permitted if it is consistent with the legislative framework. Hence, this solution only confirms the way that the state's interests are prioritised over the cultural needs of First Nations peoples. To use the words of the Commissioner, 'Little wonder then, that some critics of the FGC practice in recent years have described it as yet another instrument, although undoubtedly well intentioned, of colonisation' (2017: 25).[84]

There is a second example of the way that legal demands will take precedence over the needs and interests of First Nations peoples. Within the Integrationist model, any restorative justice agreement must be reviewed and accepted by the presiding judge or magistrate. And, as we have seen (§4.2), these authorities, given their circumscribed remit, will tend to reject any items in an agreement that are incompatible with the punitive calculus of established sentencing guidelines, even if they might be of personal or cultural significance to the participants. Indeed, there is some evidence that the more an agreement arises from a culturally authentic process and includes cultural elements, the less likely it is to be accepted.

---

84   The Commissioner makes this reflection in the context of critiquing the absence of *whānau*, *hapū* and *iwi* involvement in FGC decision-making.

> It is ironic that the format of family group conferences in Manitoba that, perhaps, most faithfully replicated indigenous cultural practice of the Ojibwa had a very low rate of acceptance by the courts for their recommendations. (Maxwell, 2008: 87)[85]

In sum, the situation is this: Over the past few decades, settler-colonialist states – such as Canada, the USA, Australia and New Zealand – have created diversionary restorative justice options such as circle sentencing and conferencing. These schemes have, in part, been justified as 'culturally appropriate' or 'decolonised' justice mechanisms that will help to address the overrepresentation of First Nations peoples in the criminal justice system. While many of those responsible for enacting these programmes may have had the best of intentions, the underlying strategy is in fact a vivid example of how settler states perpetuate the colonialist agenda. And now that the term 'restorative justice' has become virtually synonymous with the Integrationist model, it is entirely understandable that restorative justice per se should be so frequently critiqued for its collusion with the colonialist project. For example, McGuire and Palys state, without qualification:

> RJ is a colonial conception that operates to continue the assimilative goals of the state. ... Regardless of their intentions, RJ practitioners undermine the possibility for sovereign Indigenous justice. Colonial control is imminent within all RJ initiatives. (2020: 67, 68)

4.9.4 A Parallelist alternative

I have argued that the Integrationist model has not been able to ensure that restorative justice can reach its full potential in relation to meeting the needs of First Nations peoples. Circle sentencing is just as likely to fall short as conferencing schemes. And this is primarily because Integrationism cannot avoid being complicit in the state's colonialist agenda. To be clear, I am not claiming here that circle sentencing or a conferencing programme would be *no better* than the mainstream approach in this respect. As Schiff and Bazemore argue:

> While restorative community justice is far from having achieved perfection at working with and inviting the full and equal participation of indigenous and other populations or protecting the rights of such groups, it would be hard to

---

85   Maxwell's source for this finding states: 'The courts largely ignored the families' recommendations regarding cultural components, community service, and other programs' (Longclaws et al., 1996: 195).

defend traditional criminal and juvenile justice practices on the same basis.
(2015: 325)

However, the fact that the Integrationist use of restorative justice compares favourably with – or is at least no worse than – the traditional system does not entail that this is the *best* that restorative justice can offer.

But could a Parallelist model do any better? After all, the way that I have presented Parallelism so far would suggest that it, too, would be locked into the existing criminal justice system. Parallelism is not a Substitutionist approach, so it would not, even in principle, implement restorative justice as a replacement for any criminal justice system, even one that is run by a colonialist state. Again, suppose that a Parallelist restorative justice service was set up alongside the criminal justice system. Even if this service provided the flexibility for a First Nations community to design a process that would meet their cultural needs, this would not be sufficient on its own. As we have seen, the service would also need to be owned and delivered by that community. Likewise, it might be thought that, since a fully complete Parallelist model would require significant changes to the criminal justice system, this could entail the wider use of 'culturally appropriate' justice mechanisms, such as specialist courts or circle sentencing. But, again, as we have seen, these approaches ultimately reinforce the colonialist agenda.

There is, however, a quite different Parallelist approach available. To begin with, Parallelism does not entail that there must be only *one* extralegal restorative justice service, even within the same jurisdiction or geographical location. Nor does it entail that such services would deliver restorative justice in the same way, using the same standardised formats. Again, a service need not deliver only restorative justice processes. It might deliver a range of other approaches in response to social harm and only use a restorative justice process as and when needed. Or the kind of processes that it employs to address a 'crime' might include moral repair as only one of many other goals.

What this means is that a First Nations community could – even in the present situation – establish a service of their own that offers legally independent processes for dealing with (what the colonialist state has categorised as) 'crimes' and other community-identified social harms. These extralegal processes may not (or not always) include the central restorative justice objective of enabling those responsible and those who have been harmed to engage in a safe and voluntary dialogue for the purpose of working towards moral repair. But if and when they do, then this First Nations service could be regarded as taking a Parallelist approach to implementing 'restorative justice'. (I use scare quotes here to indicate that such a service might use alternative terminologies, concepts, belief systems, practices and goals that include but extend beyond moral repair).

This approach could potentially resolve most of the issues that plague the diversionary use of restorative justice with First Nations peoples. For instance, an independent First

Nations 'restorative justice' service would be free to design processes that do not conform to state-mandated practices, such as conferencing. The participants would be free to think, act and talk about what happened in a way that reflects a collectivist orientation. The service itself would be entirely owned, delivered and governed by the First Nations community. The participants would not be required to use any pre-existing state-based restorative justice service, its facilitators or venues, any state-approved training, practice guidance or accreditation. The service would not be constrained by statutory time frames and caseload pressures, and so any process could, if adequately resourced, take whatever time is necessary to ensure that the needs and interests of all participants are met. Finally, there would be no justification for the interference, regulation, authorisation or oversight by any instrument of the state. The nature of the process and its outcomes would be entirely independent and self-determined. In other words, it would fall outside the reach of the colonialist agenda and so would be far more likely to make available to First Nations people the full potential of 'restorative justice'. As Rudin, writing about the Canadian context, puts it:

> The impacts of colonialism cannot be remedied by having non-Aboriginal organisations, whether they be government or non-governmental organisations, tell Aboriginal people what they can and cannot do; that process, however well meaning, just perpetuates the colonial experience. ... In order for justice programmes in Aboriginal communities to be successful, Aboriginal people must control the alternative justice processes. (2005: 95, 109)

There is an important caveat to this suggestion. Creating a legally independent First Nations 'restorative justice' service is not yet the full-blown Parallelist model. It must also have, as its counterpart, a criminal justice system that is operating in accordance with the rule of law and due process. The problem here is that even if the existing criminal justice system was fulfilling this role to perfection, it would still be run by the colonialist state. Hence, it could not serve as a *fitting* counterpart for an independent First Nations 'restorative justice' service. The two would be inherently, and thus permanently, in conflict.

However, there is a possible alternative. I mentioned previously that Parallelism, as described thus far, would seem to be locked into maintaining (a substantially revised version of) the existing criminal justice system. But this is not entirely accurate. The Parallelist model requires *a* properly functioning criminal justice system, but this prerequisite does not rule out legal pluralism. Parallelism is compatible with two (or more) independent legal systems operating within the same geographical boundaries.[86] But in

---

86　This is not to imply that, in a legal pluralist scenario, each legal system must be paired up with only one set of restorative justice services. The same services could potentially take cases that have been processed by all

that case, all that is required for a full-blown Parallelist approach in this context is (1) an independent First Nations legal system functioning as the relevant 'criminal justice' counterpart to (2) an independent First Nations 'restorative justice' service.

This is not to suggest that there would be only one First Nations legal system or that if multiple systems were required, they would be in some sense homogeneous. As Napoleon and Friedland note, '[I]ndigenous societies, and thus Indigenous legal traditions, are incredibly diverse' (2014: 226). Nor is it to overlook or minimise the immense difficulty and struggle that would be involved in setting up such a system. Most First Nations legal traditions and customs have been severely damaged as a result of colonialism, and so an extensive process of recovery and creative development is likely to be necessary. Even so, many First Nations peoples are already working towards recovering their own sovereignty, and this includes the reinstatement and development of their own legal systems. As Napoleon and Friedland write:

> [C]olonialism has gutted, obscured, and undermined [Indigenous traditions of] social order and good governance. Today, many Indigenous people are on an important journey, with uneven progress and ongoing challenges, to recover these legal traditions as part of their decolonization and self-determination efforts. (2014: 226)

Suppose, then, that a First Nations community has created its own legally independent 'restorative justice' service as an interim measure. If, at some point in the future, this community is able to reclaim their right to deal with 'criminal justice' matters by developing and using their own legal system, then they could continue to use the existing extralegal 'restorative justice' service to address private matters, such as the need for moral repair. In other words, this First Nations Parallelist framework could be situated alongside and entirely independent of *both* the state's legal system *and* any standard extralegal restorative justice service (Figure 4.1).

_____

(or some subset) of the multiple legal systems.

Figure 4.1 A Parallelist Proposal

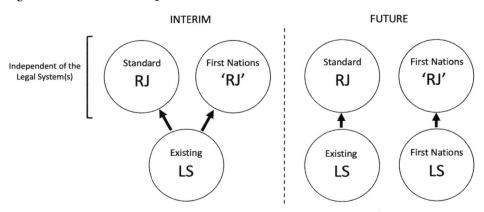

There are a number of possible responses that might be made to this kind of suggestion, four of which I will address in the following.

1. It might be argued that the legal autonomy of First Nations peoples is unrealistic. However, the UN's 2007 *Declaration on the Rights of Indigenous Peoples* recognises that 'Indigenous peoples have the right to promote, develop and maintain their ... juridical systems or customs' (Art. 34).[87] And legal pluralism of this kind is not without precedence. For example, Christopher Fromherz describes how, in 2007, the Bolivian Constitutional Assembly redesigned the country's justice system so that it would include both the existing civil law and an 'indigenous judiciary', the purpose of which would be to apply 'indigenous law and custom'. Both judiciaries would be placed on 'an equal footing', with 'exclusive and authoritative jurisdiction granted to the courts of each in their respective territories'. If any jurisdictional conflicts arose between the two, or where a court was alleged to have committed human rights violations, these would be resolved by a 'Pluri-national Constitutional Tribunal' consisting of both indigenous and civil law judges (2008: 1373, 1375-1376). These measures were finalised and enacted in Bolivia's 2009 constitution.

2. It might be thought that a First Nations legal system would be inherently restorative, and so it is unlikely that an additional extralegal process would be required. However, as Napoleon and Friedland argue, this simplistic conflation of restorative justice with First Nations justice is a mistake:

---

87 Although, as Fromherz notes, the UN *Declaration* 'is not, in and of itself, legally binding on states'. And 'nowhere does it suggest [that First Nations juridical] systems must be of an equivalent rank with ordinary state courts' (Fromherz, 2008: 1343, 1377).

> It is not that healing and restorative processes are not important, or even
> preferable, to other responses to crime within many Indigenous legal traditions.
> … [But] healing alone is not enough to prevent harm, protect the vulnerable,
> or ensure group safety in many situations, and at any rate, is a long-term
> process not a panacea. It is not logical or accurate to say that healing is the only
> legal response to crime in Indigenous legal traditions. It is more accurate to say
> that healing is the only legal response permitted to Indigenous groups within
> most states, which monopolize the use of coercive force. (2014: 238)

In other words, a self-sufficient First Nations legal system would be freed from the colonial
constraints against the use of coercive force or enforced separation. Under certain
conditions, this could conceivably include a separate policing system that operates under
First Nations law. As one example of this approach, Blagg reports that 'many Aboriginal
people in Western Australia are … developing their own forms of policing through
Aboriginal Patrols' (1997: 497). To be clear, the mainstream police retain their powers in
relation to Aboriginal people, and, at present, the Patrols see their role 'in terms of
mediation rather than enforcement' (2015: 5). But this could potentially change if they
were to operate under a separate First Nations juridical system. Thus, it is conceivable that
the methods of coercive force and enforced separation would, once again, become
legitimate options under First Nations law – especially in cases where the offender is not
(or not immediately) amenable to 'restorative justice' approaches. As Napoleon and
Friedland put it, 'When someone was waiting for or not willing to accept healing, the
principle of avoidance or separation was often employed in order to keep others safe'
(2014: 244, 245).[88]

Moreover, a First Nations legal system is very likely to include some of the key values
present in the mainstream system, such as a focus on fairness, proportionality, due process
and human rights.[89] In other words, it might still be oriented towards addressing the
public dimension of social harms. As Blagg notes in relation to the possibility of 'a
specifically Maori jurisdiction':

---

88   Cf. 'Romanticized portrayals of Indigenous peoples as living in peaceful harmony disregards the rigidity of
      some societies, existence of laws and values, and undermines our capacity to develop Indigenous Justice
      Systems today. [These Systems] will be as diverse as conceptualizations of wrongdoing and justice and
      appropriate resolution may vary considerably' (McGuire & Palys, 2020: 68). Again, 'Given the diversity of
      indigenous cultures, it is not surprising that a variety of sanctions are used by indigenous peoples within
      their specific cultural frameworks. … [S]ome sanctions are 'restorative', in the sense that a modern
      proponent of restorative justice would accept, and some, clearly, are not' (Cunneen, 2010: 115).
89   As the *United Nations Declaration on the Rights of Indigenous Peoples* states, 'Indigenous peoples have the
      right to promote, develop and maintain their … juridical systems … *in accordance with international
      human rights standards*' (Art. 34 (my emphasis)).

I am not suggesting here a return to some idealized Maori world. Aspects of traditional justice would be unacceptable to most Aboriginal and Maori people. Cultures and traditions change and adapt through narrative and other processes; current debates in New Zealand and Australia suggest that even ideas about 'parallel' systems are underpinned by reference to human rights treaties, patriarchal structures, due process, etc. (1997: 486, n. 13)

Again, Evelyn Zellerer and Chris Cunneen argue that if any separate legal system were to emerge, it would need to remove power imbalances and protect the safety of vulnerable members of the First Nations community, especially women:

If a justice initiative transfers power to a handful of already-powerful individuals within the [aboriginal] community, then there is great potential for corruption or tyranny of the less powerful. This is particularly problematic for women. ... [I]n many [aboriginal] communities, there are extraordinary levels of violence perpetrated against women, as well as high levels of tolerance for such violence. Much discussion, education, and planning is required to ensure that their interests are served and safety guaranteed. (2015: 256, 257)

But then, if the First Nations legal system is to address concerns of safety, human rights, due process and equality before the law and if it turns out that some legal sanctions can be imposed or enforced, then there might still be a need for a legally independent process that would focus on the more particularised harms experienced by individuals, extended families and local communities. If and when such a process included the objective of moral repair, then a Parallelist model would help to ensure that it does not run into the kind of problems that plague the Integrationist model.

3. There will be offenders or victims who, for whatever reason, cannot or do not wish to use either the First Nations community's legal system or its 'restorative justice' services. This may occur, for instance, where either the offender or the victim is not a member of that community. However, such cases could be accommodated with careful negotiation and the use of cross-over processes, so long as the same offence is not subject to two legal sanctions. As the UN *Study by the Expert Mechanism on the Rights of Indigenous Peoples* recommended:

Where indigenous persons are subject to both indigenous peoples' laws and also State-based justice systems for the same alleged actions, they run the risk of being subject to prosecution under two legal systems. The problem is exacerbated where the State-based system does not recognize the indigenous peoples' system. In such cases, the tribal system should be paramount. (2013: Paragraph 57)

4. Some have argued that setting up a separate First Nations legal system would require considerable government funding. A UN *Report of the Expert Mechanism on the Rights of Indigenous Peoples* (2021), for instance, includes the following recommendation:

> States should recognize in legislation indigenous peoples' own legal systems and institutions, normative and legal practices (customs and traditions) and autonomous and governmental systems and *provide adequate funding and resources* to support indigenous peoples in their pursuit of self-determination. (Para. 65, my emphasis)[90]

There are indeed a number of examples in which a colonial state has funded the creation of alternative justice schemes that are, on paper at least, under the independent control of First Nations peoples. In Canada, for instance, the Indigenous Justice Program was set up 'to allow Indigenous people the opportunity to assume greater responsibility for the administration of justice in their communities'. This has resulted in '197 community-based programmes that serve over 750 communities' (Government of Canada, 2016). However, as critics have observed, the Program did not – nor was it ever intended to – allow any First Nations community to 'develop a justice system in keeping with its own values and traditions'. Instead, it has merely 'delegated limited responsibility for administering Canadian justice' (McGuire & Palys, 2020: 65-66). In other words, 'the federal government still holds all the money, still sets all the priorities, and still effectively tells Canada's Indigenous peoples what their justice systems can look like' (Palys, 2004: 2).

This outcome only confirms that the extent to which an alternative approach is genuinely independent will depend, to a large degree, on its funding sources and, more specifically, on the conditions attached. In this respect, it might seem as if the independence of a First Nations legal system – or even an interim 'restorative justice' service – would be near impossible, given that only the state has the resources to provide adequate funding, and it would invariably demand ultimate control and oversight.

However, the reality is that colonial states rarely, if ever, provide sufficient funding for First Nations programmes to thrive over the long term, and even less so as they become further removed from the leash of government control. As Palys notes:

---

90   Cf. First Nations people in Canada 'need the socioeconomic resources to reinstitute Aboriginal criminal justice practices that for centuries kept them safe and helped them maintain their rich heritage' (Barmaki, 2021: 20).

> Any funds that do come are 'soft' funds that may or may not be there next year. No mainstream system can develop with such uncertainty. How can [Indigenous Justice Systems] be expected to do so? (2004: 2)

So it is likely that alternative, or at least additional, funding sources will need to be found. This could be achieved if First Nations communities were able to regain sovereign control over their land and its economic resources, as suggested by McGuire & Palys:

> What we need from Canada is not more prescription but rather the space to make our own decisions about how to proceed and the control over our own territories that would enable us to fund them. (2020: 75)

4.9.5 De-subjectification

I have argued that setting up 'culturally appropriate' restorative justice programmes as a diversionary option will only reinforce the colonialist agenda. Such schemes may offer a marginal improvement in terms of addressing overrepresentation. But they are effectively a 'deep colonising' strategy and so remain part of the problem.[91] The only path towards genuine decolonisation is for historical injustices to be rectified, discriminatory policies removed and constitutional reforms put in place. As the Uluru Statement, written by Australia's First Nations peoples, puts it:

> Proportionally, we are the most incarcerated people on the planet. We are not an innately criminal people. Our children are aliened from their families at unprecedented rates. This cannot be because we have no love for them. And our youth languish in detention in obscene numbers. They should be our hope for the future. These dimensions of our crisis tell plainly the structural nature of our problem. This is the torment of our powerlessness. We seek constitutional reforms to empower our people and take a rightful place in our own country. When we have power over our destiny our children will flourish. They will walk in two worlds and their culture will be a gift to their country. (ulurustatement.org, 2022)

---

91 As are 'national apologies' to First Nations peoples that are regarded or deployed by the state as an end in itself: 'This conveniently ignores the veritably universal Indigenous tenet that an apology is no more than a first step toward achieving a just resolution; "taking responsibility" also means undertaking concrete action to make things right' (McGuire & Palys, 2020: 70-71).

I have also argued that a Parallelist approach could offer a viable 'two worlds' solution for First Nations communities. Setting up an independent 'restorative justice' service could serve as an interim position while they work towards legal self-determination. Of course, as Napoleon and Friedland note, there would be many challenges to be overcome, such as the following issues:

> [L]egitimacy, conflict of laws, harmonization efforts, and, in the criminal justice field, how legitimate responses to human violence and vulnerability that require coercive force should or will be acted on. (2014: 240)

However, if at some point First Nations peoples reclaim their sovereign right to deal with 'crimes' in accordance with their own laws and customs, then, in this model, there would already exist an established 'restorative justice' service that could be immediately employed as a fitting counterpart. In the meantime, they would have an extralegal space within which they could respond to 'crimes' and other social harms that affect their community without the state's interference, regulation or control.

Indeed, there would be significant additional benefits in developing an independent 'restorative justice' service as an interim measure. We have seen that colonisation is maintained by both external and internal forms of subjugation. It is also clear that neither the external obstacles to genuine self-determination nor the internalisation of subjection will ever be fully removed by relying entirely on the state to initiate the necessary reforms. To reiterate:

First, it is in the DNA of a settler-colonialist state to put its own interests and self-preservation before those of the colonised. Hence, to whatever extent it can get away with, the state will postpone, water down, hide or obstruct any structural challenge to its sovereignty. As Shelly McGrath writes:

> [U]nlike in extractive colonies where phases of decolonization transform relations into the 'postcolonial', settler states such as Canada and Australia maintain their eliminatory agendas without any intention that the country will ever undergo meaningful or structural decolonization. (2020: 4)

Second, any structural reforms or new rights must be granted, bestowed or recognised by the state. This makes it virtually impossible for any individual to accept such 'reforms' or 'rights' without at the same time internalising the implication that they are a subject of the colonial state. As McGuire and Palys argue:

> Imposed systems of 'self-governance' that leave every change still requiring ministerial permission and fiscal control in the hands of the state further

impede the potential for fundamental change. Out of fear that they will lose funding, many First Nations elected officials 'will not rock the boat', which means real change is often either ineffective or impossible ... When we accept the colonial governments' systems of law, justice and governance – foundational cultural institutions – we remain colonized. (2020: 61)

It follows that the process of decolonisation can only be independently instigated by First Nations peoples, and in a way that reclaims and reasserts their own history, customs and laws. As Coulthard writes:

Rather than remaining dependent on their oppressors for their freedom and self-worth, ... the colonized must struggle to critically reclaim and revaluate the worth of *their own* histories, traditions, and cultures against the subjectifying gaze and assimilative lure of colonial recognition. ... [T]hose struggling against colonialism must 'turn away' from the colonial state and society and find in their own *transformative praxis* the source of their liberation ... [T]he empowerment that is derived from this critically self-affirmative and self-transformative process of desubjectification must be causiously directed *away* from the assimilative lure of the statist politics of recognition, and instead be fashioned toward our own on-the-ground practices of freedom. (2007: 454, 456.)

Thus, a Parallelist framework might, even as an interim position, be seen as one way in which First Nations peoples could 'turn away from' the 'subjectifying gaze and assimilative lure of colonial recognition' and develop their own 'on-the-ground practices of freedom'. Harold Johnson, writing about the Canadian context, argues:

We can no longer wait for Canada or the provinces to make changes. They are clearly not going to come and fix this. It is not in their interest to do so. We have to do it ourselves. We have to reclaim our jurisdiction, establish our own processes. ... We can work in collaboration with Canada and the provinces, negotiate agreements and funding, but we do not have to ask their permission; we do not need their approval. (2019: Closing Argument)[92]

---

92 Cf. 'The existence of Indigenous systems operating alongside Canada's systems should be seen as an attainable goal; we must decolonize our minds and reclaim what is rightfully ours. ... [We must] revitalize and reawaken our own ways of being in the world (McGuire & Palys, 2020: 70).

Granted, there would be many obstacles and complexities to overcome. And it will no doubt require some form of constructive but cautious engagement with the colonial state's legal and political institutions. As Coulthard acknowledges:

> Settler-colonialism has rendered us a radical minority in our own homelands, and this necessitates that we continue to engage with the state's legal and political system. What our present condition does demand, however, is that we begin to approach our engagements with the settler-state legal apparatus with a degree of critical self-reflection, scepticism, and caution that has to date been largely absent in our efforts. (2014: 179)

But suppose that First Nations peoples were able to create and maintain 'restorative justice' processes that deal with 'crimes' in a way that accords with their own customs and laws but which are entirely independent of the legal apparatus of the state. It is likely that such processes would be more authentic and meaningful to First Nations participants. Hence, they would be of a higher quality than any 'culturally appropriate' diversionary options that currently exist. Even more importantly, this Parallelist alternative could become a significant 'self-transformative' and 'desubjectifying' practice and thus a concrete step towards true autonomy. As McGrath puts it, 'only lived, self-determination strategies have the potential to decolonize inequitable relationships and create spaces of sovereignty for Indigenous peoples' (2020: 3).

5   Challenges

This chapter presents a series of key challenges that might be made to the Parallelist model and that have not already been addressed in previous chapters. It focuses on concerns that the restorative justice arm of this model could raise for victims, offenders and the criminal justice system. In relation to victims, it addresses the possibility that it could result in limited access, extended delays and safety issues. It then explores the legal risks for offenders, and concerns about reduced participation rates, informal pressures and overburdening. Finally, it explores how a Parallelist approach to restorative justice could impact criminal justice, including increased caseload pressures, its implications for the use of diversion as such, its inability to reduce penal control, the possibility that it could lead to state underreach, and the question of how it could contribute, if at all, to the systemic changes envisaged by the full Parallelist model.

5.1   Victims

5.1.1   *Limited access to restorative justice*

Suppose that Parallelism became the only model available – that is, with the Integrationist protocols phased out. It might be argued that, in this scenario, victims who would have preferred to take part in restorative justice within an Integrationist setting will feel disenfranchised. There are three reasons that might be given for this kind of preference. I will address each in turn.

1. Van Camp and Wemmers found that, when restorative justice took place in a pre-trial context in Belgium, the kind of harms that victims routinely experience in a criminal trial were pre-emptively blocked or reduced.[1]

---

1   To be clear, in this scheme, the use of pre-trial restorative justice is unlike diversion from prosecution or deferred sentencing insofar as it does not rely on the prosecutor or judge to refer a case to the programme. Either the victim or offender can 'make a request for mediation' (*Belgian Code of Criminal Procedure*, Art. 553). Moreover, if a pre-trial restorative justice process takes place, (a) this does not preclude the case from going to trial, and (b) it *may* have no impact on the legal outcome. Hence, it might be thought that the scheme operates 'independently' or in 'parallel' with the judicial system. However, as I shall argue below, the Belgian scheme is much like the *Crimes (Restorative Justice) Act 2004* (ACT) in that it does not *guarantee* legal independence, and so it is not strictly a Parallelist approach as I have defined this model (*see* §3.1.2, 'Principle 7').

> Because of an insight into the events and motives acquired through communication with the offender prior to the trial, the victims in the pre-adjudication group felt emotionally and intellectually prepared for the criminal trial. There were no surprises or shocks as far as the motives and details of the events were concerned during the trial. ... The judicial system was still perceived as impersonal and cold by a number of them, but experiences with restorative intervention preceding the trial seem to have softened the negative assessment of the criminal justice system. (Van Camp, 2014: 160-161)

It is certainly true that holding a restorative justice process in a pre-sentence context could meet specific needs that victims have, and in ways that might not otherwise be available, as the example above shows. But again, this is a 'solution' that does not actually *solve* the problem at hand—namely, how victims are treated in a criminal trial. It merely 'softens' the negative impact that the trial would otherwise have had on them. There are far more direct ways of improving the experience of victims in a court proceeding. For instance, applying the principles of therapeutic jurisprudence, together with the provision of adequate support and information, would have a significant effect in terms of helping victims to feel more 'emotionally and intellectually prepared' for the trial. This could include the prosecutor enabling victims to access details about the crime that have come to light in the investigation. That would help them to avoid being shocked or surprised by what they hear in the trial. In my own research into the use of restorative justice to address work-related death, I spoke to a prosecutor who said they could provide this kind of access:

> In some cases, the families are really intent on seeing – having access to documents and photographs. We generally will provide access to an investigation brief. We've got a policy that allows access without putting the family through, say, Freedom of Information Act, or anything like that. ... [And we will] both prepare and then debrief them in relation to showing them the brief or any photos of the scene. (Brookes, 2009: 70)

In addition, the potential benefits of any approach need to be weighed against the risks. As we have seen, when restorative justice takes place in a pre-trial or pre-sentencing setting, victims are highly susceptible to being revictimised by an insincere offender. In the example from Belgium quoted above, for instance, if a pre-trial agreement is made between the victim and the offender, they are not required to share this outcome with the judicial authorities. And even if they decide to do so, the judge may or may not take their agreement into account.[2] In other words, under Belgian law, a pre-trial agreement will not automatically result in charges against the offender being dropped or the offender being cleared of all charges or receiving a reduced sentence.[3] Nevertheless, if the participants decide to share their agreement with the court, this *could* potentially have an impact on the legal outcome. And this mere possibility is sufficient to create an opportunistic incentive for offenders. As Van Camp and Wemmers noted, for some victims who took part in the pre-trial scheme, 'an ulterior motive for participation (such as obtaining a lenient sentence) on the part of the offender was cause for frustration' (2013: 125).

2. Some victims might prefer restorative justice as a diversionary approach because they do not want the offender to receive a normal criminal justice sanction. This might occur when the offence is less serious, for instance. As Dena Gromet and John Darley found:

> At low levels of severity, when the intuitive desire to punish the offender is not strong, people feel that achieving restoration achieves justice, and they are willing to *completely forgo* more punitive, retributive measures. As crimes increase in severity, and people experience a strong intuitive desire to punish the offender, retribution will overpower restoration in a forced-choice context. If given the opportunity, however, people will choose options that allow them to achieve both retribution and restoration for high-severity offences, particularly if their attention is drawn to restorative concerns. (2009: 52a-b, my emphasis)

Suppose that a victim was willing to 'completely forgo' more punitive measures and instead take part in restorative justice as a diversionary mechanism. The problem is that not even the Integrationist model can guarantee this preference. The decision to divert a case to restorative justice is up to the court, and, even then, the offender must participate successfully if they are to avoid the usual punitive sanction. Moreover, the Parallelist model, as I have construed it, would not prevent the offender from taking part in (suitably amended) non-RJ diversionary programmes. So Parallelism does not necessarily rule out the possibility of offenders being diverted from the normal criminal justice sanction. It

---

2   *See* Art. 555 of the *Belgian Code of Criminal Procedure*. '[I]f the parties decide to inform the judge of the outcome of the mediation, then the judge can take that outcome into account in his/her decision making' (Buonatesta, Gailly & Van Doosselaere, 2018: 134).

3   'Les répondants indiquent tous avoir été informés de l'indépendance, en principe, de l'approche réparatrice par rapport au système judiciaire (par exemple, un accord entre la victime et le contrevenant ne se traduit pas automatiquement par une exonération du contrevenant, une exemption ou une réduction de peine)' (Van Camp & Wemmers, 2011: 184).

only entails that restorative justice could not be used as the means by which this is achieved (see §5.3.2).

3. If the case proceeds all the way to a sentence, then, under Parallelism as I have construed it, there would be no possibility for the victim to initiate a restorative justice process prior to that point. Yet this may be precisely the time at which it would be most helpful, in terms of recovery and healing. As Shannon Sliva, Elizabeth Porter-Merrill and Pete Lee found:

> [V]ictims' varying needs can be best supported by a range of restorative practices, available at different points in the criminal system and with different kinds of participation from the affected stakeholders. This honors the offender's right to a timely process while also honoring the victim's readiness and personal response to trauma. Victims who do not wish to participate in a restorative process at adjudication or sentencing, for instance, may later wish to participate in a post-sentencing dialogue. (2019: 490)

There are two responses that can be made here. First, it is not clear that even an Integrationist approach can offer this kind of flexibility, let alone arrange a time for restorative justice that is best suited to meet the victim's needs. In a pre-sentence context, restorative justice would only become available if and when a prosecutor or judge decides to divert the case for that purpose. The timing of this diversion will be dictated by the point at which the case happens to be in the criminal justice process. It will have virtually nothing to do with the fact that making the referral at that point in time is more likely to meet the victim's current needs. Second, there will be a tightly circumscribed time frame within which the process must be completed. But again, as we have seen, this will be determined by criminal justice priorities, such as fitting in with scheduled court dates.

And yet, it might be argued, at least Integrationism gives victims in this situation the choice of a pre-sentence context, even if the precise timing may not be perfect. This is true, but, again, the benefits must be weighed against the risks. Integrationism is far less likely to be able to ensure that the victim will not be confronted with a 'player of the system' – a situation which will do little to assist their healing from trauma and could potentially do much harm.

Finally, irrespective of the reasons why some victims may prefer to use restorative justice as a diversionary approach, it is important to recognise that there is another side to this coin. If Integrationism were to be more widely used than it is at present, there could be significantly more victims who, for whatever reason, will feel disenfranchised because they would have preferred their case to be prosecuted or sentenced in the usual way, rather than see the case dismissed or the sentence reduced as a result of a diversion to restorative justice – often without their consent or involvement (see §4.1.2). In a Parallelist model, this issue would not arise.

It should also be noted that victims who would have preferred to take part in restorative justice *as a diversionary option* would not be prevented by Parallelism from taking part in restorative justice *as such*. The extralegal option would still remain available to them, and could even occur in a pre-sentence setting – that is, either after a non-RJ diversionary programme has been completed and the case closed, or as a voluntary adjunct to a non-RJ unconditional diversionary scheme (see §5.3.2).

Ultimately, there is no perfect solution here. No matter which model is used, not every preference can be met. Hence, the decision between Integrationism and Parallelism must rest on which model is most likely, *all things considered*, to meet the needs of those concerned.

5.1.2   Extended delays

One challenge that might be made to Parallelism is that, if it were implemented, this would lead to prolonged delays before victims can gain access to restorative justice. And this could, in some cases, mean that the recovery needs of victims are less likely to be met. Since Integrationism can offer restorative justice as a diversionary option, it will occur sooner and, hence, would appear to be superior to Parallelism in this respect. There are four possible responses a Parallelist could make to this challenge.

1. The evidence suggests that, for minor cases, restorative justice processes are more likely to be effective if they commence within three months from the offence (Denkers & Winkel, 1998; Norris & Kaniasty, 1994). In §3.1, I suggested that the Parallelist principle of legal independence could be secured if restorative justice takes place once a case has actually or effectively exited the justice system. Thus, the process could be held at any time after the police decide not to make an arrest, or a prosecutor decides not to file charges or the charges are unconditionally dismissed in a subsequent hearing. These contexts are most likely to be available for less serious crimes and when the crime was committed by young people or first-time offenders. But then it follows that, on a Parallelist model, these access points would make it possible for minor cases to access a restorative justice option just as quickly as any Integrationist scheme employed to cater for this category of offences.

2. Where a case would ordinarily have been diverted from prosecution to restorative justice, a Parallelist would advocate using a non-RJ diversionary programme instead (see §3.1 and §5.3.2). Then, after this programme has been completed and the case closed, an extralegal restorative justice process could be made available. The start date of restorative justice would, on this approach, clearly be later than the standard Integrationist model. But the extent of the delay will depend on the diversionary programme that is used. For

instance, it might involve a limited number of community service hours or a specific reparative task to be completed within a relatively small time frame. In such cases, the comparative delay for a Parallelist approach would be minimal.

I have also suggested that the Parallelist model could offer restorative justice as a voluntary adjunct to a lengthy non-RJ unconditional diversionary programme, since, if a case were referred to such a programme, it would have effectively exited the system. Such programmes are likely to be relatively uncommon or reserved for only minor offences. Nevertheless, this option, if available, would mean that the delay would again be no more protracted than an Integrationist approach to this level of offending.

3. With respect to more serious offences, the evidence suggests that it is far more important to ensure that people feel they have sufficient time to prepare for any restorative justice process and that the timing suits their needs, than it is that the process should commence as soon as possible after the offence.[4] Indeed, research has found that 'victims' willingness to participate in [restorative justice] increased over time after more harmful offenses, whereas it decreased when offenses inflicted less harm' (Zebel, Schreurs & Ufkes, 2017: 385). In other words, it is not a forgone conclusion that a Parallelist model would suffer from longer delays than Integrationism if the timescales for both were dictated solely by the needs of participants, rather than criminal justice priorities. Shorter timescales cannot be advanced as a reason to prefer Integrationism if it can only achieve this result by overriding the needs of victims.

4. Unless legislation is put in place that compels the court to defer eligible cases to restorative justice, it is likely that many, if not most, serious offences will not be deferred for this purpose. Sherman and Strang, for example, noted the difficulty in persuading the judiciary to adjourn cases to allow restorative justice to take place:

> For several years, in 2001-04, police and Home Office officials asked the magistrates' courts not to sentence cases 'there and then' when offenders offered guilty pleas, and where no [pre-sentence report] would be requested – the majority of the adult convictions for eligible cases. Instead, police asked the courts to adjourn the cases for sentencing four weeks later, to allow time to organise RJ before sentence. Court officials said they would do so, but in

---

4   It is worth noting that an English study of an Integrationist restorative justice pilot scheme found that 'there is quite a broad time span [from the time of the offence] in which restorative justice is felt to be helpful' (p. 39). When participants were asked 'Do you think the conference was held at the right time after the offence?' 76% of offenders and 72% of victims felt that the timing 'was about right', but 17% of offenders and 22% of victims thought it was 'too long after'. Only 1% of offenders and 3% of victims thought it was 'too soon after'. (p. 37). However, it is difficult to draw any specific conclusions from these figures about what is the best time after the offence to hold a conference, since these answers are not correlated with the actual timescales to which the respondents were referring. The report merely indicates that the times ranged from 'weeks' to 'years' (Shapland et al., 2007: 39).

practice the courts continued to sentence 'there and then'. Even a meeting of some 200 magistrates with the Lord Chancellor failed to change the local custom, which made RJ-before-sentence impossible to organise in the majority of eligible cases. (2007: 36)

In this kind of scenario, an Integrationist model will be, for the most part, limited to offering restorative justice as a component of the sentence. But then it follows that in the majority of offences that result in a sentence, the delays that can be expected when a post-sentence approach is employed would be no worse than Integrationism.

5. In more serious cases, sentencing can take over a year to eventuate. For example, in 2021 it was reported that, in the UK, 'Victims, witnesses and defendants are waiting longer for their cases to be heard as the number of cases older than a year increased from 2,830 to 11,379 (302%)' between March 2020 and June 2021 (National Audit Office, 2021: 7). This might be due to the complexity of an investigation, but it could also arise as a result of systemic issues, such as under-resourcing, mismanagement, political interference and the subsequent backlog of cases. On first glance, it might seem that, since these are the kind of cases that have not yet actually or effectively exited the system, victims who would prefer to take part in restorative justice earlier would be prevented by a Parallelist approach from doing so. There are two responses that a Parallelist could make to this objection.

First, if sentencing has been delayed due to a protracted investigation, then this would usually mean that the offender has chosen to plead not guilty in court.[5] But in cases where the diversion occurs in the context of a deferred (or adjourned) sentence, some Integrationist schemes require that the offender plead guilty in order to be eligible for restorative justice as a diversionary approach.[6] Thus, in such jurisdictions, if the offender contests the charges, an Integrationist approach will not be available in any case. Assuming the offender is found guilty, a post-sentence approach will be the only option. Hence, Integrationism will not resolve this particular problem. In other jurisdictions, the offender can still participate if they do not plead guilty but are nevertheless found guilty.[7] But in that case, any (deferred sentence) diversion to restorative justice will need to wait until the court has proven the offender's guilt. Thus, if the only cause for a prolonged delay is the time taken to investigate the case and prove the offender guilty, then the Integrationist model will not be substantially quicker than a Parallelist (post-sentence) approach.

---

5   It is true that, in inquisitorial regimes, court magistrates may 'conduct a profound search for the truth, regardless of whether a defendant admitted guilt during the pre-trial investigation'. Yet, in practice, 'genuinely probing trials take place only in those few cases in which the defendant actively contests the charges against him' (Goldstein & Marcus, 1977: 265, 270; Van Camp, 2014: 49).

6   *See*, for example, New Zealand's *Sentencing Act 2002*: adjournment for a restorative justice process may take place: 'if – (a) an offender appears before the District Court at any time before sentencing; and (b) the offender has pleaded guilty to the offence' (s.24A.1).

7   As in the *Crimes (Restorative Justice) Act* 2004 (ACT).

Second, even if the investigation was itself a relatively simple matter, the entire judicial process leading up to the sentence could still have taken an inordinate amount of time merely due to a lack of resources, long-established traditions, administrative negligence and so on. In such cases, victims who would have preferred to take part in restorative justice earlier would indeed have legitimate grounds for frustration. But it is important to pinpoint the cause of this issue. If it were not for the deficiencies in the justice system, then there would be no such excessive delays. In other words, this problem is not a built-in feature of either Integrationism or Parallelism but is instead due to an entirely contingent situation.

Nevertheless, I would argue that, by contrast with Integrationism, the Parallelist model comes with the kind of theoretical resources that could offer a solution to this issue. The Integrationist model has only one mechanism for dealing with flaws in the criminal justice system: it simply diverts as many cases as possible. Parallelism takes a different approach. It explicitly acknowledges the value and legitimacy of a properly functioning justice system, and so this model will not be fully realised until the necessary reforms (or transformations) have taken place. In other words, removing a deficiency, such as unwarranted judicial delays, is both essential to and justified by the Parallelist model. Hence, if Parallelism were to be adopted, the actual cause of excessive delays to restorative justice would *thereby* need to be addressed directly, rather than merely side-stepped.[8]

But what would a Parallelist propose in the meantime? After all, I have argued that one of the advantages to this model is that the restorative justice arm can be implemented without needing to wait for the justice system to be reformed (or transformed). So, is there an interim solution that might shortcut or reduce these unwarranted delays? Unfortunately, in this case, it is hard to imagine how this might be possible. If the judicial authorities have determined that a case is serious enough to warrant a sentence, then it would, by definition, remain (actually and effectively) in the system until sentencing. So any earlier pre-sentence use of restorative justice would not be possible, whether the model is Integrationist or Parallelist.

In sum, the worst that can be said of the Parallelist approach, as I have construed it, is this: In cases where the offender contests the charges, then the time at which restorative justice can take place might turn out to be considerably later than participants would have wanted, due to unnecessary delays in the judicial process – a situation that would be addressed if the Parallelist model were to be fully implemented. But compare this limitation with the 'time window deadline' that is built into Integrationism, where the provision of a restorative justice process is 'determined by the date at which the next step in the process must occur by law' (Sherman & Strang, 2007: 36-37). It must, for instance, be situated after

---

8   Jason Payne, for instance, provides a useful summary of approaches that could be used to address factors that contribute to trials not proceeding as scheduled (Payne, 2007: 59-72).

arrest, but before prosecution, or after conviction, but before sentencing, or after the sentence commences, but before a probation plan is put in place, and so on.

5.1.3   Risk management issues

One concern that could be raised about the Parallelist model is that, if restorative justice is removed from a diversionary framework, this will leave victim participants subject to a number of risks. For instance, the process could involve meeting the offender, and so victims may have concerns about their physical safety. This is one of the reasons why Integrationist schemes employ police officers as facilitators or invite them to be present as attendees or observers. But a Parallelist approach is designed to make a clear demarcation between a criminal justice orientation and the private sphere of restorative justice. So police officers would not serve as facilitators; nor would they be invited to attend, unless it was in an entirely private capacity.

However, the issue of safety can be – and routinely is – effectively addressed by other means. The facilitator will conduct a thorough risk assessment of the offender. If there were any significant doubts, the facilitator would not proceed. Again, if the process is being held in a post-sentence context, then the facilitator could organise any meeting prior to the offender's release from prison. The meeting could also be held within a building that has security guards. Alternatively, the participants could use a shuttle dialogue process instead of a face-to-face meeting. This kind of safeguarding is advocated by Nikki D'Souza and Xavier L'Hoiry in their discussion of the understandable reticence that victims of Serious and Organised Crime might have in meeting the offenders in a post-sentence context, 'given the serious physical and/or psychological harm [they have] suffered' (2021: 237). Thus, they suggest 'alternative forms of RJ such as shuttle mediation or letters of apology' (p. 238), as well as 'extensive preparatory work, risk assessment, the sharing of multi-agency intelligence and bespoke safeguarding' (p. 236).

Another related concern might be whether a Parallelist approach can assure victims that they will not encounter an offender who is insincere or participating for inappropriate reasons. Even if a restorative justice process took place in a Parallelist context, an offender could turn out to be less than fully authentic. Before addressing this issue, an important distinction needs to be made. An offender might be completely open and honest, and yet they could still be *perceived* by the victim as being insincere. As Miller noted, in describing a post-sentence programme:

> Evaluating whether apologies are sincere is subjective; an offender may offer a
> very sincere apology, yet the victim may hear it as disingenuous (as did one of
> the [programme's] victims whose mother was murdered). (2011: 163)

The question here, then, is whether Integrationism or Parallelism is more likely to ensure not only that offenders are genuine but also that, when they *are* sincere, they are more likely to be *perceived* as such by victims. In this respect, it would appear that, all else being equal, Parallelism has a clear advantage.

First, in an extralegal context, the offender knows that they will not be receiving any legal benefits by participating, and, indeed, as we shall see, they might even be putting themselves at some legal risk. It follows that Parallelism removes even the possibility of this kind of ulterior motive. Of course, other unacceptable motives or intentions might remain, but a Parallelist context makes it far more likely that proper screening and extensive preparation will be undertaken, since the process would not be subordinated to criminal justice priorities, such as timescale restrictions.

Second, the victim is also, for the same reasons, far more likely to receive whatever level of preparation and support they need to obtain the full potential of the process. Most importantly, they can be assured that there are no legal benefits or threats that could, at some level, be motivating the offender's participation or their display of remorse. This will automatically remove a significant and not unreasonable cause for suspicion, and so make it easier for them to hear a sincere expression of apology for what it is.

5.2   OFFENDERS

5.2.1   Risk of self-incrimination

When restorative justice is used in response to a crime, the process will usually focus on the incident for which the referral was made (call this the 'RJ offence'). One advantage of a Parallelist approach is that there is no possibility of self-incrimination with respect to the RJ offence. For the case to have exited the system, in the sense required by the model, there must be no possibility that the RJ offence can be reopened and prosecuted. If the process takes place in a post-sentence context, then the case will have effectively exited the system, since that offence cannot then be re-prosecuted.

But there is a related concern that might be made to the Parallelist model. Suppose that, during the course of a restorative justice process, the offender confesses to an additional as-yet-undetected or unprosecuted crime. The other participants could potentially report the offence to the police or serve as a witness to the admission in any subsequent legal proceeding. In §3.1, I argued that even a signed confidentiality agreement would not prevent this from occurring. There may be some jurisdictions that currently have (or would be willing to create) legal safeguards that could protect the offender from this kind of self-incrimination, but this is likely to be rare.

In response to this issue, a Parallelist will take the view that, if it is in the public interest for an offence to be prosecuted – as would be the case for a homicide, child abuse or sexual assault, for instance – then the law should be enforced. Hence, the judicial authorities should be able to access any evidence of additional crimes so that they can determine the most appropriate legal response (see §3.1.2, 'Principle 6'). And indeed, most Integrationist schemes already have this kind of policy in place. For example, in New Zealand, participants are informed prior to the conference that 'the disclosure of other offending may be reported to the Police' (Ministry of Justice, 2004: 21). But then it follows that Parallelism is likely to be identical to most Integrationist schemes, insofar as the offender would not be protected from this kind of self-incrimination.

Nevertheless, one might think that this remains a challenge for Parallelism, even if it is one that it shares with Integrationism. As Samantha Buckingham argues, under such conditions, an offender 'would be foolhardy to participate or would be chilled from participating in a meaningful and open way' (2013: 876). For instance, there might be cases where the offender would find it difficult to explain how they came to commit the RJ offence without mentioning other prior offences. Or the victim, in attempting to understand the character or motives of the offender, might ask a probing question about their history. Anything but a straight answer could easily undermine the victim's confidence in their honesty. As Goldsmith et al. write:

> In a process where the success of the process relies in large part on the development of trust, apparent 'evasiveness' by [the] offender when asked questions like 'have you done this before?' can significantly harm the trust building process that takes place in the conference. (2005: 23)

There are several ways of approaching this issue. Regardless of the model being used, it is always best practice for facilitators to discuss precisely this kind of scenario when preparing participants. In some cases, the participants may come to an agreement beforehand that the conversation will only focus on the RJ offence and that any additional offences will only be referred to if they have already been dealt with by the justice system.[9] If the offender is caught off guard in a meeting, and does not know how best to answer a question about their prior offending, a facilitator could pause the discussion to check that the offender is willing to speak about such matters and possibly to remind the group about the limits to confidentiality and any agreements that might have been made about focusing on the RJ offence.

---

9   This will be considerably more difficult in cases of repeat offending against the victim, such as domestic violence. But, as I have argued elsewhere, extreme caution should be taken in using restorative justice in such cases, and even then, the format used must have been appropriately modified (*see* Brookes, 2019b).

In some cases, the offender may decide to take the risk of incriminating themselves if being open and transparent about their past will help to meet the recovery needs of the victim. In my research into work-related death, I spoke with a defence lawyer whose clients included companies facing the possibility of prosecution. The lawyer took the view that a client could, for moral reasons, choose to prioritise the needs of the bereaved family over the legal risks of speaking openly to them about what happened:

> There's been a couple of cases in which I've said, 'Look I can't give you moral guidance. I'll tell you what the legal position is.' Some clients have said to me: 'Well, what would you do?' And I've said: 'I'd go and talk to the family. To hell with the legal.' (Brookes, 2009: 80)

In sum, given the possibility of enabling the participants to self-manage this kind of issue, there is little reason to suppose that it would, in general, prevent offenders from participating, or from doing so in a 'meaningful and open way'.

5.2.2   Risk of appeals or litigation

The Parallelist model is designed to remove any possibility of an offender choosing to participate in order to gain some legal advantage. Ensuring that the case has actually or effectively exited the system is designed to achieve this goal. This should, in most cases, also remove the legal risk of speaking openly to the victim about the crime. If the case has been unconditionally dismissed or already sentenced, then this will usually mean that it cannot be reopened or re-prosecuted.

However, depending on the legal system or the reason why the case was closed, there could theoretically be cases where a victim agrees to participate because they are hoping to discover new leads or obtain additional evidence so that they can ask the prosecutor to consider appealing the sentence as unjustly lenient. Or again, suppose an offender fails to pay the restitution amount agreed to in a restorative justice process, or the victim is, for whatever reason, not satisfied with the criminal justice outcome and the option of an appeal is not open to them. In such a case, they might exercise their right to bring civil proceedings against the offender and use whatever admissions or information they have gleaned from the restorative justice process to make their case. Indeed, Ann Skelton and Cheryl Frank argue, unless victims are required to 'waive' this right, then offenders should be legally advised not to take part or at least not to agree to pay restitution, given the risk that they could 'later be sued through the civil process' (2004: 204).

It might be thought that a Parallelist model could avoid these scenarios by creating legislation that is not dissimilar to existing diversionary restorative justice schemes, such as the following provision:

> Any statement, confession, admission or information made or given by a child during the giving of a caution or a conference under this Act is not to be admitted in evidence in any subsequent criminal or civil proceedings. (*Young Offenders Act 1997* No 54 (NSW), s.67.1)[10]

However, this option is not unproblematic. As we have seen, this kind of legislation rarely removes the legal risk entirely, since the offender's admissions could easily assist in the discovery of evidence that is available outside the process itself and, hence, would be admissible in court (see §3.1.2, 'Principle 6').

An alternative would be to use more informal methods. For instance, the facilitator could, in the initial introduction and preparation phases, advise the participants that, while making an appeal or taking civil action are not necessarily inappropriate in themselves, using the process as a means of collecting evidence for such purposes would be contrary to the values and objectives of restorative justice. They could also require that all participants sign a confidentiality agreement that includes something like the following statement: 'I will not subpoena the Facilitators to testify or produce records at any hearing.' (Reed College, 2019: Supporting Document II). This agreement may not be legally watertight, but it will at least put the signatories on notice that if they have other intentions, they will not be participating in good faith.

In addition, the facilitator or any legal counsel would be highly negligent if they did not advise a victim who might be considering an appeal or civil action that they should take into account the limitations and likely consequences of their doing so. For example, in a document designed to explore policies and practices that would enhance the prosecution of sexual violence, two suggestions are made on how best to advise victims who might wish to pursue a civil case – both of which would seem to be valid in the majority of criminal cases:

> [A]lthough civil avenues are open to the victim, if the defendant is of modest means, how much is a victim likely to recover even if they were to sue? Where the defendant has resources, explaining the financial and emotional costs of the victim pursuing a criminal and even civil case can help demonstrate how

---

10   Ireland's Diversion Programme has a similar wording: 'No evidence shall be admissible in any court of any information, statement or admission disclosed or made only in the course of a conference or of the contents of any report of a conference' (*Children Act 2001* [Ireland], Pt. 4, s.50).

unlikely it would be for a victim to endure the litigation process unless their claim was valid. (AEquitas, the Justice Management Institute & the Urban Institute, 2020: 71-72)

But suppose it somehow becomes clear to a facilitator that the victim is nevertheless intending to use the process to gather evidence for legal purposes. In that case, they would need to reiterate to the victim that this is not the purpose of restorative justice. In some cases, the victim will then withdraw. But they could instead take the facilitator's advice on board and proceed in good faith. However, they might then change their minds as a result of what they hear. So while this kind of informal safeguard can certainly minimise the legal risks, it is not bulletproof.

While the two options above should not necessarily be ruled out, there is another approach that would be more consistent with the Parallelist model. A victim should not be forced to choose between taking part in restorative justice and exercising their right to pursue criminal justice or take civil action. This is especially important in cases of corporate wrongdoing, work-related death, institutional child abuse, war crimes and historical injustices, where a pre-emptive 'restorative justice' process might be exploited by offenders to evade the public censure their actions deserve or the cost of fair and proportionate reparations. If victims wish to ask the prosecution to consider appealing the sentence or if they want to pursue civil action after a criminal case has closed, then they should not be required to waive these rights simply in order to take part in a private dialogue that has no objective other than to attain some measure of personal healing and moral repair. But given the issues raised in the foregoing, it is very likely that, in such a scenario, the optimal solution for all concerned would be to draw on the Guiding Principles set out in §3.1. In other words, the restorative justice process should, wherever possible, take place *after* any appeal or civil action has been actually or effectively completed.

In sum, the legal risk for offenders will be present, to varying degrees, in both the Integrationist model and the Parallelist model. So the offenders should always be encouraged to take legal advice before participating. But what gives the Parallelist model its distinctive advantage is that, unlike Integrationism, it is immune from the compromises and distortions that almost invariably result from attaching legal benefits to restorative justice.

5.2.3   Lower participation rates

One challenge that could be made to a Parallelist model is that, because it rules out the incentive of any legal advantage, fewer offenders will opt to take part in restorative justice. There are several responses that could be made here.

First, in view of the damage that such incentives can do to the restorative justice process, then if the rate of offender participation decreases, so be it. Adhering to core ethical values and optimising the quality of the process are far more important than getting as many bodies as possible onto the restorative justice conveyer belt.

Second, even if prioritising case numbers could be justified, it is not clear that using a legal carrot-and-stick would be the most effective approach. The numbers being processed by the Integrationist model are still comparatively small – especially when it comes to victim participation rates. This could well be due to the resistance that Integrationism faces from criminal justice professionals and victims, both of whom, as we have seen, have good reason to be wary. Even offenders who might otherwise have participated could be opting out because of how they might be perceived by the victim (see §4.5). If a Parallelist approach was presented to these groups as an option, they might well reconsider.

5.2.4   Voluntariness

In §4.5.4, I considered a battery of responses that an Integrationist could make to the concern that a diversionary approach is not fully voluntary. But there are two related challenges that could be made to the Parallelist alternative.

1. It could be argued that if restorative justice was 'purely voluntary', as in Parallelism, then offenders could just 'do nothing and forget about it', as Braithwaite puts it. Whereas in the Integrationist model, there are 'deterrent elements' that would make 'doing nothing' a far less attractive option (2018: 71).

It is true that an offender who declines restorative justice in an extralegal context could 'do nothing and forget about' the harm that they have caused the victim, without incurring any legal consequence. But it is precisely the absence of this kind of legal threat that makes it possible for Parallelism to achieve the full potential of restorative justice. The decision to take part in restorative justice would be made for the right reasons, and not, as with Integrationism, due to the coercive pressure of a legal Sword of Damocles.

2. It might be argued that, even within a Parallelist model, there remain other types of non-judicial or informal pressures – for instance, from families or facilitators – that cannot be wholly eradicated. Hence, as Zernova and Wright put it, a 'completely voluntary restorative justice may be an unrealistic ideal' (2007: 97). This may be true, but it is not clear how this fact renders the kind of voluntarism possible under Parallelism no better than (or just as problematic as) that espoused by Integrationism.

First, the problem of informal pressure is of a quite different order to the problem of state coercion, for all the reasons given earlier. For example, suppose the victim proposes a reparative task for the outcome agreement. If the offender believes that the task is unreasonable or disproportionate, then it is far more likely that they will feel free to negotiate honestly and openly with the victim about this matter, rather than acquiesce out of fear for what the legal alternative might turn out to be. As Tony Ward and Robyn Langlands argue:

> The danger is that offender wishes will be trumped by those of the community and victim(s), and that the option to either accept an outcome or return to court is really a form of subtle coercion. (2008: 361)[11]

Second, informal pressure is far more likely to consist of legitimate and helpful moral education than it is of punitive threats – particularly if restorative justice is divorced from any legal proceedings. The offender may still feel a moral obligation to repair the harm they have caused in a way that the victim suggests, but this is the kind of 'pressure' that the offender *ought* to feel. It arises from their own moral conscience, not a legal Sword of Damocles hanging over their heads.

5.2.5 Risk of overburdening

Christopher Bennett objects to using a Parallelist approach in a post-sentence setting on the grounds that undertaking both a state sanction and a restorative justice meeting with the victim would be 'in their different ways, quite onerous' and that 'this could lead to quite a burden being placed on offenders' (2006: 128). For this reason, he rejects the post-sentence option in favour of an Integrationist approach:

> One possibility, for instance, is that restorative justice be offered as a voluntary and optional addition to the sentence for those who want it. … But such an arrangement would be an imperfect one in the sense that any involvement in restorative justice would be strictly additional to the sentence and would place an extra burden on the offender who decides to comply. A better solution might be to find a way of counting involvement in restorative justice as part of the discharge of a sentence for those who want it while not prejudicing those who do not. (2008: 177)

However, on a Parallelist model, the 'burden' of a restorative justice meeting with the victim is not 'placed' on the offender. It is freely taken on by the offender as a way of discharging their own active responsibility to repair the harm they have done to the victim.

---

11   Cf. '[C]oercion, pressure and fear of being pursued or punished severely might encourage young offenders to restore more than they think is just' (Eliaerts & Dumortier, 2002: 210). Again, 'fairness dictates that the reparation should not be excessive even if a contrite offender agrees to it' (Wright & Masters, 2002: 55).

In other words, this is not a case of unfairly doubling up or overextending the offender's obligations in the aftermath of their crime. As I suggested earlier, Parallelism is the view that, if one citizen harms another in a way that breaks the law, they thereby acquire both civic (passive) and moral (active) obligations. And these obligations cannot be optimally discharged at the same time or by using the same kind of process. So, as 'onerous' as it might be to undertake both, this is unlikely to put off a genuinely repentant offender – especially once they understand that doing both will give them the chance to meet all of their obligations, both civic and moral. Put another way, if the offender's remorse truly is sincere, then they are likely to feel that it would be an even greater burden to bear if they did *not* also take part in a restorative justice meeting.

5.3   CRIMINAL JUSTICE

5.3.1   Caseload pressures

It might be argued that if a Parallelist framework were ever to be rolled out more widely, then the problem of increasing caseload pressures would also apply. And yet it would be unrealistic to expect that the funding and resources for restorative justice would ever be sufficient to match the growing need. This is especially the case given that a Parallelist model is designed to be driven by participant needs, and so would be inherently open-ended with respect to timescales. Miller, for instance, describes the post-sentence programme 'Victims Voices Heard' (VVH) in the following way:

> Since the VVH program is an independent, nonprofit program that exists separately from the state criminal justice apparatus, its flexibility and time-consuming nature is not threatened by bureaucratic pressures to resolve cases more quickly or to expand the number of individuals it serves. By not being under the auspices of the state, the program is free of any quota constraints or other exigencies of government-funded programs. A more formalized program might lose the open-ended structure of the preparation process and sacrifice the depth of the process for breadth. (2011: 174)

Hence, the financial and staffing resources required to complete each restorative justice process on a Parallelist model are likely to be considerably higher than they would be in any Integrationist model.

We can grant that this is likely to become a pressing logistical issue for the Parallelist model, as it would be for any emerging non-profit service. But this situation needs to be assessed in terms of how it compares with the alternative. For the Integrationist model, an expanding caseload would not only raise resourcing issues for restorative justice. It would also impose enormous pressures and costs upon the criminal justice system. For instance, the relevant judicial authorities would need the time and resources to incorporate referral decisions and case reviews on top of their existing schedules and on a more routine basis. In addition, there would inevitably be a sharp increase in caseload pressures for restorative justice services that would only arise due to their need to comply with criminal justice timescales and quotas. Moreover, the procedural routinisation and restrictions required to fit in with these external pressures will, as we have seen, only diminish the quality and effectiveness of restorative justice. These are all burdens that would be absent from the Parallelist model.

5.3.2   Non-RJ diversionary programmes

In §3.1 ('Principle 9'), I suggested that one way of implementing Parallelism would be to situate restorative justice either after a non-RJ diversionary programme has been completed and the case closed, or as a voluntary adjunct to a lengthy non-RJ unconditional diversionary scheme. But there is an important challenge that could be made to this proposal.

A great many of the objections that I have made in this book to the use of restorative justice as a diversionary option could apply equally to non-RJ diversionary programmes, as they are currently used. So as a matter of consistency, a Parallelist should insist that any non-RJ diversionary programme avoid these same objections. In particular, they would need to ensure that all participants, whether offenders or victims, are rendered equal before the law (as argued in §4.1); any requirements are proportionate and consistent (§4.2); there are adequate due process protections (§4.3);[12] the programmes do not result in net widening and other forms of state overreach (§4.4); they avoid compulsory attitudinising (§4.5) and revictimisation (§4.6); the programmes' values and objectives are not compromised by criminal justice priorities, such as timescales and caseloads (§4.7); the programmes are not infected by the discriminatory practices and attitudes that plague most criminal justice systems (§4.8); and they do not perpetuate or reinforce any colonialist

---

12   The use of existing diversionary programmes is largely justified on the grounds that they are more likely to reduce recidivism than the usual punitive sentences available to the court. However, such programmes are – like the Integrationist use of restorative justice – criminal justice disposals, and so should be subject to all the constraints implied by the rule of law. Hence, while the focus on reducing recidivism is important, it should not take priority over, let alone justify, the neglect of due process, proportionality, consistency and so on.

agenda (§4.9).[13] Yet it is highly doubtful that, in the short term, existing non-RJ diversionary programmes will be modified in these ways, assuming it is even possible to do so.

Even so, not unlike using restorative justice in death penalty cases, I think that, on balance, the interim solution I have proposed in §3.1 is a compromise that can be justified. Any diversionary programme is far more likely to avoid most of the concerns listed earlier or, at least to a far less significant degree, if it does *not* include a restorative justice component. The potential for revictimisation, disproportionate outcomes, state overreach, self-incrimination or compulsory attitudinising is especially acute when restorative justice occurs in an Integrationist context. This has a great deal to do with the distinctive array of moral and psychological resources that are required to move towards authentic moral repair. But it is especially due to the involvement of a victim in a legally conditional setting. This is why the Parallelist can accept the need for non-RJ diversionary programmes in the interim – even though they are likely to remain subject to serious objections – while still maintaining that it would be better if restorative justice is *not* employed as a diversionary programme. This is because the quality and effectiveness of a non-RJ programme will not suffer *to the same degree* as restorative justice would if it was used as a diversionary programme.[14]

So how would diversionary approaches be used, if at all, once the systemic reforms that would be required to fully implement the Parallelist model are in place? There are several possible answers to this question, some of which will depend on the particularities of the relevant legal system or local conditions. So in offering the following two suggestions, I am not thereby excluding the possibility that other options may be more effective or realistic.

1. Many existing non-RJ diversionary programmes are focused on meeting the criminogenic needs of particular offenders. Such interventions include mentoring, job skills training, drug rehabilitation, mental health programmes, family group decision-making and so on. But these are precisely the kind of programmes that are susceptible to the issues listed earlier. However, there is a potential solution. Assuming these programmes are supported by evidence of effectiveness and are tailored to the specific needs of individuals, they could be placed in the same category as publicly funded healthcare. That is, it could be seen as a responsibility of the state to ensure that offenders are enabled and

---

13   *See* Farrell, Betsinger and Hammond (2018), on both the potential harms of diversionary programmes, which include 'Net widening', 'Increased recidivism', and 'Inequitable access and use' (pp. 4-5), as well as best-practice solutions (pp. 12-13). However, it should be noted that this list of 'potential harms' does not include all of the issues that I listed above (e.g. concerns about due process). One reason for this is, as I have suggested, that it is extremely difficult to avoid such issues, given the nature of diversionary approaches in general.

14   One objection to this approach is that non- RJ diversionary programmes may be less effective than restorative justice in reducing recidivism and enabling victims to recover. But even if this were true, the Parallelist approach here involves offering restorative justice *after* the non- RJ diversionary programme has been completed and the case closed. So the beneficial outcomes of restorative justice would still be available.

encouraged to engage in activities that are likely to reduce their risk of reoffending. But like healthcare, the state's use of its coercive power in attaining this goal is more than likely to be counterproductive. Hence, a crime should serve as a legitimate reason for making state-funded resources available to offenders as a voluntary (legally unconditional) service that operates alongside, but is entirely separate from, the criminal justice process.[15]

In other words, like restorative justice, there should be no legal eligibility criteria other than the fact that they have committed a crime. These resources should not be conceived of or utilised as a form of punishment; nor should noncompliance be met with a punitive response. Hence, these programmes should not be used as diversionary mechanisms but instead be made available to offenders to help them escape the cycle of reoffending. Many offenders are already deeply disadvantaged by structural injustices, a lack of adequate social support, and highly restricted life opportunities. Crime could be seen as a trigger that alerts the state to the fact that, with respect to the offender in question, it has failed in its responsibilities, and so it should remedy the situation to whatever extent possible by deploying its resources more effectively. Criminal incidents should also signal to the state that it has failed in its duty to protect the victims. And so, as Susan Herman has argued, its response to any crime – whether or not the offender is prosecuted – should include:

> a focused effort to help ensure the victim's safety, to help the victim recover
> from the trauma of crime, and to provide resources to help the victim rebuild
> his or her life. (2004: 79)

2. If a non-RJ diversionary programme were to be used within a Parallelist model, then the concerns listed earlier could potentially be minimised if it was focused only on victim restitution or community reparation. But these tasks must have been assessed as fair and proportionate by the appropriate judicial authorities, in line with due process, and they must not involve any compulsory attitudinising, state overreach, discrimination and so on.

Of course, such a diversionary programme would in effect be equivalent to a criminal justice sanction. However, this is the de facto status of most diversionary schemes in any case, but without adequate due process protections and so on. Thus, a 'diversion' would, on this proposal, serve as an intermediate sanction – more than a police warning and less than the expected sentence. The goal would be to ensure that the criminal justice system can impose a fair and proportionate sanction for crimes that would otherwise warrant a more burdensome sanction, but for the presence of various mitigating factors.

---

15 Offering such programmes while the case is still in the system would be possible since they do not involve contact between the offender and the victim, and, hence, many of the concerns that attach to the use of restorative justice while a case is still pending fall away.

In this respect, there is one option that could assist any shift from Integrationism to a Parallelist model. Many diversionary programmes that currently pass under the name of 'restorative justice' could transition into the kind of intermediate sanction envisaged here without undergoing radical changes. Such schemes already have a very low victim participation rate. For instance, in the early 2000s, the victim attendance rate in the Thames Valley Police initiative in restorative cautioning was about 14%. Fifteen years later, the rate had changed very little, with 'victims rarely attending panel meetings' (Hoyle & Rosenblatt, 2016: 39). Partly as a consequence, such schemes tend to focus on community reparation. So it would only require relatively slight adjustments in government policy or legislation to convert this kind of 'restorative justice' scheme into the purely reparative 'diversionary' programme suggested here. Restorative justice could then be offered after the offender has completed this kind of programme and exited the system.

5.3.3   Reducing penal control

One disadvantage of the restorative justice arm of Parallelism is that, unlike Integrationism, it seems incapable of reducing the state's penal control over offenders. The mechanism for reducing penal control will have been the judicial decision to remove the case (actually or effectively) from the system, rather than restorative justice per se.

There are three responses that can be made to this challenge. First, while it may be true that using a Parallelist approach would not *reduce* penal control, it also would not, in itself, *increase* it – as can occur when a diversionary approach is used. Put another way, the restorative justice arm of the Parallelist model, regardless of the context, would not carry any risk of widening or tightening the criminal justice net.

Second, the Parallelist view on 'penal control' is that it is not always illegitimate. When (and only when) it is in the public interest to employ the coercive powers of the state – as in cases of sexual assault, child abuse or homicide – then the Parallelist would argue that restorative justice should not be used as a way of circumventing 'penal control'.

Third, and most importantly, the Parallelist model assumes that, if the criminal justice system were operating as it should – with all the necessary reforms (or transformations) in place – then 'penal control' would only be used as a last resort and in a comparatively small number of cases. For instance, many 'crimes', such as trivial misdemeanours and victimless behaviours, would be decriminalised. As Douglas Husak has argued, 'A substantial amount of contemporary punishments are unjust because they are inflicted for conduct that should not have been criminalized at all' (2008: 3). Again, the state would turn its attention to addressing social-structural injustices, rather than sweeping its victims under the rug of mass incarceration. Finally, the normative goal of sentencing would be redirected from administering a punitive calculus, to repairing the harm. In other words, if the criminal justice reforms envisaged by Parallelism were carried out, this would radically reduce the amount of unwarranted 'penal control'.

5.3.4   State underreach

I have argued that, unlike Parallelism, using restorative justice as a diversion from prosecution can result in net widening or net tightening. But it might be argued that there is one use of the diversion from prosecution pathway that does not fall foul of this objection. Many offences are sufficiently serious to warrant prosecution, and yet the usual criminal justice methods are, for whatever reason, unable to achieve this outcome. For instance, it may be that the charges are dismissed due to the lack of witnesses or the offender might have absconded. Thus, suppose that offenders in this category were offered restorative justice as a diversion from prosecution so long as they declined to deny responsibility. In such a case, the offender might accept the offer since they would no longer be pursued by the criminal justice system. The courts might prefer this option since it would avoid the cost and effort of attempting to achieve a prosecution, which is unlikely in any event.

In a scenario such as this, Integrationism could retain the diversion from prosecution referral route without widening the criminal justice net, since the offences in question were serious enough to warrant prosecution. If anything, the Integrationist model would be helping to strengthen the net where it is needed. Offences that would otherwise have either evaded prosecution or that would have required an expensive outlay are not only 'brought to justice' but also dealt with in a way that meets the needs of all concerned.

On the face of it, this would appear to be a powerful argument against Parallelism and in favour of Integrationism. Legal independence, I have suggested, would be extremely difficult, if not unattainable, when cases are still pending. They must actually or effectively exit the system. But if so, it follows that Parallelism would not be able to 'mop up' those offences that *should* have been captured by the criminal justice net but have, thus far, escaped. The Integrationist model, on the other hand, can contribute to preventing precisely this kind of state underreach and, hence, would seem to have a significant advantage over Parallelism in this respect.

To assess this kind of argument, it will be useful to have some evidence before us. Sherman and Strang cite five randomised controlled trials showing that, when restorative justice is offered as a diversion from prosecution, this results in more offences being 'brought to justice' than would otherwise have been the case, given that most offenders manage to evade prosecution:

[O]ffenders in five controlled tests in New York City and Canberra readily took responsibility for serious crimes and 'declined to deny' their guilt – choosing instead the prospect of participation in deciding what should be done about their crimes. ... One of these tests was conducted in Brooklyn, New York, where prosecutors approved a high volume of serious felonies to be diverted to victim-offender mediation. These cases were all felonies, or crimes punishable in New York State by more than one year in prison. ... In the Brooklyn experiment (Davis, et al., 1980), for example, almost three out of four cases randomly assigned to prosecution as usual were never brought to justice. Dismissals and absconding accounted for most of the case attrition. In the RJ (mediation) group, by contrast, 56% of the offences completed the process. From the perspective of both victims and offenders, it seems fair to say that these mediation cases were 'brought to justice'. Certainly, victims were more satisfied in these cases than in the prosecution cases (p. 51). When the percentage of randomly assigned cases that were resolved in each group is compared as a ratio, the odds of bringing the crime to justice were over 2 to 1 in favour of RJ. (2007: 13, 82)

It is important to be clear about the problem for which the Integrationist model is being advanced as a 'solution' here. One issue is that a large proportion of serious offences are not being 'brought to justice' in the sense of the offenders *being prosecuted*.[16] So one question that should be addressed is whether the offer of restorative justice as a diversion from prosecution is the optimal way of tackling *this* particular problem. The evidence clearly suggests that the Integrationist approach is having success of a certain kind, but it is not at all clear that it is solving the problem at hand. Sherman and Strang suggest that restorative justice can help to 'bring more offenders to justice', but it is obviously not doing so by *prosecuting more offenders*. Indeed, the evidence suggests that, if given the option, offenders are more likely to opt for restorative justice rather than submit themselves to prosecution. But in that case, expanding the Integrationist model would only increase this issue, since even fewer offenders would end up being prosecuted.

So what would count as a solution? Sherman and Strang suggest one likely cause of this problem. To achieve a criminal conviction, they observe, requires that key parties are in attendance at court over multiple days at exactly the right times. If certain individuals,

---

16   It might be argued that the high attrition rate in the prosecution group could have been due to the defendants being 'factually innocent'. But Sherman and Strang counter this objection by arguing that the 'random assignment' of offenders to each group means that 'the proportion of truly innocent defendants should have been roughly the same in each group' (2007: 82).

such as witnesses, fail to turn up, this can prevent a conviction. As Sherman and Strang put it:

> Consider how many people must appear at exactly the right time on how many different days in order to achieve a criminal conviction at trial. Every one of those deadlines holds the potential of losing the case to justice. (2007: 82)

Diverting cases to restorative justice 'lowers that risk level', they argue, by 'lowering the number of times and dates, and even more by making it predictable – and convenient – to the key parties concerned' (p. 82). But clearly, restorative justice does not thereby lower the risk level of losing a criminal conviction at trial. It only lowers the risk of participants failing to complete a restorative justice process.

In other words, restorative justice may have certain procedural or administrative advantages over the court system, but this does not make it any more likely that serious offenders will be convicted. A genuine solution would involve reforming the court system so that trials are more predictable and convenient. This is not as farfetched as one might imagine. For example, in 2003, witness care units were piloted in five criminal justice areas in England and Wales. The impact over a six-month period was reported in an independent evaluation by Robyn Holder:

> [W]itness attendance at court up nearly 20 percent. The number of trials which had to be adjourned to a later date as a result of witness difficulties down 27 percent. A 17 percent drop in 'cracked' trials where the witness withdrew their statement or didn't attend. A 10 percent increase in the number of 'positive cracked' trials due to late guilty pleas. A seven fold increase in the take up of victim personal statements. More victims and witnesses attending pre-trial court visits. (2008: 106-107)

It might be argued that the problem at hand is not the lack of a sufficient number of prosecutions, but rather the proportion of offenders who are not 'brought to justice' *of any kind*, whether by means of prosecution or otherwise. And Integrationism does appear to provide a solution to *this* problem. After all, as Sherman and Strang argue, 'From the perspective of both victims and offenders, it seems fair to say that these [restorative justice] cases were "brought to justice"' (2007: 82). And in the Brooklyn trial, when the percentage of cases that were prosecuted is compared as a ratio to the percentage of completed restorative justice cases, then 'the odds of bringing the crime to justice were over 2 to 1 in favour of RJ' (p. 82). By contrast, Parallelism can only bring to (restorative) justice cases that have already received a (criminal) justice response of some kind. So Integrationism has the advantage of bringing cases to (restorative) justice that were not also brought to (criminal) justice.

This does not of course entail that Integrationism is likely to bring more cases to (restorative) justice than Parallelism *in total*. The cases in question here are only those that the court believes it cannot successfully prosecute, and so it decides to use a diversionary approach instead. But this would only amount to a small fraction of the total number of criminal cases. Even when it comes to cases that the court believes *can* be prosecuted, Integrationism is still limited to only those offences that the court decides are suitable for diversion, whether from prosecution, deferred sentence or by some other mechanism. Granted, this could, in some jurisdictions, come to include a sizable portion of the total number of criminal cases. However, on Parallelism, a restorative justice service can, in theory, accept virtually any case that has passed through the justice system, including both pre- and post-sentence cases. Thus, the Parallelist model would always have access to a larger pool of potential cases. So it could be argued that this advantage overrides the fact that Parallelism cannot access a comparatively small number of unprosecutable (or still pending) cases.

But even if Parallelism resulted in a lower number of referrals than Integrationism, it is still possible to show that Integrationist's so-called advantage is deeply problematic. The Integrationist claims to bring (restorative) justice to victims and offenders who would otherwise have received no 'justice' whatsoever. But what is the quality of restorative justice that is in fact being offered in this context? We have already discussed this issue at some length. But here it will be useful to mention one consideration, partly because it is raised by Sherman and Strang themselves.

Consider the offender's motives for participating in restorative justice as a diversionary option. Given the odds against prosecution ('three out of four cases'), why would offenders bother with restorative justice? Sherman and Strang suggest one possible motivation: offenders know that they might escape prosecution, but they cannot be certain. Opting to take part in restorative justice puts an end to the matter. If they complete the process successfully, the courts will not pursue them any further. As Sherman and Strang put it:

> The fact that many more offenders take responsibility for the crimes with RJ ... may simply indicate their preference for a path of least resistance. If RJ makes it quicker and easier for them to 'give it up' and get it over with, they may prefer to game the system that way rather than by playing cat and mouse with the court process. Evidence of such attitudes may be indicated by the substantial differences in rates of guilty pleas across demographic groups and regions within Britain. Whether or not we want defendants to think in such terms will not change the truth about how they in fact make such calculations. (2007: 82)

But if this explanation is right, then the fact that restorative justice was even offered to such 'players of the system' is of serious concern. Perhaps this is why, in the Brooklyn trial, only 56% of the cases that were assigned to restorative justice offences 'completed the process'. But it is very likely that offenders would still have made this kind of 'calculation' even in the successful cases. And, as we have seen (§4.5 and 4.6), such a motivation, even if accompanied by other more worthy incentives, cannot help but have an impact on the quality and effectiveness of restorative justice. But then, the likelihood that, in this context, offenders are 'gaming the system' merely confirms how Integrationism enables and encourages restorative justice values and objectives to be co-opted or traded away for other purposes. Parallelism would not be subject to this kind of extraneous incentive and, hence, in this respect, is more likely than Integrationism to protect and enhance the integrity of restorative justice. This capacity is of such value and importance that it must surely override the fact that Parallelism cannot access unprosecutable cases.

It might be argued, in response, that even if the restorative justice on offer is of a lower quality, it is better than nothing. At least on the Integrationist model the offenders in question are brought to justice *of some kind*. But this response assumes that a diversion to restorative justice is the only option. As I have already argued, a Parallelist could, as an interim solution, advocate the use of non-RJ diversionary schemes, given that they are, in certain respects, less likely to suffer from the kind of problems built into the use of restorative justice as a diversion. For instance, most would not involve victims, thereby avoiding the secondary harm that is likely to be caused by an offender who is 'gaming the system'.

However, the objection that I want to highlight here is the impact that the net-strengthening advantage of Integrationism is likely to have on the criminal justice system. A useful place to start is Sherman and Strang's argument that diverting cases to restorative justice is likely to be cheaper than prosecution:

> Diverting more cases from court that would ultimately be dismissed might bring down the costs of prosecution with no impact on offences brought to justice. It could even raise the count of total offences brought to justice, while bringing down the cost per offence brought to justice. These costs would include legal aid solicitors and barristers, court security and clerical personnel, and time spent by police and prison officials in going to and from court. The costs of organising a single RJ conference appear likely to be far less, even with substantial monitoring of post-conference compliance with agreements. (2007: 86)[17]

---

17   It should be noted here that this cost-benefit analysis is not uncontroversial. For instance, Shannon Sliva, Mariah Shaw and Tyler Han found that prosecutors rejected the notion that 'referring cases to a restorative

But you get the quality of 'justice' that you pay for. If it is genuinely in the public interest to hold offenders to account before the law, then the procedures required to bring them to (criminal) justice should be properly resourced, rather than side-stepped. If, as Sherman and Strang suggest, it is true that most factually guilty offenders will admit responsibility under the right conditions, then the criminal justice system needs to be reformed (or transformed) so that it can realise precisely this set of conditions. What choices would offenders make if they could be assured that the courts would treat them and their loved ones with dignity and respect? What if the court system was adequately staffed and resourced, so that it could offer a more predictable and convenient service to victims and witnesses? What if all offenders were given access to proper legal representation? What if they knew that they would be judged in accordance with the principles of due process and that their sentence would be reasonable, humane and proportionate?

In this respect, it is Parallelism that appears to have a significant advantage over Integrationism. The Parallelist model regards restorative justice and criminal justice as playing distinctive but equally essential roles in bringing offences to 'justice' in the fullest sense. But any Parallelist would also be aware that most criminal justice systems, as they currently operate, are far from fulfilling their indispensable societal role. And this is why, to a significant extent, serious offences are able to evade prosecution. But Parallelism cannot be said to have been fully implemented unless precisely this kind of shortcoming is remedied. Integrationism, by contrast, is a model that can only offer a way of circumventing the problems that plague the criminal justice system, and, thus, it provides no theoretical requirement or incentive to address them.

Enabling offenders to take responsibility for their actions in a restorative justice process is certainly a good that cannot be ignored. But this way of addressing crime deals primarily with the private dimension of crime, not the public. One should not be advanced at the expense of the other. Why implement a model that will only further erode an already-much-degraded justice system? Restorative justice should not operate as a competitor to criminal justice but as an equal partner.

5.3.5   *Parallelism as a driver for reform*

One challenge to Parallelism that might be made is that it is difficult to see how implementing the restorative justice arm of this model will make it any more likely that

---

process is less costly than prosecution'. As one interviewee from a District Attorney's Office explained, 'The cheapest thing for a district attorney to do is to prosecute the case. You file it, you set it for trial, and it either plea bargains or goes to trial. It's much more time intensive to do an assessment, approve a case for restorative justice, and make sure that the defendant complies with the requirements, which is really taking over work that used to be done by the probation department. So basically we're frontloading the work that used to be done later, and we have to figure out how we're going to fund it' (Sliva et al., 2020: 534-535).

desperately needed changes to the criminal justice system will be implemented. The Parallelist answer, and a constant refrain in this book, is that the role of restorative justice is not to rescue a dysfunctional justice system. Its only purpose is to offer individual victims and offenders a safe and voluntary opportunity to work towards repairing the moral harm that was caused by the crime. No matter how extensively it is implemented, this kind of process simply does not have the capacity to bring about the wide-sweeping cultural and legal reforms that most criminal justice systems require. And whenever restorative justice is press-ganged into this role, the collateral damage is profound. Not only is the full potential of restorative justice squandered, but an even greater strain is placed upon a justice system that is already struggling to hold onto its fundamental principles.

The Parallelist model, taken as a whole, is neither a band-aid nor a quick-fix. It is a comprehensive long-term vision for how justice, in the fullest sense, can be realised in the aftermath of a crime. Its central guiding aspiration is to repair the harm that was caused, including both its public and private dimensions. But it follows that, to achieve this goal, implementing restorative justice is not enough. We also need to create a humane, properly functioning, repair-oriented criminal justice system.[18]

18　As well as a range of other informal responses, of course, such as victim support services, substance misuse programmes, justice reinvestment schemes and so on.

6   CONCLUSION

My aim in this book has been to show that the way in which restorative justice is situated in relation to criminal justice can have a significant impact on the quality and effectiveness of both approaches. In particular, I have tried to make the case that the optimal relationship, in this respect, is one of maximal separation, rather than integration. In practice, this means that restorative justice would no longer be used as a diversionary approach but would instead need to become a legally independent service.

I have also argued that this is most likely to be secured by making restorative justice available after a criminal case has *actually* exited the justice system. This could theoretically occur at almost any stage of the criminal justice process, depending on the legal system in question. For instance, a case could exit the system after the police decide not to make an arrest or the prosecutor decides not to file charges (perhaps after a non-RJ diversion from prosecution programme); it could occur after charges are dropped or dismissed in an initial appearance or at a preliminary hearing or before a trial; it might take place after a waived sentence (perhaps after a non-RJ deferred sentence programme) or when a sentence has been completed (post-release). But whenever or however the exit occurs, the crucial requirement is that, so far as the justice system is concerned, no legal benefits will be attached to any subsequent restorative justice process.[1]

I have also suggested two exceptions to this rule, given that, in some cases, it would deny timely access to restorative justice. These are situations in which a criminal case has, in legal terms, *effectively* exited the system – that is to say, where the offender is still 'in' the justice system, but restorative justice can take place without the offender thereby gaining any legal benefits. Specifically, restorative justice could be offered as a voluntary adjunct to either (1) a sentence, such as a prison term or a reparation order, or (2) a lengthy non-RJ unconditional diversionary programme, such as a six-month substance misuse programme.

In making these recommendations, I accept that there could potentially be other settings in which legal independence could be better or equally well secured. This might, for instance, be due to distinctive features of other legal systems and cultures. In other words, the case for Parallelism in this book does not hinge entirely upon whether the settings presented in the foregoing would be the best (or the only workable) ways of attaining legal independence within whatever jurisdiction or legal system is of most relevance to the reader. The defining feature of Parallelism is its claim that the optimal

---

1   This is not to suggest there would be no legal risks. In §5.2.2, I addressed the issue of appeals and litigation, and argued that there is a good Parallelist solution to both.

relationship between restorative justice and criminal justice is one of legal independence. I have set out a series of Guiding Principles, together with examples and suggestions that may provide some assistance in realising this goal (§3.1). But given the immense number of variables at play, how that relationship can be best achieved in practice will, in the end, need to be a matter for each jurisdiction to determine for itself.

My hope is that, in light of the material presented in this book, the Parallelist model will be deemed sufficiently plausible to warrant further empirical investigation. For instance, an existing diversionary restorative justice scheme could trial the addition of extralegal referral protocols and then compare the results. In this conclusion, however, I want to reiterate that Parallelism is far more than a mere procedural or administrative adjustment. It entails a broader normative vision about what is required for justice to be done in the aftermath of criminal wrongdoing.

In his seminal book *Changing Lenses* (1990), Howard Zehr describes restorative justice and criminal justice as being like two very different lenses. The vision of justice that Parallelism offers would accept this distinction, but with one crucial alteration. To continue with Zehr's ocular analogy, restorative justice and criminal justice, as conceived in the Parallelist model, are not to be understood as two competing lenses, only one of which will enable us to see clearly. Instead, we need both, but just not at the same time or for the same purposes.

Thus, Parallelism might be compared to bifocal glasses. The criminal justice system can be aptly construed as 'farsighted'. In each of its decisions, it must take into account the interests of each and every citizen of the state – and not just the particular interests of the individual offender or victim in question. It must, in effect, act as if they were any member of the citizenry. The criminal justice system must censure wrongful acts with equality and fairness, without fear or favour. No matter who stands before the law, regardless of how powerful or wealthy they happen to be, their treatment must be the same. It is for this reason that the decisions and actions of the criminal justice system will often seem abstract, remote, disempowering and even dehumanising to those directly involved. The more extreme end of these qualities could, no doubt, be significantly reduced with various reforms. But most of the abstract or remote features are likely to remain. This is not necessarily due to the inertia, conservatism, elitism or hard-heartedness of the legal profession. Rather, it is due to the fact that many of these impersonal characteristics are a direct and inevitable consequence of the criminal justice system's 'farsighted' focus on serving the public interest.

Restorative justice is not uninterested in wider societal needs. Indeed, any society without restorative justice would be considerably poorer. However, in terms of its procedural focus, restorative justice is invariably 'nearsighted'. It is primarily interested in meeting the needs of private citizens. It serves 'the micro-communities of place or relationships which are directly affected by an offence', as Zehr puts it (2002: 28). It takes into account their unique histories, personalities and the specifics of the offence that has caused harm. A restorative justice process is not, in itself, designed to serve the interests of the public at large. And the moment it is employed to this end, it will lose its way.

In the aftermath of a crime, 'justice', in the fullest sense, requires both perspectives. It must be both 'farsighted' and 'nearsighted'. This is why we need both restorative justice and criminal justice. However, like the two segments of a bifocal lens, we will only be able to 'see' each perspective with the clarity that is possible if we use them separately. Thus, to give restorative justice and the criminal justice system the best chance of working together to bring about this more holistic vision of justice, we need to ensure that they can operate independently.

Bibliography

ACT Department of Justice and Community Safety. (2006). *First phase review of restorative justice*. Canberra: Department of Justice and Community Safety. Revision: 3. 21 December 2012.

ACT Restorative Justice Sub-Committee. (2003). *Restorative justice options for the ACT issues paper*. Australian Capital Territory, Canberra: Department of Justice and Community Safety.

AEquitas, the Justice Management Institute, & the Urban Institute (2020). *Model response to sexual violence for prosecutors (RSVP model): an invitation to lead. Volume I: prosecution practices*. Washington: Department of Justice, Office on Violence Against Women.

Agnihotri, S. & Veach, C. (2017). Reclaiming restorative justice: an alternate paradigm for justice. *CUNY Law Review*, 20, 323-350.

Ahren, M. (2004). Indigenous people's culture, customs, and traditions and customary law: the Saami people's perspective. *Arizona Journal of International and Comparative Law*, 21(1), 63-112.

Allan, A., de Mott, J., Larkins, I.M., Turnbull, L., Warwick, T., Willett, L. & Allan, M.M. (2021). The impact of voluntariness of apologies on victims' responses in restorative justice-findings of a quantitative study. *Psychiatry, Psychology, and Law*, 29:4, 593-609.

Alternatives. (2017). *Inspiring the future: Alternatives' restorative justice work at Paul Robeson High School 2014-2017*. Chicago: Alternatives, Inc.

Amstutz, L.S. & Zehr, H. (1998). *Victim-offender conferencing in Pennsylvania's juvenile justice system*. Harrisburg: Commonwealth of Pennsylvania.

Andersen, J.D. (2003). *Victim offender settlements, general deterrence, and social welfare*. The Harvard John M. Olin Discussion Paper Series: No. 402 01.

Andvig, E., Koffeld-Hamidane, S., Ausland, L. & Karlsson, B. (2020). Inmates' perceptions and experiences of how they were prepared for release from a Norwegian open prison. *Nordic Journal of Criminology*, 22:2, 203-220.

Anyon, Y., Gregory, A., Stone, S., Farrar, J., Jenson, J.M., McQueen, J., Downing, B., Greer, E. & Simmons, J. (2016). Restorative interventions and school discipline sanctions in a large urban school district. *American Educational Research Journal*, 53(6), 1663-1697.

Armour, M. (2015). *Ed White middle school restorative discipline evaluation: implementation and impact, 2014/2015, sixth, seventh, & eighth grade*. Austin: University of Texas-Austin, The Institute for Restorative Justice and Restorative Dialogue.

Ashworth, A. (2002). Responsibilities, rights and restorative justice. *The British Journal of Criminology*, 42(3), 578-595.

Ashworth, A. (2003). *Principles of criminal law* (4th ed.). Oxford: Oxford University Press.

Ashworth, A. (2010). *Sentencing and criminal justice* (5th ed.). Cambridge: Cambridge University Press.

Avieli, H., Winterstein, T.B. & Gal, T. (2021). Challenges in implementing restorative justice with older adults: institutional gatekeepers and social barriers. *The British Journal of Social Work*, 51(4), 1445-1462.

Barmaki, R. (2021). On the incompatibility of 'western' and aboriginal views of restorative justice in Canada: a claim based on an understanding of the Cree justice. *Contemporary Justice Review*, 25:1, 24-55.

Bazemore, G. (2006). Review of Karp, D.R. & Allena, T. (2004). Restorative justice on college campuses. *Contemporary Justice Review*, 9(4), 443-448.

Becroft, A. (2017). *Family group conferences: still New Zealand's gift to the world?* Wellington: Office of the Children's Commissioner.

Bennett, C. (2006). Taking the sincerity out of saying sorry: restorative justice as ritual. *Journal of Applied Philosophy*, 23(2), 127-143.

Bennett, C. (2008). *The apology ritual: a philosophical theory of punishment*. Cambridge: Cambridge University Press

Berg, M. (2011). *Popular justice: a history of lynching in America*. Chicago: The Rowman & Littlefield Publishing Group.

Black, H.C. (2009). *Black's law dictionary* (9th ed.). St. Paul: West Publishing Co.

Blad, J. (2003). Community mediation, criminal justice and restorative justice: rearranging the institutions of law. In L. Walgrave (ed.), *Repositioning restorative justice* (pp. 191-207). Cullompton: Willan Publishing.

Blagg, H. (1985). Reparation and justice for juveniles. *British Journal of Criminology*, 25, 267-279.

Blagg, H. (1997). A just measure of shame? Aboriginal youth and conferencing in Australia. *The British Journal of Criminology*, 37(4), 481-501.

Blagg, H. (2015). *Models of best practice: aboriginal community patrols in Western Australia*. Crawley: The University of Western Australia.

Boersig, J. (2005). Indigenous youth and the criminal justice system in Australia. In E. Elliott & B. Gordon (eds.), *New directions in restorative justice* (pp. 115-133). London: Willan Publishing.

Bolitho, J. (2019). Complex cases of restorative justice after serious crime: creating and enabling spaces for those with disability. In T. Gavrielides (ed.), *Routledge international handbook of restorative justice* (pp. 159-176). Milton: Routledge.

Bonig, R. (2013). Re-investing in justice: finding a better way to prevent crime. *Bulletin (Law Society of South Australia)*, 35(4), 12-14.

Boonin, D. (2008). *The problem of punishment*. Cambridge: Cambridge University Press.

Boutellier, H. (2006). The vital context of restorative justice. In I. Aertsen, T. Daems & L. Robert (eds.), *Institutionalizing restorative justice* (pp. 25-43). London: Willan Publishing.

Bovens, M. (1998). *The quest for responsibility: accountability and citizenship in complex organisations.* Cambridge: Cambridge University Press.

Bowen, H., Boyack, J. & Hooper, S. (2000) *New Zealand restorative justice practice manual.* Auckland: Restorative Justice Trust.

Bowen, H. & Thompson, T. (1999). Restorative justice and the New Zealand Court of Appeal's Decision in the Clotworthy Case. *Journal of South Pacific Law,* 3(1).

Boyes-Watson, C. (2004). What happens when restorative justice is encouraged, enabled and/or guided by legislation? In H. Zehr & B. Toews (eds.), *Critical issues in restorative justice* (pp. 227-238). Monsey: Criminal Justice Press.

Boyes-Watson, C. (2019). Looking at the past of restorative justice: normative reflections on its future. In T. Gavrielides (ed.), *Routledge international handbook of restorative justice* (pp. 7-20). Milton: Routledge.

Braithwaite, J. (1989). *Crime, shame and reintegration.* New York: Cambridge University Press.

Braithwaite, J. (1997). Restorative justice and a better future. The Dorothy Killam Memorial Lecture. Halifax, Nova Scotia: Dalhousie University.

Braithwaite, J. (1999). Restorative justice: assessing optimistic and pessimistic accounts. In M. Tonry (ed.), *Crime and justice: a review of research, vol. 25* (pp. 1-127). Chicago: University of Chicago Press.

Braithwaite, J. (2002a). In search of restorative jurisprudence. In L. Walgrave (ed.), *Restorative justice and the law* (pp. 150-167). Cullompton: Willan Publishing.

Braithwaite, J. (2002b). *Restorative justice & responsive regulation.* Oxford: Oxford University Press.

Braithwaite, J. (2002c). Setting standards for restorative justice. *British Journal of Criminology,* 42(3), 563-577.

Braithwaite, J. (2006). Accountability and responsibility through restorative justice. In M.W. Dowdle (ed.), *Public Accountability: Designs, Dilemas and Experiences* (pp. 33-51). Cambridge: Cambridge University Press.

Braithwaite, J. (2018). Minimally sufficient deterrence. *Crime and Justice,* 47(1), 69-118.

Braithwaite, J. (2019). The future of restorative justice. In T. Gavrielides (ed.), *Routledge international handbook of restorative justice* (pp. 1-3). London: Routledge.

Braithwaite, J. & Mugford, S. (1994). Conditions of successful reintegration ceremonies. *British Journal of Criminology,* 34(2), 139-171.

Broadhurst, R., Morgan, A., Payne, J. & Maller, R. (2018). *Australian capital territory restorative justice evaluation: an observational outcome evaluation.* Canberra: Australian National University and the Australian Institute of Criminology.

Brookes, D. (2009). *Restorative justice and work-related death: consultation. Report.* Melbourne: Creative Ministries Network.

Brookes, D.R. (1998). Evaluating restorative justice programs. *Humanity & Society*, 22(1), 23-37.

Brookes, D.R. (2019a). *Beyond harm: toward justice, healing and peace.* Sydney: Relational Approaches.

Brookes, D.R. (2019b). Restorative justice and domestic violence. (Unpublished).

Brookes, D.R. (2021a). Moral grounds for forgiveness. *International Journal of Applied Philosophy*, 35(1), 97-108.

Brookes, D.R. (2021b). Forgiveness as conditional: a reply to Kleinig. *International Journal of Applied Philosophy*, 35(1), 117-125.

Brookes, D.R. & Kirkwood, S. (2007). Will the victim statement scheme secure greater participation for victims in the criminal justice process? *Criminal Justice Scotland*, November, 1-6.

Brookes, D.R. & McDonough, I. (2006). The differences between mediation and restorative justice/practice. (Unpublished).

Brown, J.G. (1994). The use of mediation to resolve criminal cases: a procedural critique. *Emory Law Journal*, 43(4), 1247-1310.

Buckingham, S. (2013). Reducing incarceration for youthful offenders with a developmental approach to sentencing. *Loyola of Los Angeles Law Review*, 85(3), 801-884.

Buonatesta, A., Gailly, P. & Van Doosselaere, D. (2018). Restorative justice in France and French-speaking Belgium: not on the same track? *The International Journal of Restorative Justice*, 1(1), 132-137.

Burnett, N. & Thorsborne, M. (2015). *Restorative practice and special needs: a practical guide to working restoratively with young people.* London: Jessica Kingsley Publishers.

Buss, S. (1999). Appearing respectful: the moral significance of manners. *Ethics*, 109(4), 795-826.

Caruso, G.D. (2021). *Rejecting retributivism: free will, punishment, and criminal justice.* Cambridge: Cambridge University Press.

Castiglione, J.D. (2010). Qualitative and quantitative proportionality: a specific critique of retributivism. *Ohio State Law Journal*, 71(1), 71-125.

Choi, J.J. & Severson, M. (2009). "What! What kind of apology is this?": the nature of apology in victim-offender mediation. *Children and Youth Services Review* 31, 813-820.

Choi, J., Bazemore, G. & Gilbert, M. (2012). Review of research on victims' experiences in restorative justice: implications for youth justice. *Children and Youth Services Review*, 34(1), 35-42.

Christie, N. (1977). Conflicts as property. *British Journal of Criminology*, 17(1), 1-15.

Clairmont, D. (2005). Penetrating the walls: implementing a system-wide restorative justice approach in the justice system. In E. Elliott & R. Gordon (eds.), *New directions in restorative justice* (pp. 245-265). Cullompton: Willan Publishing.

Clamp, K. (2019). Restorative policing for the 21st century: historical lessons for future practice. In T. Gavrielides (ed.), *Routledge international handbook of restorative justice* (pp. 177-192). London: Routledge.

Coates, R.B. & Gehm, J. (1985). *Victim meets offender: An Evaluation of victim-offender reconciliation programs*. Valparaiso: PACT Institute of Justice.

Corpus Juris Secundum. (1961). *Criminal law*. Volume 22. Brooklyn: American Law Book Company.

Coulthard, G.S. (2007). Subjects of empire: indigenous peoples and the 'politics of recognition' in Canada. *Contemporary Political Theory*, 6, 437-460.

Coulthard, G.S. (2014). *Red skin, white masks: rejecting the colonial politics of recognition*. Minneapolis: University of Minnesota

Council of Europe Committee of Ministers. (1999). *Recommendation no. R (99) 19 of the committee of ministers to member states concerning mediation in penal matters*. Strasbourg Cedex: Council of Europe Publishing, 15 September.

Council of the European Union. (2012). *Directive 2012/29/EU of the European parliament and of the council of October 2012 establishing minimum standards on the rights, support and protection of victims of crime, and replacing Council Framework Decision 2001/220/JHA*. Official Journal of the European Union, L. 315: 57-73.

Covey, H.C. & Eisnach, D. (2021). *Daily life of African Americans in primary documents*. Santa Barbara: Greenwood, an imprint of ABC-CLIO, LLC.

Crawford, A. (2002). The state, community and restorative justice: Heresy, Nostalgia and butterfly collecting. In L. Walgrave (ed.), *Restorative justice and the law* (pp. 101-129). Cullompton: Willan Publishing.

Crawford, A. & Newburn, T. (2003). *Youth offending and restorative justice: implementing reform in youth justice*. Cullompton: Willan Publishing.

Crown Office and Procurator Fiscal Service. (2001). *Prosecution code*. Edinburgh: Crown Office.

Cunneen, C. (1997). Community conferencing and the fiction of indigenous control. *Australian & New Zealand Journal of Criminology* (Australian Academic Press), 30(3), 292-311.

Cunneen, C. (2002). Restorative justice and the politics of decolonization. In E.G.M. Weitekamp & H. Kerner (eds.), *Restorative justice: theoretical foundations* (pp. 32-49). Cullompton: Willan Publishing.

Cunneen, C. (2010). The limitations of restorative justice. In C. Cunneen & C. Hoyle (eds.), *Debating restorative justice* (pp. 101-187). Oxford: Hart Publishing.

Cuppini, A. (2021). A restorative response to victims in proceedings before the international criminal court: reality or Chimaera? *International Criminal Law Review*, 21(2), 313-341.

Currie, E. (2005). *The role of forgiveness and repentance in sentencing* (Unpublished MA dissertation). King's College London, UK.

Daly, K. (2002). Restorative justice: the real story. *Punishment & Society*, 4(1), 55-79.

Daly, K. (2003). Mind the gap: restorative justice theory in theory and practice. In A. von Hirsch, J. Roberts, A. Bottoms, K. Roach & M. Schiff (eds.), *Restorative justice and criminal justice: competing or reconcilable paradigms* (pp. 219-236). Oxford: Hart Publishing.

Davis, F. (2014). Discipline with dignity: Oakland classrooms try healing instead of punishment. *Reclaiming Children and Youth*, 23(1), 38-41.

Davis, R., Tichane, M. & Grayson, D. (1980). *Mediation & arbitration as alternatives to criminal prosecution in felony arrest cases: an evaluation of the Brooklyn dispute resolution center* (First Year). New York: Vera Institute of Justice.

Davison, M., Penner, A.M. & Penner, E.K. (2022). Restorative for all? Racial disproportionality and school discipline under restorative justice. *American Educational Research Journal*, 59(4): 687-718.

D'Souza, N. & L'Hoiry, X. (2021). An area of untapped potential? The use of restorative justice in the fight against serious and organized crime: a perception study. *Criminology & Criminal Justice*, 21(2), 224-241.

de Waal, F. (2006). *Primates and philosophers: how morality evolved*. Princeton: Princeton University Press.

Delgado, R. (2000). Goodbye to Hammurabi: analyzing the atavistic appeal of restorative justice. *Stanford Law Review*, 52(4): 751-775.

Denkers, J.M. & Winkel, F.W. (1998). Crime victims' well-being and fear in a prospective and longitudinal study. *International Review of Victimology*, 5(2): 141-162.

Dignan, J. (2003). Towards a systemic model of restorative justice. In A. von Hirsch, J. Roberts, A. Bottoms, K. Roach & M. Schiff (eds.), *Restorative justice and criminal justice: competing or reconcilable paradigms* (pp. 135-156). Oxford: Hart Publishing.

Doob, A. & Webster, C. (2003). Sentence severity and crime: accepting the null hypothesis. *Crime and Justice: A Review of Research*, 30, 143-195.

Duff, A. (1986). *Trials and punishments*. Cambridge: Cambridge University Press.

Duff, A. (2003). Restoration and retribution. In A. von Hirsch, J. Roberts, A. Bottoms, K. Roach & M. Schiff (eds.), *Restorative justice and criminal justice: competing or reconcilable paradigms* (pp. 43-60). Oxford: Hart Publishing.

Duff, A. (2007). *Answering for crime: responsibility and liability in the criminal law*. Oxford: Hart Publishing.

Eden, M. (2018). Teachers nationwide say Obama's discipline 'reform' put them in danger. So why are the unions fighting DeVos on repeal? *The 74 Media Inc.*, April 2.

Eliaerts, C. & Dumortier, E. (2002). Restorative justice for children: in need of procedural safeguards and standards. In E.G.M. Weitekamp & H. Kerner (eds.), *Restorative justice: theoretical foundations* (pp. 204-223). Cullompton: Willan Publishing.

Elias, R. (1993). *Victims still: the political manipulation of crime victims.* Newbury Park: SAGE.

Elias, S. (2001). Lecture on the occasion of the John Robson lecture for the Napier Pilot City Trust, April 24.

Elias, S. (2018). *Fairness in criminal justice: golden threads and pragmatic patches.* Cambridge: Cambridge University Press.

Epstein, R.A. (2005). *What Do We Mean by the Rule of Law?* Wellington: New Zealand Business Round Table.

Equal Justice Initiative. (2017). *Lynching in America: confronting the legacy of racial terror* (3rd ed.). Montgomery: Equal Justice Initiative.

Eriksson, A. (2009). A bottom-up approach to transformative justice in Northern Ireland. *International Journal of Transitional Justice*, 3(3), 301-320.

Fanon, F. (1968). *The wretched of the earth.* New York: Grove Press.

Farrell, J., Betsinger, A. & Hammond, P. (2018). *Best practices in youth diversion: literature review for the Baltimore City Youth Diversion Committee.* Baltimore: The Institute for Innovation & Implementation, University of Maryland School of Social Work.

Fromherz, C.J. (2008). Indigenous peoples' courts: egalitarian juridical pluralism, self-determination, and the United Nations Declaration on the Rights of indigenous peoples. *University of Pennsylvania Law Review*, 156(5), 1341-1381.

Fry, D.P. & Soderberg, P. (2013). Lethal aggression in mobile forager bands and implications for the origins of war. *Science*, 341, 270-273.

Gavrielides, T. (2022). *Power, race, and justice: the restorative dialogue we will not have.* New York: Routledge.

Geeraets, V.C. (2016). Fictions of restorative justice, Vincent Geeraets. *Criminal Law and Philosophy*, 10(2), 265-281.

Gerkin, P.M. (2009). Participation in victim-offender mediation: lessons learned from observations. *Criminal Justice Review*, 34(2), 226-247.

Goldsmith, A., Hasley, M. & Bamford, D. (2005). *Adult restorative justice conferencing pilot: an evaluation—final report.* Adelaide: South Australian Courts Administration Authority.

Goldstein, A.S. & Marcus, M. (1977). The myth of judicial supervision in three "inquisitorial" systems: France, Italy, and Germany. *The Yale Law Journal*, 87(2), 240-283.

González, T. (2020). The legalization of restorative justice: a fifty-state empirical analysis. *Utah Law Review,* 2019(5), Article 3, 1027-1067.

Government of Canada. (2016). *Indigenous Justice Program.* Ottawa: Department of Justice Canada.

Grant, R. (1992). Honesty, honour and trust. In D. Anderson (ed.), *The loss of virtue.* London: Social Affairs Unit/National Review Books.

Green, S. (2007). The victims' movement and restorative justice. In G. Johnstone & D. Van Ness (eds.), *Handbook of restorative justice* (pp. 171-191). Cullompton: Willan Publishing.

Gromet, D. & Darley, J. (2009). Retributive and restorative justice: importance of crime severity and shared identity in people's justice responses. *Australian Journal of Psychology,* 61(1), 50-57.

Gross, H. (1979). *A theory of criminal justice.* Oxford: Oxford University Press.

Halliday, J. (2001). *Making punishments work: report of a review of the sentencing framework for England and Wales.* London: Home Office.

Hampton, J. (1984). The moral education theory of punishment. *Philosophy and Public Affairs,* 13, 208-238.

Hartmann, A. (2019). Victims and restorative justice: bringing theory and evidence together. In T. Gavrielides (ed.), *Routledge international handbook of restorative justice* (pp. 127-144). Milton: Routledge.

Havel, V. (1978). The power of the powerless. In J. Vladislav (ed.), *Living in the truth: twenty-two essays published on the occasion of the award of the Erasmus Prize to Václav Havel* (pp. 36-122). London: Faber and Faber.

Hawkins, K. (2003). *Law as last resort: prosecution decision-making in a regulatory agency.* Oxford: Oxford University Press.

Herman, J.L. (2005). Justice from the victim's perspective. *Violence Against Women,* 11(5), 571-602.

Herman, S. (2004). Is restorative justice possible without a parallel system for victims? In H. Zehr & B. Toews (eds.), *Critical issues in restorative justice* (pp. 75-84). Monsey: Criminal Justice Press.

Hodgson, J. (2022). *Gender, power and restorative justice: a feminist critique.* Cham: Springer International Publishing AG.

Holder, R. (2008). *The quality of justice: operation of the victims of crime act 1994 in the Australian Capital Territory 1996-2007.* Canberra: ACT Government, June.

Holloway, K. (2018). In America, prisoners with money can pay their way to a nicer stay. *Salon,* 13 January.

Holtermann, J. (2009a). *Everything you always wanted to know about restorative justice (but were afraid to ask)* (PhD thesis). Roskilde: Department of Culture and Identity, Roskilde University.

Holtermann, J. (2009b). Outlining the shadow of the axe—on restorative justice and the use of trial and punishment. *Criminal Law and Philosophy*, 3, 187-207.

Home Office. (2001) *Home office crime reduction programme: restorative justice. project specification*. London: Home Office.

Howard, J.W. & Pasternak, A. (2021). Criminal wrongdoing, restorative justice, and the moral standing of unjust states. *The Journal of Political Philosophy*, 1-18 (online).

Hoyle, C. (2010). The case for restorative justice. In C. Cunneen & C. Hoyle (eds.), *Debating restorative justice* (pp. 1-100). Oxford: Hart Publishing.

Hoyle, C. & Rosenblatt, F.F. (2016). Looking back to the future: threats to the success of restorative justice in the United Kingdom. *Victims & Offenders*, 11(1), 30-49.

Hoyle, C., Young, R. & Hill, R. (2002). *Proceed with caution: an evaluation of the Thames Valley police initiative in restorative cautioning*. Oxford: Joseph Rowntree Foundation.

Husak, D.N. (2008). *Overcriminalization: the limits of the criminal law*. New York: Oxford University Press.

Jacobson, J. & Hough, M. (2007). *Mitigation: the role of personal factors in sentencing*. London: Prison Reform Trust.

Johnson, H.R. (2019). *Peace and good order: the case for indigenous justice in Canada*. Toronto: McClelland & Stewart.

Johnstone, G. (2007). Critical perspectives on restorative justice. In G. Johnstone & D. Van Ness (eds.), *Handbook of restorative justice* (pp. 598-614). Cullompton: Willan Publishing.

Johnstone, G. (2017). Restorative justice for victims: inherent limits? *Restorative Justice: An International Journal*, 5(3), 382-395.

Jones, V.N. & McElderry, C.G. (2021). Social work and reparations: applying a restorative justice approach. *Journal of Ethnic & Cultural Diversity in Social Work*, 1-10 (online).

Joyce, R. (2006). *The evolution of morality*. Cambridge: The MIT Press.

Justice Committee. (2016). *Restorative justice: fourth report of session 2016-17*. London: House of Commons.

Karp, D.R. & Allena, T. (eds.). (2004). *Restorative justice on the college campus: promoting student growth and responsibility, and reawakening the spirit of campus community*. Springfield: Charles C. Thomas Publisher Ltd.

Kelly, E.I. (2018). *The limits of blame: rethinking punishment and responsibility*. Cambridge: Harvard University Press.

Kelly, E.I. (2021). From retributive to restorative justice. *Criminal Law and Philosophy*, 15(2), 237-247.

Kirby, A. & Jacobson, J. (2015). *Evaluation of the pre-sentence RJ pathfinder: February 2014 to May 2015*. Project report. London: Restorative Solutions.

Kissel, M. & Kim, N.C. (2018). The emergence of human warfare: current perspectives. *American Journal of Physical Anthropology*, 168(S67), 141-163.

Krygier, M. & Winchester, A. (2018). Arbitrary power and the ideal of the rule of law. In C. May & A. Winchester (eds.), *Handbook on the rule of law* (pp. 75-95). Northampton: Edward Elgar Pub., Inc.

La Prairie, C. (1999). Some reflections on new criminal justice policies in Canada: restorative justice, alternative measures and conditional sentences. *Australian & New Zealand Journal of Criminology*, 32(2), 139-152.

Langbeinm J.H. (1978). Torture and plea bargaining. *The University of Chicago Law Review*, 46(1), 3-22.

Lanni, A. (2020). Taking restorative justice seriously. *Buffalo Law Review*. Harvard Public Law Working Paper No. 21-17.

Laxminarayan, M. (2014). *Accessibility and initiation of restorative justice*. Leuven: European Forum for Restorative Justice.

Lenta, P. (2021). Can transitional amnesties promote restorative justice? *Critical Review of International Social and Political Philosophy*, 1-27 (online).

Levrant, S., Cullen, F.T., Fulton, B. & Wozniak, J.F. (2003). Reconsidering restorative justice: the corruption of benevolence revisited? In G. Johnstone (ed.), *A restorative justice reader: texts, sources, context* (pp. 417-425). Cullompton: Willan Publishing.

Liebmann, M. (2007). *Restorative justice: how it works*. London: Jessica Kingsley Publishers.

Lilles, H. (2002). Circle sentencing: part of the restorative justice continuum. *International Institute of Restorative Practices News*.

Little, S., Stewart, A. & Ryan, N. (2018). Restorative justice conferencing: not a panacea for the overrepresentation of Australia's indigenous youth in the criminal justice system. *International Journal of Offender Therapy and Comparative Criminology*, 62(13), 4067-4090.

Longclaws, L., Galaway, B. & Barkwell, L. (1996). Piloting family group conferences for young aboriginal offenders in Winnipeg, Canada. In J. Hudson, A. Morris, G. Maxwell & B. Galloway (eds.), *Family group conferences: perspectives on policy and practice* (pp. 195-205). Annandale: The Federation Press.

Love, C. (2002). Māori perspectives on collaboration and colonisation in contemporary Aotearoa/New Zealand child and family welfare policies and practices. Paper presented at the Policy and Partnerships Conference. Wilfrid Laurier University, Waterloo.

Magee, B. (1998). *Confessions of a philosopher: a journey through western philosophy*. London: Phoenix.

Marshall, T. (2003). Restorative justice: an overview. In G. Johnstone (ed.), *A restorative justice reader: texts, sources, context* (pp. 28-45). Cullompton: Willan Publishing.

Mathiesen, T. (2006). *Prison on trial* (3rd ed.). Winchester: Waterside Press.

Matthews, R. (2006). Reintegrative shaming and restorative justice: reconciliation or divorce? In I. Aertsen, T. Daems & L. Robert (eds.), *Institutionalizing restorative justice* (pp. 237-260). London: Willan Publishing.

Maxwell, G. (2008). Crossing cultural boundaries: implementing restorative justice in international and indigenous contexts. *Sociology of Crime, Law and Deviance*, 11, 81-95.

Maxwell, G. & Morris, A. (1993). *Families, victims & culture: youth justice in New Zealand*. Wellington: Social Policy Agency and Institute of Criminology, Victoria University of Wellington.

McAsey, B. (2005). Critical evaluation of the Koori court division of the Victorian magistrates' court. *Deakin Law Review*, 10(2), 654-685.

McCold, P. (2000). Toward a holistic vision of restorative juvenile justice: a reply to the maximalist model. *Contemporary Justice Review*, 3, 357-414.

McCold, P. (2003). A survey of assessment research on mediation and conferencing. In L. Walgrave (ed.), *Repositioning restorative justice* (pp. 67-120). Cullompton: Willan Publishing.

McCold, P. & Wachtel, B. (1998). *Restorative policing experiment: the Bethlehem police family group conferencing project*. Pipersville: Community Service Foundation.

McCullough, M. (2008). *Beyond revenge: the evolution of the forgiveness instinct*. San Francisco: Jossey-Bass.

McGowan, M. (2021). George Pell: news organisations fined more than $1m over reporting of sexual abuse verdict. *The Guardian*, 4 June.

McGrath, S. (2020). Decolonizing 'justice' in settler-colonial states: a transnational study. (Unpublished).

McGuire, M. & Palys, T. (2020). Toward sovereign indigenous justice: on removing the colonial straightjacket. *Decolonization of Criminology and Justice*, 2(1), 59-82.

McIvor, B., ed., (2018). *First peoples law: essays on Canadian law and decolonization* (3d ed.). Vancouver: First Peoples Law Corporation.

Miers, D., Maguire, M., Goldie, S., Sharpe, K., Hale, C., Netten, A., Uglow, S., Doolin, K., Hallam, A., Enterkin, J. & Newburn, T. (2001). *An exploratory evaluation of restorative justice schemes*. Crime Reduction Research Series Paper 9, Home Office, UK.

Miller, S.L. (2011). *After the crime: the power of restorative justice dialogues between victims and violent offenders*. New York: New York University Press.

Miller, S.L. & Hefner, M.K. (2015). Procedural justice for victims and offenders? Exploring restorative justice processes in Australia and the US. *Justice Quarterly*, 32(1), 142-167.

Ministry of Justice. (2004). *Restorative justice: best practice in New Zealand*. Wellington: New Zealand Government.

Ministry of Justice. (2014). *Presentence restorative justice*. London: Ministry of Justice.

Ministry of Justice. (2020). *Restorative justice impact of section 24A of the sentencing act 2002 on reoffending*. Wellington: New Zealand Government.

Ministry of Justice. (2022). *New Zealand crime and victims survey. Cycle 4 survey findings. Descriptive statistics. June 2022. Results drawn from Cycle 4 (2020/21) of the New Zealand crime and victims survey.* Wellington: Ministry of Justice.

Minow, M. (1998). *Between vengeance and forgiveness: facing history after genocide and mass violence.* Boston: Beacon Press.

Monbiot, G. (2007). Libertarians are the true social parasites. *The Guardian*, 23 October.

Morris, A. (2003). Critiquing the critics: a brief response to critics of restorative justice. In G. Johnstone (ed.), *A restorative justice reader: texts, sources, context* (pp. 461-476). Cullompton: Willan Publishing.

Morris, A. & Maxwell, G. (1998). Restorative justice in New Zealand: family group conferences as a case study. *Western Criminology Review*, 1(1): 1-17 (online).

Morris, R. (2000). *Stories of transformative justice.* Toronto: Canadian Scholars' Press.

Moyle, P. (2013). *From family group conferencing to Whanau Ora: Māori social workers talk about their experiences* (Unpublished Master's thesis). Massey University, New Zealand.

Moyle, P. (2014). Maori social workers' experiences of care and protection: a selection of findings. *Te Komako, Social Work Review*, 26(1), 5-64.

Moyle, P. & Tauri, J. (2016). Maori, family group conferencing and the mystifications of restorative justice. *Victims and Offenders: Special Issue: The Future of Restorative Justice?* 11(1), 87-106.

Murphy, J.G. (1988). Forgiveness and resentment. In J.G. Murphy & J. Hampton (eds.), *Forgiveness and mercy* (pp. 14-34). New York: Cambridge University Press.

Mustian, A.L., Cervantes, H. & Lee, R. (2021). Reframing restorative justice in education: shifting power to heal and transform school communities. *The Educational Forum* (West Lafayette, Ind.), 86(1), 51-66.

Napoleon, V. & Friedland, H. (2014). Indigenous legal traditions: roots to renaissance. In M.D. Dubber & T. Hörnle (eds.), *The Oxford handbook of criminal law* (pp. 225-247). Oxford: Oxford University Press.

National Audit Office. (2021). *Reducing the backlog in criminal courts.* London: Ministry of Justice and HM Courts & Tribunals Service.

Nocella, A.J. II (2011). An overview of the history and theory of transformative justice. *Peace & Conflict Review*, 6(1), 1-10.

Norris, F.H. & Kaniasty, K. (1994). Psychological distress following criminal victimization in the general population: cross-sectional, longitudinal, and prospective analyses. *Journal of Consulting and Clinical Psychology*, 62(1), 111-123.

O'Connell, T., Wachtel, B. & Wachtel, T. (1999). *Conferencing handbook: the new real justice training manual.* Pipersville: The Piper's Press.

O'Dwyer, K. (2005). Victim-offender mediation with juvenile offenders in Ireland. In A. Mestitz & S. Ghetti (eds.), *Victim-offender mediation with youth offenders in Europe: an overview and comparison of 15 countries.* Dordrecht: Springer.

Office of the Children's Commissioner. (2017). *Fulfilling the vision: improving family group conference preparation and participation*. Wellington: Office of the Children's Commissioner.

Ohbuchi, K., Kameda, M. & Agarie, N. (1989). Apology as aggression control: its role in mediating appraisal of and response to harm. *Journal of Personality and Social Psychology*, 56(2), 219-227.

Olsaretti, S. (1998). Freedom, force and choice: against the rights-based definition of voluntariness. *Journal of Political Philosophy*, 6(1), 52-78.

Olshak, R.T. (2006). Review essay [Review of the book *Restorative justice on the college campus*]. *ACResolution*, 4(1), 6.

Olson, J. & Sarver, R.S. (2022). How restorative are you? Introducing the restorative index. *Victims & Offenders*, 17(6), 941-973.

Palys, T. (2004). Resolving conflicts involving Indigenous peoples: lessons from the search for 'indigenous justice' in Canada. Intervention to the U.N working group on indigenous populations at its 22nd session; 19-23 July; Geneva, Switzerland.

Palys, T. & Victor, W. (2008). "Getting to a better place": Qwi:qwelstóm, the Stó:lō, and self-determination. In Law Commission of Canada (ed.), *Indigenous legal traditions* (pp. 12-39). Vancouver: UBC Press.

Paul, G.D. & Borton, I.M. (2021). *Creating restorative justice: a communication perspective of justice, restoration, and community*. Lanham: Lexington Books.

Payne, J. (2007). *Criminal trial delays in Australia: trial listing outcomes*. Research and Public Policy Series No. 74. Canberra: Australian Institute of Criminology.

Penning, M. (2016). *Written evidence for justice select committee inquiry into restorative justice*. London: Ministry of Justice.

Perán, J.O. (2017). Pragmatic abolitionism? Defining the complex relationship between restorative justice and prisons. *Restorative Justice*, 5(2), 178-197.

Petteruti, A. (2011). *Education under arrest: the case against police in schools*. Washington, DC: Justice Policy Institute.

Pfander, S.M. (2020). Evaluating New Zealand's restorative promise: the impact of legislative design on the practice of restorative justice. *Kōtuitui: New Zealand Journal of Social Sciences* (Online), 15(1), 170-185.

Pinker, S. (2021). *Rationality: what it is, why it seems scarce, why it matters*. London: Allen Lane.

Platt, J. (2006). Beyond evangelical criminology: the meaning and significance of restorative justice. In I. Aertsen, T. Daems & L. Robert (eds.), *Institutionalizing restorative justice* (pp. 44-67). London: Willan Publishing.

Prichard, J. (2010). Net-widening and the diversion of young people from court: a longitudinal analysis with implications for restorative justice. *Australian & New Zealand Journal of Criminology*, 43(1), 112-129.

Radzik, L. (2009). *Making amends: atonement in morality, law, and politics.* Oxford: Oxford University Press.

Reed College.(2019). Restorative justice policy. In The Office of the Dean of Faculty (ed.), *Guidebook.* Portland: Reed College.

Reimund, M.E. (2004). Confidentiality in victim offender mediation: a false promise? *Journal of Dispute Resolution*, 2004(2), 401-427.

Report of the Expert Mechanism on the Rights of Indigenous Peoples. (2021). *Efforts to implement the United Nations declaration on the rights of indigenous peoples: indigenous peoples and the right to self-determination.* A/HRC/48/75 August.

Restorative Justice Services in the Children's Hearings System. (2005). Edinburgh: Scottish Executive.

Retzinger, S.M. & Scheff, T.J. (1996). Strategy for community conferences: emotions and social bonds. In B. Galaway & J. Hudson (eds.), *Restorative justice: international perspectives* (pp. 315-336). Monsey: Criminal Justice Press.

Reutter, D. (2015). For shame! Public shaming sentences on the rise. *Prison Legal News*, February, p. 38.

Rishmawi, M. (2018). The rule of law and human rights. In C. May & A. Winchester (eds.), *Handbook on the rule of law* (pp. 357-379). Northampton: Edward Elgar Pub., Inc.

Roach, K. (2006). The institutionalization of restorative justice in Canada: effective reform or limited and limiting add-on? In I. Aertsen, T. Daems & L. Robert (eds.), *Institutionalizing restorative justice* (pp. 167-193). London: Willan Publishing.

Roberts, J.V. & Erez, E. (2004). Communication in sentencing: exploring the expressive function of victim impact statements. *International Review of Victimology*, 10(3), 223-244.

Robinson, P.H. (2003). The virtues of restorative processes, the vices of 'restorative justice'. *Utah Law Review*, 2003(1), 375-388.

Robinson, S.-A. & Carlson, D. (2021). A just alternative to litigation: applying restorative justice to climate-related loss and damage. *Third World Quarterly*, 42(6), 1384-1395.

Roche, D. (2003). *Accountability in restorative justice.* Oxford: Oxford University Press.

Rodriguez, N. (2005). Restorative justice, communities, and delinquency: whom do we reintegrate? *Criminology & Public Policy*, 4(1), 103-130.

Rose, D.B. (1996). Land rights and deep colonising: the erasure of women. *Aboriginal Law Bulletin*, 3(85), 6-13.

Rosenblatt, F.F. (2015). *The role of community in restorative justice.* New York: Routledge.

Rossi, R. (2008). Meet me on death row: post-sentence victim-offender mediation in capital cases. *Pepperdine Dispute Resolution Law Journal*, 9(1), 185-210.

Rudin, J. (2005). Aboriginal justice and restorative justice. In E. Elliott & B. Gordon (eds.), *New directions in restorative justice* (pp. 89-114). London: Willan Publishing.

Saulnier, A. & Sivasubramaniam, D. (2015). Effects of victim presence and coercion in restorative justice: an experimental paradigm. *Law and Human Behavior*, 39(4), 378-387.

Schiff, M. (2013). Institutionalizing restorative justice: paradoxes of power, restoration and rights. In T. Gavrielides & V. Artinopoulou (eds.), *Reconstructing the restorative justice philosophy* (pp. 153-178). Farnham: Ashgate Publishing.

Schiff, M. & Bazemore, G. (2015). Dangers and opportunities of restorative community justice: a response to critics. In G. Bazemore & M. Schiff (eds.), *Restorative community justice: repairing harm and transforming communities* (pp. 309-332). New York: Routledge.

Schmid, D.J. (2003). Restorative justice: a new paradigm for criminal justice policy. Victoria University of Wellington. *Law Review*, 34(1), 91-134.

Schneider, E. (1991). The violence of privacy. *Connecticut Law Review*, 23, 973-98.

Schwartz, M. (2010). Building communities, not prisons: justice reinvestment and indigenous over-imprisonment. *Australian Indigenous Law Review*, 14(1), 2-17.

Scottish Parliamentary Corporate Body. (2002). *Justice 2 committee, 22nd meeting, session 1, 5 June*. Norwich: The Stationery Office Ltd.

Shapland, J. (2003). Restorative justice and criminal justice: just responses to crime? In A. von Hirsch, J. Roberts, A. Bottoms, K. Roach & M. Schiff (eds.), *Restorative justice and criminal justice: competing or reconcilable paradigms* (pp. 195-217). Oxford: Hart Publishing.

Shapland, J., Atkinson, A., Atkinson, H., Chapman, B., Dignan, J., Howes, M., Johnstone, J., Robinson, G. & Sorsby, A. (2007). *Restorative justice: the views of victims and offenders. The third report from the evaluation of three schemes*. Ministry of Justice Research Series 3/07. London: Ministry of Justice, June.

Shapland, J., Atkinson, A., Colledge, E., Dignan, J., Howes, M., Johnstone, J., Pennant, R., Robinson, G. & Sorsby, A. (2004). *Implementing restorative justice schemes (crime reduction programme). A report on the first year*. Home Office Online Report 32/04. London: Home Office.

Shapland, J., Robinson, G. & Sorsby, A. (2011). *Restorative justice in practice*. London: Willan Publishing.

Sheehan, A. & Dickson, D. (2003). *Criminal procedure: Scottish criminal law and practice series*. Charlottesville: Lexis Law Publishing.

Sherman, L. & Strang, H. (2007). *Restorative justice: the evidence*. London: The Smith Institute.

Skelton, A. (2019). Human rights and restorative justice. In T. Gavrielides (ed.), *Routledge international handbook of restorative justice* (pp. 32-42). Milton: Routledge.

Skelton, A. & Frank, C. (2004). How does restorative justice address human rights and due process issues? In H. Zehr & B. Toews (eds.), *Critical issues in restorative justice* (pp. 203-213). Monsey: Criminal Justice Press.

Sliva, S.M. & Lambert, C.G. (2015). Restorative justice legislation in the American states: a statutory analysis of emerging legal doctrine. *Journal of Policy Practice*, 14(2), 77-95.

Sliva, S.M., Porter-Merrill, E.H. & Lee, P. (2019). Fulfilling the aspirations of restorative in the criminal justice system? The case of Colorado. *The Kansas Journal of Law & Public Policy*, 28(3), 456-504.

Sliva, S.M., Shaw, M. & Han, T.M. (2020). Policy to practice: an implementation case study in restorative justice. *Contemporary Justice Review: CJR*, 23(4), 527-543.

Smith, J.M. (2021). The formerly incarcerated, advocacy, activism, and community reintegration. *Contemporary Justice Review: CJR*, 24(1), 43-63.

Smith, N. & Weatherburn, D. (2012). Youth justice conferences versus children's court: a comparison of re-offending. *Crime and Justice Bulletin* No. 160. Sydney: NSW Bureau of Crime Statistics and Research: 1-24.

Smith, P. S. & Ugelvik, T. (2017). *Scandinavian penal history, culture and prison practice: embraced by the welfare state?* London: Palgrave Macmillan.

Strang, H., Sherman, L.W., Mayo-Wilson, E., Woods, D. & Ariel, B. (2013). *Restorative justice conferencing (RJC) using face-to-face meetings of offenders and victims: effects on offender recidivism and victim satisfaction—a systematic review*. Oslo: The Campbell Collaboration.

Study by the Expert Mechanism on the Rights of Indigenous Peoples. (2013). *Access to justice in the promotion and protection of the rights of indigenous peoples*. A/HRC/24/50 July.

Sullivan, D. & Tifft, L. (2001). *Restorative justice: healing the foundations of our everyday lives*. Monsey: Willow Tree Press.

Suzuki, M. & Wood, W. R. (2017). Co-option, coercion and compromise: challenges of restorative justice in Victoria, Australia. *Contemporary Justice Review*, 20(2), 274-292.

Sykes, G. (1958). *The society of captives*. Princeton: Princeton University Press.

Tasioulas, J. (2007). Repentance and the liberal state. *Ohio Journal of Criminal Law*, 4, 487-521.

Tauri, J.M. (2009). An indigenous commentary on the standardisation of restorative justice. *Indigenous Policy Journal* (Online), 20(3): 1-24.

Tauri, J.M. (2014). An indigenous commentary on the globalisation of restorative justice. *Faculty of Social Sciences* – Papers. 3197.

Tauri, J.M. (2015). 'Beware justice advocates bearing gifts': a commentary on the glorification of family group conferencing. *New Zealand Sociology*, 30(1), 183-190.

Tauri, J.M. (2019). Restorative justice as a colonial project in the disempowerment of Indigenous peoples. In T. Gavrielides (ed.), *Routledge international handbook of restorative justice* (pp. 342-358). Milton: Routledge.

Thames Valley Partnership. (2013). *Wait 'til eight – an essential start-up guide to NOMS RJ scheme implementation*. London: National Offender Management Service.

The Economic and Social Council. (2002). *United Nations declaration of basic principles on the use of restorative justice programmes in criminal matters*. Resolution 2002/12.

The Scottish Government. (2019). *Restorative justice: action plan*. Edinburgh: APS Group Scotland.

Thompson, P.N. (1997). Confidentiality, competency and confusion: the uncertain promise of the mediation privilege in Minnesota. *Hamline Journal of Public Law and Policy*, 18, 329-375.

Tonry, M. (2014). Can deserts be just in an unjust world. In A.P. Simester, A. Du Bois-Pedain & U. Neumann (eds.), *Liberal criminal theory: essays for Andreas von Hirsch* (pp. 141-165). Oxford: Hart Publishing.

Tränkle, S. (2007). In the shadow of penal law: victim-offender mediation in Germany and France. *Punishment and Society*, 9(4), 395-415.

Trounstine, J. (2018). Fighting the fees that force prisoners to pay for their incarceration. *Prison Legal News*, 29(11), 30-31.

Ulurustatement.org. (2022). What did the Uluru Statement say about sovereignty? Retrieved from: <https://ulurustatement.org/education/faqs>.

Umbreit, M.S. (1990). The meaning of fairness to burglary victims. In B. Galaway & J. Hudson (eds.), *Criminal justice, restitution, and reconciliation* (pp. 47-57). Monsey: Criminal Justice Press.

Umbreit, M.S. (2000a). Restorative justice conferencing: guidelines for victim sensitive practice. Balanced and Restorative Justice Project, Florida Atlantic University, USA.

Umbreit, M.S. (2000b). Reply to Radalet and Borg. *Homicide Studies*, 4(1), 93-97.

Umbreit, M.S. (2001). *The handbook of victim offender mediation: an essential guide to practice and research*. San Francisco: Jossey-Bass.

Umbreit, M.S. & Armour, M.P. (2011). *Restorative justice dialogue: an essential guide for research and practice*. New York: Springer Publishing Company.

Umbreit, M.S., Vos, B., Coates, R.B. & Armour, M.P. (2006). Victims of severe violence in mediated dialogue with offender: the impact of the first multi-site study in the U.S. *International Review of Victimology*, 13(1), 27-48.

United Nations Declaration on the Rights of Indigenous Peoples. (2007). GA Resolution 61/295 (Annex), UN Doc A/RES/61/295.

Van Camp, T. (2014). *Victims of violence and restorative practices: finding a voice*. London: Routledge.

Van Camp, T. & Wemmers, J.-A. (2011). La justice réparatrice et les crimes graves. *Criminologie*, 44(2), 171-198.

Van Camp, T. & Wemmers, J.-A. (2013). Victim satisfaction with restorative justice: more than simply procedural justice. *International Review of Victimology*, 19(2), 117-143.

Van der Merwe, A. & Skelton, A. (2015). Victims' mitigating view in sentencing decisions: a comparative analysis. *Oxford Journal of Legal Studies*, 35(2), 355-372.

Vanfraechem, I. (2003). Implementing family group conferences in Belgium. In L. Walgrave (ed.), *Repositioning restorative justice* (pp. 313-327). Cullompton: Willan Publishing.

Vasiliev, S. (2015). Victim participation revisited: What the ICC is learning about itself. In C. Stahn (ed.), *The law and practice of the international criminal court* (pp. 1133-1202). Oxford: Oxford University Press.

Victim Support UK. (2003). *Policy on restorative justice in criminal justice*. London: Victim Support.

Victims Services and Criminal Law Review. (2014). *Sentencing information package*. New South Wales: NSW Department of Justice and NSW Sentencing Council.

von Hirsch, A. (1993). *Censure and sanctions*. Oxford: Oxford University Press.

von Hirsch, A., Ashworth, A. & Shearing, C. (2003). Specifying aims and limits for restorative justice: a "making amends" model? In A. von Hirsch, J. Roberts, A. Bottoms, K. Roach & M. Schiff (eds.), *Restorative justice and criminal justice: competing or reconcilable paradigms* (pp. 21-41). Oxford: Hart Publishing.

Wachtel, T. & Mirsky, L. (2005). *Burning Bridges*. Bethlehem: International Institute of Restorative Practices (Video).

Walgrave. L. (ed.). (1998). *Restorative justice for juveniles: potentialities, risks and problems for research*. Leuven: Leuven University Press.

Walgrave, L. (1999). Community service as a cornerstone of a systemic restorative response to juvenile justice. In G. Bazemore & L. Walgrave (eds.), *Restorative juvenile justice: repairing the harm of youth crime* (pp. 129-154). Monsey: Criminal Justice Press.

Walgrave, L. (2001). On restoration and punishment: favourable similarities and fortunate differences. In G. Maxwell & A. Morris (eds.), *Restorative justice for juveniles: conferencing, mediation and circles* (pp. 17-37). Cambridge: Hart Publishing.

Walgrave, L. (2002). Introduction. In L. Walgrave (ed.), *Restorative justice and the law* (pp. xv-xix). Cullompton: Willan Publishing.

Walgrave, L. (2003). Imposing restoration instead of inflicting pain. In A. von Hirsch, J. Roberts, A. Bottoms, K. Roach & M. Schiff (eds.), *Restorative justice and criminal justice: competing or reconcilable paradigms* (pp. 61-78). Oxford: Hart Publishing.

Walgrave, L. (2007). Integrating criminal justice and restorative justice. In G. Johnstone & D. Van Ness (eds.), *Handbook of restorative justice* (pp. 559-579). Cullompton: Willan Publishing.

Walgrave, L. (2021). *Being consequential about restorative justice*. The Hague: Eleven International Publishing.

Wallis, P. & Tudor, B. (2008). *The pocket guide to restorative justice*. London: Jessica Kingsley Publishers.

Ward, T. & Langlands, R.L. (2008). Restorative justice and the human rights of offenders: convergences and divergences. *Aggression and Violent Behavior*, 13(5), 355-372.

Weatherburn, D., Hua, J. & Moffatt, S. (2006). How much crime does prison stop? The incapacitation effect of prison on Burglary. *Crime and Justice Bulletin* No 93. Sydney: NSW Bureau of Crime Statistics and Research: 1-12.

Wemmers, J. (2002). Restorative justice for victims of crime: a victim-oriented approach to restorative justice. *International Review of Victimology*, 9(1), 43-59.

Wemmers, J. & Canuto, M. (2002). *Victims' experiences with, expectations and perceptions of restorative justice: a critical review of the literature*. Ottawa: Department of Justice.

Whittaker, A. (2017). White law, blak arbiters, grey legal subjects: deep colonisation's role and impact in defining aboriginality at law. *Australian Indigenous Law Review*, 20, 4-47.

Willemsens, J. (2003). Restorative justice: a discussion of punishment? In L. Walgrave (ed.), *Repositioning restorative justice* (pp. 24-42). Cullompton: Willan Publishing.

Willis, R. & Hoyle, C. (2022). The good, the bad, and the street: does "street culture" affect offender communication and reception in restorative justice? *European Journal of Criminology*, 19(1), 118-138.

Wilson, D.B., Olaghere, A. & Kimbrell, C.S. (2017). *Effectiveness of restorative justice principles in juvenile justice – a meta-analysis*. Fairfax: George Mason University.

Wong, D.S.W. & Lui, W.C.Y. (2019). Restorative justice in Chinese communities. In T. Gavrielides (ed.), *Routledge international handbook of restorative justice* (pp. 299-312). London: Routledge.

Wood, W. R. (2014). Justice reinvestment in Australia. *Victims & Offenders*, 9(1), 100-119.

Wood, W. R. & Suzuki, M. (2016). Four challenges in the future of restorative justice. *Victims & Offenders*, 11(1), 149-172.

Woolf, H.K. (2002). Restorative justice project. Open letter, 14 February.

Wright, M. (1996a). *Justice for victims and offenders: a restorative response to crime* (2nd ed.). Bristol: Open University Press.

Wright, M. (1996b). Can mediation be an alternative to criminal justice? In B. Galaway & J. Hudson (eds.), *Restorative justice: international perspectives* (pp. 227-239). Monesy: Criminal Justice Press.

Wright, M. (2003). Is it time to question the concept of punishment? In L. Walgrave (ed.), *Repositioning restorative justice* (pp. 3-23). Cullompton: Willan Publishing.

Wright, M. & Masters, G. (2002). Justified criticism, misunderstanding, or important steps on the road to acceptance? In E.G.M. Weitekamp & H. Kerner (eds.), *Restorative justice: theoretical foundations* (pp. 50-70). Cullompton: Willan Publishing.

Yeong, S. & Moore, E. (2020). Circle sentencing, incarceration and recidivism. *Crime and Justice Bulletin* No. 226. Sydney: NSW Bureau of Crime Statistics and Research: 1-22.

Young, R. & Hoyle, C. (2003). New improved restorative justice? Action-research and the Thames Valley initiative in restorative cautioning. In A. von Hirsch, J. Roberts, A. Bottoms, K. Roach & M. Schiff (eds.), *Restorative justice and criminal justice: competing or complementary paradigms?* (pp. 273-291). Oxford: Hart Publishing.

Zebel, S., Schreurs, W. & Ufkes, E.G. (2017). Crime seriousness and participation in restorative justice: the role of time elapsed since the offense. *Law and Human Behavior*, 41(4), 385-397.

Zehr, H. (1990). *Changing lenses: a new focus for crime and justice*. Scottsdale: Herald Press.

Zehr, H. (2002). *The little book of restorative justice*. Intercourse: Good Books.

Zehr, H. (2019). Foreword. In T. Gavrielides (ed.), *Routledge international handbook of restorative justice*. London: Routledge.

Zellerer, E. & Cunneen, C. (2015). Restorative justice, indigenous justice, and human rights. In G. Bazemore & M. Schiff (eds.), *Restorative community justice: repairing harm and transforming communities* (pp. 245-263). New York: Routledge.

Zernova, M. (2016). *Restorative justice: ideals and realities*. London: Routledge.

Zernova, M. & Wright, M. (2007). Alternative visions of restorative justice. In G. Johnstone & D. Van Ness (eds.), *Handbook of restorative justice* (pp. 91-108). Cullompton: Willan Publishing.

Zhang, Y. & Xia, Y. (2021). Can restorative justice reduce incarceration? A story from China. *Justice Quarterly*, 38(7), 1471-1491.

Index

Studies in Restorative Justice (Series Editors: Estelle Zinsstag and Tinneke Van Camp)

Monographs and edited collections
Iain Brennan and Gerry Johnstone, *Building bridges*, 2019, ISBN 978-94-6236-882-8
Annemieke Wolthuis and Tim Chapman (eds.), *Restorative justice from a children's rights perspective*, 2021, ISBN 978-94-6236-227-7
Derek R. Brookes, *Restorative justice and criminal justice*, 2023, ISBN 978-94-6236-418-9

Anthologies
Lode Walgrave, *Being consequential about restorative justice*, 2021, ISBN 978-94-6236-235-2
Kathleen Daly, *Remaking justice after sexual violence*, 2022, ISBN 978-94-6236-226-0